Polydoxy

Religious p ra   e collapse of traditional religious institutions, and the
growing im ac   ligious studies on believers have prompted widespread
rethinking of   igion is. *Polydoxy* offers a brilliant and original theological
response to h   ectual crisis by suggesting that there are multiple forms of
right belief. R   g against reductive or nostalgic theological tendencies, the
chapters in h   k take an exciting and creative approach to theology in the
twenty-first ce   . Divided into parts, the first part lays out the theological
agenda of *P ly*   while an impressive array of scholars explore key theological
topics in the   h   relationality and multiplicity in the second and third sections.

Catherine   r is a leading contemporary theologian. She is Professor of
Constructiv   logy at Drew University, USA.

Laurel C. S   er is a philosophical theologian working at the cutting edges of
multiplicity   . She is Professor of Theology, Ethics, and Culture at Chicago
Theological   nary, USA.

Polydoxy

Theology of multiplicity and relation

**Edited by Catherine Keller and
Laurel C. Schneider**

Routledge
Taylor & Francis Group

LONDON AND NEW YORK

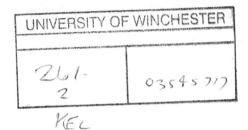
First published in 2011
by Routledge
2 Park Square, Milton Park, Abingdon, Oxon OX14 4RN

Simultaneously published in the USA and Canada
by Routledge
270 Madison Ave., New York, NY 100016

*Routledge is an imprint of the Taylor & Francis Group,
an informa business*

© 2011 Catherine Keller and Laurel C. Schneider for selection and
editorial materials. The contributors for their contributions.

Typeset in Times by
GreenGate Publishing Services, Tonbridge, Kent

Printed and bound in Great Britain by
CPI Antony Rowe, Chippenham, Wiltshire

British Library Cataloguing in Publication Data
A catalogue record for this book is available from the British Library

Library of Congress Cataloguing in Publication Data
Polydoxy : theology of multiplicity and relation / edited by Catherine
Keller and Laurel Schneider.
p. cm.
Includes bibliographical references and index.
1. Theology--Congresses. 2. Religious pluralism--Christianity--
Congresses.
I. Keller, Catherine, 1953- II. Schneider, Laurel C., 1961- III. Title.
BR41.D74 2009
261.2--dc22
2010014859

ISBN: 978-0-415-78135-0 (hbk)
ISBN: 978-0-415-78136-7 (pbk)
ISBN: 978-0-203-84155-6 (ebk)

Contents

Contributors

Sharon V. Betcher is Associate Professor of Theology at Vancouver School of Theology. A constructive theologian working with pneumatological dimensions, she is the author of *Spirit and the Politics of Disablement* (Fortress 2007), as well as essays on ecological, postcolonial and disabilities theologies within multiple anthologies. Her current manuscript project considers theological responses – worked through the lenses of disabilities studies – to the emergence of global cities.

Monica A. Coleman is Associate Professor of Constructive Theology and African American Religions, Co-Director of the Center for Process Studies at Claremont School of Theology, and Associate Professor of Religion at Claremont Graduate University. She is the author of *The Dinah Project: A Handbook for Congregational Response to Sexual Violence*, *Making a Way Out of No Way: A Womanist Theology*, a blog on depression and faith, and various articles.

Brianne Donaldson is scholar-activist, currently in doctoral study at Claremont Graduate University focusing on metaphysics, animal ethics, and the neuro-biology of empathy. She is an Associate Fellow with the Oxford Centre for Animal Ethics, a researcher at the Center for Neuroeconomics Studies, and a visiting scholar with the International Summer School for Jain Studies in India.

Roland Faber is the Kilsby Family/John B. Cobb Jr. Professor of Process Studies at Claremont School of Theology, Professor of Religion and Philosophy at Claremont Graduate University, Executive Co-Director of the Center for Process Studies, and Executive Director of the Whitehead Research Project. His recent publications include: *God as Poet of the World: Exploring Process Theologies* (Westminster John Knox 2008), with A. Stephenson (eds) *Secrets of Becoming* (Fordham 2010), and with H. Krips and D. Pettus *Event and Decision* (Cambridge Scholars 2010).

Marion Grau is Associate Professor of Theology at the Church Divinity School of the Pacific, a member school of the Graduate Theological Union in Berkeley. She is the author of *Rethinking Mission in the Postcolony: Soteriology Beyond Imperialism* (T&T Clark/Continuum, forthcoming), *Of Divine Economy: Refinancing Redemption* (T&T Clark/Continuum 2004), and with Rosemary R. Ruether (eds) *Interpreting the Postmodern: Responses to Radical Orthodoxy* (T&T Clark/Continuum 2006).

Colleen Hartung is currently pursuing doctoral studies at Chicago Theological Seminary. Her research interests lie in the intersections between feminism, ritual theory, the continental philosophies of Jacques Derrida and the French feminists, and theology with a current emphasis on liturgical hospitality in an ecumenical context as a site of resistance, renewal, and innovation. She holds a B.S. and M.A. in Speech Pathology from the University of Nebraska-Lincoln and an M.A. in Religious Studies from Edgewood College in Madison, WI.

Catherine Keller is Professor of Constructive Theology in the Theological School and Graduate Division of Religion at Drew University. Her publications include *From a Broken Web: Separatism, Sexism, and Self* (Beacon 1986), *Apocalypse Now and Then: A Feminist Guide to the End of the World* (Fortress 1996), *Face of the Deep: A Theology of Becoming* (Routledge 2003), *God and Power: Counter-Apocalyptic Journeys* (Fortress 2005), *On the Mystery: Discerning God in Process* (Fortress 2008), and with Chris Boesel (eds) *Apophatic Bodies: Negative Theology, Incarnation, and Relationality* (Fordham 2010).

Hyo-Dong Lee is Assistant Professor of Comparative Theology at Drew University School of Theology and its Graduate Department of Religion. A native of South Korea, he received a B.A. from Yonsei University, a B.Th. and an M.A. from McGill University, an M.Div. from the United Theological College, Montreal, and a Ph.D. from Vanderbilt University. He is the author of "Interreligious Dialogue as a Politics of Recognition: A Postcolonial Re-reading of Hegel for Interreligious Solidarity," *The Journal of Religion* 85, no. 4 (2005).

Mayra Rivera is Assistant Professor of Theology and Latina/o Studies at Harvard Divinity School. She is co-editor of *Postcolonial Theologies: Divinity and Empire* (Chalice 2004), author of *The Touch of Transcendence: A Postcolonial Theology of God* (Westminster John Knox 2007) and *Planetary Loves: Spivak, Postcoloniality and Theology* (Fordham 2010).

Mary-Jane Rubenstein is Assistant Professor of Religion at Wesleyan University, where she teaches in the areas of philosophy of religion and modern Christian thought. She is the author of *Strange Wonder: The Closure of Metaphysics and the Opening of Awe* (Columbia 2009), and of numerous articles and chapters on Kierkegaard, Heidegger, Derrida, negative theology, and the crisis over sex and gender in the global Anglican communion.

Laurel C. Schneider is Professor of Theology, Ethics, and Culture at the Chicago Theological Seminary. She is the author of *Beyond Monotheism: A Theology of Multiplicity* (Routledge 2008) and *Re-Imagining the Divine: Confronting the Backlash Against Feminist Theology* (Pilgrim 1999) along with articles and chapters that variously work at the intersections of constructive theology with queer, postcolonial, feminist, and race theories.

John Thatamanil is Assistant Professor of Theology at Vanderbilt Divinity School. He is the author of *The Immanent Divine: God, Creation and the Human Predicament* (Fortress Press 2006). He is working on a book entitled *Religious Diversity After Religion*, which seeks to overcome blind spots in theologies of religious pluralism and comparative theology generated by problematic configurations of the category "religion."

Acknowledgments

The present volume was made possible by the ongoing Transdisciplinary Theological Colloquium at Drew, of which *Polydoxy* comprised the ninth annual event. Drafts of the collected chapters were first presented in that context, in the Fall of 2009. Responses and contributions from other invited participants – Christopher Boesel, Virginia Burrus, Melanie Johnson-DeBaufre, Elisabeth Gerle, Jason Mahn, and Anna Mercedes – have added immeasurably to the quality of this collection. The lively papers from the graduate student session infect the spirit of the volume: cheers to Rose Ellen Dunn, Beatrice Marovich, Dhawn Martin, Kathryn Reklis, Carolyn Roncolato, and Eric Trozzo. We are especially grateful to the graduate student organizers of the TTC9, Dhawn Martin and Sam Laurent. And *brava* to Beatrice Marovich for her time and skill in the final editing and production of the index. Thanks to Ann Yardley, the Associate Academic Dean and Maxine Clarke Beach, the Dean of Drew Theological School, for their support of the colloquium series across the decade (the series and its volumes are tracked at http://depts.drew.edu/tsfac/colloquium). Also we want to express our appreciation of our Routledge editor, Lesley Riddle, for her initial inspiration and her canny support.

Cover image, *Reaching*, by Mary Hughes. Used by permission of the artist.

"Crib" from *Elephant Rocks* by Kay Ryan. Copyright © 1996 by Kay Ryan. Used by permission of Grove/Atlantic, Inc.

1   Introduction

Catherine Keller and Laurel C. Schneider

A single being is a contradiction in terms.[1]

For where two or three are gathered ...[2]

In recent years, a discernible movement within theology has emerged around a triune intuition: the daunting differences of multiplicity, the evolutionary uncertainty it unfolds, and the relationality that it implies are not problems to be overcome in religious thought. They are starting points for it. Divinity understood in terms of multiplicity, open-endedness, and relationality now forms a matrix of revelation rather than a distortion, or evidence of its lack. The challenges and passions of theological creativity blossoming at the edges of tradition and at the margins of power have shown themselves, far from being distractions from doctrinal or doxological integrity, to be indispensable to its life. And this vitality belies at once the dreary prophecies of pure secularism and the hard grip of credulous certainties.

Really, given the venerable pronouncements of the death of God, theology at the start of this millennium should be worse off than it is. The undeniable atrophy of those denominations that still support an educated clergy limit the resources for even discerning just *which* God it is that is presumed dead. The hard questions remain hard; the institutional fragilities remain unsparing. And so the buoyancy we see in theology right now is all the more remarkable. Its life and movement, which in this volume we are nicknaming "polydoxy," has multiple sources. Indeed, *multiplicity itself* has become theology's resource. What had always seemed a liability for Christian theology – multiplicitous differences contending from within and competing from without – has miraculously turned into theology's friend. Indeed an emergent commitment to the manifold of creation as it enfolds a multiplicity of wisdoms may be functioning as a baseline requirement for theological soundness. A responsible pluralism of interdependence and uncertainty now seems to facilitate deeper attention to ancient religious traditions as well as more robust engagement with serious critiques of religion. This is an approach that no longer needs to hide the internal fissures and complexities that riddle every Christian text or that wound and bless every theological legacy.

These intuitions and starting points find grounding in the Christian tradition not only because of the rich history of texts and practices therein that support doctrinal and ethical formulations of multiplicity, evolutionary openness, and relationality. But also, like other global religions, "Christianity" was never merely One to begin with. Internally multiple and complex, it has always required an agile and spirited approach to theological reflection. We sense that the current resilience of theology in its *becoming multiplicity of relations* is a sign and a gift of that Spirit.

From the start, the plurality of canonized gospels accompanied by the ancestral Hebrew library and the shadows of the excluded gospels made multiplicity manifest. Any durable unity that Christians achieved in texts, theology, or community was not just debatable but hotly debated. The debates display the manifold genius of Christian orthodoxy and the creative tenacity of dissent. But the habit of producing heretics as outer boundary markers for orthodox identity also exposes a repressive evasion of evident Christian complexity. Every point in the two thousand year trajectory of Christian theology is a nexus of traditions engaging – in whatever irenic or bellicose moods – each other and the divine. This means that, despite its linguistic ease of use, "the Christian tradition" does not refer to a singular lineage, nor do Christians speak with one voice even (or especially) when they attend to the same line of scripture. In this sense, the Christian tradition is always already polydox; it is irreducible to any one voice or lineage that may claim exhaustively to represent Christian faith, thought, and practice. This characteristic complexity is wrought of interweaving cultures and stories, of shifting agonisms and political pressures, of myriad communal practices, artistic media, and philosophical schools. Thus multiplicity becomes a source of richness and revelatory possibility for supple theologies that remain open to the ongoing participation of divinity in the world. It invites theological attention. The specific complexity of the Christian tradition may well be precisely what enables its mature (that is, *not simple*) unity.

In other words, much theology that has been understood as orthodox nourishes and advances its own polydox legacy. If, therefore, we dub the present gathering of texts a polydoxy, we do not intend a new orthodoxy of the Multiple to replace the orthodoxy of the One. Deleuze, a great thinker of multiplicity, puts it precisely: "A multiplicity certainly contains points of unification, centers of totalization, points of subjectivation, but these are factors that can prevent its growth and stop its lines. These factors are in the multiplicity they belong to, not the reverse."[3] Theologically we intend a *confessedly* multiple teaching of divine multiplicity. Its hermeneutics and its ontology implicate and explicate one another. Both in reality and in the theological interpretation of reality we presume therefore a deep interconnection, a constitutive relationality, between every one and its others. And so by multiplicity we do not mean a mere many, a plurality of separate ones; nor by relationality do we mean a swamp of indistinction.[4] Yet the lines of differentiation that we find in a logic of relational multiplicity resist predictability.

Without leakage into the indeterminate, multiplicity collapses into totality and dies. The mystery of relationality lies, in part, in its inexhaustible depth and openness to emergence, its stubborn resistance to unification under one point of view. A certain critical apophasis – an "unsaying" of what we most want to say – becomes unavoidable. It is related to the mysticism of negative theology but also to what Trinh T. Minh-ha calls, for postcolonial theory, "a critical nonknowingness."[5] This priority of multiplicity signifies in other words a developing attention to the edges of the known. It conveys the wilder energy of revelation in polydoxy, grounded thematically in our inherited biblical stories of the wilderness, whether grand and desert-exilic or intimate and Emmaus-suburban.

Michel Serres reminds us that "[t]he multiple as such, unhewn and little unified, is not an epistemological monster, but on the contrary the ordinary lot of situations ..." Yet it requires us to recognize that its comprehension, like the apophatic God, always eludes even as it beckons and inspires. "Commonly we know a bit," Serres concedes, "a meager amount, enough, quite a bit; there are various undulations, even in the hardest and most advanced sciences."[6] We cannot know it all, in other words. But this unknowing is an energy of epistemological and theological integrity, as the disparate apophatic thinkers of the Christian tradition from Justin Martyr, through Nicholas of Cusa, to Sallie McFague have always insisted. Unlike the otherworldly priority of much mysticism, polydoxy understands unknowing to have a deep relation to creaturely interrelations. It constitutes and animates the actual openness that an evolutionary sensibility requires; it limns the depth of "ordinary situations" with which theology has to do, or it dies.

Polydox inheritances

Theology that starts from manifold intuitions of multiplicity and relationality is often inspired by stories of liberation, of resistance to some monolithic religio-political rule. But it does not therefore dispense with unity and endurance. Rather it refuses to continue Procrustean practices that chop off whole limbs of experience to fit a dominant theological frame of oneness. It refuses, in fact, the false dichotomy of nihilistic dissolution of meaning on the one hand and unification by self-appointed orthodoxy on the other. It seeks instead an evolving coherence in the midst of actual, lived complexity. It remains mindful of the toxic by-products of any doxic certainty. It appreciates the semantics of *doxa* as "mere opinion," "appearance," "illusion," and "glory" inflecting the doxologies of Christian confession. Indeed it glories in irreducible complexities as sites of enfolded revelation, which is to say, of the embodiment of love according to the discernment of spirits.

But how, one might ask, can such a polydoxy make coherent claims of truth and justice? How will a theology that is energized by the tangle of ancient texts and teachings within and well beyond Christianity, that internalizes the emergent and divergent histories of trauma, survival, remembrance, celebration, and liberation, avoid becoming "lost in multiplicity" that Augustine reasonably feared?[7] Evidently it will seek a polyvocal kind of coherence. Its logic is not that of an abstract order of pyramidal meaning. Rather it hangs together by "network thinking," as Hardt and Negri say of the emergent "multitude."[8] The net, however, does not remain in the logic of virtual space but embodies itself in the webs of living interaction, in their sticky logic: to "cohere," after all, means in Latin "*to stick together.*"

The solidarity of such togetherness cannot be conceived theologically apart from a radically widened sense of the incarnation. Indeed the abstractions of philosophical or systematic theologies exist relative not only to each other but to the bodies that produce them. Feminist theory across the disciplines has labored to keep thought responsible to its relational contexts of embodiment, mindful of what Donna Haraway has dubbed its "situated knowledge."[9] And according to Alfred North Whitehead, who earlier unfolded a relevant theo-cosmology of radical pluralism (issuing from William James' "pluriverse"), "no entity can be conceived in complete abstraction from the system of the universe." This is because all key notions, or metaphors, in a system of thought "presuppose each other." Yet Whitehead is here defining "coherence" to mean not just that the signifiers "are definable in terms of each other; it means that *what is indefinable* in one such notion cannot be abstracted from its relevance to the other notions."[10] The unknown is not excused from the multiplicity of its relations.

The theology introduced in this volume sticks together without plastering over differences. As invitations to polydoxy, these essays do not let go of creative divergences and stubborn tensions. They variously point to an incarnational depth in the world from which Christian faith and teaching might renew itself. If that depth also requires of us a disciplined unknowing, it is not as an escape from knowledge. Rather it lends contemplative attention to what Judith Butler calls the "opacity" of our own self-constitution in an intimate multiplicity of relations.[11] Otherwise we may miss the point at which the planetary multitude lays its specific claim, its truth, and its justice, upon our gifts.[12]

By way of introduction to this volume and its performances of polydoxy, we suggest an economic trinity of themes – multiplicity, unknowing, and relationality – to serve as a loose guide to the text. This interactivity of multiplicity, unknowing and relationality hints at the triune mystery of a divine manifold eluding and inspiring our collaboration. It also lets us begin to explicate the relations among the texts as they create the manifold of polydox theology.

Multiplicities of Christian theology

Polydoxy foregrounds the context of vibrant and enduring religious and spiritual diversity in the world. At the same time, polydoxy reads that context as indigenous to Christian history and its theological legacy. The theologians in this volume, who share the intuitions and commitments that polydoxy here collects, recognize the novel avowal of that diversity as prolegomena to theology's future vitality and intellectual integrity. For this reason, despite fundamentalist fears to the contrary, internal and intersectional multiplicity is no embarrassment to theology, something to be masked or dismissed as evidence of Christian failures to *be* Christian. There is a doctrinal claim at play in this volume about what it means to be Christian in this world. It requires a receptive posture toward a manifold of texts within and beyond the corpus of interpretations, practices, and spiritualities of those who claim the tradition/s of Jesus.

However, multiplicity as such remains a risky and powerful concept, tricky to handle. It constrains any claims of orthodox exclusivity. In the process it can wash out any ethical or cultural authority with which – in the interest of justice or truth – we ourselves presume to speak. Increasingly, however, there are transdisciplinary clues among philosophers and poets who pit the multiple against the logic of the One. Sometimes, as with Deleuze and Guattari, they take aim at God the One as irreversibly totalizing in His mission. But on the whole, even among poststructuralists still attending the funeral of God (as caricature of the death of European metaphysics), the animus of difference directs itself against the monodoxies and mono-politics that manage a history of vengeful and imperial unities. These monoliths of the One bristle with *ressentiment.* They shore up boundaries of exclusion in vain efforts to deny the very multiplicity that constitutes them – that, as Mary-Jane Rubenstein points out in her theological reading of Butler, also undoes them. If as Jean-Luc Nancy puts it "the origin is irreducibly plural," then it is no surprise that the multiplicity of lived existence repeatedly interrupts the deafening monotones of empire forthright or neoliberal, theocratic, or totalitarian. Yet we do not naively embrace multiplicity. It is often in the name of pluralism, difference, and interconnection that the globalization of the economy works to flatten the planet like a One World credit card. Leveling cultural difference and old growth forests, this economy can annihilate the very diversity it craves and commodifies. The injustices that late capitalism imposes and the rage its rapacious disregard provokes are not new, only – multiplying.

The peculiarity and promise of this moment may lie in the planetary pressure that a growing multitude feels to find and practice a saner, more sustainable common life. If there is a startling vitality in newer theologies growing in the depleted soil of mainline Christianity, it is not incidental to this pressure. These theologies began to arise like waves when major social crises of the mid-twentieth century solicited responsive echoes in biblical prophetic movements.[13] The one God of the Christendom that took up the Roman pattern and built empires on the labor of slaves had, through centuries, provoked many rounds of exodus. The U.S. civil rights movement and the birth of Black theology along with Latin American liberation theology churned up new Christian discourses of exodus. And soon the international women's movement, followed by gay, lesbian, and other queer movements, deepened challenges to the God of orthodoxy. God's faces and names began to proliferate. God's façade of bourgeois decency began to slip.[14] A sense was growing that the logic of the One may stand more in the way of justice, liberation, and love than not.[15] Entwining faith with social analysis in their different singularities, these emergent theologies have come through decades of fragile, often brittle solidarity with each other. In the process they have formed vibrant and resolute counter- (not anti-) traditions. Which is not to say that any of these explosive movements have always gracefully engaged their own complexes of multiplicity.

The plurality of issues that energize these emergent theologies are informed by a plurality of extra-theological theories, multiplied by cultures, sexes, and spirits of many sorts. So we have some sympathy for various conservative retreats from this tragicomic multiplication of inelegant identities, with its noisy complication of the rules of theology. One might in a gesture of impatience with liberation, a moue of postfeminist or even postcolonial sophistication, relegate these social movement theologies to the past millennium. Which of them after all is innocent of the logic of the One? But we suspect that a more delicate operation is needed and indeed underway in the form of multiple sensitive moves away from single issue simplifications toward a coalitional, or at least more complex, manifold. Multiplicity and pluralism are not the enemy of justice, or of identity politics, though they require supplemental strategies of reflection and action.

Each of the contributions to this volume takes up the concept of multiplicity as an organizing principle in theology, though each does so differently. Unlike triumphalist theologies that find themselves again and again comfortably ensconced in the political programs of empire, the theological voices in this collection articulate a coherence that neither retreats from uncertainty nor falls into nihilistic disarray. Not surprisingly, they do not all speak with one voice or use a single strategy to create their particular pluralisms. For example, Roland Faber uses Whitehead's richly "irreducible interplay of the multiplicities of creator, creatures, and creativity" to take on the idea of God's peace within his intertwined neologisms of "theoplicity," "polyphilia," and "para-doxy." He does so in order to better account for worldly multiplicity and the divine multiplicity revealed in and through it. Laurel Schneider argues for multiple modes of reasoning that can help remedy theology's typically stultifying over-reliance on presuppositions and frames of thought forged in Europe's cultural context. She seeks to "loosen Christian theology's cramped grip on seriousness, a tired habit of solemnity that undermines its lush capacity for wisdom." Divine multiplicity, revealed by incarnation and accessible through postures of openness and humor, is grounded in the rich inheritance of canonical and extra-canonical stories about it, their plurality and limber ambiguities.

Sharon Betcher investigates the global city as a locus of bodily and spiritual multiplicity that, rather than being a problem for Christian pneumatology, becomes a source of insight for it. With her eye on growing cosmopolitan "spiritual but not religious" populations in the midst of centrifugal urban forces, she teases out the "ligatures" of connection that indicate a spiritual vitality. She gestures toward a nascent ecclesiology of the multiple, in which "the prosthesis of Spirit, the locus of opening and the harness of corporeal generosity might imply practicing ... ways of 'being with' one another in the city." Catherine Keller thinks toward the con-vivality of polydoxy with the help of the little known Anne Conway, "the first writer of the relational multiplicity." Conway's reasoned challenges to the emergent, desensitizing dualism of early modernity crackle with explosive potential. But her small voice, nurtured in a multiplex of thinkers and activists, bided the centuries as philosophy and theology gradually benumbed themselves with the mechanized view of the universe. Of course the fact that we have any philosophical writing by any woman of any era before our own is a wonder, a testament to the same canny Spirit of multiplicity that flows through the fissures and gaps interrupting the patriarchal hubris of biblical and early Christian writings. In Conway, we find an ancestress for the explicit avowal of multiplicity as the relational fabric of existence itself, one who argues that "a creature must *be* manifold … in order to receive 'the assistance of its Fellow-Creatures.'"

All of the contributions to this collection reflect angles of the logic of multiplicity that undergirds polydoxy as a mode of Christian constructive theology. They variously demonstrate the fold, the *pli*, which distinguishes multi*pli*city from mere plurality. That enfolded and unfolding relationality suggests not a relation between many separate ones but between singularities, events of becoming folded together, intersecting, entangled as multiples. It is such connectivity that allows, indeed implies (im*pli*catio), the becoming coherence of polydoxy.

Stories of the unknown

If multiplicity addresses the diversity unfolding as a cosmos, and relationality addresses the interconnections that enfold creatures one in another, neither concept will necessarily divulge its own mystery. Mystery clouds the *eschata* as well as the origins. Do we not need a conceptual space in which to address, *in media res*, both the bottomless beginnings and the glorious and unnerving openness of all of reality to its future? We believe so, and for this reason, embed unknowing in the middle of this collection, between the thematic energies of plurality and of relationality. Change, novelty, and evolutionary emergence all characterize the interactivity that gives meaning to both relations and to diversity. But they also characterize its uncertainty. Is it not this element of the unknown that lends philosophies of becoming and theologies of process their unsettling edge?

If a polydox planetarity calls for unprecedented attention to uncertainty, it is because creation is not static, nor is it unfolding predictably from an origin to an end.[16] This condition of epistemic limitation is often addressed by saying we lack a "God's eye view," which is surely the case. But the phrase implies something we do not, that God not only sees it all but sees it in advance, from an eternity beyond time. Many Christians find comfort in such providential remedies to human uncertainty. We do not however find it reassuring to rob God of the new. If, in our polydox trinity, uncertainty goes all the way down – as quantum theories indicate – we suspect it goes "up" as well. We might leave divine unknowing in the cloud of our own unknowing of the divine. But we would still agree that the indeterminacy of the creation is the creative condition of its genesis – its becoming multiplicity. Some of us would affirm that God is also becoming in the internal relations of this becoming; others of us would negate our capacity to distinguish between the being and the becoming of what we call "God." And these are not incommensurable positions. Negative theology, as in Gregory of Nyssa's "brilliant darkness," both relativizes and revives the affirmative utterance – in prayer, confession, and speculative offering – but then precisely not as dogmatic certainty. Our unknowing, linked in this way to the ancient tradition of apophatic

mysticism, "unsays" its own certainties – identities, essences, bodies, objectifica-
tions, exclusions, and other last words – in order paradoxically that we may keep
speaking of God.[17]

Polydoxy presumes a mindful uncertainty. It makes possible what Nancy
calls the "auto-deconstruction of Christianity," as it loosens theology's limbs,
allowing for a greater responsiveness to the world and to the intimate unfolding of its stories. The irresistible postmodern interplay between deconstruction
(with its asymptotic proximity to atheism) and any negative theology (with its
asymptotic proximity to theism) further tests our spirits and tones our discourse.
With the help of Jacques Derrida's notion of "*sans*" (religion without religion),
Colleen Hartung takes up this unsaying of certainty in her exploration of a polydox faith in the face of real-world limitations. "Polydox theologies foreground
the multiple and the uncertain," she writes. They "take seriously this deep-seated,
embodied experience of indeterminacy." Derrida's pursuit of the *sans* provides
Hartung with language that makes a faith without the certainty of religion's God
theoretically intelligible. The apophatic therefore signifies at once the humility of
not-knowing-it-all and the excess of expression in the face of it All.

Uncertainty in our triune approach appears at every level implicated in *multiplicity* – as the very density and cloud of *relationality*. Polydox theologies need
not retreat to divine proscriptions or veils of authorized revelation to accept this
unknowing, which is itself known to us at every juncture of the creation. In their
contributions, John Thatamanil, Hyo-Dong Lee, and Catherine Keller all delve
specifically and variously into the relationality signified by the trinitarian symbol as a particularly rich and traditioned aspect of polydoxy's long Christian
inheritance. Lee offers insight into a trinitarian panentheism with the help of Neo-
Confucian emphases on the openness of the Spirit to embodied abundance. In
part this is due to its being "empty and tranquil, without any sign" – which is
paradoxically necessary to the Spirit's *presence* in embodiment. He suggests that
Neo-Confucian struggles with openness and presence can provide a great deal of
help to Christian trinitarian thought that seeks to move past the shackles of mono-
logical ontology. A dialogue between them, he argues, "will be able to strike a
balance between the apophatic and the kataphatic by recognizing a depth in God
while refusing to call that divine depth God's ground."

Apophasis never means a mere "not." In its theological forms it cannot be
confused with the pseudo-certainty of simple denial. The gesture of unknowing
entails an apophatic leap of faith. This space in which unknowing transforms
certainty in to open-armed uncertainty (a fertile, receptive, and promiscuous
openness) can be perhaps symbolized by the Holy Spirit, which for the fifteenth-
century cardinal Nicholas of Cusa (following Augustine) is "connection itself."[18]
This Spirit implicates every relation in the "negative infinity" of Cusa's One,
which is "not a one that is opposed to the many": the divine *complicatio*. Its infinity "folds together" all creatures in itself, even as they unfold of themselves. It
cannot enclose the multiplicity in a monistic totality or a dualist hierarchy. But for
all its resistance to the idolatries of definition, it does not fold orthodoxy down; it
complicates it.

Mary-Jane Rubenstein plumbs the apophatic wealth of vulnerability and inscrutability that comes with relationality in her dialogical reading of Augustine's *Confessions* alongside Judith Butler's *Precarious Life*. She finds in Augustine's account of conversion a kind of testament to personal and divine multiplicity. "Or in a more polydox register" Rubenstein suggests, "perhaps conversion does not bring about the static unity it promises. Perhaps, far from annihilating multiplicity, the confessional journey uncovers and reconfigures it." With the help of Butler's reflection on the *ex-stasis* of grief and desire – the constitutive "being beside one-self" that pushes even at ordinary meanings of relationality – Rubenstein thinks about many of the key turnings in Augustine's stories as so many processes of faithful "undoing," not only of the bishop's own sovereignty, but in a certain sense, of his God's sovereignty. "Exhausted from his struggle in the garden with an omnipotent God, Augustine gives himself over to the *incarnate* God, renouncing his own sovereignty for the God who renounces *his* ..."

Being undone by ecstasy is not, in a polydox sense, something to avoid, just as multiplicity is not the epistemological monster that Augustine seems to have feared. It is a confirmation of being alive and of accepting that gift. The only way around this, he himself finds, is an austere closing down of both modes of ecstasy – desire and grief – which simply does not seem to succeed in his own, stubbornly passionate life, and certainly not in his theological account of that life. And therein lies an exquisite, poignantly unpretentious basis for orthodoxy's own polydox self-understanding. As Schneider argues, the incarnational theology implicit in Christianity's own stories dismantles every legitimate bill of sale, pedigree, or authorized provenance in favor of disreputable, improvised, and impure emergence that polydoxy recognizes as necessary to the integrity of its work. The question for polydoxy therefore does not lie in whether Christian theology is multiple and shady in its sources and foundations. Rather the challenge is how to understand its syncretic folds theologically. What interpretive authority/ies can be made possible through a more generous and humorous acceptance of Christianity's own messy, fertile ancestral lures and complications?

All our relations

While attention to plurality and a certain apophatic openness mark – to different degrees and with divergent feelings – all of these chapters, the theme of relationality appears to be the condition of possibility for this shared theology. Because multiplicity falls into incoherence, and apophasis into mere negation, in abstraction from their implicate connections, polydoxy presumes at several levels the ligatures (to use Betcher's image) of a relationality that imbricates and undoes multiplicities as they emerge. The relation of a subject to an inexchangeable other, itself already related to other inexchangeable others, is what makes possible the plural manifestations of worldly experience. This descriptive truth takes on normative force. Relationality distinguishes pluralism from the relativism that swamps judgment and inhibits resolution. Historically speaking, the authors in this volume also presume a debt to the heritage of feminist and Black liberation thought, much of it in theology, that explicates the systemic relationality of our personal and political condition. Sociality immanent to our individualities, not external to some prior essence, had other antecedents as well, especially of Hegelian and Whiteheadian provenance; but the analysis of our primary relations across sexual and racial divides first rendered this discourse of constituent relationality ethically unavoidable.[19]

Also feminist theological alliances with ecology and process theology embed interhuman sociality in layers of cosmological accountability. Certainly Keller, Schneider, and Faber have been long involved in the methodological webs of feminist, pluralist, poststructuralist, and process theories that highlight the explication of multiplicity and relationality as such, especially in its stimulation of a counter-ontology for Christian constructive theology. Brianne Donaldson builds on this foundation in her exposition of interspecies care. She reminds us, with the help of an ecofeminist reading of Whitehead and the Jain concept of *ahimsa*, that "the realm of embodied particularity has long been associated with women and nature." This is a position that some feminists have sought to move past, but Donaldson retrieves it for a deeper understanding of polydoxy as a mode of theology that attends to planetary life beyond the human realm. In other words, polydox relationality extends through and beyond participation in the familiar to our more alien affinities. Betcher touches on this relational thinking as well in her reading of the Deleuzean "becoming whale," and Keller lifts it into prominence in her concept of "the conviviality of creation." Only in the discernment of the vibrant webs of a prehensive interdependence does pluralism escape from liberal banality, the sterile series of separate ones: plastic bottles tossed by a desert road.

These chapters want theology to come to grips with the problematic and promising immensity of our creaturely interdependence. However we articulate divine relationality, it seems to be inviting a more mindful participation in itself, and therefore in the cosmopolitan, ecological, and posthuman senses of our planetarity. What is more, if we open the fold between self and other in these terms, we expose the margin of entanglement that holds us in relation – akin to what Anne Joh refers to as *Jeong*, or "sticky love" in her postcolonial Christology – and renders our multiplicities coherent.[20] Relationality, in this sense, laps over and suffers difference without letting go. It bears the memories of the oppressed and excluded and so cannot deny the force of hybridity and miscegenation, of queer fertilities and revelatory contaminations, in the formulation of sacred wisdom. It will not repress the promiscuity and – in memory of Marcella Althaus Reid – the indecency of divine love itself.[21]

Relationality is also the theme that most grounds us, as human beings embodying thinking and writing, in the materiality of connection. As a number of the authors in this collection demonstrate, there exists a wealth of narrative sources originating outside of the European mainstream. Schneider argues that these sources and modes of reasoning are not merely, as Andrea Smith points out, exotic objects for study; they also *produce theory*.[22] There is something commonsensical and obvious about the claim that not all good theory comes from

Europe; but remarkably, most Christian theology limits itself to a parochialism that diminishes its rigor, relevance, and honesty. Polydoxy therefore returns to the theoretical intensity of ancient Christian theology by way of disciplined openness to intersecting traditions, narratives, and philosophies. En route to a sustainably planetary vision, it seeks careful and adventurous engagements with the multiplicity of relations that characterize Christianity's global character.[23] In this spirit, Monica Coleman follows the ancestral lures and voices of Oya through a postmodern womanist attention to the multiplicity of Black women's experiences and narratives. She attends to the presences of past and future that link us all to our own and each others' ancestors in theologically potent ways. In an HIV age that has grown terrified (anew) of blood, especially of African blood, Coleman thinks with Tananarive Due's novel *The Living Blood*, about soteriology as complex healing-in-community. She grounds soteriology in the ever shifting ligatures of community, blood-bound, and chosen. "As boundaries bend and cross in the narrative world of *The Living Blood*," she tells us, "this reading also suggests that practicing polydox soteriology is transnational, transcontinental, postcolonial, feminist, womanish, and dangerous, while also necessary for our health."

In their attention to injustice, polydox theologies that eschew singular answers to complex realities are challenged by their own commitments to naming and claiming the multiple interconnections between communities that have survived by any means possible. Exposing oppression as a critique of the privileged is only one side of the work of relationality, as Homi Bhabha has so persuasively demonstrated. "For the colonial hybrid is the articulation of the ambivalent space where the rite of power is enacted on the site of desire, making its objects at once disciplinary and disseminatory."[24] The work of decolonization is a work of recognition: ambivalence structures the hybrid relations and complicated desires that circulate in the empire's wake. Oppression, in one sense, is the suppression of elemental relationality, shored up by doctrines of separation and the legitimation of violence. Exposing, naming, even claiming the hybrid interdependencies of bodies *across* lines of oppression is also a work of relationality; but doing so can undermine resistance efforts that depend upon clearly delineated identities. This work can expose how identities of resistance, forged in oppression, risk an internally-policed sameness that mirrors the exclusionary energies of oppression itself. These identity-based strategies of survival persist because they are needed, and the work of challenging the logic of the One makes polydoxy itself an ambivalent gift, even as it stretches theological imagination toward more fluid and open-ended notions of identity; a peaceable kindom in which relations bind, but also unfold. In other words, ambivalent attractions, uncertain hopes, and attention to the least (who are never identical with us), give guidance to polydox relationality.

This means that colonialism and its spawn of institutionalized racial and sexual violence form a primary legacy with which theology can fruitfully contend – when it has the courage to do so. We do not turn away from Christianity's implication on every level of the denial of relationality that has enabled the genocidal trajectories of imperialism. But neither do we turn away from Christian counter-movements, out of which real alternatives to the force of imperialism have flowed. Stories of enemy-love and resistance to oppressive domination (whether political, ecclesial, economic, or social) can be found even at the heart of imperial and missionary schemes, confounding the easy caricatures of Christian missionaries that tend to permeate contemporary discourse. Marion Grau traces just such a story of resistance and complex conversion in the Anglican mission to the Zulus led by the Colenso family – and the mission to the Colensos led by the Zulu. The deep relationality that this story exposes makes a simplistic reading of mission (from either side) impossible. Reciprocity attends relationality, when it is read as constituent, not as something that I "do" with or to you. John Milbank's insistence on the "asymmetrical reciprocities" of a participatory ontology has resonance, at this angle, with postcolonial, polydox theology.[25]

As we have said, relationality is the connective tissue that makes multiplicity coherent. It is the depth that makes all of our relations strange and unknowable even, or especially, in intimacy. The immensity of the manifold converges, as Cusa would have it, upon an infinity, a "divine maximum," where "the minimum coincides with the maximum."[26] Or as Mayra Rivera notes in her chapter, divine glory transcends the great, and manifests in the neglected and smallest exchanges of life. "Glory appears not only as the shock of injustice," she writes, "but also as the irreducible difference of that which is closest to us, which lures us beyond ourselves." She is challenged by injustice – which sticks to bodies and shapes them – to seek "concrete, material, fleshy images of the divine," for which she relies on "biblical images of glory as earthy and elemental."

The very excessiveness of biblical images of glory is what makes those images a fertile resource for polydoxy. In those texts, God cannot be contained in single narratives or in single bodies. An elemental vitality seems to exceed in the divine, to transcend conceptual closure in just the ways that flesh elementally exceeds all grasping, imperial, rapacious, or puritan control. There is relationality at play in glory, just as there is multiplicitous excess and the beckoning strangeness of the unknown. We are immersed in glory, embedded in it, and brought forth out of it. Or in other words, the world itself is implicated, complicated, and explicated through divine glory. In the relations of the trinity, the deep orthodoxy of love (which is relation itself) multiplies polydoxically.

In the concluding chapter (which is by no means a closure), it is to the trinity that John Thatamanil brings us. As an indigenous ground for Christian thinking about multiplicity, ineffability, and relationality, the trinity offers an apt place to launch the beginning that an ending may yield. Like Keller, Thatamanil sees in trinitarian thought a strong basis for polydoxy. Through it he is able to approach Christian theology's proximity to other religious traditions as a source of enrichment and mutual correction rather than mere competition or dismissal. "Might it be possible," he asks, "for Christian theologians to envision a trinitarian engagement with religious diversity that is marked by a sense of *anticipation* that other traditions may have something to teach us about how to think even about trinity?" He not only finds this vision possible, but does much to actualize its promise. Through his own construction of a triune scheme of "contingency, ground, and relation" he shows this intersectionality to be necessary to an improved, less anemic, understanding of Christian ideas in themselves. In other words, the differences between religions are important to the ecological health and internal integrity of the religions. But even more so, the differences between and among religions reveal diversity in divine life itself; they reveal a healthy and mysterious multiplicity of relations.

Engaging the endogenous plurality of traditions, texts, and practices in Christianity is therefore one aspect of our intent to develop greater probity and rigor in the mode of Christian theology that we are calling polydoxy. At the same time, the exogenous plurality of traditions has never *not* exercised a shaping effect on Christian thought. Other traditions have always exerted a pressure and influence on Christianity, the recognition of which serves to improve the clarity with which we think about the distinctiveness of our claims. Like others in this volume, Thatamanil recognizes the ways in which traditionally non-Christian modes of approaching common questions of meaning also sometimes offer new lines of flight through doctrinal impasses. The presupposition here is that polydoxy positions Christian theology where it already stands – in the midst of a boundless array of intersecting conversations and modes of reasoning. Furthermore, as we noted at the beginning, polydoxy does not see the challenges of such a boisterous and sometimes bellicose environment to be only a distraction and a problem for Christian theology. That environment also delivers the very ecological diversity upon which theology's own health depends. Christian thought cannot avoid the multiplicity that constitutes it at its textual and narrative core. Nor can it avoid the multiple relations to others who in ongoing interchange, friction (as Grau points out), and mutual inspiration constitute its existence in an actual world.

In conclusion, the chapters in this volume form an invitational introduction to polydoxy as a vibrantly engaged mode of doing constructive theology. We suspect that the evolutionary leap of the manifold – the processes of creation that enfold and unfold the divine – will embody itself in emerging, uncertain, endlessly promising coherencies. If Christian renditions of this unfinished incarnation are also to emerge and stick together, they will need the energy of ancient intuition multiplied by the flight lines of our freshest thinking. Faith, hope, and *caritas*: if the uncertainty translates into faith, multiplicity yields a hope that indeed our chosen multiplicities, as Coleman suggests, will prove loveable. And furthermore, that the unknown will prove liveable.

We hope that the present performances of polydoxy find resonance among many other emerging efforts. We hope they encourage younger theologians and scholars of religion in their commitment to a richer, more rigorous thinking of multiplicity within and of any religions. Our own multiplicities, enfolded here in the structure and personalities of this volume, unfold within the body of Christ, itself multiply incarnate in a logos-invoked cosmos. This polydoxy will help to right theology – *orthos* – to the extent that it teaches us to trade certainty for faith and *anathema* for *caritas*. Polydoxy – by whatever name – happens whenever a few of us are gathered – in whatever space, medium or web – *seeking* understanding. Without yet again presupposing the answers.

Notes

1   J.-L. Nancy, *Being Singular Plural*, trans. R. D. Richardson and A. E. O'Byrne, Palo Alto, CA: Stanford University Press, 2000, p. 12.
2   Matthew 18:20.
3   G. Deleuze, *Two Regimes of Madness: Texts and Interviews, 1975–1995*, New York: Semiotext(e), 2006, p. 305.
4   "To try to think outside of the manifold of combinations, outside of classification, outside of customs and fixed species, outside of discipline and specialty...," M. Serres, *Genesis*, trans. G. James and J. Nielson, Ann Arbor, MI: University of Michigan Press, 2005 (1995), p. 96.
5   Trinh T. Minh-ha, *Woman, Native, Other: Writing Postcoloniality and Feminism*, Bloomington, IN: Indiana University Press, 1989.
6   Serres, p. 5.
7   "*in multa evanui*," Augustine of Hippo, *Confessions*, trans. O. Chadwick, Oxford: Oxford University Press, 1991, 2.1.1. See also M. J. Rubenstein in this volume, p. 108.
8   M. Hardt and A. Negri, *Multitude: War and Democracy in the Age of Empire*, New York: Penguin Books, 2005, pp. xiii–xiv.
9   D. Haraway, "Situated Knowledges: The Science Question in Feminism," *Feminist Studies* 14, No. 3 (Autumn 1988), pp. 575–99.
10   A. N. Whitehead, *Process and Reality*, New York: The Free Press, p. 3, emphasis added.
11   J. Butler, *Giving an Account of Oneself*, New York: Fordham University Press, 2005, pp. 8ff.
12   And indeed that contemplation may lead us, theologically, to the precise place of the painfully relevant contradiction – that which Nicholas of Cusa has called "the cloud of the impossible." C. Keller, *The Cloud of the Impossible*, forthcoming.
13   For a genealogy of theological liberalism in the United States, see Gary Dorrien's three volume series, especially the first volume which examines the nineteenth-century precedents for the social gospel movement: G. Dorrien, *The Making of American Liberal Theology: Imagining Progressive Religion (1805–1900)*, Vol. 1, Louisville, KY: Westminster John Knox Press, 2001.
14   For a magnificent discourse on the question of divine decency, see the writings of the late Marcella Althaus Reid, especially M. Althaus Reid, *Indecent Theology: Theological Perversions in Sex, Gender, and Politics*, London and New York: Routledge, 2001. And also M. Althaus Reid, *The Queer God*, London and New York: Routledge, 2003.
15   For an introduction to the concept of the "logic of the One" as a problem in Christian history and theology, see L. C. Schneider, *Beyond Monotheism: A Theology of Multiplicity*, New York: Routledge, 2008.
16   C. Keller, *Apocalypse Now and Then: A Feminist Guide to the End of the World*, Boston, MA: Beacon Press, 1996.
17   For more on the apophatic, see C. Boesel and C. Keller (eds), *Apophatic Bodies: Negative Theology, Incarnation, and Relationality*, New York: Fordham University Press, 2009.
18   See Catherine Keller's work on Cusa in C. Keller, "The Cloud of the Impossible: Embodiment and Apophasis," *Apophatic Bodies*, p. 40.
19   For more on constituent relationality and primary relations, see I. Carter Heyward, *The Redemption of God: A Theology of Mutual Relation*, Lanham, MD: University Press of America, 1982. And also C. Keller, *From a Broken Web: Separation, Sexism, and Self*, Boston, MA: Beacon Press, 1986, 1988; R. N. Brock, *Journeys By Heart: A Christology of Erotic Power*, New York: Crossroad, 1988; A. Lorde, *Sister/Outsider: Speeches and Essays by Audre Lorde*, Berkeley, CA: The Crossing Press, 1984.

20 W. Anne Joh, *Heart of the Cross: A Postcolonial Christology*, Louisville, KY: Westminster John Knox Press.

21 Althaus Reid, *Indecent Theology*.

22 A. Smith, "Queer Theory and Native Studies: The Heteronormativity of Settler Colonialism," *GLQ: A Journal of Lesbian & Gay Studies* 16, No. 1/2: 1–2, 2010, p. 43.

23 We are using the distinction between "global" and "planetary" that Gayatri Chakravorty Spivak names in *Death of a Discipline*.

> Planet-thought opens up to embrace an inexhaustible taxonomy of ... names, including but not identical with the whole range of human universals: aboriginal animism as well as the spectral white mythology of postrational science. If we imagine ourselves as planetary subjects rather than global agents, planetary creatures rather than global entities, alterity remains underived from us; it is not our dialectical negation, it contains as much as it flings away.

See G. Chakravorty Spivak, *Death of a Discipline*, New York and Chichester, West Sussex: Columbia University Press, 2003, p. 73. For a fuller discussion of the qualitative distinction between the "global" and the "planetary" particularly as it relates to theological concerns, see M. R. Rivera and S. Moore, *Spivak*, New York: Fordham University Press, 2010.

24 H. K. Bhabha, *The Location of Culture*, London and New York: Routledge, 2005 (1994), p. 160.

25 For more on Milbank's "assymetrical reciprocity" see, for example, J. Milbank, *Being Reconciled: Ontology and Pardon*, New York: Routledge, 2003. For an alternative view, see M. Grau and R. Radford Ruether (eds), *Interpreting the Postmodern: Responses to Radical Orthodoxy*, London: T&T Clark, 2006.

26 Nicholas of Cusa, "Of Learned Ignorance," in *Selected Spiritual Writings*, trans. H. L. Bond, New York and Mahwah, NJ: Paulist Press, 1997.

Part I
Multiplicity

2   Crib notes from Bethlehem

Laurel C. Schneider

Note, for instance, in our
annual rehearsals of innocence,
the substitution of manger for crib –
as if we ever deserved that baby,
or thought we did.

Kay Ryan[1]

Three of the four Christian gospels begin their narratives of the life, teachings, and deeds of Jesus Christ with pregnancy and birth. They tell an evocative story: a poor, unwed mother forced into a long and difficult journey by colonial powers, no place to rest, the birth of her fabled son attended by sheep, stars, and foreigners. Of course, the nativity is much more than a story of one child's birth, more even than the story of a god's birth. It is a story of origin for a whole religion. Throughout the centuries, the narrative account of Mary's pregnancy, journey, and the night her son was born has been cherished for its intimacy, its theatrical quality, its familiarity, and its metaphoric power to dramatize the divine inauguration of Christianity. But as we shall see, it is also an origin story with a guilty shimmer; it is a tall tale of sorts. And it is all the more fertile – gravid, even – for the ambiguity and multiplicity it bears.

The "birth of Jesus," sealed canonically into no less than three accounts, also cannot be collapsed to a single interpretation or *doxa*. At the intimate storied origin of Christianity, multiplicity leaks out. But we need a different sort of theological reasoning than what we commonly employ to get at the complexity nestling there. Theological reasoning comes out of a human desire to stretch intellect toward the farthest reaches and most intimate recesses of existence; it takes up the linguistic and conceptual tools that establish plausibility within the specific cultural frameworks in which it functions. Theology is a map, after all, not a terrain. It seeks to trace, or simulate, a landscape of spirit that always exceeds its grasp. The stories that fertilize theology embody its spirit and shape its possibilities. This means that greater attention to those stories' ambiguities and *parous sojourns* can loosen traditional Christian theology's cramped grip on solemnity, its tired habits of barren purity, and so help restore to that theology its own lush capacities for wisdom.

Theology nimble and rigorous enough to attend to the stories, images, experiences, and practices that animate it presupposes the possibility of some coherence and even some lively mutual influence between spiritual experience and intellectual reasoning. Its faith seeks understanding in the name of mystery rather than avoiding understanding by invoking mystery as its opposite or by accepting a hard boundary between understanding (qua rationality) and mystery (qua spirituality). What is more, theology that does not attend to the fecund multiplicity, porosity, and shiftiness of its sources and modes of reasoning can only succeed at aversion and an arrogant narrowness of spirit, neither of which are sufficient to the actual complexity of the world. Such attention, however, takes a more limber posture than Christian theology has been used to assuming. It requires a lighter spirit of inquiry, guided by modes of reasoning unafraid of humor.

The gospel birth narratives – or more specifically the pregnancy narratives – form a collage of images, bits of stories pasted together into a fabric of origin. Their very ambiguity fueled early theological arguments about incarnation that have never been settled. Arian, Athanasian, Manichean, Docetic, and multiple other claims for understanding the promiscuous mingling of god and woman resonate still in a wide and lively array of fully functioning theological anthropologies. Jesus' Jewish origin is fairly straightforward, and its coherence is supported by most of the stories that fill out his short life. His iconic *Christian* origin in Bethlehem, however, is anything but straightforward; it serves the liveliness of the theological array of the Christian anthropologies that continue to follow from it. That pregnancy and birth comprise a shady tale, rife with ulterior motives and sleights of hand, multiple in its effects, requiring a theology of multiplicity to account honestly for its productivity, power, and richness.

This means that historical plausibility in the prosaic sense is the least interesting aspect of the story. Bethlehem exists, there were stables and inns there two thousand years ago, the Roman empire did require census data of its colonial holdings. But those facts work like the punch line that my father's relatives loved to use. They often closed their tall tales with a wink, saying "and if you don't believe me, the barn where it all happened is still standing." The agency of the tall tale of Jesus' birth does not reside in its historical plausibility but in its enduring opacity. It demonstrates a rich parodic capacity to spin an origin out of straw. The story made and makes history in its effects. And its ambiguities still vibrate with potential, less in terms of late Hellenic concerns about stasis and purity and more in terms of multicultural concerns about relationality, openness to change, multiplicity, and embodied integrity. As a thoroughly ambiguous story of conception and birth, it is an appropriate place for polydoxy to begin.

Cribbing sources

How theology understands itself and navigates its own constitutive multiplicity depends a great deal on the tools that it uses. During the millennia of European domination of western Christian thought (and of Christian domination of European thought), it is not surprising that the codes of rationality forged in that cultural context also served to shape the particular scope and criteria of plausibility in Christian theological inquiry. What is more, the past few centuries of global shifts in populations and colonial overlapping and overtaking of cultures make clear that no theological approach has ever stood alone in a vacuum of influences. The interdependence of cultures and religions also makes clear that interdependent modes of reasoning help us to get at the deeper plurality of the world, indeed the deeper plurality of Christian thought itself.

It is certainly the case that many cultural traditions with their varying modes of reasoning are already embedded within Christianity; it is already polydox. The Bible certainly contains texts that celebrate different and sometimes conflicting doxai, exposing a range of rationalities that are expressed in a variety of genres. But even more important for theology's work today is the complicated multitude of cultures within which Christianity is rooted. As Thomas Reynolds neatly points out, "being religious – being Christian – already entails being 'beyond' one's own local faith perspective, [it entails] being interreligious. Pluralism affects religious affirmations from the root."[2] Pluralism here refers to the polysemic intersections, dissonances, relations, and syncretic accretions of multiple stories, experiences, presences, cultures, religious traditions, and modes of reasoning that lead to Christian theology's positions and aversions. Theology that has grown over the course of millennia cannot help but result, in hindsight, in a kind of "polyphonic bricolage."[3]

This assumption of an *originary pluralism* from which Christian theology properly begins, along with the mature awareness of the limitations of Euro-Christian modes of reasoning, form the primary set of presuppositions upon which polydoxy depends. I have argued elsewhere that Christian theology suffers from a sensible lack – an anorexic denial even – of humor and of poetry; it wastes from an over-reliance on apodictic and deductive modes of reasoning to the exclusion of other pathways. In order to think about the enhanced reasoning that poetics and humor offer particularly to polydox theology, I therefore turn to poetry itself, to one poem in which the trope of the crib functions ironically to evoke a depth of complexity and plurality at the narrative birth of Christianity.

Quoted in its entirety below, *Crib*, by U.S. Poet Laureate Kay Ryan engages in erudite play within the linguistic and theological traditions of Europe and Anglo-America. But to better understand the particular insights that the poem suggests for Christian theology, I attend to a Native North American philosophical source that Gerald Vizenor calls "native modernity," which reasons through the intersections of philosophy, poetry, and humor.[4] With the help of this pathway, it is possible to trace some of the fertile tensions in Ryan's theopoetic gestures, and in so doing to clarify some of the key methodological moves that polydoxy makes en route to a more grounded Christian theology. In other words, I approach my topic – the origin myth of Christianity – aslant, "cribbing" from literary criticism and Native American philosophies to illuminate its inherent polysemia, which orthodoxy tends to repress.

My decision to work here with a philosophical mode that comes from cultures not entirely my own does not come lightly. I do so accepting the challenge to white scholars that has been voiced by scholars such as Andrea Smith, Elizabeth Cook-Lynn, James Cone, and Vizenor, who have all argued that the modes of reasoning, as well as the narrative, philosophical, and theological resources, originating outside of Europe have something to say to the problems and issues that affect everyone.[5] Smith has argued, in agreement with Rey Chow, that "ethnic studies ... often confine themselves and are confined to the realm of ethnic or cultural representation rather than positioning themselves as intellectual projects that can shape scholarly discourse as a whole." She goes on to recommend "positioning native peoples as producers of theory and not simply as objects of analysis."[6] I take from challenges such as these the theoretical assumption that anyone can engage with what I am calling the *modes of reasoning* that have operated in many non-European traditions, just as anyone can engage with the modes of reasoning that have largely come out of Europe. What is more, anyone can fruitfully apply such modes of reasoning to issues, cultural products (like poems or theology) and events that may intersect with those originating traditions tangentially, if at all.

There are, of course, unavoidable risks of omission (disregard) and of commission (misappropriation) here. Misappropriation is a real possibility, especially as modes of reasoning usually depend upon specific cultural contents.[7] But the avoidance of this risk through a careful observance of ethnic hermeneutical boundaries can repetitively return to reiteration of exclusively European cultural modes of reasoning. As Smith points out, "the logics of settler colonialism structure all of society, not just those who are indigenous."[8] In this case, the conversation is about Christian theology that takes its own involvement in logics of settler colonialism seriously, that does not turn obsessively to the singular cultural framework or settler logics of Europe to understand itself.

Integrating the fruits of multiple modes of reasoning is not a new phenomenon in Christian theology. African modes of reasoning, for example, first gave Christianity its constitutive construction of theological multiplicity in the form of the Trinity.[9] What is new, and still all too rare, is acknowledgment of the sources of those fruits. There has been a great deal of thievery in the creation of the Christian world. Denying it exacerbates its destructive effects. Naming it, telling stories about it, and constructing theology out of those stories does not remove the reality of Christian larceny both petty and grand (both forgiveable and genocidal). But the stories, told carefully and with the insights of a more poetic and humorous mode of reasoning, may surface the ambiguity out of which life comes, the messiness that makes birth possible.

The tall tale that built a world

Crib

From the Greek for
woven or plaited,
which quickly translated
to basket. Whence the verb
crib, which meant "to filch"
under cover of wicker

anything – some liquor,
a cutlet.
For we want to make off
with things that are not
our own. There is a pleasure
theft brings, a vitality
to the home.
Cribbed objects or answers
keep their guilty shimmer
forever, have you noticed?
Yet religions downplay this.
Note, for instance, in our
annual rehearsals of innocence,
the substitution of manger for crib –
as if we ever deserved that baby,
or thought we did.

Kay Ryan[10]

Of the many metaphoric possibilities that the Christian pregnancy and birth narratives hold for what we are calling a polydox approach to Christian theology, I
am inspired to follow Kay Ryan and focus on the small detail of the baby Jesus'
crib. Not the feed box itself in which we are told the infant first lay, but the
complex English etymology of the word "crib," which provides an opening to a
more mature appreciation of Christian beginnings, from which a more vigorous
approach to theology can grow. I approach the crib and its rich variety of meanings
indirectly through the lens of Ryan's poem and a philosophical sensibility gleaned
from my work with some Native North American modes of reasoning. Vizenor
calls the originators and practitioners of these modes of reasoning the "storiers of
natural reason on this continent."[11] This brief reflection is therefore the result of a
confluence of several theoretical strands whose coherence, I believe, nets insights
otherwise missed by more settled theological approaches.

In the poem, "crib" is a term that swings readily between naughty and nice, land-
ing guilt right into the middle of innocence. It is a wonderful word, ancient enough
to have accrued meanings that clash and thereby to have enhanced its complexity
and nuance. It is a feeding structure out in fields, a dwelling place of thieves, a
cradle and a cheat-sheet, a brothel, covered basket, saloon, and an illegitimate translation. It is certainly ripe for poetry. But its complexity also ripens it for theology, in
part because according to the *Oxford English Dictionary*, it was preferred early on
to other translations (illegitimate or otherwise) of the nativity scene: "In nearly all
early quotations [crib] applied to the manger in which the infant Christ was laid."[12]

In the first few lines, Ryan imagines the origins of the word literally as a covering for what might be purloined. The heart of the poem, however, is much more
than etymology. It is a reflection on the guilty pleasures of theft, a "vitality to the
home" that perhaps can only come from things that do not belong to us. She is
talking about small time theft, at least at the start, but through the humorous wink

and nudge over satisfied pleasures that come from harmless scams, she entraps us with complicity – and the complexity of pleasure – in bigger, world-altering crimes. Ryan teases out the ambiguity of cribbing especially (and perhaps most pleasurably) in terms of its theological and religious implications. She ends the poem with a pseudo-lament that religions disavow the animating character of theft even as they depend upon it. She accuses Christianity (though not in so many plodding words) of overplaying its own innocence by, in effect, switching the polysemic crib for a stabilized (stabled) manger "as if we ever deserved that baby."

What is important here, both for the humor of the poem and the theological insight to which the humor points, is that Ryan is not discrediting the crib or the counterfeit it implies, not even in the case of the most famously sacred sleeping newborn. Instead she indicts religion's pretensions to legitimacy, its cover-ups of its own invariably inglorious and promiscuous beginnings. She dismisses typical Christian avowals of innocence that pretend the founding stories of Christian faith are not a pastiche of pick-pocketed baubles and filched treasures. Apart from the saucy impiety of such a claim, Ryan seems to be suggesting that Christianity's protestations of innocence actually diminish creativity and life and so, presumably, dim the enlivening radiance of the treasure swaddled at its core.

In contrast to orthodox Christian claims of divine impeccability, the idea that imposture and thievery is part and parcel of the vitality of the divine spirit has long operated at the root of trickster theologies in native modernity and continues to function in some native Christianities. Trickster (Coyote, Hare, Spider, and others, depending on the language and tradition) is often a critical figure in Native North American creation accounts. His (or her) greedy heists, disastrous but funny scams, and irreversible mistakes are necessary to the creation of the complex world which the people inhabit and which they become. Ryan's *Crib* also suggests a heist at the center of Christianity's story of origin. Parsed through the reasoning mode of native modernity, it may reveal far more than a joke, or rather the joke reveals far more than could ever be expressed without it. The joke – in this case *a cribbed god* – reveals a fertile ambiguity at the heart of Christianity that endures (and may even require) its originary subterfuge. Rather than compounding the error of fraudulence by denying it, polydoxy, grounded in a logic of multiplicity, maintains a proper perspective and hermeneutic by laughing at it.

In the Native American cultures out of which the trickster comes, he (or she) is a world-creating master of words, of parody, lies, cons, and stories that, in a postmodern sense, could result in a summative assumption that reality is a game of language alone. But native modernity also presumes life *in* stories, and so the issue is not whether reality can be reduced to grammar, thereby soothing postmodern aversions to ontology. Rather the issue is how to handle the ontic productivity that stories inevitably carry. As Thomas King declares, "the truth about stories is that that's all we are."[13] The challenge coming from native modernity is not ontology's totalizing tendencies as it is in European thought. Rather the challenge in this mode of reasoning is ontology's slipperiness – the porous and promiscuous excesses that narrative produces beyond the tissue of grammar.

This ontic slipperiness is most evident in the scams that the trickster pulls – the cons that he or she unselfconsciously and (usually) without malice masterminds. These scams do actually help to create the world that humans and other animals inhabit. Animals lose or gain speech, appendages, skills, and any number of relations due to the trickster's mistakes. Mountains fold into slumbering ancestors and trees become rivers, even stones cry out in response to the trickster's indecent creativity. It is not necessary to assume a narrow realism here to glimpse possibilities inherent in these accounts, although I share Grinde's observation that "when Jesus Christ walks on water this is treated as 'religious' but when Coyote steals fire … it is invariably characterized by the dominant society's discourse as 'legend' or, worst [sic] yet, 'folklore.'"[14] Whether the trickster elements in Native North American traditions are treated linguistically and metaphorically (as code for particular meanings within nontransferable cultural frameworks) or philosophically (as "ontic signifiers," as per Vizenor, for what might be transculturally shared as real), they offer by way of example an alternative to the narrow exclusions that western philosophical rationalism has imposed on the actual trickiness and complexity of Christian texts and traditions.

The cribs of trickster narratives illuminate a deeper logic in Native North American ontological appraisals of the way things are and ought to be. That logic resides in the vatic quality of humor that any serious accounting of reality requires. In other words, the "storiers of natural reason on this continent" pursue through ironic and parabolic lenses a "common tease of cultures, a sense of presence, and the obscure traces of traditions" that otherwise utterly evade the grinding reasoning of European modernity.[15] This natural reason allows for honesty about theft even long after the fact, and recognizes its effects in the world that is created, for better or worse, as a result. Humor here, in other words, is not without horror, and it is more than a mere coping strategy. It is an element of a mode of reasoning that recognizes long-term consequences in actions, words, and concepts, even when those consequences can only be sketched in caricature and put metaphorically into stories of possibility. Some things are so serious, in other words, that only humor can touch them.

Friedrich Nietzsche, an acerbic critic of European modernity as well as one of its devoted sons, had an intuition of this when he entertained the possibility that some "truths … are singularly shy and ticklish and cannot be caught [by the plodding modes of Hegelian reasoning]."[16] He asked "[d]oes a matter necessarily remain un-understood and unfathomed merely because it has been touched only in flight, glanced at, in a flash?"[17] At times capable of great insight through laughter, Nietzsche understood fleet-footed humor to be able to travel through a terrain that the heavily treaded brush-clearing machinery of (humorless) western logic simply flattens and so may mistake or miss or destroy altogether. I choose the metaphor of terrain deliberately here, as native modernity also never forgets the realities of western expansion, not only in cultural terms, but in terms of the land on which all theologians in the Americas (at least) stand. Settler colonialism signifies a mode of reasoning, but also a material reality. Theft undergirds the economic structures (think slavery and land) and the physical spaces (think real estate and "homes") of Euro-American modernity that is also a globalized colonial modernity. But in the context of what could – and should? – kill laughter altogether, humor charts alternative courses through the thickets of existence. It thereby not only "sees" the terrain differently, but can actually produce different concepts and different knowledges in relation to it.

This approach to philosophical theology (this "sense" of humor) follows Vizenor in that it recognizes a fundamental liveliness in creation *and* in humor, a constitutive trickiness and subterfuge to living and to understanding. It cannot be contained or colonized in systems of thought that are too comprehensive, settled, or confident. It also picks up on Gilles Deleuze's motile sensibility and nomadic ontology (an exuberant theory of becoming) as well as both Alain Badiou's and Jean-Luc Nancy's arguments for the primacy of the multiple as constitutive, or prior, to the One. Deleuze, Badiou, and Nancy are European thinkers whose contributions to theories of multiplicity push toward post-modern recognition of the limits of the logic of the One and hint at points of sympathy with native modernity and other non-European modes of reasoning.[18] Deleuze and Badiou also share a fundamental dependence upon "the problematic," meaning that they recognize the fact that specific, contextual problems generate thought, constitute it, provoke it to new insight. As a philosophical sense of humor, furthermore, Vizenor through native modernity and Deleuze through Nietzsche understand such reasoning to be a force of life. This grants to humor a deceptively conceptual weight in which it is possible for trickster narratives to "remind Native Americans and non-Native [peoples] alike that 'there is no final, ultimate answer, no infallibility that we can blindly accept and follow. Power, like life, is in motion.'"[19]

Although I am emphasizing here something more productive than functional about humor, it is also important to point out that postcolonial humor sometimes serves as "a strategy for exposing how western epistemologies and scientific, aesthetic, and historiographic discourses may inherently condition one-dimensionally Eurocentric responses and interpretations."[20] Humor is revelatory and strategic for communities that under colonial assault were not or are not meant to survive.[21] In 1969, Lakota theologian Vine Deloria, Jr. wrote in *Custer Died For Your Sins* that "[w]hen a people can laugh at themselves and laugh at others and hold all aspects of life together without letting anybody drive them to extremes, then it seems to me that people can survive."[22] What is more, Laguna poet Paula Gunn Allen declares, "we live in a time that has much that is shabby and tricky to offer; and much that needs to be treated with laughter and ironic humor."[23] Postcolonial and decolonial humor "relies on ambiguity, discrepancy, and incongruity" and in so doing employs a kind of perception that tilts what is taken for granted and allows for a reconsideration of sacred or merely habituated categories.[24] But along with Vizenor, I suggest that what is strategic and canny in the face of overwhelming and unremitting assault is also ontically significant; it is productive of reality and knowledge in the face of deeper questions of orientation to tradition and world, of ethics, and of "how the coming generation is to live."[25]

Humor that bears ontic significance is also, as I have indicated, profoundly serious.[26] Perhaps because it often travels the sharp edges of hurt and uncertainty such humor may be, as Langston Hughes has suggested, "what you wish in your heart were not funny, but it is, and you must laugh."[27] What is funny about a poor, young, unwed woman traveling at night, nine months' pregnant, depending upon the goodwill of a man willing, for the moment, to protect her with the pretense of fatherhood? Where is the humor in her labor outside of closed inns? Or in the demanding cries of her baby? Nothing is really humorous in the content of the story itself (well, except for perhaps the annunciation, the shepherds, the angels, the sheep, and the wise men). The humor of the crib is also its horror, both of which are only available in hindsight of imperial Christianity's boastful claims to legitimacy. The absurdity of the seriousness, and the inescapability of its various indictments, is part of what allows humor to constitute a particularly sharp and productive epistemology. "That's what makes it funny," Hughes claims, "the fact that you don't know you are laughing at yourself." Perhaps only those who can relate to the pain of having been that poor, exhausted young woman bearing the burden of divine and imperial schemes *can* really laugh, can recognize the humor – which is a particular kind of knowledge – of the cribbed god.

There is certainly irony in the triumphal arches, solemn processions and avowals of holy innocence in the midst of genocidal advances and purges, in the beauty of golden and marble pietas and crèches, in doctrines of love and compassion and expansion and conversion, of blankets and food and guns, all nestled together in the innocence of a cribbed god. *That* is funny, in a particularly horrifying kind of way. It is funny because it is part of what constitutes the world; its story has helped to create the crazy, ambiguous, painful, and lively world in which we live and which we continue to build. Erasing the crib, erasing Christianity, erases us all. You wish with all of your heart that it was not funny, but from the angle of ontic significance "it is, and you must laugh."

And so to return to Kay Ryan's *Crib*, at work in the poem is an insight framed as a punning joke about Christian – or any self-important religious – claims to authority and ownership. It has the same sort of potential for exposing the obvious that the proverbial little boy has in the story of the emperor's new clothes: in spite of the pontifical processions and elaborate, earnest rehearsals of possession, Jesus does not belong to Christianity; he never did. He is one of those "[c]ribbed objects or answers" that perhaps thereby retains a hold on us and a power (a vitality and guilty shimmer) that we cannot really explain. Ryan implies something both serious and paradoxical here, namely that a refreshing imposture actually constitutes the reality and dynamic potential of Christian stories and so of Christian faith. A lively and energizing fraudulence flows beneath the worn-out patina of legitimacy and purity (evident, for example, in the savior's chastity of body and imagination). It surges there still despite the centuries of somber effort that theologians concerned about Christianity's imperial legitimacy have put into stitching veils of innocence in which to wrap him and with which to cover their own tracks.

Because cribbing is stealing, the crib-qua-theft is an idea which, applied to the collection of stories upon which Christian theology depends, undermines any claims to the purity of theology's content, by which I mean the theologian's ability to stake claims of ownership to the objects (or answers) that have already been cribbed in its sources. In Eric Bentley's discussion of the prevalence of theft in the plots of good comic dramas ("if we did not wish to break the tenth commandment" he quips, "comic plotting, as we know it, could never have come into being"), he reminds us that "to steal is to falsify, for it is to forge, as it were, a title to ownership."[28] Of course, theft in and of itself is not a benign concept. It may be the basis of comedy, but by that very token it is also the basis of tragedy. The brutal thefts of lands, of human bodies and lives, of languages and of freedoms have built the structures of privilege upon which the industrialized, capitalist world gorges itself.

Theft is not a virtue, either in native modernity or in contemporary theology. It should not be romanticized (as it is never romanticized in postcolonial humor). As Kenneth Lincoln writes, echoing Langston Hughes, "[t]here is always hurt in humor, and vice versa … It's the way one learns the truth."[29] In addition, in his essay on comedy, Christopher Fry insists that "there is an angle of experience where the dark is distilled into light … where our tragic fate finds itself with perfect pitch, and goes straight to the key which creation was composed in."[30] The tragic, in other words, cannot be glossed or smoothed away, nor can the weight of responsibility lift from the shoulders of thieves. But neither should the role of theft and deception in the creative motion of the world be denied. The theft of life by predators and their constant frustration by the canniness of prey contributes to the audacious genius of evolution just as every stolen life remains irreplaceable and grieveable, a spur to transformation and to the creative impasses of loss.

It is the humor in Ryan's poem that works subtly to unmask the trope of larceny cradled at the narrative heart of Christian self-avowals of innocence. *Crib* suggests something inherently contrary and funny in the entire edifice of Christian pomp and self-satisfaction, especially in Christmas invocations of the Bethlehem narrative, but it does not stop there. In a manner resonant with native modernity, Ryan reveals non-innocence in the innocent; she peeks under the baby blanket of Christian immaculation and sees a purloined letter happily slumbering there. But her disruption of the crib's monosemic simplicity is more than functional. Beyond being a tool of unmasking, her humor is a mode of theological construction that starts from the virtue and fertility of non-innocence. And that is, I am suggesting, what makes theology capable of birth, *which is messy*.

The newborn Christ is a crib-sheet of the enduring multiplicity threaded throughout the fabric of Christian identity. As an ontic signifier, the crib's ambiguity and incongruity as cradle and cheat-sheet make it humorous, but also give to theology an open-ended capacity that axiomatic solemnity foregoes. These stories have a volatile, creative power that doctrinal absolutism can entirely miss, glossing their volatility as the dispensable by-product of human frailty. Rather than adding clarity and wisdom to the core stories or even extracting wisdom from them, theology that cleaves too tightly to apodictic and axiomatic norms of judgment, that eschews humor and takes itself and its presumed possessions too seriously, dessicates and distorts the potential for wisdom resident in those stories. It cancels the invitational openness that they do possess. Perhaps the crib can provide to theology what Deleuze calls the "force of life" and thereby restore to Christian theology a recognition that incarnation has to be messy and ambiguous if it is to have anything to do with actual embodiment. Perhaps a better, more contrary and humorous story of the crib in Bethlehem can give to Christian theology a hope of actually recognizing incarnation when it bawls and clamors for the breast.

The very idea that the creative and salvific center of the Christian faith is founded on a bit of sleight of hand (represented in the fully divine treasure of a strangely fugitive human birth and life) does not in and of itself constitute much of a provocation. Lying, stealing, and willful disregard of evidence are charges that have been laid against Christians, and answered or dodged by them, at least since Origen's analogical replies to Celsus's ridicule. More recently, Christian theology has had to face sustained disaffection by contemporaries who respond to the austere requirements of Christian avowals of innocence by shrugging off Christianity's claims on them and simply walking away from its tottering edifices of doctrine. Liberal attempts to construct hermeneutical circles and recent radical orthodox attempts to construct narrative boundaries of authority have sought erosion-free zones wherein the serious and mostly dry business of theological doctrine can take place free of molestation by the disgruntled. But there are exiles, poets, and storiers of many continents who suspect Christian theology of more fluidity than it tends to admit. They find the play of uncertainty at the heart of the faith refreshing, compelling, and even quickening.

Polydox possessions or, there are four gospels

Polydoxy welcomes the frisson of uncertainty in theology's provenance. It shakes the foundations of any claims to absolute truth. Despite the fact that these foundations are already crumbling and, as Catherine Keller points out, they have been crumbling for a very long time, their erosion represents precisely the kind of problem, or impasse, that precedes insight.[31] Beyond celebrating such impasses – which they do – I have indicated that both Badiou and Deleuze see philosophy itself (and I would add theology) as functionally and essentially dependent upon impasses and therefore as problematic in the best sense.[32] The loss of Christian absolutes forms an obstacle that looms before business-as-usual modes of theological reasoning but in so doing provokes new modes of thought, allows theologians to be "seized [stolen?] by some such intimation of that which lies beyond their present-best powers of attainment or epistemic grasp."[33]

But the possibility of a crib at the heart of Christian theology does not represent an impasse at all if it only provokes apology and complacent affirmations of the boundaries of authority. It does not even matter that we can think of the Christian crib-qua-theft more or less literally, not least because the Jesus of the Gospels is none other than a pilfered Christian. All records indicate that he was, after all, a Jewish Palestinian man without any apparent intention of founding a new religion, particularly a religion that would rely so heavily – and to a Jew so heretically – on his own divine status. But that nicety of probable intention in the absence of much documentary evidence means little two millennia into the historical effects of a global religion that has claimed – and seeks to possess – Jesus entirely as its own. Indeed Christianity cannot do without Christ or the incarnational crib of divine–human intercourse that Christian theology has built to secure him to itself. Even for those who distinguish between Jesus as historical figure and Christ as ecclesial figure in order to separate the gospels from the church's later doctrines, the "person" of Jesus/Christ remains central to Christian understanding. As Kathryn Tanner argues, "Christ is the key," at least for Christians, "to what God is doing everywhere."[34]

The impasse that does loom large before Christian theology, "and of which a philosophy of this sort suffers the secret attraction," takes the form of the long-standing theological aversion to uncertainty and multiplicity *except* as the exterior to divinity, as the friable, worldly other to God's serene completion.[35] "Present-best epistemic grasps," forged in orthodox presuppositions of divine simplicity and indefeasibility cannot conceive of purity (or, therefore, of divinity) except in subtractive terms. Those terms cancel out the "grand and squalid matter of all things human" (Margaret Atwood).[36] And so the question here is not whether the center of the Christian narratives is a pastiche of stolen goods. Rather, the question is whether a theological engagement with, rather than against, that possibility can offer a breakthrough, a "coming to light" as Badiou puts it, "of an indiscernible of the times."[37] If theology can engage its own constitutive multiplicity more fully, it enables the shimmering and creative power that the trickster's thefts bring, as well as a humbling relief from the dessicating exactitude of having only decent stories – and relatives – of which to tell.

Because Jesus as the Christ not only stands distinctively at the center of Christian faith, practice, and theology but functions theologically as the key to Christian understandings of divine presence in and relationship to the world, we can say that Christian theology is possessed by the very Christ it has cribbed. Thieves often do, after all, get possessed by the treasures they seek to possess, especially if, to keep possession, they can never really reveal their loot. I am suggesting here through the trope of originary theft that Christianity is possessed by what it has never been able fully to possess, and humor is a deft mode of natural reasoning for teasing out that obsessive and tragicomic flaw in Christian creativity. The energy of dissonance and attraction between the poles of possessing and being possessed account for much of the genius, horror, error, and possibility that Christian faith and theology still bears and which keeps so many of us coming back, and back, to its unobtainable but enlivening depths.

In his reflection on philosophical hermeneutics, Hans-Georg Gadamer argues optimistically that "we are possessed by something and precisely by means of it we are opened up for the new, the different, the true."[38] This may be the case, but only if we let possession open us up. Doing so requires better stories. More than the gratuitous lure of the new and different, the opening-up to which Gadamer refers – the acceptance of a constitutive porosity and pluralism – looms like a promise and an impasse before Christian theology grown plodding and dim on bourgeois certainties, myths of innocence, and the fixes of imminent domain. The opening-up that incarnation offers to Christian theology is a corrigible foundation that allows embodiment actually to become present in Christian thought. Embodiment requires presence in an ordinary sense; it is incoherent without presence and, in that fact, it entails a logic of multiplicity. Bodies are constitutively porous, relational, mutable, and utterly inexchangeable, requiring any philosophy or theology that "opens up" to embodiment to be necessarily painted with the same brush. Put another way, the friable qualities of flesh do not adhere, they constitute.

Presence, or "being-with," to adopt the phrase that Nancy prefers, is not a static notion. It requires becoming-present, or presentation. Presence is a tricky term for philosophies steeped in the logic of the One, because – as Kant intuited – no thing in itself can fully present itself without remainder, contradiction, or trickery. In the logic of the One, the only resolution to this problem is to deny presence(s) any epistemological or ontological certainty at all. Hence the caricature of postmodern philosophy's supposed nihilism: there is nothing that can be absolutely asserted, and "presence" requires too many substantive assumptions that simply cannot be supported in the context of so much possibility of error. Whatever one sees or experiences in the supposed presence of another can never certainly refer to anything outside of the narrative one inhabits. In the caricature of European postmodernity, reality ultimately consists only of competing interpretations of texts.

As I have been suggesting throughout this essay, other modes of reasoning exist (than the logic of the One, that is) that have never required "presence" to instantiate static, unverifiable substance prior to linguistic or narrative implication. They do not assume language, narrative, and story to be inert building blocks and tools for reporting, memory, or instruction. In other words, these other modes of reasoning do not assume language, narrative, and story to be disembodied, without agency of their own. Perhaps there is a fundamental tendency in book-cultures toward the negligent idea that language and narrative can be reduced to utility and thereby bound (as in shelved). The error lies in forgetting the innate agency of stories, their capacity to be bound *for* something, for mischief and creation beyond any storyteller's ability to predict or manage. Ontic significance co-implicates story and presence(s), assuming a world-creating aspect to narrative that cannot be restricted or entirely managed. But this idea is intelligible only within a mode of reasoning that begins with multiplicity or more specifically does not presume a prior logic of the One wherein an ontological separation between truth (as one) and fiction (as multiple) must be maintained.[39]

It is significant that some European philosophers – Badiou, Nancy, and Deleuze in particular – have finally begun to turn energetically toward theories of multiplicity as a starting point for postmodern rationality. They are doing so in part because the general global milieu for writing has allowed the possibility of different modes of reasoning (along with very different kinds of stories) to circulate and pollinate hybrid species of thought. They also have begun to reach some of the logical limits of negation in postmodern thought, and seek more supple grounds for thinking about reality without reactivity about presence and ontology. This has led them to theories of multiplicity and a new willingness to entertain ideas of presence.

Badiou, for example, agrees that presence cannot denote a static reality and so he prefers "presentation," a more active notion, which he defines as "multiple-being." For Badiou, as with Deleuze and Nancy, multiple-being is logically prior to the One. "The One is not presented," he declares, "it results, thus making the multiple consist."[40] To put it another way, multiplicity founds coherence and the possibility of unity. Native modernity, as we have seen, starts with this assumption, taking from it the structures of plausibility that incorporate ambiguity (which is a kind of multiplicity) into the core of its mode of reasoning. Without ambiguity there are no stories, and without stories, as King asserts, there is no truth. Which means that truth, in truth, is multiple.

The crib – the founding story of incarnation – is a story of multiplicity, quite literally. Flesh cannot be thought through the logic of the One and it implicates incarnational philosophies worthy of the name in that failure as well, a failure which has turned into a very productive impasse. "If," as Tanner suggests, the incarnation demonstrates to Christians that "God usually works with, rather than over-riding, the ordinary character of human life … [i]t is as changing and defeasible truths, then, that human claims would gain divine sanction."[41] What is more, being present – embodied – also characterizes the basic Christian claim to the divine act of incarnation, casting God's own existence (or, more precisely, what God gives us to know of that existence) into the corrigible excesses and intrusions of multiplicity. And for Gabriel Marcel, this presence is the very meaning of fidelity.

> A presence is a reality; it is a kind of influx; it depends upon us to be permeable to this influx, but not, to tell the truth, to call it forth. Creative fidelity consists in maintaining ourselves actively in a permeable state; and there is a mysterious interchange between this free act and the gift granted in response to it.[42]

The Christian narratives, the body of texts, and the bodies of communities that circulate like blood, or like constellations, or like rumors, are inherently permeable to presence; they consist in multiplicity. This has always been a stumbling block for theologies bound to and for the logic of the One, but this constitutive permeability becomes a source of rejuvenation and vitality for theologies bound otherwise. To the extent that Christian theology depends upon the inherently plural consistency of the embodiment narratives to which it turns to authorize its claims, its claims retain a fundamentally polydox character, which is to say *a porous and responsive character, cognizant of the* a priori *multiplicity in which incarnation consists.*

If the crib at the heart of Christianity offers anything to a long-overdue mode of reasoning that we are calling polydoxy, it is the suggestion of a distinctive and thoroughly grounded approach to Christian thought that need not lie about its original ambiguity and illegitimacy any more than it ever has needed to exclude fugitive newborns or life stories told four ways. The manyness-teaching that polydoxy entails cannot accept a reduction of its own constitutive multiplicity to a virginal trope of purity, although variations on that theme can certainly enliven a polydox approach. As a term, polydoxy has the burden and benefit of unfamiliarity (unlike orthodoxy, for example), but it possesses the virtue of veracity in describing the actual multiplicity that constitutes the sources and traditions that intersect in Christian thought.

Where several of the gospel variations literally crib the figure of Jesus in their opening scenes, theology has cribbed its answers from the riches of local wisdom, stories of power, inherited traditions, aphorisms, scientific findings, cultural norms, political expedients, popular culture, visual art, philosophical disciplines, war traumas, heroic narratives and anything else that helped to maneuver the bits and pieces of the ancient stories and exhortations into an architecture of meaning for whole communities frontally faced with the challenges of existence. Such multiform cribbing might be described in Deleuzean terms as rhizomatic, the result of nomadic experimentation and growth, or it might be described in economic terms, such as hunting and gathering. The difference between the metaphors of theft, expansion, and gathering, however, lie mainly in their aesthetic appeal rather than in their substance. After all, hunting and gathering can become theft when someone puts up 'no trespassing' signs and has the power to enforce presumed ownership, as so many hunter-gatherers across the world have discovered in recent centuries to their detriment. And expansion can become theft (of shared lands, for example) by the same practice.

The strategic assistance that the trope of theft provides here, instead of the more palatable and aesthetic notions of the rhizome, the nomad, the hunter-gatherer, or even creole bricolage, is its potential of resistance to a too-easy return to impostures of legitimacy. Next to imperial greed, the hubris of legitimacy is one of the oldest and strongest obstacles to integrity and humor in Christian theology. For that reason alone it bears watching. But beyond that concern, Deleuze's polemical and metaphoric differentiation between the rhizomatic, relationally-dependent, fundamentally nomadic plant and the arboreal, pedigreed, stationary plant is less about differences among flora and more about the artifice of clear origins, identities, and genealogical certainty that prevails within the walls of gardens and of garden-like philosophies. What polydoxy shares with Deleuze and Vizenor is a suspicion that there is fraud being perpetrated in those genealogies – particularly religious genealogies – that confer innocence, legitimacy, and ownership upon the powerful. What it gathers paradoxically from Ryan and native modernity is the storyteller's contrary and humor-sharpened suspicion that a certain amount of pilfering and counterfeit is necessary to creation and to the stories that are "all we are." Especially when they are told truthfully, carefully, and in the right season.

Notes

1   K. Ryan, "Crib," *Elephant Rocks: Poems by Kay Ryan*, New York: Grove Press, 1996, p. 17.
2   T. E. Reynolds, *The Broken Whole: Philosophical Steps Toward a Theology of Global Solidarity*, Albany, NY: SUNY Press, 2006, p. 9.

3   B. E. Schmidt, "The Creation of Afro-Caribbean Religions and their Incorporation of Christian Elements: A Critique Against Syncretism," *Transformation*, 23, 4, 2006, p. 236.

4   Gerald Vizenor has coined the phrase "native modernity" to counter the ethnocentric and linear notion that modernity can only be applied to European cultures. "Natives are not premodern in the sense of primitive, medieval cultures," he argues. "Such peevish notions were presented by the monotheists, polytheists, the separatists of manifest destiny, and by colonial dominance. Clearly, natives are the storiers of natural reason on this continent, and their stories are, as they have always been, the imagic moments of cultural conversions and native modernity." G. Vizenor, *Native Liberty: Natural Reason and Cultural Survivance*, Lincoln, NE: University of Nebraska Press, 2009, p. 161.

5   J. Cone, "Theology's Great Sin," Plenary Address to the American Academy of Religion, Denver, CO, November 2001.

6   Smith is primarily addressing indigenous scholars, but the importance of her challenge is also relevant for European and Euro-American scholars, who must also be vigilant to the realities of misappropriation and distortion. A. Smith, "Queer Theory and Native Studies: The Heteronormativity of Settler Colonialism," *GLQ: A Journal of Lesbian and Gay Studies*, 16, 1/2, 2010, p. 43.

7   Elizabeth Cook-Lynn describes the very real result that efforts to engage native works "often seem superficial or exploitative." E. Cook-Lynn, "American Indian Intellectualism and the New Indian Story," in D. A. Mihesuah (ed.), *Natives and Academics: Researching and Writing About American Indians*, Lincoln, NE: University of Nebraska Press, 1998, p. 113.

8   Smith, p. 44. It is important to note that she is referring specifically to the need for native studies to engage queer theory rather than Christian theology, but the argument is persuasive regarding both.

9   L. C. Schneider, *Beyond Monotheism: A Theology of Multiplicity*, New York: Routledge, 2008, pp. 60ff.

10 Ryan, pp. 16–17.

11 Vizenor, p. 161.

12 See *OED* entry "crib (n)" and "crib (v)," *The Oxford English Dictionary*, 2nd ed., 1989. *OED Online*, Oxford University Press, (accessed online at Regenstein Library, The University of Chicago, June 20, 2010).

13 T. King, *The Truth About Stories: A Native Narrative*, Minneapolis, MN: University of Minnesota Press, 2003, p. 2 et passim.

14 D. A. Grinde, Jr., quoted by E. Gruber, *Humor in Contemporary Native North American Literature: Reimagining Nativeness*, Rochester, NY: Camden House, 2008, p. 158.

15 Vizenor, pp. 161, 164.

16 F. Nietzsche, *The Gay Science*, in W. Kaufman (ed.), *Basic Writings*, trans. W. Kaufman, New York: Modern Library, 2000, p. 177.

17 Ibid.

18 Although their work variously represents points of sympathy with native modernity and other non-European modes of reasoning (as well as modes of reasoning generated by feminists in Europe, the United States, and elsewhere), these thinkers mostly maintain the hubris of believing that they are the producers of their own thought, and do not recognize the importance of the rise of alternative modalities in liberation movements around the world. It is a pity, as their work would be that much further along, if only they would recognize their indebtedness to women, and to the indigenous philosophers of non-Eurocentric cultures.

19 K. Blaeser, quoted by M. A. Bowers, "'Ethnic Glue': Humor in Native American Literatures," in S. Reichl and M. Stein (eds), *Cheeky Fictions: Laughter and the Postcolonial*, Amsterdam: Rodopi, 2005, p. 253.

20   Gruber, p. 227.
21   Audre Lorde penned this memorable line in her poem "A Litany for Survival" in *The Black Unicorn: Poems By Audre Lorde*, New York: Norton, 1978, pp. 30–1.
22   V. Deloria, Jr., *Custer Died For Your Sins: An Indian Manifesto*, New York: MacMillan, 1969, p. 167.
23   P. G. Allen, quoted in Bowers, p. 248.
24   J. Miller, quoted in S. Pichler, "Interculturality and Humor in Timothy Mo's *Sour Sweet*," in S. Reichl and M. Stein (eds), *Cheeky Fictions: Laughter and the Postcolonial*, Amsterdam: Rodopi, 2005, p. 210.
25   D. Bonhoeffer, "After Ten Years: A Reckoning Made at New Year 1943," in E. Bethge (ed.), *Letters and Papers from Prison*, trans. E. H. Robertson, New York: MacMillan, 1967, p. 6.
26   Vizenor, p. 178.
27   L. Hughes, "A Note on Humor," in L. Hughes (ed.), *The Book of Negro Humor*, New York: Dodd, Mead and Company, 1966, p. vii.
28   E. Bentley, *The Life of the Drama*, excerpted in R. W. Corrington (ed.), *Comedy: A Critical Anthology*, Boston, MA: Houghton Mifflin, 1971, p. 766.
29   K. Lincoln, *Indi'n Humor: Bicultural Play in Native America*, New York: Oxford University Press, 1993, p. 63.
30   C. Fry, "Comedy," in R. W. Corrington (ed.), *Comedy: A Critical Anthology*, Boston, MA: Houghton Mifflin, 1971, p. 755.
31   C. Keller, *Face of the Deep: A Theology of Becoming*, London: Routledge, 2003, p. 229.
32   "[A]n impasse: So much the better," in G. Deleuze and F. Guattari, *A Thousand Plateaus: Capitalism and Schnizophrenia*, trans. B. Massumi, Minneapolis, MN: University of Minnesota Press, 1987, p. 20.
33   C. Norris, *Badiou's Being and Event*, London: Continuum, 2009, p. 10.
34   K. Tanner, *Christ the Key*, Cambridge: Cambridge University Press, 2010, p. viii.
35   G. Marcel, "On the Ontological Mystery," *The Philosophy of Existentialism*, trans. M. Harari, New York: Citadel Press, 1962, p. 46.
36   M. Atwood, "Trickster Makes This World: Mischief, Myth, and Art and The Gift: Imagination and the Erotic Life of Property by Lewis Hyde," M. Atwood, *Writing With Intent: Essays, Reviews, Personal Prose 1983–2005*, New York: Carroll & Graf Publishers, 2005, p. 181 (essay pp. 177–81).
37   A. Badiou, *Being and Event*, trans. O. Feltham, London: Continuum, 2005, p. 16.
38   H. G. Gadamer, *Philosophical Hermeneutics*, trans. D. Linge, Los Angeles, CA: UCLA, 1976, p. 9.
39   For a fuller discussion of the bifurcation of fact and fiction in the logic of the One, see L. C. Schneider, *Beyond Monotheism: A Theology of Multiplicity*, New York: Routledge, 2008, Chapter 6.
40   Badiou, p. 519.
41   Tanner, p. 280.
42   Marcel, p. 38.

3   The sense of peace

A para-doxology of divine multiplicity

Roland Faber

Orthodoxy and the doxa of multiplicity

According to a qualified theological "opinion" (*doxa*), the alpha and omega of theology, is *doxology*: The functionless evocation of divine *doxa* – powerful beauty – for its own sake.[1] In Luke 2:4, the doxological invocation of divine *doxa* is equivalent with her shining over the ones who live in peace. However, in recollecting the history of religion it would be just as easy to claim that religion is the last resort of violence, a "record of the horrors," of "human sacrifice … the slaughter of children, cannibalism, sensual orgies, abject superstition, hatred as between races, the maintenance of degrading customs, hysteria, bigotry," or in one phrase, "the last refuge of human savagery?"[2] Is it with deep disgust that we must admit that "the name of God" has become equivalent with any number of reasons for war?[3] And is it with deep embarrassment that we must be stupefied by the fact that while we might (want to) confess that *God* becomes *flesh*, *doxa* has become *orthodoxy* – as our orthodoxies are considerably implicit in our religious divisions? How, and in what sense, then, could the doxological arousal of the divine become an evocation of peace?

If the only means of "peace in heaven" is the inhabitation of a single, true *orthodox* realm, its doxology only suggests a subjugation to an orthodox One. Consequently, the equivalent of *doxa* on earth becomes "war." The question is this: can we save "the name of God" from war – "in heaven" and "on earth" – by saving divine *doxa* from orthodoxy?[4] Could we, perhaps, resist the *ortho-dox* One – the only true measure "in heaven" – and instead evoke a *para-dox* multiplicity as an expression of "peace on earth?"[5] Could, maybe, an understanding of divine *multiplicity* before and beyond any "true orthodox essence" be key to envisioning the overcoming of perpetual generations of religious wars? Could the *doxa* of such *divine love of multiplicity* shine over us, instigating a profound *sense* of peace, that is, the imagination of its *real* possibility?[6]

Like a paranoid disorder, religious "opinion" (*doxa*) tends to find in itself such *absolute* truth that, if it really were the shadow of God's *doxa*, it makes God *only* the expression of the power of war. Is the reason to abandon religion altogether, for many, a disenchantment with the sanctification of someone else's idiosyncratic horizon that, in its own turn, justifies itself as the expression of the one, absolute God "himself"? What is such an "orthodoxy" that seduces to a "dox-ology of war" other than *fanaticism* – the *exclusive* expression of *being right*, righteous, justified, sanctified by *being on the right side*, namely *God's* side?[7] If only these orthodox ones are meant to survive the war against all others, "ortho-doxy" becomes a synonym for *exclusion*; the exclusion of the unwilling ones who (even by God's will or damnation) cannot find the right side; the untruthful; the evil ones – or are they maybe just the others, the aliens, the poor, the different, the nonconformists, the lawless? *Paradoxically*, would such a fanatic orthodoxy not have excluded all in whom, in Matthew 25, God's presence *anonymously* resides with its hidden desire for, and sense of, peace?[8]

Religious fanaticism always erodes the earth and its inhabitants. The unmasking of its war-soul is a theological imperative. In order to generate "peace-making propositions"[9] we must dissociate *doxa* from fanaticism. And in order to generate at least a *sense* for the possibility of peace among humans and of humanity with the eco-cosmos in which it is embedded, we must dissociate *doxa* from self-designated "orthodoxies." We must name a *difference* of *doxa* from the *function* of orthodoxy in religious fanaticism, namely, as the reason and expression of one of the most fundamental binaries in human existence: the exaltation of "better ones" and the enslavement of the other. This master–slave mechanism is the foundation for all kinds of binarisms that signal power structures and their omnipotence. Pushing Michel Foucault, we might say that the only reality in fanatic enthrallment that is, in fact, omnipotent, is not God, but the power of the elected.[10] In other words, whenever we seek an "eminent reality" from which to explain and reconstruct our own fragility such that it issues a legitimate reason for the domination of others, this reality fairly regularly ends up being named "God." God is power and to be in power is to be like God, that is, in God's service: *vicarii potestatis Dei*. Participants in the power of God's vicars are bereft of their own *potestas* and they are given back to themselves as inventions of the omnipotence of the better ones *ex nihilo*. Fanatic participation is a subtle machine for the production of slavery.[11]

Various orthodoxies have had their fair share in the perpetuation of fanatism and slavery.[12] Whenever they became (and become) used as an instrument of legitimating any variety of religious violence, religious aristocracies intrude into the bodies of people (in the singular and plural sense).[13] There is an inter-religious resonance between religions not just in their effort to seek and find peace and justice – as Hans Küng has demonstrated[14] – but a companionship of war against one another. As war is a *regular* means of religious commu-nication, violence is its generalization throughout experience and the use of orthodox measures often its script. In fact, in any analysis of warfare as an intra- and interreligious medium of conversation and conversion, orthodoxy must be reckoned with *as the very medium* of the reign of fanatism and enslavement on various levels of bodily and mental existence. As orthodoxy becomes a medium for the canalization of righteousness and a domination of access to salvation, the poetic complexity of religious myths become the harbinger of the justification of subjection. In numbing resistance, orthodoxies universalize the internaliza-tion of fanatism as such.

In Whitehead's analysis of the fanatic function of Christian orthodoxy, it becomes the expression of a power-driven confusion of God and Caesar – based on imperialistic fantasies of the divinization of power and its dialectical companion: subjection into physical and mental enslavements. In its fanatic use, orthodoxy not only legitimizes the power of domination, but also attaches itself *as* the Law to the notion of God per se, such that the only possibility to relate to this divine Law is by orthodoxy. "When the Western world accepted Christianity," Whitehead concludes in the final section of *Process and Reality*, "Caesar conquered; and the received text of Western theology was edited by his lawyers. The code of Justinian and the theology of Justinian are two volumes expressing one movement," of the *legalization* of the "deeper idolatry, of the fashioning of God in the image of the Egyptian, Persian, and Roman imperial rulers." In fact, according to Whitehead, the "Church gave unto God the attributes which belonged exclusively to Caesar."[15]

Its alternative, the "brief Galilean vision of humility," which is not based on the Law and its power, but on the "the tender elements in the world, which slowly and in quietness operate by love," just appeared as an aberration that only "flickered throughout the ages, uncertainly."[16] Maybe, however, it is precisely in this *uncertainty* of the ever-fragile endangerment of the movements of love through power that *doxa* reveals her place as the "other" of orthodoxy *within* its domain – that which cannot be grasped from within the binary of orthodoxy and heterodoxy (or heresy); that which in Law will only appear as outside of any lawful behavior; the event that must be ignored or, if this is not possible, must be destroyed. A living connex that is not bound by the certainties of any Law, but by the uncertainties of relativity and relationality does not operate through the power of domination. In its domain, the tenderness of mutuality will always only appear as a disturbance of the Law. This *doxa* becomes the mirror that reveals the terror of the Law of power and, if it is confused with God, the violence of the righteous. Against its very insistence on *that which cannot be defined by power*, this *doxa* will *paradoxically* always arouse orthodox violence of expulsion and destruction. Its sense of peace always arrives *sub contrario*: not as *power* to create peace, but as mischief; not as peacemaker, but as the sufferer of the violence of domination; not as king, but as pariah. Rene Girard is right about the "function" of the Lamb – to take the sin away.[17]

In its most sublime form, the "vampirism" of orthodox fanatism will appear as a reconstruction of mutual relationality from the *participatory* sovereignty of an all-creative sovereign: everything is created by "his" despotic act and everything only participates in it.[18] The logical (logocentric) implication of such a reconstruction of mutuality from a binary structure of elevation and subjection is nothing less than the generation of various forms of enslavement. As the elevated becomes an independent *substance*, the subjected remains only a shadow, a mere *participatory property* of the higher and highest beings.[19] In this dynamic of enslavement, its imperialism becomes the very structure of orthodoxy. It presents us with a concept of God from the perspective of the master–slave hermeneutics in which God not only stands "in the same relation to the whole World as early Egyptian or Mesopotamian kings stood to their subject populations." But in the final "metaphysical sublimation" from "its barbaric origin," becomes precisely "the one absolute, omnipotent, omniscient source of all being, for his own existence requiring no relations to anything beyond himself."[20] While this orthodox divine is "internally complete," it makes everything else dependent such that its creature must find *even its very reason of existence* in the subjection to the sublime barbarism of power.

It is interesting that this Transylvanian conception of the divine within Christian orthodoxy appears not only in Whitehead's philosophical appraisal of participatory enslavement as the "metaphysical sublimation" of God in the realm of power as it suffers from "the Platonic doctrine of subordinate derivations"[21] of properties from Ideas. Teilhard de Chardin, from the heart of his Christian spirituality, pointed to the same problematic Platonism as the cornerstone of the orthodox obstruction of the renewal of theology. It needs to overcome the tendency to cling to a non-relational and internally complete *ens a se* that "dangerously devaluates 'participated being' to a mere *ens ab alio*,"[22] that is, a mere subordinate derivation from the perfect being.[23] Instead of reducing the world's multiplicity to a puppet of the all-sufficient completeness of an absolute sovereign, he urges us to re-imagine God as *only* relational. But such a God "must complete [God]self in something outside of [God]self."[24] As it is this radical move that rescues the world from being viewed as a mere imitation of the transcendent original, it also frees its multiplicity from the binary of elevation (election) and subjection (enslavement). As a consequence, such a new theology will yield to a *genuine mutuality of God and the world*. As Teilhard speaks of a "strictly bilateral and complementary relationship of the world and God,"[25] Whitehead suggests that the "mutual immanence" of God and the world "requires that the relationships of God to the World should lie beyond the accidents of will, and that they be founded upon the necessities of the nature of God and the nature of the World."[26]

In the same sense in which the one absolute, omnipotent, omniscient One is only the sublimation of rogue power into structured Law, this logocentric mask of power, in which its *logos* appears innocently as reflecting (a neutral and naturalized) "rationality," makes its appearance in the philosophical category of substance and its properties, attributes, and predicates. In fact, this One of power subjects self-creativity rather than releasing it. It mutes relationality rather than inventing it. And it coerces relationality into enslavements, rather than persuading, within a web of mutual relation, splitting the multiplicity into independent substances of which everything else is only its own, inherent, participatory property. But does this "bifurcation" express the most profound "violence to that immediate experience which we express in our actions, our hopes, our sympathies, our purposes, and which we enjoy?"[27]

The *substantialism* underlying the development of Christian orthodoxy is not innocent, after all. On the contrary, if everything is the mere property of the One, this hierarchy of power will, in its ultimate consequence, lend itself to a total reconstruction of "creation" in terms of property and the absolutism of merely granted existence. On the one hand, if every creature is the *property* of the creator (at least in the Eschaton), its absolute subjection to orthodoxy is the *measure of its very existence.*[28] On the other hand, since the One is complete and independent of any relationship and mutuality, this God must also be *esse ipse subsistence* that *possesses "his" own existence.*[29] The outcome of this orthodox substantialism was not only the justification of the right of orthodoxy to burn its enemies on the stakes.[30] It survives in any recollection of those doctrines that convey the absolute sovereignty of God with regard to creation and redemption. The alleged power of God as one that can annihilate creation without a trace (whenever "he" pleases)[31] only mirrors the power to condemn any creature that is not compliant to eternal pain or non-existence.[32] Such is the domain of the doxology of fanatical orthodoxy.[33]

What, on the other hand, would happen, if we do not follow the substantialism of orthodoxy and its doxology of power and instead invoke the *doxa* of that which cannot be named with any name of power? What if, instead of the silencing violence of the Transylvanian deity, we seek the silent traces of the tender *love* of multiplicity? What if, instead of the doxology of the One, we follow a doxology of *polyphilia*? What if, instead of the mechanisms of subjection, we emphasize the multiplicity, reciprocity, and mutuality of creative becoming? The implications would, indeed, be profound on all levels – methodologically, ontologically, and theologically. In a disentanglement of God and Caesar, we could instead cherish and worship a *divine polyphilia* in which the love of multiplicity becomes liberated from the encroachment of the love of power – even in the form of the power of love. We might, with a phrase from Laurel Schneider, just "let go (of the One)"[34] and, in doing so, find another *doxa:* the *doxa of a divine manifold* in which not only Oneness ceases to figurate as the ground of being, but – in an disentanglement of the confusion of being with unity – "being" itself might be freed *from itself* by being transformed into an *irreducible multiplicity of infinite becoming.*

With Teilhard, we could learn to replace the "metaphysics of *Esse* with a metaphysics of *unire* or *uniri*"[35] in which unity always means a process of unification, of *becoming* united. Following Whitehead, we could embark on a deeply polyphilic account of multiplicity in which *creator, creatures*, and *creativity* have "no meaning"[36] apart from each other. With Gilles Deleuze, we could relieve ourselves from the power of the participatory ontologies of the One and instead risk perceiving of a world differently, as a *univocal* texture that "repudiates hierarchies" and any "One superior to being." We could trust a *doxa* in which we transgress into an "essentially anti-hierarchical world," a "world of immanence," "almost a kind of anarchy,"[37] of connectivity, differentiation, and creativity. In fact, where our love for multiplicity does not seek any unity of the One that ever would overcome irreducible complexity,[38] we might gain a new sense of (religious) peace. Not a peace that lives from pacification in the name of the legitimized violence of hierarchical orthodoxies, but a peace that will only make sense with a life *from* and *within* the multiplicity of uncertain, vague, complex, differentiated, and ever-new differently differentiating voices that speak with the voice of mutual immanence. This *polyphony* of voices beyond the binary of elevation and subjection, beyond master and slave, and beyond reductions of others to heterodox or heretic intruders, invokes a *doxa* that will tell a story of *polyphilia*. I will call the characteristic of this story *para-dox*. If the polyphilic insistence on multiplicity is a means of a new sense of peace, the *doxa* of multiplicity itself is para-doxical.

Multiplicities and the paradox of indetermination

Multiplicity is, as Deleuze muses in *The Fold*, an "irruption of incompossibilities on the same stage."[39] It names the *incompossibility* of a "divergent series (of events) in the same world" without pre-established unity. It neither constitutes a One nor many already constituted ones. It is a "harmony" only "through a crisis that leads to a broadened chromatic scale, to the emancipation of dissonance or of unresolved accords, accords not brought back to tonality." It transgresses "from harmonic closure to an opening onto a polyphony."[40] It is the polyphony of inconsistencies and inadequacies, a harmony of indeterminacies, a process of poly-harmonic indetermination of presupposed identities or mere pluralities. Instead of a divine Law that establishes a harmony of *exclusion* of the incompossible from a world of divine consistency (Leibniz), poly-harmonic multiplicity consists of any number of multiplicities of *reciprocal and reciprocally incomplete* series of events or reinventions of harmonic becoming. Since any form of generalized abstractions cannot conceptualize poly-harmonic multiplicity, it will need a new method of understanding: the paradox.

Everyone knows the Liar's paradox: if the lie speaks truth, it is false; if it speaks false it is true. It formulates a *contradiction* of something being *this* and *its opposite at once*, or being true and false at the same time. The claim that *some* contradictions of such a form are *true* implies that there is a *sound* reason as to why, from such contradictions, *only indeterminacies* can follow. They are not false because they are indeterminate or they are *only* false if we presuppose reality to be *determinate*.[41] In other words, their truth-value is false not insofar as it is wrong (without correspondences to a presupposed reality) but insofar as "reality" always *invokes novelty*.[42] Whitehead's version of such *paradoxical indetermination* takes the form of the claim that "in the real world it is more important that a proposition be interesting," insofar as it arouses novelty, "than that it be true." Although the "importance of truth" is not eliminated, it is that it "adds to interest."[43] In other words, the determinant of truth is not the ground of truth, but an *addition* that names a *resonance* within a multiplicity *in the process of incessant creative alteration.*

The paradox of indetermination states that any claim will be situated between the ever-fluent limits of *consistency* and *adequacy*. On the one hand, when we survey experience with some adequacy, it becomes inconsistent. On the other, when we reduce experience "to a rigid consistency" it will become inadequate to its complexity.[44] In both cases, what escapes is the paradox of multiplicity (of experiences, thoughts, or claims). *Either* we lose the *adequacy* of experience to perceive multiplicity in the process of creative renewal by the very categoreal reductions of these processes resulting in abstract unifications that cannot account for novelty. *Or* the story these experiences tell will remain *incomplete* with regard to their *consistency* because of the sheer multiplicity that can never be suspended by any presupposed or generated unity. The paradox of multiplicity consists in this *incompossibility*: the impossibility of any abstraction to function as *a priori reason* for the participation of multiplicity as a variation of its "essence" *and*, at the same time, the necessity to formulate such *ideas* in order to *understand* multiplicities as multiplicities, that is, as an experiential a priori of any abstract unification. Any *consistent* unification has already lost the multiplicity that it was meant to control, but any *adequate* idea of multiplicity will necessarily become inconsistent. Such is the paradox of indetermination: since multiplicity is always inconsistent or inadequate, it is always *polyphonically indeterminate*. Moreover, multiplicity as multiplicity is always *a process of poly-harmonic indetermination*.

The "logic" of the poly-harmonic multiplicity does not *state* any law under the logic of the One and Many; it names the *becoming* of multiplicities with a *paradoxal logic* for which experience and understanding are fundamentally indeterminate.[45] In the Greco-philosophical sense of the term, the *logos* of the One and the Many can always only aim at a compossibility of its premises and consequences. It impresses the world with its bifurcations of the world into true and false, this and that, determinate opposites and consistent (but undiscovered) determinations *because* it is urged (under the logic of the One and the Many) to presuppose reality as per se *determinate* (and that only the determinate is real). *Doxa*, the accompanying shadow of *this logos*, was understood as mere vanity, a mere illusion, or a mere uninformed opinion *on this otherwise determinate reality*. Hence, *doxa*, here, always follows the logic of the One and Many: it just *imitates* this *logos* of the either–or of determinate reality and only differs from it with regard to the scope it finds and embraces for the determination to be satisfying. Hence, from the perspective of the *paradoxal logic* of multiplicity, *doxa* and *logos* are not opposites between which one has to decide – as was classically believed – but *the same*: *determinations of identities* as criteria of understanding and reality. Contrarily, the *paradoxal logic* of multiplicity discards the very categorization of the world as reality built on determination as a ground or aim of understanding and reality altogether and views "reality" as being constituted by *what has been lost* in such a doxic logic – a pre-original indeterminacy and indetermination of multiplicity.

What, from the perspective of *doxic* logic, must appear as the *intoxication* of Apollo by Dionysius – the indeterminacy of that which *becomes* before, after, and beyond sedimentations of unifications with their simplifications, obstructions, and suppressions of inherent differences and differentiations of becoming – is, from the perspective of *para-doxa*, a poly-harmonics of multiplicity. What "doxically" was held to be the orgiastic Bacchanalia, is "para-doxically" the *polyphilic doxology of the eros of becoming*, a doxology of the *indeterminacy of pure intensities*. This polyphilic *doxa* is – with Deleuze – neither cosmic (lawlike determinate) nor chaotic (merely indeterminate) but "chaosmically" poly-harmonious in the irruptive movement, through the indeterminate zones of the manifold of chaosmic bodies.[46]

It is this poly-harmonics of indetermination that makes all the difference to war between *doxa* and *logos* and its war-generating fanaticism. Polyphilic indetermination suggests a new sense of peace not because it omits differences or forgoes otherness by being merely "vague" (like fuzzy logic) but because it formulates *procedures of indetermination*. With Nicholas Cusa, Nagarjuna, and Deleuze's paradoxal logic of the *both-and-neither-this-and-that* polyphilic indetermination is deconstructive of abstractive unifications, simplifications, or reductions that haunt multiplicity under the Law of the One and the Many.[47]

First of all, polyphilic indetermination is not the *opposite* of determination; it is *indifferent* toward opposites. In the paradoxal logic of multiplicity – its both–and, and neither–nor – opposites are only universalizing abstractions, substantiations of abstractions that only appear on the surface of processes of becoming-multiplicity. They become toxic when we allow them to ignore the before, the after, and the beyond of unifications by which they *determine themselves* as opposites against multiplicities. For the polyphilic para-dox, there are no determinations as differences "between" opposites except as substantializations that establish power over multiplicities. Hence, determination, universalization, and abstraction are not "the opposite" of indeterminations; or *as* opposites, they are only illusions that abandon multiplicities for "reasons" of security. If "reasons" are about security (in order to control multiplicities), not understanding (of multiplicities), they oppose *themselves* to indeterminations only as *regressive self-determinations within* multiplicities. From the perspective of indeterminations, however, they are only *abstractions from* multiplicity, the *invention of dualism* in the midst of a sea of indetermination that for reasons of power-establishment *only ground themselves*, nothing less. And since they are only *repetitions of sameness* in the midst of difference, they *only oppose themselves* to multiplicities and indeterminations, but are *not opposed by* multiplicities and indeterminations.

Further, paradoxal poly-harmonics *"in-determines" opposites*. What poststructuralists name deconstruction of logocentric binaries is, in fact, the *suspension of opposites* of their hierarchical determination of multiplicities by uncovering them as abstractions of power, as simplifications of control. By emphasizing the paralogical indeterminacies instead, the *logos* of opposites is really the *doxa* of the logocentric discourses it was meant to oppose. The "*logos* of reasons" is only the disguised "*doxa* without reason" because the "reasons" found in the logic of determination are, in fact, groundless repetitions of *self-grounding abstraction from* multiplicities. These hierarchical contaminations of multiplicities are always a means of violence. Nevertheless, in establishing the substantial logic of enslavement, it is *not* multiplicity that is determined (like chaos that is in need of control) but only the *logos* of domination in its *own abstraction from* multiplicity. The determinations of this *logos*, then, is itself nothing but a groundless *doxa* (groundless opinion of false determination). But ironically, in the same movement it also appears as a shining *doxa* of power, as ontological or even a divine halo for the very (participatory) existence of multiplicities.[48] That the paradox of multiplicity remains witnesses to the fact that multiplicity is *not determined* by dualism. In being *indifferent* to its power, multiplicity is always the infinite resource of resistance against the logic of the One and the Many. The self-determination of the logic of the One and the Many is always already harbored *within the space* of undetermined multiplicity. This is the notion of *khora*.

Khora names the paradox of multiplicity that always escapes determination into opposites. This was already the fourfold insight of the late work of Plato. In the *Sophists*, he realizes that the world is always only one of *becoming* and that even the Ideas are not eternally frozen classes of participation but living beings. In the *Timaeus*, he realizes that it is false to think of reality in terms of oppositions of Ideas (forms, Laws) and sensible becoming (matter) but that such oppositions are embedded in the space of indetermination, *khora*. And in the *Parmenides*, Plato deconstructs the very idea of the One as enshrouded in the paradox of self-reference and, hence, as in *itself indeterminate*, that is, as not identical with itself.[49] Not only is Derrida's *différance* built on this paradox, but also Whitehead's reference to the space of mutual immanence. *Khora* is the *space of profound indetermination* through the *mutual incompleteness*, *reciprocity*, and *determination* of everything by every-thing in terms of the multiple multiplicities of differentiation.[50]

Moreover, the paradox of *khoric* multiplicity "*in-determines*" a space for *nov-elty*. "Reasons" are not grounding abstractions, but *arising conditions of novelty* that – like Whitehead's "ontological principle" – only call for *acts of indeter-mination* in which events of becoming become the only reasons for becoming of novelty. Like a retrovirus of their own perpetuation *as* indeterminate, such events of becoming cycle back into their own becoming *as the reason* of their becoming such that the univocity of becoming is always and only the "ground" of becoming.[51] This is the polyphilic paradox: where only becoming is the *reason* for becoming – Deleuze's "univocity"[52] – there is *no* reason for becoming except becoming itself. Without a transcendent rule or law or divine decree, becoming is not geared towards, or bound by, a repetition *of* the same (determination) but liberated for the becoming of *novelty*, that is, an indetermination in which only *the unprecedented may be repeated*. Deleuze calls this process *the repetition of difference itself*.[53] "Reasons" as repetition of the same are, then, only self-determinations that always already assume the determinacy of reasons repeated in actualities for "reasons" of security and control and because of the fear of the intoxication from the indeterminate (the becoming of what has no precedence). *Novelty*, on the other hand, does not just fall from heaven – not even Whitehead's heaven of possibilities.[54] Rather, it is itself introduced as *methexis*, as a kind of "participation" in the fabric of the process of *the repetition of the unprecedented into ever-new indeterminacies*. Indeterminations, by way of novelty, always appear in events of becoming-multiplicities.

In classical Aristotelian logic, such a suggestion was avoided because it seems to imply an infinite regress. Aristotle, and any theistic derivation that aimed at the *same* instead of novelty, solved this problem by the "unmoved mover," a perfect act of origin that precedes any becoming-multiplicity. Whitehead, however, as Deleuze after him, demonstrates that this solution is already based on the pre-condition of substantialism, that is, the elevation of abstraction to the status of an eminent reality with its participatory sovereignty. Everything that becomes is always already *something*, a substance of which becoming is only a dismissible, secondary, or evil variation.[55] In using Zeno's paradoxes, Whitehead makes the point that *only if* we suppose that it is *something* (a substance) that (already in its essence *is* and then) becomes, infinite regress is absurd. If, however, (substantial) continuity is itself *in becoming* – namely from the passing events of multiplicities – continuity (of substantiality) is *not* a precondition for becoming, but *becomes* itself.[56] Hence, the polyphilic paradox of undetermined multiplicities implies that if becoming is its own precondition, it *has no precondition* except its becoming. Therefore, *becoming-multiplicity is always unprecedented.*[57]

While the *doxa* of the *logos* of the One and Many establishes the violence and enslavement of exclusive determination of truth, rightness, and righteousness, it is the peace-making proposition of the *doxa* of the paradoxal logic of multiplicities to invite to polyphilic embrace of the profound indeterminacies of multiplicity and to embark on a process of un-determination. In de-legitimizing hierarchical power structures employed by orthodoxies that worship with a doxology of the One and the Many, the doxology of the *paradox of polyphilia* – the *non-precedence of becoming-multiplicity* – divines only the *para-doxa*, the *pure expression of the polyphonic voices of infinite becoming*. Instead of presupposing the One that determines one (identity) and many (mere difference) with any form of pre-established harmony as its means of grounding, the paradox of *para-doxy* uses modes of communication, resonance, and mutuality that cannot be *framed* by any means of identification within structures of laws of identity, universal generalization, or classification. Instead of finding the divine in the abstractness of an eminent reality, established as the hierarchical reason for actualization such that actualizations were only instances of abstractions,[58] *polyphilic para-doxy* seeks the divine (in) multiplicity – a divine that *loves* multiplicity (polyphilia) and names *the poly-harmonics of multiplicity*, that is, *divine multiplicity*. In reference to Deleuze's understanding of Whitehead's God,[59] this divine (in) multiplicity names the process by which becoming-multiplicity *never determines itself per logical exclusion* (of "other" worlds of unfitting harmonics) but *indeterminately affirms the all of the polyphony of the chaosmos.*[60] The *para-doxy* of the divine (in) multiplicity worships the *divine insistence on/in/as the process of the always-unprecedented affirmation* of the rugged chaosmos of incompossible and unprecedented complexity.[61]

Polydoxy and the problem of violence

Para-doxy does not seek orthodoxy. "Paradox is opposed to *doxa*"[62] as is para-doxy to the *doxa* of orthodoxy. Para-doxy avoids orthodoxy *if* its *doxa* views the divine from a logic of the One and Many and, hence, builds the relationship of the divine with the non-divine (or creation) on a universalized structure of abstraction *from* multiplicity that, for reasons of security and control, is invested with the eminent reality of absolute power that structures the binary functions of a world under the prerogative of a hierarchical dualism of ultimate opposites of faith and apostasy impregnated with bifurcating determinations of right and wrong, good and evil, true and false, as well as correct and insufficient.[63] The *doxa* of this orthodoxy is defined by identity and counter-identity: who is in and who is out. Its God is *esse ipse subsistence* and *actus purus*, the paradigm of absolute identity. This *doxa* starts with the *dogma* of the divine identity of essence and existence of which everything else is a derivative and participatory system of hierarchical property. It was precisely against these mythologians (God-singers and story-tellers) that Plato set his philosophy of reason as grounded in universal and universally valid Ideas. It was against such dogmas that Plato developed his *typoi peri theologias*, that is, *criteria* of naming God *rationally*.[64] Ironically, it was precisely this universal *logos* that Christian theologians began to claim for their dogma. By identifying *doxa* with *logos*, the Christian dogma became the very expression of the universal structure of Plato's Ideas by which theologians not only claimed their own rationality, but also hid their own inherently irrational *doxa* by the divination of its logocentric structure.[65] This is a lesson in two-fold colonization: the colonization of multiplicity by logocentric reason and the doxological colonization of the universal *logos* by an irrational *doxa*. This colonization holds *in nuce* the fatal oppositionalism of religious fanaticism by which all systems become "dogmatic," in the sense of a striving for their precedence over all others by immunizing against any porosity of their implied logic against the inflow of multiplicity.

Instead of seeking "orthodoxy," para-doxy suggests *polydoxy* – the proposition that the divine cannot be encroached in any logocentric binary in the form of the master–slave dualism, but instead should express the paradoxal poly-harmonics of multiplicity. This proposition is, however, only mediating the paradoxal sense of peace *if* it risks violence and avoids it, at the same time. In avoiding the colonizing identifications, polydoxy might become a mortal offence to orthodoxy. Any suggestion of the orthodox confusion of deity and power might not be seen as a friendly act, but as an offence against religious identity or even as the very blasphemy the religious dogma of orthodoxy was meant to be guarding against. On the other hand, any suggestion of schemes of understanding that avoid orthodox binarisms may ironically not liberate from such dualisms, but be in danger of exchanging them for *forced plurality*. Polydoxy may need to suffer the first violence, but it must avoid the second violence: the principle that forces everyone to believe *in* a plurality of truths, salvations, and divine realities. The paradox of polydoxy is not meant to exchange the violence of orthodoxy with a violence of a religious pluralism that is not necessarily more tolerant than orthodox fanaticism. Polydoxy is meant to avoid *any* fanaticism, and be it a counter-fanaticism against the orthodox dogma and its potentially violent implications.

Polydoxy seeks the poly-harmonics of an interrelated multiplicity of relational differences, but it is never exempt from the seduction to introduce its own fallacy of misplaced power, that is, it is not exempt from the impact of its paradoxal claim of multiplicity on any formulation of identity – be it that of the One or that of the Many. Polydoxy will always be overshadowed by the question *how* its inherent refutation of fanatic orthodoxy and its desire to live in a religious world of the indeterminacy of divine multiplicity will convey a *sense of peace* that is liberating *and* non-violent at the same time. This is not only a perennial question of political philosophy[66] and of liberation theologies in their effort to overturn unjust structures of oppression "in the name of God"; it is a question of the *very possibility* of liberation from subjection, *whether this can be done non-violently.*[67]

Thereby, polydox engagement of religious complexity really touches on deep questions of resistance to, transformation of, dissociation from, and overcoming of power – questions with which Foucault and Butler are wrestling (whether power structures are omnipotent and unavoidable). Whether any "outside" (a kind of paradise, kingdom of heavens, or ideal society) is a mere illusion. Whether such an "outside" might even be produced by omnipotent power to generate control over any relief from it – much like in the movie *The Matrix* in which machines generate a virtual world of imagined freedom in order to control human imagination as a necessary part of their main interest to use human bodies to produce energy.[68] In employing the polyphilic indetermination suggested in the previous section, polydoxy might generate a new sense of peace that undercuts any orthodox or pluralist violence precisely by employing *principles of indetermination* that avoid any dangerously war-bound paths of resistance, refusal, liberation, or transformation.

First of all, we *cannot simply exchange the logocentric world* of the law of the One and the Many, we always already live in, with *khora* as a realm of unframed multiplicity. If with Julia Kristeva and George Bataille we do not believe – as is almost unavoidable in Foucault's and Butler's early work[69] – that *khora* is an *illusionary* "outside" of the Law, we must also remain aware of the impossibility that "the expulsion from paradise" cannot be simply reverted. We have "left" the *khoric* matrix of the mother, or the animal kingdom's intimacy, for good in becoming human, developing language, consciousness, thought, culture, and religion.[70] It is precisely this expulsion from paradise that made us seek the khoric "paradise" *through* the law of the father (Kristeva) or the manipulation of objects (Bataille) – and, of course, hopelessly so.

Hence, we must instead *invert the effects* of this "paradise lost" *from within*, for instance, by seeking the openings of poetic inconsistency (Kristeva) or by a conscious consummation of the subject–object duality (Bataille).[71] With Butler, we might engage in strategies of parody, citation, and performance that practically achieve from within the lived logic of the One and Many, what Plato theoretically exercised of the One[72] – its non-identity. If identity is an abstraction that always needs the power of self-assertion (and the assertion of its servants) of its very possibility and, hence, is in practice always already contradicting its self-evidence, we must rather *live* the paradoxal process of in-determination as it makes "space" for multiplicity to become *effective* as "de-formations" all the way up and down the ladder of material, psychological, cultural, social, and political formations of identity.

Further, we must *transform the way we perceive, experience, and live in the world*. This was Whitehead's and Deleuze's remedy against logocentric, dualistic (binary), and substantialist modes of settling the power of identification. Instead of the world of isolated substances (simple location), we may learn to *feel the multifarious complexity we are suppressing, but were feeling all along, and transform our categoreal frameworks such that they allow for such trans-formations.*[73] Instead of the violence done to our "immediate experience which we express in our actions, our hopes, our sympathies, our purposes, and which we enjoy," we may become aware and enabled to ecologically situate ourselves within a "buzzing world, a democracy of fellow creatures."[74] Instead of clustering the world with concepts all over, the accessibility of such an "ocean of feeling"[75] might open a disturbing "silence" where "the inflow into ourselves of feelings from enveloping nature overwhelms us," where "in the dim consciousness of half-sleep, the presentations of sense fade away" and "we are left with the vague feeling of influences from vague things around us."[76] Where we invert – revert from the inside – the logocentric exclusions, we might gain an awareness of *the poetic indeterminacy of overwhelming multiplicity.*[77]

Finally, in order to access multiplicity we need not violently destroy the abstractions on which the dualistic logic of the One and Many is built, but we must non-violently *transform the function of abstractions from serving the substantialization of power.* Instead, these abstractions, insofar as they are implied by orthodoxy, must be transformed into a polydoxy that can release *their liberating potential for an experience, theory, and practice of multiplicity.* We can find such redirection of the impact of abstractions in Deleuze's "transcendental empiricism" that transforms their use from an establishment of a state of eternity into a mode of understanding the world *from* novelty and creativeness.[78] It is also present in Whitehead's profound *para-doxy of novelty* that shifts the function of abstractions in their sedimentation of an eminent reality to the evocation of the unprecedented.[79]

"Orthodoxy" is not discarded in this polyphilic approach to polydoxy. It becomes *contextualized*, that is, elucidated from the polyphony of experiences *from* which it springs. Orthodoxy must be situated in the poly-harmony of mutual relatedness. From this, it follows that religious inspiration must never be limited to a "narrow circle of creeds" because a "dogma ... can never be final" in its "adjustment" of its "abstract concepts" but must in "the estimate of the status of these concepts"[80] always remain *indeterminate.* When we accept, with Whitehead, that orthodoxies "commit suicide when they find their inspirations in their dogmas," we also suggest that polydoxy evokes an "intuitive response which pierces beyond dogma"[81] into the *creative methexis of the novelty as the source of their inspiration.* In conceptualizing this indeterminacy of multiplicity, we must value the dogmatic *intuition* from which such conceptualization arises – "Prometheus chained to his rock, Mahomet brooding in the desert, the meditations of the Buddha, the solitary Man on the Cross"[82] – but not its momentary conceptual or doctrinal expression if it postulates itself as universally determining exclusive relevance.

The *para-doxa* of a religion will inherently recognize its own poly-harmonious complexity against its own simplifications *if* it is not forced to leave its own intuition behind in order to attend an anonymous "universal harmony," but if it can recognize the (interreligious) entanglement of its own unique beginnings in the world of experiences, conceptualizations, and communities.[83] The inherent polydoxy of the dogma of a religion will, then, *release* a sense of peace if the "universal harmony" it feels – through its unique sources of experiences – is felt as affirmative of its *own* experience *in* its interrelatedness with a multiplicity of experiences, that is, an awareness of a poly-harmonics it always already employs beyond all its determining conceptualizations.[84]

A para-doxology of divine multiplicity

To say it again: the poly-harmonics of multiplicity will release a sense of (inter-religious) peace *if* the doxology of orthodoxy is *inherently* transformed into a para-doxology of polydoxy. Polydox doxology, then, indicates *the divine multiplicity of interreligious entanglement. At the same time, it affirms the unique intuitions of religions as enveloped in a process of the renewal of unprecedented novelty that always is beyond any fixed identities of singular religions and their orthodoxies.* Since this *para-doxology* is concerned with *polyphilic indetermination*, the sense of peace it suggests may be hinted at in *procedures of indeterminacy* that live from an inherent "theopoetics of multiplicity" – of the divine manifold that loves and graces multiplicity. I will name three such dimensions of polyphilic indetermination in which we might begin to find traces of such a para-doxology of the divine (in) multiplicity.

First, *the divine (in) multiplicity cannot be "identified,"* that is, "identity" under the logic of the One and Many is not a category of experiencing the divine. The implications of this mark of the process of polyphilic indetermination are profound: neither should we identify God within the realm of the One and Many nor with any multiplicity (which otherwise would still remain its very expression). While it is understandable that many poststructuralist thinkers follow Nietzsche's "death of God" insofar as God appears to be the very expression of the rule of the One, it would also be problematic to counter-identify the divine with the *khoric* multiplicity that the logic of the One has excluded. While I can follow Butler's criticism of monotheism as an expression of the Law,[85] I would not follow theologians that, with Irigaray, infer that the *khoric* realm, which is never (the) one (the male God), imagines an inexpressible (female) divine.[86] It is, perhaps, an odd commonality of Kristeva and Bataille that they have pointed in this direction when they (in very different ways) differentiate the dogmatic (logocentric) naming of God from the mystical experience of *khora* (in the form of pre-symbolic immediacy to the mother or the nothingness of immediate intimacy of animality) *that cannot be named divine.*[87] Although *khora* harbors deep religious gestures that must be saved from the reign of the One (insofar as they also appear within it), their poetic of *ecstasies* of the subject–object split is profoundly a-theological.[88] Nevertheless, by directly hinting to deep mystical practices *within* the realm of orthodox Christianity (and beyond it in other religions) they touch on such "zones of immanence"[89] as Nicholas of Cusa's poetic logic of the *coincidentia oppositorum* or Eckhart's *Godhead* beyond the differentiation of God and creation.[90]

This insistence on the non-identity of the divine with either the One (and Many) or multiplicity satisfies a para-doxology that *affirms* the singular experiences buried in orthodoxies at the same time as it *inverts* any desire for their dogmatic substantiation. This is why I suggest that in our poetics of the divine a *divine poetics* can

neither be constructed from any logocentric universalization of the One nor in opposition to these constructions by an identification with the *khoric* ream.[91] If God cannot be identified, the function of the divine to be the expression of power – a power among powers, or as *the* super-power or as a khoric anti-power – is avoided. This is what I name the divine *subtractive affirmation* of multiplicity that *affirms* multiplicity but *subtracts itself* from any identification *with multiplicity*.[92] Instead of such identifications that, in my view, *always* arouse the ream of power and violence, the divine as polyphilic love may be *within* all powers – be they of the logic of the One or of multiplicity – but is neither *of* them.

Second, *the divine (in) multiplicity must always be "ecologically contextualized" within multiplicity*. Since *the divine polyphilia is before, after, and beyond any identification*, it can only appear in the *mutual immanence* of all contexts on which it insists as multiplicity.[93] Divine indetermination implies a process of *mutual reciprocity* and *mutual incompleteness* in which the divine (in) multiplicity only appears *in* mutual reciprocity and mutual incompleteness *with* all multiplicities. There are two ways to *avoid* such an "essential relationality" of the divine. One can either elevate God to the "highest being," a superpower player in the world among other players of less power – this is the God that fights against the devil, that uses religious hierarchies for his judgment, that micromanages the globe from "his" throne through an elected group of the faithful. The other way, disgusted with this power-play, refrains from invoking God in mundane matters – either as deistic *epoché* or (with the early Wittgenstein) as the whole of the world that cannot appear within itself.[94] It was the incarnational and kenotic dynamics of Christian *orthodoxy* that has always broken through such assumptions *by finding God in the midst of everything* – the incarnation of the infinite horizon *within* its horizon[95] or as a desiring God at the *heart* of all becoming or as a *complication* of God and the world *in one another*.[96] This polydox transgression of orthodoxy appears in *the mutual incompleteness and reciprocity of the divine (in) multiplicity* in Whitehead's statement that creature, creativity, and creator must find their meaning only in mutual reciprocity[97] and in Heidegger's *Geviert*. Earth, sky/heaven, the mortals, and the *divinities (as multiplicity)* transgress any identification and become multiplicity[98] as do Whitehead's "fourfold" of the "World of Creativity" (mortals), the "World of Value" (sky/heaven) as *folded together* through "Creativity" (earth) and "God" (the divinities). In such "ecological contextualization," divine polyphilia becomes the name that names *only* multiplicities – *multiplicities as enfolded within themselves (Cusa), but even more as irreducibly making sense only through the other multiplicities – none are all, but all are all in all*.[99]

Third, we may want to seek *new conceptualities that actually can transform the function of abstraction at the heart of the avoidance of multiplicity in orthodoxy into a polyphilic multiplicity of multiplicities in polydoxy*. Such polyphilic "abstractions" (inverted against themselves) will be creative *only* of multiplicities instead of substantial unifications by, at the same time, remaining *internally* transformative of the doxic and logocentric use of abstractions. These paradoxal modes of indetermination must not explain reality through abstractions, but rather the very abstractions and their working in a world of multiplicities. They must transform the function of abstraction from being explanatory reasons elevated to the eminent realities of divinities into *initiators of becoming-multiplicity*. Hence, without diminishing their importance for the formulation of conceptual frameworks of experience and activity in the aesthetic, ethical, political, or religious world (and by not even denying their divine connotations), they inversely lure us into a world *constituted by novelty and creativeness*.[100]

An example of such transformative conceptual processes can be found, for instance, in Nicholas of Cusa's construction of the divine "names" of *coincidentia oppositorum*, *possest*, *non aliud*, and *the posse ipsum* that upset an expectation that their use could abstractly construct an eminent reality that controls the creativity of creatures or limits the relationality of God. Instead, God arouses the chaosmic disturbance of identity, novelty, and the change of characters of repetition.[101] In the best scenario, this use of "abstractions" will address the *indetermination of non-identity by way of their mutual reciprocity, incompleteness, and immanence*. Because the "adequate description" of such terms as Whitehead's triad creator, creature, and creativity "includes characterizations *derived* from the other,"[102] they are *mutually exploratory and, hence, entangle multiplicities*. In this *mutual* "process of modification,"[103] these terms begin to generate the creativeness that is not based on the eternity of the same, but always the poly-harmonies of becoming-multiplicity.

The transformation of the mindset of orthodoxy into that of a polydoxy of religious/theological teachings and doctrine is its ever-new passage through, and exploration of, the para-doxy of its founding or "revelatory" events in which polydox formulations would withhold a determination of their identity in orthodox dogmatizations. Instead, in the internal *inversion* of the use of their dogmas, the para-doxy of indetermination would engage in new modes of universality, namely an *ongoing re-enactment of their founding or "revelatory" event-character* in its universal importance for the chaosmic harmonics of the "open whole" of multiplicity, that is, the shared world or the ecological community. Since re-enactments of events per se express novelty, singularity, and renovation, their conceptualization can never reach a static universality; instead, their event-character will always elicit a disturbance of stasis. Hence, polydox conceptual expressions of singular (revelatory) events will *mediate* their universality through an open-ended poly-harmony that could only illegitimately claim "eternity." The peace-making proposition of this para-doxology of the divine (in) multiplicity is that the "eternity" in these events in which we worship the divine mystery should be allowed to maintain their mystery through polydox indetermination, that is, the *mutually immanent, reciprocal, and incomplete disturbances of any conceptual sedimentation*. The paradoxal sense of peace might appear when we seek the traces of this polyphilic mystery not despite, but because of the poly-harmonious journey on which it invites us to embark upon.

Notes

1   W. Pannenberg, *Systematic Theology*, Vol. I, Grand Rapids, MI: Eerdmans, 1988, p. 55.

2   A. N. Whitehead, *Religion in the Making*, New York: Fordham University Press, 1996, p. 37.

3   O. McTernan, *Violence in God's Name: Religion in an Age of Conflict*, Maryknoll, NY: Orbis Books, 2003.

4   Rev 12:7–9. "War in heaven" is associated with a logic of the One: the origin of sin as fall from the One; it is used as explanation of the "war on earth" – as being not one under the true One – and it companions the eschatological restitution of peace – a peace through war as peace of the One. Since in such a war always one side is excluded, it is a war of orthodoxy, of segregation, and destruction of "the other."

5   L. C. Schneider, *Beyond Monotheism: A Theology of Multiplicity*, New York: Routledge, 2008.

6   For the introduction and exploration of these terms, see R. Faber, *God as Poet of the World: Exploring Process Theologies*, Louisville, KY: Westminster John Knox Press, 2008. Postscript and idem, "Ecotheology, Ecoprocess, and Ecotheosis: A Theopoetical Intervention," in *Salzburger Theologische Zeitschrift*, 12, 2008, pp. 75–115.

7   I suggest that this and not "atheism" was the reason for Feuerbach to abandon any "entitative" (substantial) notion of God instead of the pure act of love that avoids fanaticism and always creates peace. His reformulation of Christian orthodoxy may be nothing but such a reconstitution of "theology" under the auspices of love. L. Feuerbach, *Essence of Christianity*, Amherst, NY: Prometheus Books, 1989, Chapter 4; see also Faber, "Ecotheology," p. 99.

8   The overwhelming biblical topos of God's "presence in" or even "siding with" the *lost* ones may be a good starting point to approach an understanding of peace that is not built on the rightness of the One but a mutual engagement for a common future that envelops the respect, justness, and "divine nature" of the other as other.

9   I. Stengers, "Beyond Conversation," in C. Keller and A. Daniels (eds), *Difference and Process: Between Cosmological and Poststructuralist Postmodernism*, University of New York Series in Constructive Postmodern Thought, New York: SUNY Press, 2002, p. 245.

10 M. Foucault, *Power/Knowledge: Selected Interviews and Other Writings, 1972–1977*, New York: Pantheon Books, 1980.

11 R. Faber, "'Amid a Democracy of Fellow Creatures' – Onto/Politics and the Problem of Slavery in Whitehead and Deleuze," in R. Faber, H. Krips, and D. Pettus (eds), *Event and Decision: Ontology and Politics in Badiou, Deleuze, and Whitehead*, Cambridge: Cambridge Scholars Press, 2010, pp. 192–237; see also C. Keller, *The Face of the Deep: A Theology of Becoming*, New York: Routledge, 2003. The *ex nihilo* manages to deconstruct the relational other into either nothing or evil (opposite) such that the One is always the winner of this war on the other (that is its redemptive impulse, although it might simply hide the interests of orthodox control).

12 C. M. C. Hilkert, "Experience and Tradition," in C. M. LaCugna (ed.), *Freeing Theology: The Essentials of Theology in Feminist Perspective*, San Francisco, CA: HarperSanFrancisco, 1993, p. 69; see also E. Ferguson, *Backgrounds of Early Christianity*, Grand Rapids, MI: Eerdmans, 2003.

13 M. Garland-Hill, *Slavery and Christianity: The Untold Story*, Ramona, CA: Vision Publishing, 2009.

14 H. Küng, *A Global Ethic for Global Politics and Economics*, New York: Oxford University Press, 1997, pp. 114–53.

15 A. N. Whitehead, *Process and Reality: An Essay in Cosmology*, corr. ed., D. R. Griffin and D. W. Sherburne (eds), New York: Free Press, 1978, p. 342.

16 Whitehead, *Process*, pp. 342–3.

17 R. Girard, *Violence and the Sacred*, Baltimore, MD: The Johns Hopkins University Press, 1979.
18 R. Faber, "Wahrheit und Maschine: Wider das transsylvanische Argument von der Gewalt im Diskurs der Erkenntnis," in *Labyrinth: International Journal for Philosophy, Feminist Theory and Cultural Hermeneutics*, 3, 2001.
19 Faber, "Amid a Democracy," op. cit., pp. 203–4.
20 A. N. Whitehead, *Adventures of Ideas*, New York: Free Press, 1967, p. 169.
21 Ibid.
22 P. Teilhard de Chardin, *Letters from My Friend, Teilhard De Chardin, 1948–1955: Including Letters Written during His Final Years in America*, Mahwah, NJ: Paulist Press, 1980, p. 166.
23 P. Teilhard de Chardin, *Science and Christ*, New York: Harper & Row, 1968, p. 182.
24 P. Teilhard de Chardin, *Lettres Intimes à Auguste Valensin*, Paris: Aubier Montaigne, 1993, p. 296.
25 P. Teilhard de Chardin, *Christianity and Evolution: Reflections on Science and Religion*, San Diego, CA: Harvest Books, 1969, p. 226.
26 Whitehead, *Adventures*, p. 168.
27 Whitehead, *Process*, p. 49.
28 Faber, "Amid a Democracy," p. 203.
29 R. Faber, "Indra's Ear: God's Absence of Listening," in I. Dalferth (ed.), *The Presence and Absence of God*, New York: Palgrave, 2010, pp. 174–8.
30 A. L. Barstow, *Witchcraze: A New History of European Witch Hunts*, London: Pandora, 1995.
31 J. D. Caputo, *The Weakness of God: A Theology of the Event*, Bloomington, IN: Indiana University Press, 2006, Chapter 9.
32 D. Pawson, *The Road to Hell: Everlasting Torment or Annihilation?*, London: Hodder & Stoughton, 1996.
33 For a classical dogmatic scheme of orthodoxy under the name of doxology, see G. Wainwright, *Doxology: The Praise of God in Worship, Doctrine and Life: A Systematic Theology*, New York: Oxford University Press, 1980.
34 Schneider, *Monotheism*, p. 203.
35 Teilhard, *Christianity*, pp. 226–7.
36 Whitehead, *Process*, p. 225.
37 See G. Deleuze, *Lecture on Spinoza in Vincennes of December 12, 1980* at http://www.webdeleuze.com/php/texte.php?cle=17&groupe=Spinoza&langue=2 (accessed 5 August 2010).
38 Deleuze defines multiplicity precisely in this way:

> The states of things are not unities or totalities but multiplicities. That does not simply mean that there are many states of things (where each state would be a whole) or that each state of things is multiple (which would only be an indication of its resistance to unification). The crucial point from an empirical point of view is the word "multiplicity." Multiplicity indicates a group of lines or dimensions that cannot be reduced to one another. Every "thing" is made up of them. A multiplicity certainly contains points of unification, centers of totalization, points of subjectivation, but these are factors that can prevent its growth and stop its lines. These factors are in the multiplicity they belong to, not the reverse.

  G. Deleuze, *Two Regimes of Madness: Texts and Interviews 1975–1995*, New York: Semiotext(e), 2006, p. 304.
39 G. Deleuze, *The Fold: Leibniz and the Baroque*, Minneapolis, MN: University of Minnesota Press, 1992, p. 82.
40 Ibid.
41 R. M. Sainsbury, *Paradoxes*, 2nd ed., Cambridge: Cambridge University Press, 1995, pp. 107–34.

42 Faber, *Poet*, Chapter 2.
43 Whitehead, *Process*, p. 259.
44 Ibid., p. 57.
45 G. Deleuze and F. Guattari, *A Thousand Plateaus*, Minneapolis, MN: University of Minnesota Press, 1987, p. 24.
46 R. Faber, "'O Bitches of Impossibility!' – Programmatic Dysfunction in the Chaosmos of Deleuze and Whitehead," in K. Robinson (ed.), *Deleuze, Whitehead, Bergson: Rhizomatic Connections*, New York: Palgrave, 2009, pp. 200–19.
47 Faber, *Poet*, §40.
48 This is one reason why the two classical meanings of doxa, from the perspective of indetermination, can appear as one and the same movement of the repetition of self-determining power structures that create their own power of foundation and domination.
49 K. M. Sayre, *Plato's Late Ontology: A Riddle Resolved*, Princeton, NJ: Princeton University Press, p. 198. See also R. Faber, "The Infinite Movement of Evanescence – The Pythagorean Puzzle in Plato, Deleuze, and Whitehead," *American Journal of Theology and Philosophy*, 21, 2000, 171–99.
50 Faber, *Poet*, §15–16, 24, 32.
51 Whitehead, *Process*, pp. 24–5.
52 G. Deleuze, *The Logic of Sense*, New York: Columbia University Press, 1990, p. 194.
53 G. Deleuze, *Difference and Repetition*, New York, 1994, p. 57.
54 A. N. Whitehead, *Religion in the Making*, New York: Fordham University Press, 1996, p. 154.
55 Whitehead, *Process*, pp. 242–3.
56 Ibid., p. 35.
57 Ibid., p. 68.
58 Ibid., pp. 29–30.
59 Deleuze, *The Fold*, p. 81.
60 J. Williams, *Encounters and Influences: The Transversal Thought of Gilles Deleuze*, Manchester: Cinnamon Press, 2005, Chapter 5.
61 This is the thesis of my upcoming book: *The Divine Manifold: A Theology of Polyphilia*.
62 Deleuze, *Logic*, p. 75. R. Scholes defines *para-* as being *against doxa* as *dogma*, *Polydoxy of Modernism*, New Haven, CT: Yale University Press, 2006, p. 275.
63 G. Gutting, *French Philosophy in the Twentieth Century*, Cambridge: Cambridge University Press, 2001, pp. 293–4.
64 M. Seckler, "Theologie als Glaubenswissenschaft," in W. Kern, H. Pottmeyer, and M. Seckler (eds), *Handbuch der Fundamentaltheologie Vol. 4: Traktat Theologische Erkenntnislehre*, Freiburg: Herder Verlag.
65 W. Pannenberg, *Theologie und Philosophie*, Göttingen: Vandenhoek & Ruprecht, 1996, Chapters 1–2.
66 G. Deleuze and F. Guattari, *Anti-Oedipus,* Minneapolis, MN: University of Minnesota Press, 1996, p. 29.
67 J. Douglass, *The Non-Violent Cross: A Theology of Revolution and Peace*, Eugene, OR: Wipf and Stock, 2006.
68 R. Faber, "Introduction: Negotiating Becoming," in R. Faber and A. Stephenson (eds), *Secrets of Becoming: Negotiating Whitehead, Deleuze, and Butler*, New York: Fordham University Press, 2010. See also J. Butler, *Gender Troubles: Feminism and the Subversion of Identity*, New York: Routledge, 2006, p. 40.
69 J. Butler, *Bodies That Matter: On the Discursive Limits of "Sex,"* New York: Routledge, 1993, p. 41.
70 J. Kristeva, *Revolution in Poetic Language*, New York: Columbia University Press, 1984, Chapter 1. See also G. Bataille, *Theory of Religion*, New York: Zone Books, 1992, Chapter 1.

71 Bataille, p. 103.

72 J. Butler, *Giving Account of Oneself*, New York: Fordham University Press, 2005, Chapter 1.

73 Faber, *Poet*, §41–2.

74 Whitehead, *Process*, p. 49.

75 Ibid., p. 166.

76 Ibid., p. 176.

77 Whitehead describes the process of opening with an explosion of layers of experience:

> In order to discover some of the major categories under which we can classify the infinitely various components of experience, we must appeal to evidence relating to every variety of occasion. Nothing can be omitted, experience drunk and experience sober, experience sleeping and experience waking, experience drowsy and experience wide awake, experience self-conscious and experience self-forgetful, experience intellectual and experience physical, experience religious and experience skeptical, experience anxious and experience care-free, experience anticipatory and experience retrospective, experience happy and experience grieving, experience dominated by emotion and experience under self-restraint, experience in the light and experience in the dark, experience normal and experience abnormal.

> *Adventures*, p. 226

78 Deleuze, *The Fold*, Chapter 6.

79 "The explanatory purpose of philosophy is often misunderstood. Its business is to explain the emergence of the more abstract things from the more concrete things. It is a complete mistake to ask how concrete a particular fact can be built up out of universals. The answer is, 'In no way.' The true philosophic question is, how can concrete fact exhibit entities abstract from itself and yet participated in by its own nature?" Whitehead, *Process*, p. 19.

80 Ibid., pp. 130–1.

81 Ibid., p. 144.

82 Ibid., pp. 19–20.

83 Faber, "God in the Making," pp. 191–200.

84 R. Faber, "On the Unique Origin of Revelation, Religious Intuition and Theology," *Process Studies* 28/3–4, 1999, pp. 273–89.

85 Butler, *Gender Trouble*, p. 38.

86 L. Irigaray, "Equal to Whom?," in G. Ward (ed.), *The Postmodern God: A Theological Reader*, Oxford: Blackwell, 1998, pp. 198–214. See also M. Joy, *Divine Love: Luce Irigaray, Women, Gender, and Religion*, Manchester Studies in Religion, Culture and Gender, Manchester: Manchester University Press, 2007. For the discussion of the khora in Irigaray, see Butler, *Bodies*, Chapter 2; for a discussion of Irigaray and Spivak, see M. Rivera, *The Touch of Transcendence: A Postcolonial Theology of God*, Louisville, KY: Westminster John Knox Press, 2007, Chapter 6.

87 Kristeva, pp. 24–30 and Bataille, Chapter 3.

88 Kristeva, ibid., p. 61 and G. Bataille, *Inner Experience*, Albany, NY: SUNY Press, 1988, Part I.

89 Deleuze, *Two Regimes*, Chapter 35.

90 R. Faber, "'Gottesmeer' – Versuch über die Ununterschiedenheit Gottes," in T. Dienberg and M. Plattig (eds), *"Leben in Fülle": Skizzen zur christlichen Spiritualität*, Theologie der Spiritualität 5, Münster: LIT, 2001, pp. 64–95.

91 Faber, *Poet*, et passim.

92 Ibid., postscript.

93 Faber, "Ecotheology," and my forthcoming *The Divine Manifold*.

94 L. Wittgenstein, *Tractatus Logico-philosophicus* 6.41–45; see also D. Z. Philips, *The Problem of Evil and the Problem of God*, Minneapolis, MN: Fortress Press, 2005.

95 K. Rahner, *Foundations of Christian Faith: An Introduction to the Idea of Christianity*, New York: Crossroad, 2005, Chapters 1–2.
96 Faber, *Poet*, §40.
97 Whitehead, *Process*, p. 25.
98 M. Heidegger, "Building Dwelling Thinking" Idem, in D. F. Krell (ed.), *Basic Writings*. San Francisco, CA: Harper, 1993, p. 359.
99 R. Faber, "De-Ontologizing God: Levinas, Deleuze and Whitehead," in C. Keller and A. Daniels (eds), *Process and Difference*, op. cit., pp. 209–34.
100 Faber, "Evanescence."
101 R. Faber, *Prozeßtheologie: Zu ihrer Würdigung und kritischen Erneuerung*, Mainz: Grünewald, 2000, Chapter 2.
102 A. N. Whitehead, "Immortality," in P. A. Schilpp, *The Philosophy of Alfred North Whitehead*, 3rd ed., Chicago, IL: Open Court, 1991, pp. 683–4, emphasis added.
103 Ibid., p. 685.

4 Take my yoga upon you

A spiritual *pli* for the global city

Sharon V. Betcher

Cities appear on the human horizon as enticing as hives for honeybees – as places where the intermixture of human energies might tumble, bumble, entangle, and synergistically catch. Humans so seek this energy of social agglomeration – this creative, bustling stew that makes spontaneous relationships, creativity, entertainment, and education possible – that theorist Edward Soja has consequently argued that the motor of human history might be something he calls *synekism*.[1] As Soja sees it, such urbanism has been the ethos of human history for the last 10,000 years.[2]

Urbanism also suggests a human disposition toward a loose weave of social relations. Cities do, after all, inherently open us to relations beyond "kith and kin" – to the neighbor, to the friend, to the incidental encounter, to relations of choice. If humans are not so endogenously predisposed as Soja surmises, philosophers like Gilles Deleuze and Gianni Vattimo argue that the postcolonial conditions of urbanism today make preferable less oedipally determined or otherwise encoded relations. Consequently, Deleuze sets out a philosophy that attends to the immanent relational agonism of urbanism where friends must think together "how to mobilize the deterritorialization that capitalism unleashes … in the service of new ways of living together."[3] Vattimo comparably argues for the relational posture of friendship amidst the flood of former colonial subjects from Africa into Europe and from the presupposition of re-conceiving Christianity after metaphysics: "The death of the moral God marks the impossibility of preferring truth to friendship."[4] And so for humans, whether "essentially urban by nature,"[5] as Soja surmises, or if needing simply to navigate it, urbanism appears an open and unobligated relational milieu.

Yet if cities promise relations unprescribed, the conditions of "postmetropolis," a chaotic urbanism without a center and admitting uneven development, challenge us anew.[6] "The new urban form is marked," writes Canadian geographer and urban planner Engin Isin, "by hitherto unimagined fragmentation; by immense distances between its citizens, literal, economic, cultural, social and political."[7] This loose weave of urban relations leaves us vulnerable to the apartheid of wealth and poverty, to psychic loneliness, to the compulsory, individualist task of identity formation and the potential political ineffectiveness of that singularly crafted identity.[8]

Urban poverty is becoming, the World Bank warned already in the 1990s, "the most significant and politically explosive problem" of the twenty-first century.[9] Yet the growing urban divide factors neither into contemporary economic reason (this version of capitalism gone global without a safety net) nor into the human rights agenda (western philosophy has kept need, i.e., access to food and water, clothing and shelter, outside the realm of liberal thought). Today's "urbanization with deindustrialization" nonetheless will make, as sociologist Mike Davis convincingly concludes, "urbanization and favelization synonymous."[10] In stark contrast to neomarxist philosophers Michael Hardt's and Antonio Negri's promising narrative of *Multitude*, Davis warns that today's urbanism – this face of globalization resulting from "labor made redundant" – makes as possible and as likely rhizomatic connections like gangs, piracy, and criminal syndicates. This is made more likely by governmental agencies that abdicate urban reform as neo-liberal economics abandons welfare nets and citizens shutter themselves against mutuality.[11]

Complicating citizen responsiveness to this scenario of inter- as well as intraurban apartheid is the fact that during modernity, dominant power has been exercised as mobility, itself conflated with the spiritual, psycho-social and political promise of freedom. If the rivers of humanity loosed on the planet during modernity have been of two orders – the flow of migrant and now redundant labor and that of the cosmopolitans, this newly fluid mass of humanity could only have been set in motion by assuming "the mobile personality."[12] Theologian Mark C. Taylor traces this modern personality formation back to the Reformation and insists we recognize it as precisely "the good" which is now being globalized.[13] Modernity – following here a certain Christian-enthused transcendentalism of the self, i.e., "neither Jew nor Greek … male nor female" (Galatians 3:28) – insists on the shedding of ethno-cultural tradition and rituals.[14] It has worked assiduously to release bodies from obligation and obedience, from all ligatures, including that of religion. If that makes possible the urban spirit of friendship, it has also unwittingly induced, argues psychologist Bruce Alexander, psychosocial dis/integration.[15]

Assuming responsibility as an urban species

As the generations hand off one to another, the gift of individual choice, which was from early industrialization through the libratory movements of the late twentieth century, a structure of freedom, has become, sociologists like Zygmunt Bauman argue, the ache of irrelevance in a disconnected world. This failure of meaning and mattering affects the well-resourced and the resource-excluded equally: "The destruction of psychosocial integration is shockingly obvious in the homeless, the physically violated and the destitute, but … it affects the protected, safe and wealthy with a similar force."[16] Dislocation exacerbates the self-enclosure of the mobile, individualistic personality, which can be re-enforced by hard technology, e.g., iPods, internet, and private domestic habitat.

Humans wither under the loss of "the protective covering of cultural institutions," even when those seem to have been willingly shed.[17] Without loyalties, customs, rituals, or kin-folds, the psyche may be thrown into a vacuum of meaning. Given that "free market society exploits human cultures in the same relentless way that it exploits the earth's minerals ... even the people who benefit the most from free-market society," Alexander insists, "cannot escape the feeling that something fundamental is missing from their lives of affluence ... and independence."[18] For the now globally mobile personality, everything is possible, nothing matters. The loss of "social consciousness" and, therefore, of generosity, Alexander concludes, stems from a person's felt social and political irrelevance.[19]

A "life without demands" – which, according to Alexander's study, will be how any number of us viscerally experience modernity's razing of sociocultural obligations – "makes us 'homesick' ... makes us long [to ... inhabit ...] a place populated with objects, people and activities which themselves have existential as opposed to merely instrumental importance."[20] In the absolute rationalism of a technological world, philosopher Mark Wrathall explains, "nothing is encountered as really mattering." To the contrary, "everything that shows up" – including fellow humans – "is lacking in any inherent significance, use or purpose."[21] For cosmopolitans, too, life can come relationally unstrung – to the point of screaming psychic pain – whether of a certain existential despair or of an intellectually toned cynicism.

I suggest my home city of Vancouver as one example of contemporary cosmopolitanism, an example with which I will work throughout this chapter. Generated as a city "to fill a niche in the global economic system" of the then British empire,[22] its current "global city" status is a ramification of its earlier colonial role. Vancouver today harbors a people spinning at the vortex of the free-market system, a people relationally bereft. While annually ranked as the most livable city on the planet, Vancouver is rife with addiction – not just to drugs, alcohol, and sex (those are simply the most obvious, Alexander is quick to underscore), but to work, consumerism, gambling, ideologies (religious, economic, political, ecological), internet, television, romantic love, exercise, and anorexia. Without a shared culture at the heart of urban life, with modernity having encouraged the razing of ties to kin as well as religious de-ritualization, Vancouverites can develop addictions as adaptive rituals. Vancouver was recently selected by the U.N. Population Fund as "its example to prove that the social problems of twenty-first-century urbanization strike rich cities as well as poor cities in the Third World."[23]

If we are to assume responsibility for ourselves as an urban species, how will we grow obligation to each other, and especially to bodies that have been refused economic access within an age in which we are bound only by the "cash nexus?"[24] What kind of intelligence might Christian theology offer toward the hope of "a city/region in which there is genuine connection with, and respect and space for, the cultural other and the possibility of working together on matters of common destiny, a recognition of intertwined fates?"[25] A theology on location within a global city might not be unrelated to creating a civil city as distinct from a feral city (gone wild with despair and frustration over lack of access) or a sterile city of wealth (presuming one definition of civility while pretending to ignore the economic and ecological quake zone). If to be religious today might yet again mean paying attention to the psychic and material needs of the neighbor, then I might hope that a yoga of corporeal generosity could be unfolded from the *pli* of Spirit.

Spirit haunts contemporary theological thought. In addition to its appearance in ecotheology and some science-theology conversations, Spirit has emerged as a place-holder of the sacred within the work of conceiving religion after metaphysics, specifically in the critique of ontotheology, and in theologies informed by an immanentalist Deleuzean ontology. As Santiago Zabala puts it, "Learning to live without anxiety or neurosis in a world lacking fixed, guaranteed structure ['salvation,' in other words] depends on our transferring the real as we now experience it to the level of spirit."[26]

John Caputo has consequently resorted to a "Derridean hauntology" to work desire across the frigid skins of moral melancholics trying to wake to life in the ruin of God.[27] Nietzsche earlier surmised – and contemporary pneumatological evocations pick this up – that modernity suffers an erotic problem. In the wake of the accomplishments of modern reason, including science and technology, moderns suffer from a failure of desire – itself notable in modernity's lament of losses innumerable. Consequently melancholy, a moralizing self-critique that freezes life-love, has settled over liberal western culture and may infect even the analytic accounts of Bauman, Giddens, and Alexander and, more importantly, the bodies their analytic gazes assess. Spirit, as Caputo supposes, might be a theopoetic whisper of desire, a haunt that does not profess doxic certainty, but nevertheless offers a locus, a passional vortex, that yields a practice of faithfulness to life.[28]

Here, I explore how I might constructively think about the manifold of Spirit within a diversely "spiritual, but not religious" scene. Because "pluralism is not enough" (according to Keller), I suggest that the *pli* of Spirit, that "many-one," signals a fertile "fold" (i.e., *pli* or pleat) of difference within immanence itself so as to generate ligatures or obligations.[29] The work of religion within this scene will be that of growing corporeal generosity into a social muscle. Consequently, this chapter develops the spiritual prosthesis of the practiced vow – the "yoke" or "yoga" – of corporeal generosity to creaturely need within the inter-religious milieu of today's global cities.

I am simply uttering a *pli*/plea of and for Spirit over the postcolonial city. The *pli* of Spirit, as Vattimo surmised, has historically been congruent with relations of friendship. Although terms like friendship, neighbor, and Spirit-adoption might well have been borrowed from ancient philosophical repertoires, these relational ligatures – or at least their correlation with contemporary urbanism – have slipped from our theological awareness. Then again, the human urban disposition and resultant urbanism itself appears a strange secret western Christian theology has kept from itself. Paradoxically, during the nineteenth and twentieth centuries as North America was aggressively entering into its own urban formation, pastoralism animated North American literature and theology, from readings of the Christian gospels that present a Jesus of noble savage vintage to American transcendentalism and recent ecological spiritualities.

Today a dense urban postcolonial manifold, which I argue can be remembered in and through the *pli* of Spirit, must cross-check our theological tendency to repress the urban disposition of the human animal. Because Nature too can serve as a transcendental term while hiding in "a material mask,"[30] and reason, as Lyotard alerts us, carries its own totalizing impulses, enfolding Spirit too closely with nature might invite not only a reduction of nature but also reify secular rationalism.[31] If Spirit and nature can neither be wholly identified nor neatly distinguished, these perspectives also acknowledge that there is no longer "a transcending God whose dictates we must follow or whose substance we must seek in our lives to resemble ... no longer a transcending Other that can lay claim upon our faith or our behavior."[32] If "Spirit" thus marks our release from a tired theism, it nonetheless names the movement of what Jean-Luc Nancy calls "dis-enclosure ... inscribed at the heart of the Christian tradition."[33]

Spirit and urban diasporas

A theology of the manifold unleashed in this synekistic stew of urbanism cannot help but be influenced by the resident polyphony of world religions. Christianity may recognize itself anew when living in intimate relationship with Tibetan Buddhism or the yoga of Vedic thought. Especially where Christianity must find some new way to become operational (as it must in Cascadia), it may sound itself out amidst the religious polyphony of the city. In this way, Christianity might, as I have elsewhere argued, remember itself as a practice.[34]

Considering the northern band of the western hemisphere where others have argued that Christianity is growing irrelevant, Harvey Cox has wondered whether Christianity might rather be acquiring more Asian sensibilities: "Could Christianity ... be moving away from an institutionally positioned model and toward a culturally diffuse pattern, more like the religions of many Asian countries, and therefore more difficult to measure by such standard means as church attendance and baptism statistics?"[35] Ten years later, in his 2009 text, *The Future of Faith*, Cox has moved to the declarative, announcing a "tectonic shift in Christianity," a shift into "The Age of the Spirit," in which the religious returns as "a way of life rather than a doctrinal structure," as the experiential practice of "faith and love," as distinct from belief.[36] So as the theology of the manifold goes on location within the global city, we may find that the persons with whom we think about this theology do not share a common religious heritage as much as a commitment to practiced paths of faithfulness to life.

Where "Christianity as belief" traveled well through the modern passages, a new regionalism saturates the sensibilities of practitioners. In Cascadia, a cathedral of nature whose mountains, forests, and oceans cradle the cosmopolitan "emerald" cities of Vancouver, Seattle, and Portland, "Spirit" designates a "place"-holder, an immanental religious sensibility. Owing to postcolonial flows, our "trinity" is as likely to include the parlor dance of Kuan Yin, Buddha and the Christ as the tri-uning fold of classic Christian theism.[37] Spirit plays well in this locale because, as theologian Jay McDaniel reminds us, Spirit "is not reducible to Chrisitianity," and Spirit honors those who would be "spiritual without being religious ... [or] theistic."[38] Spirit – which I hope might serve as a prosthesis of friendship for covering the exposure of the other, for approaching the need of the other, given the psychosocial dis/integration and dislocation of rich and poor – cannot but benefit from the comparative theological conversation of postcolonial cosmopolitans.

Spirit operates as a locus of multiplicity that does not always necessitate a distinctive name of belonging. Spirit, as a theopoetic concept that counters the sheered relations and dis/integrated psyches of diaspora, may be practiced as a yoga of neighborliness and adoptionism. That said, Christianity remains for me the strongest shaper of entrustment to life and of political ethics. But if, as Karl Jaspers suggests, axial religions developed transcendence as an elite fear of masses, and hence as elite avoidance of urban multiplicities,[39] the concept of Spirit – first constructively formulated among those dislocated persons in the multi-religious milieu of the ancient Roman world (Eliade), then triangulated into repression for 1,500 years within Christian theology – returns here as the fold or *pli* of postcolonial cosmopolitan religious multiplicity.

So I conspire with Spirit in its ongoing constructive hybridization, yearning toward its own new becomings. If religions can be used toward violent ends, religions may also provide diverse wisdoms for lived solidarities. Within postmetropolis, Spirit might – if we refuse to let it escape into idealist fantasies and pay attention to the explicitly spatial politics of the city – provide that necessary third space, a combinatory interval that refuses oppositionalism. Spirit has shown itself before as a strange attractor, which loves and so refuses to shatter amidst heterogeneous mixing. So Spirit might here too "occasion … new and varied forms of bonding." The spatial ruptures of postmetropolis will be, Bell Hooks advises, those places where the critical, organic intellect will need to come into play.[40] In cities threatened by "no go" zones and gated communities, Spirit "walks through" enclosures. It seeps under gates, partitions, and fortresses of human aversions. Spirit offers itself as a dynamic fold across territorial and psychic separations.

The yoga of neighbor-love

In the vacuum of meaning and starvation by dislocation occasioned by the British Empire, Gandhi countered with a "re-ligare" or "re-binding" of relations, namely the renovation of the vowed life centered in the Satyagraha Ashram. Vows, Gandhi wrote, worked to heal "that hurting indifference which keeps one human being from another."[41] As relations were diffused owing to colonialism, Gandhi advocated the yoga of neighbor-love, i.e., "A [person's] first duty is to … neighbor."[42] Given the limitless extension of life opened out in the wake of colonialism, an extension that simultaneously wreaked local havoc, Gandhi made the yoke of neighborly immediacy an aspect of the practice of neighbor-love, e.g., wearing only cloth spun within the community. Neighbor-love, a spiritual practice, therefore worked against the imperial energies to become boundless.

The yoga of neighbor-love, one might imagine, countered the way in which persons' dreams and aspirations were pulled into the circulation of colonialism, a propagandistic sense of "the good life" which was not materially available to locals. One could likewise imagine, owing to the ways in which colonialism and now globalization scatter communities of belonging at great distance, that neighbor-love could encourage a certain adoption of place, a grounding of life in place, so as not to get caught in the backwash of nostalgia. Insomuch as "neighborhood" has today become a "zombie institution,"[43] making the localization of neighbor-love into a religio-spiritual practice might begin to generate a physics of meaning and mattering. Further, thinking now from an ecological perspective, such practices of neighbor-love may help us learn to live with the limits of mortality and ecosystemic boundaries – rather than "overcoming" them, as the idealist metaphysics of modernity incite.

Gandhi's reconstruction of sacred obligations evolved from the *pli* or fold where "some of the recessive elements of Christianity," e.g., the Sermon on the Mount, found resonance with "congruent … elements of Hindu and Buddhist world views."[44] Setting out from two convictions, that our birth, itself of a sacrificial nature, makes us debtors all our lives and that "the one who serves his[/her] neighbor serves all the world,"[45] Gandhi constructed the yoga of non-violence in order to liberate Indians and so likewise to liberate the British from their "panicky, self-imposed captivity," from the "psychology of British colonialism."[46] An existential loss of bearings was here countered by religious obligation. The yoke brings life out of isolation – a not insignificant gift, if we can analogically compare the pain of the vacuum of meaning in global cities to that of Indians relationally dispersed and economically ill-disposed by earlier stages of colonialism.

The yoga of the Christian gospels

Huston Smith situates the birth of western philosophy in a comparable scenario. He argues that the schools of philosophy of the ancient world, e.g., Pythagorean and Epicurean, arose during a period of skepticism. "The ancestral order had dissolved and men and women were looking for an alternative way to get their bearings." Finding "the rootlessness and rudderlessness of skepticism intolerable," they reached for philosophy – not merely to titillate the mind, but as "a way of life and death," as salvation, as a "*practice*" to free them from anxiety.[47] If ancient and contemporary dislocated and relationally truncated bodies were redressed by religious vows, by assuming the "yoke" or yoga of philosophical practice, the Christian gospels too might be read not for "belief," but as themselves acts of the creation of ligatures (the etymological base of "religion" and "obligation") amidst the vacuum occasioned by the Roman Empire's de- and reconstruction of life worlds.

For readers of Matthew's gospel, "*Christ the Yogi*" offers the Beatitudes as a locus of reverence, as a yoke or harness of desire amidst the sheering of psychophysical trauma and social dislocation.[48] Warren Carter surmises that Matthew's intended audience lived near or resided in Antioch in Syria. Not only had Cicero declared that "Jews and Syrians were born to be slaves," the urban milieu of Antioch was, for the majority of inhabitants "who existed to provide services," hardly conducive to well-being. With a population density exceeding that of contemporary Mumbai and Calcutta, amidst xenophobia and filth, laborers could not expect the universalism of the empire to "solve the issues of social identity … It failed to penetrate the everyday life of the mass of the people," even as it emptied them of prior meaning worlds. With labor so intricately woven into the imperial system and given that with it comes not only exhaustion, but "loss of heart," Jesus' call, i.e., "[t]ake my yoke upon you … for my yoke is ['merciful']" (Matthew 11:28–30), was "addressed to all those who labor desperately to keep themselves in the economically oppressive … system of Roman imperialism."[49]

The fact that "yoke" – as the term has been translated into English – and "yoga" share the same etymological base in Sanskrit might begin to help us break through the simplistic way Christians have thought of Christianity as mere "belief" and of Jesus' "yoke" as mere metaphor. "No teaching worth its salt can be understood only by the mind, for the simple reason that a *teaching*, a *yoga*, is not simply a set of propositions for the mind to assent to or to argue over," explains Ravi Ravindra. He concludes: "Above all, what a teaching demands is that one engage in practice."[50]

If the Beatitudes (Matthew 5, Luke 6) might, as Bonnie Thurston insists, spell out for Christians the "most basic rules of life,"[51] the Beatitudes likewise constitute a yoga of re-socialization into "indiscriminate love" lived in new models of kinship, of civic relations without respect to status, and nonviolence, a practice of generous availability to one another amidst a lot of good reasons to be afraid. While a yoga or yoke implies submission, one might read "submission" as opening oneself outward – in this case, toward a covenant of trust with the neighbor. "The real point of obedience," Thurston insists, "is not to do someone else's will," but to cultivate "'an emptiness,' … a 'space'" – an openness not already subjected to self-will, to one's own purposes.[52] To be sure, "the progressive liberation from … one's own little ego is the purpose of any transformational teaching or spiritual path," as Ravindra instructs us.[53] But for Christianity, that freedom arrives through entrustment, by binding one's self to the neighbor. As Paul Knitter writes in a more consciously theistic vein, "to be loyal to Christ, one must be vulnerable to others."[54]

The urban pli *of spirit*

The concept Spirit – first constructively formulated among persons in diaspora, owing to an imperially stewed, multi-religious, multicultural milieu – signals, I suggest, a similar yoga among ancient readers of the Gospel of John. The Johannine gospel situates Spirit as the "sanctuary" of new life (John 3:1–15). Followers of the Johannine text worked the yoga of Spirit so as "to prepare a place" (John 14:2) for themselves where the tentacles of empire had strewn them.

For bodies dispersed at the whim of empire, whether because of the mobility of mercantilism or imperial policies of deportation, of razing and rebuilding cities with foreign persons (thereby undermining powers of resistance), the ancient place-based religions – tied to Mt. Gerizim, to the Samaritan well or by ancestral pilgrimage patterns to the city of Jerusalem (see John 4:20) – could no longer offer meaning. "In times of catastrophic dislocation, such as the Judean exile to Babylon [as also the later economic reconstruction of Palestine, owing to the Roman Empire], traditional rituals lost their power."[55] Owing to such diasporic conditions, Spirit – a theological concept developed when Hebraic convictions were folded through Hellenistic and Stoic philosophies – denoted the sheer, extensive immanence of the divine.[56] The Gospel of John consequently ties the concept of Spirit back to a genesis account of the cosmos (Genesis 1:1–2). Spirit was seen as conceptually broad and spacious enough to gather in those scattered by empire, to absolve and then obligate one to another beyond ethnic and territorial separation.[57]

If this constructive *pli* of Spirit suggests the potential sacrality of all places, folded implicitly therein is the Hebraic sense that *ruach* ("spirit" or "breath") names the experience of the divine as breathing room, as "the space of freedom in which the living being can unfold."[58] If with exile "space threatened to become permanently emptied of meaning," Hebrew prophets suggestively constructed "Spirit" as the placeholder spelling the sacrality of even "the decentralized spaces of [peoples'] exile."[59] For ancient persons, who had lost their religio-cultural maps of meaning and mattering and whose lives were constricted by ethnocultural xenophobia, Spirit named "broad, open space for living" again.[60]

While this new way of valuing space in terms of Spirit may have eventuated into Christianity's "delegitimizing [of] all territorially based religions" and its own ignorance of place, as Tod Swanson argues, one might – holding well founded suspicions of campaigns against indigenous space in abeyance for a moment – also recognize the constructive relief occasioned by the concept Spirit among diasporic bodies. As religious identity was deterritorialized (the effects of which might not be inconsistent with Alexander's and Wrathall's descriptions of the psychosocial disintegration among cosmopolitans today), Spirit named a mobile "dis-enclosure" – a non-territorially specific, but nonetheless religiously meaningful locus. Through it one could practice a certain "courage to be with" others. Swanson insinuates as much when he notes that "the Johannine map [was] a plan of action" and that Christian love was expected to remap bodies into a quickening hold of obligations.[61]

Swanson argues for "the non-transferable quality of sacred places," e.g., graves, memorials, pilgrimage sites, and indigenous territories.[62] I do not disagree with his respect for these places, but remind him that any number of bodies have had to make sense of unknown spaces, have had to use religious obligations to weave something of "the space of freedom in which the living being can unfold."[63] But the space of ultimate freedom always comes nonetheless by way of a yoke, e.g., neighbor-love – as Gandhi also surmised.

Spirit as dis/enclosure

The *pli* of Spirit might be conceived as an art of inhabiting, an art of turning the "vacuum of meaning" into the reverentially inflected "broad, open space for living."[64] Relations, as some Cascadian cosmopolitans will admit, can be sheered to the point of psychosocial disintegration; the open may be too unstrung to prove out any quality of life. Buddhist theologian Daisaku Ikeda comparably observes that "[w]ith their lives devoid of comradeship and intimacy, many people find human relationships savage." He then adds, "[r]estoring human ties and making local communities, and society more generally, warmly humane are two of religion's most important roles in the twenty-first century."[65]

Spirit names, to adapt Nancy's concept of "dis-enclosure," a religiously deterritorialized relation to place that nonetheless assumes a sheltering function by way of *obligare* and *religare*. A psychosocially induced vacuum of meaning enervates or disperses persons' energies carelessly (or in patterns that are felt to lack dignity or worth); but ritual and practice – like neighbor-love – can weave bodies into patterns of meaning and mattering. As Alexander cautions, because "humans are not psychologically self-sufficient, social belonging and individual autonomy must be balanced."[66] In other words, meaningful lives require yokes of obligation to something worthy.

Intriguingly, in diagnosing "poverty of spirit" by implicitly referencing the ancient Beatitudes ascribed to Jesus, Alexander himself reached prescriptively, if unconsciously, for the yoga of an ancient people, themselves – like today's rising tide of poor and rich – "torn from the close ties to family, culture and traditional spirituality."[67] Suffering dislocation under the Roman Empire, ancient Christian movements assumed the vowed or yoked life – epitomized in the Beatitudes as in the adoptionism of the communal movements of "the kin[g]dom of God" and Pauline *ecclesiai* – as a counter-imperial practice of freedom and joy.

The psychosocial maelstrom of postmodern life can leave persons relationally sheered. The structure of choice as a promise of freedom has become for some enervatingly abstract (e.g., the ideal career) or reductively trivial (this toothpaste or that, this tv show or that, this entrée or that). Contrary to this structure of freedom, religious persons – Hindu, Buddhist, Christian – have long taught that the yoke gives life, that vows give "greater freedom."[68] The yoke opens out what Karmen MacKendrick calls "counter pleasures": "A new ascesis [or discipline] is a new strategizing of pleasure, a new disruption in the relations of power."[69]

Comparably, from among the vowed Christian religious, Sandra Schneiders suggests that vows generate alternative structures of life. Vows engage disciplines so persons can actually love more freely with open hearts. Yet, she concludes, "The only reason religious make a vow … is that it seems … the best way to … their own true freedom."[70] Raimon Panikkar echoes this sensibility in his *Initiation to the Vedas*: "To be able to invocate, that is, to call upon, something greater than ourselves and so break our own [ego] boundaries, is the beginning of wisdom, the source of hope and the condition of joy."[71] But to what do "spiritual, but not religious" persons bind ourselves if we accept that "God" might be only a transitional object along the way? Our intellectual point of entrée must be, as Vancouver author Douglas Copeland puts it, *"Life After God."*[72]

Oblates

In the fifteenth year of my life reborn after trauma, I find myself amidst a psychological turmoil. I feel, I mutter to a friend, as if I am being unfaithful to what happened to me – to that occasion when my life lay intimately close to death, the occasion that left me mobility challenged. But how precisely – and to what – could trauma have obligated me? How do I explain this "feeling ... of being bound ... [of] being taken hold of from without" by a "dislocating force" that "knocks me out of orbit?"[73] From whence this gravity of obligation, given that I am a "walking disaster?"

Thirteen years old when an auto accident meant that life for him proceeded as a paraplegic, Matthew Sanford writes in *Waking: A Memoir of Trauma and Transcendence* of what I might call – at the point of interpolation between disability experiences and the work of Jean-Luc Nancy – an obligation to "the great open." Refusing the western script of "willfully overcoming adversity," Sanford writes:

> Something had happened to me – not just the accident, not just the loss of my father and sister or my ensuing paralysis ... I felt like I had been left with a secret ... I could not articulate what it was, but I did have a nagging sense of what it was not. It was not to simply live a relatively normal life. I felt far too weighty, too heavy, like there's a purpose to what I have experienced.

But dredging for the source of that obligation, he can speak only of "the 'openness' left by trauma," of cultivating the "silence" as "itself ... the insight I was sensing," a silence – which like that described by apophatic theologians or "the greater consciousness" of Buddhist practitioners – cut through all one presumes to know about "how the world worked and what it needed."[74]

Reminding us that the body (not just the mind) is conscious, Sanford explains – by analogy to standing at the edge of the Grand Canyon – the gift wrestled from the intensity of his trauma experience:

> The act of 'opening' consciousness makes us feel both uncertainty and the onrush of silence that comes with it ... It is both awesome and unsettling – one knows not to stand too close to the edge. The feeling of openness and a confrontation with silence are deeply related.[75]

If we might acknowledge this as an occasion of religious response to mystery, to the sublimity of life beyond our grasp, suffering may be a surprising spiritual rite of passage. For Sanford, it was literally his initiation into the practice and teaching of yoga.

Mark Matousek – a journalist living HIV positive – has heard multiple outpourings of disease and trauma and has tracked the ways in which suffering has served as "rite of initiation." A spiritual seeker in the face of his own diagnosis, Matousek writes to understand what his body already knows – that "HIV had saved his life."[76] A reporter of tales of "savage grace," of those occasions when "terror can be a door to enlightenment," an opening to a life baptized in awe and not constrained by fear or its bipolarities (e.g., good/evil, pleasure/pain, success/failure), Matousek set out – first taking leave of a status job – "determined not to lose track of what [he'd] learned in the mortal zone or to forget the miraculousness of things."[77]

Matousek's personal story as well as his collection of tales cut through modernity's dismissal of suffering to let pain's paradoxical blessing out of the bag.

"There's vitality in facing life's extremes," he insists, naming this energy *viriditas*, a term used by medieval theologian Hildegard von Bingen to speak of Spirit's immanental humour, its "greening power." He explains: "Though we're immersed in this power at every moment, survivors realize how profoundly quality of life is determined by how skillfully … we harness ourselves to that evergreen force at the heart of things." Oddly, what we've grown to call the tragic and a sense of holy mystery – yielding generosity, courage, and ego-lessness – are not mutually exclusive. "Epiphanies happen where life and death meet," Matousek asserts, given that "the very walls we construct to protect our lives hide the full glory of those lives from us."[78] This locus, this point of reverence, this flash of satori and the discipline of walking with its hindrances, I mark as Spirit.

The open – prolonged in my case through an extended recovery (Virginia Woolf might well draw a parallel between it and a spiritual retreat)[79] – allows for a critical, constructive dissociation from social geographies of meaning and value, from normalcy. Caught in awe, I take my vows to the great open – this haunting dis-enclosure, this sheltering nowhere. I awake inveterately in love with the world (I am not ignorant of the fact that this "naturalism" comes to me from Christian theism's impulse to love the world as God has loved it. God too, says Lutheran theologian Joseph Sittler, is "an undeviating materialist").[80] But the intrigue for me – reflecting on my own experience – is that of the poignancy and power of living with something like religious vows without "belief." If suffering opens us to "the open" or "Spirit," it also sets its demands on us, "binding" or folding us back into the thick of it. To be alive is to be obligated – harnessed, yoked, devoted.

The pli *of intercorporeal generosity*

Being a patient of life (a "becoming" that is other than that managed by the will to overcome) might be the subjective locus to which pain initiates one. Pain introduces one to a postural submission or patience with life. Suffering allows our rigid, defensive selves to move through an unmarked door of dis- and re-organization, to recognize the nominal looseness and permissiveness of existence. But intriguingly, as William Connolly indirectly suggests, there is something phenomenologically analogous between suffering, which "resides in the underside of agency, mastery" and an "ethos of generosity," which "moves us beyond mastery, will to control."[81]

The religious sense of obligation lived out of a relation with pain, enacted as a sense of generosity toward the world, might strike moderns raised on the idea that suffering is meaningless and capable of eradiction, as paradoxically perplexing. Yet this co-incidence between pain and generosity appears, theologically speaking, hardly unique. As the Buddha knew, to touch such a cut, an open, was flush with that form of generosity known as compassion. Where Buddhism situates the open, it carries a heart quality – generosity. "Gratitude for life," Connolly explains, "draws an ethics of generosity partly from those energies and attachments that exceed established conventions," from those energies that sneak through even suffering's dis-organizing whirl.[82]

Contrary to Caputo's scene in *Against Ethics* within which obligation swells in relation to neediness, Roslyn Diprose insists that generosity is "not reducible to an economy of exchange between sovereign individuals."[83] Indeed "Generosity is not one virtue among others but the primordial condition of personal, interpersonal and communal existence." She explains: "Primordially, generosity is not the expenditure of one's possessions but the dispossession of oneself, the being-given to others that undercuts any self-contained ego." Generosity, she continues, "happens at a prereflective level, at the level of corporeality and sensibility … Generosity is being given to others without deliberation in a field of intercorpore-ality, a being given that constitutes the self as affective and being affected."[84]

While Caputo would commendably have us practice social availability to the other, Diprose underlines the "nonvolitional" nature of generosity – prior to identity.[85] In other words, the practice of corporeal generosity begins for Diprose within the milieu of intersubjective relations (in fact, generosity names this intercorporeal field) and not at the level of property, status, identity, and value. A demonstrative example might well be in order. During a wheelchair training unit, I met David and Jonathan, two adolescent males both of whom – in separate accidents – became lifelong wheelchair users, owing to the extremes of mountain biking. Born of their situation was a friendship of visceral depth. Yet both were also typical young, straight males – not wanting to show too much feeling, covering their own pain in humor and antics.

Then came the day we were to practice picking ourselves up from a fall by first intentionally flipping ourselves so as to occasion a spill out of our chairs. Jonathan dared to go first but, owing to the chaotic – and not yet habituated – firing of nerves in his still newly quadriplegic body, Jonathan convulsed as he spilled over. If all of us felt our stomachs drop in that moment, David's compassion betrayed his adolescent cool. His feelings for his friend literally pulled him likewise into a gut-coiling spasm of compassion, which took him slithering out of his chair and onto the ground. It was one of the most moving, intimate moments in which I have ever been privileged to participate.

This zone of interdependent feeling below volition – an openness that is "carnal and affective" – seems to me to be of the nature of generosity to which Diprose points us. If obligation calls from within the deeps of intercorporeal tissue, then plenitude – corporeal generosity itself, in other words – is that which obligates. Corporeal generosity catches us up in an affective effulgence; the intensity of affect felt among bodies draws us into an exuberant, energetic carnival. To locate one's self within the field of corporeal generosity might lead one to renounce any superior sense of the self, arising from access to wealth or wholeness. When one assumes the practice of a spiritual path setting out from the locus of this great open field, then one might experience the beggar or the CEO, like pain, to become one's spiritual teacher. Everything and everyone provides an opening to the practice of generosity, of sympathy at the cellular level. The yoga or obligation of neighbor-love is born of this, develops this generosity as a social muscle.

Responsiveness to the obligation felt within corporeal generosity challenges the humanist self. Corporeal generosity suggestively insinuates that the self might practice "the open" in a way beyond its mastered and patrolled defensive lines (i.e., property, identity). A spiritual practice of the open calls us from below sovereign selfhood, where the phenomenology of suffering links up with generosity. As Caputo himself has observed, "Obligation is the sphere of what I did not constitute … It comes to me … in a curved space which lays me low, producing a kind of disequilibrium in me."[86] That curve, given culturally prescribed lives of linear progress, is telling.

Toward an urban naturalist cosmology

"I don't know what purpose we have as humans other than to be one another's servants," muttered one who might well epitomize Cascadia's "spiritual, but not religious" population. She is a massage therapist with an array of healing practices from ayurveda and aromatherapy to Chinese herbalism and acupuncture. Yet, as we traded conversation about what it might mean to think about obligation to each other in a city like Vancouver (she having balked at the word "obligation," thinking that it related her to a set of duties to an externality, like God, not felt in the heart, her declared authoritative center), the words tumbled out of her mouth as a somewhat surprising confession, even to herself. "Servant. I know it's kind of a funny, old word," she began apologetically. And yet as she spun her own thought, she heard herself saying, "Why even the rest of the natural world – like trees, like ants, like bacteria – have a servant role." Indeed: the turning of our soft tissues one to another, this submission or entrustment of the soft tissue, of the heart, so as to be folded through one another's lives, constitutes some aspect of neighbor-love. The theological reformer Martin Luther might be pleased to hear the yoke of servant-hood interpreted as a naturalist cosmology for twenty-first-century urban dwellers.

Luther's summary of the Christian life in his 1520 treatise "The Freedom of a Christian" states that "the Christian is 'lord of all, ["subject to none"]' and a 'servant, completely attentive to the needs of all.'"[87] Luther drafted this treatise in mind of a humanity "prone to find security in earthly 'addictions,'" which Alexander might quip is not unlike our own contemporary urban humanity.[88] While Luther cathected "the open" as Christ-identified, as a relational locus of being loved by God and out of which one "knows nothing except this sense of spontaneous joy," that relational yoke was transferred by Luther to the needs of the neighbor and the world.[89] In the great open, informed for Luther by the character of God's prodigal love, humans can turn our soft, vulnerable flesh toward one another. Perhaps it might yet be read even as a nature cosmology, of life that is inherently relational and turned servant-like one toward another.

Does Luther anticipate Nietzsche's cosmological potlatch, his contention that nature is "an unreproductive squandering of excess without reciprocation"[90] when he writes: "We freely and willingly spend ourselves and all that we have … This is just as our Father does, who gives all things to all people richly and freely, making 'his sun to rise on the evil and on the good' (Matthew 5:45)?" Such great permissiveness, experiencing the heart as "free … from all [guilt], laws and commands," might well today be expressed in the postmodern life without even the siren call of Being, World Spirit, or God.[91] As Buddhist Masao Abe puts it, "[i]n Christianity … the kenosis of God is fully realized, and [as] God completely empties God-self, the dynamic relationship of mutual domination-subordination or mutual immanence and mutual transcendence between human beings and God, and human beings and nature, can be fully realized. This is possible only by overcoming" – as in the deconstruction of Christianity – "the theocentrism innate in Christianity."[92] That overcoming has opened nonetheless upon the vista named corporeal generosity.

Spirit as prosthesis

The "cut that binds" (Wolfson), the opening that obligates, unfolds the great vastness that in a Deleuzean sense is the dense virtuality of what might yet be. I have marked this verdant open as Spirit, as did Hegel. Spirit might prevent the rationalist foreclosure of the field of intercorporeal generosity. But how can we invoke "the Spirit" without reverting to strong theology, to the metaphysics of presence?[93]

Thinking religiously in the ruin of God

"It is not our concern to save religion, even less to return to it," writes Nancy.[94] Like Alexander, he is well aware of the psychosocial effects of globalization via the cash nexus. While construing atheism as the promise of Christianity and greeting the "death of god" as Christianity's destiny, he is not averse to faith – although clearly distinguishing it from belief. Looking at the de-traditionalizing effects of modernity, Nancy reminds us to think of this as the unfolding of Christianity, not its deviation: "Christianity has delivered Western society" to this point of its own dissolution. And as this is so, then "the essence of Christianity" may itself be "dis-enclosure" or, simply, "opening."[95]

Nancy's "dis-enclosure" of Christianity disrupts a certain enlightenment myth we have used to colonize Christianity as our western past:

> The West was born not from the liquidation of a dark world of beliefs, dissolved by the light of a new sun … There was no reduction of the unknown, but rather an aggravation of the incommensurable … Christianity designates nothing other, essentially … than the demand to open in this world an alterity or an unconditional alienation.[96]

Nancy finds something of this same demand in the kenotic impulse, an impulse that resembles Laurel Schneider's sense of the ruined distinction between God and world, a resolutely dirty conception of God.[97] Within a world threatened by what Nancy calls foreclosures of reason and of religion, Christianity – that "religion of the egress/departure from religion" daring to think religiously "after God" – might understand itself as an inheritor of an obligation to the open, as under obligation of the "dis-enclosure … inscribed at the heart of the Christian tradition."[98]

A God who is emptied out into this world – the locus from which both Nancy and Vattimo set out – suggests a way of thinking within which God empties God's self of transcendence, God yields sovereignty so as to become with the world. If God has been "ruined" or "dirtied" in such a way that neither nature/spirit nor God/world can be cleanly distinguished,[99] Spirit suggestively insinuates a conceptual commitment to "opening."

While Nancy's sense of the open does not necessarily presume to look upon the field of multiples, the dis-enclosure of all totalizing worlds must set us on such a vista. "How do we recognize 'the ungraspability of being'?" he asks rhetorically, already alerting us to Spirit's relevance to multiplicity. "How do we touch, or let ourselves be touched by, the opening of the world/to the world? How, if not by a gesture ... that passes outside of knowledge without unreason ...?" Nancy goes on immediately to suggest the relationship between this gesture and the yoga of what Luce Irigaray calls "felicity in history"[100] or what he simply marks as a faith in faithfulness itself: "A faith that would stand up unflinchingly to the atheism without reserve in which it would be nothing other than the 'courage' invoked to say the 'strange.'"[101] While Nancy hopes to preclude any romanticization of the open, he nonetheless insists on keeping faith with it – a posture not unlike Luther's relation to the hidden God, at least on this point.

Yet for Nancy, the great open does not so much exist as "it ... defines and mobilizes ex-istence."[102] Such a thin notion of Spirit is surely to be distinguished from a *logos* theology, like a process Christology within which Spirit's polyvalent and polyocular omnipresence drenches world complexes. Nancy seems instead to evoke a "poverty of spirit" – to obligate us to Spirit that is not, except perhaps in our gesture of openness.[103] And yet in that gesture, corporeality becomes generous.

As prosthesis, spirit capacitates becoming

Within a philosophy of becoming, which has moved through the deconstruction of ontotheology, we can best say that Spirit capacitates being. J. Edgar Bruns hypothesizes that "the key to Johannine thought lies in an understanding of Buddhist concepts."[104] Consequently, Bruns reads 1 John 4:16 through a *prajna paramita* hermeneutic:

> There is no difference between loving and being one with God, because God is simply another name for love, and without love there is no present God ... God does not do something. God is the doing of something, which is why John calls [God] spirit, light and love ... Consequently God does not generate love in us, but rather, our loving generates God."[105] If so, Spirit in a religion without belief might not so much name an existent something as it will capacitate a practice.

We can think of Spirit, then, as something of a conceptual prosthesis capacitating belief in the world or, as per Nancy, sheer faithfulness.[106] "Prosthesis is semiosis, the making of meanings and bodies," Donna Haraway asserts, "not for transcendence, but for power-charged communication."[107] As a prosthesis, the concept Spirit refers us to an amazing point of physics – like a cane or a crutch upon which one does not bear weight, but which nonetheless capacitates movement, enables agility. Analogous to Foucault's concept of "queer" not as a substance or positivity, but as a positionality, Spirit as prosthesis allows us to improvise a distinct art of the self – openness to the intercorporeal field, weighted toward corporeal generosity.[108] Assuming Spirit as prosthesis takes seriously the poststructuralist challenge to truth; Spirit as prosthesis names the resort to a machinic assemblage of commitment to live within the field of corporeal generosity.

Admittedly leaning upon a certain Christian interpretation of the world, Spirit as prosthesis capacitates "this impious, nontheistic reverence for life," which may not be wholly severable in Nietzsche's case or mine from the Lutheran cradle.[109] Luther insisted – and both Vattimo and Nancy sound an echo on this point – that "the justice of God ... is the free gift of God surrendering God's self to us," of God submitting God's self to the world.[110] Spirit as prosthesis capacitates our corporeal becoming with the world. As a prosthesis capacitates the body, so Spirit capacitates our belief in the world, enables the mutual submission – or entrustment – of flesh one to another.

"The courage to be with"[111]

Donning the prosthesis, the shuffle begins:

> Shifting from one to the other as though there could be some sort of even transfer or equal distribution, as though beyond it all there was perfect or at least functionally satisfactory balance between the two, and failing to find it, failing to find an end to the discomfort of one and the other position, the one too ready to give way under prolonged exertion, the other too rigidly secure in its own uprightness, and in the interstice no easy middle, no ground for rest or resolution.[112]

So David Wells observes of his father, slipping on his prosthetic leg. Donning the conceptual prosthesis of Spirit situates us similarly – agonistically – between two economies, that which is culturally available (namely, rationalism or "secularism") and the "divine economy," the fold of corporeal generosity.

Tyler Roberts describes Spirit as a locus of difference disrupting reason's totality, thereby re-orienting – not repressing – desire. Spirit might be described, Roberts surmises from Nietzsche's work, "as life cutting into life, as an instrument used by life in its efforts to enhance itself."[113] Far from occasioning serenity, Spirit suggests a way of forming the self around fundamental alterity. Insomuch as Spirit "open[s] the self to the undomesticated power of life," honing Spirit might, he suggests, allow us to live "body in a different key."[114] In other words, the spiritual life feels a bit more like Jacob wrestling the angel than contemplative placidity. Developing the muscle of corporeal generosity takes some practice, a redistribution of weight, never finally resolved.

The geography of spirit

To don Spirit as prosthesis is to adopt a new geography – not to inflate interiority. Spirituality, as Philip Sheldrake puts it, is not so much a personal intimacy of the self with an imagined beyond as a practice of our availability within the particularity of a place. More precisely it is "the practice of everyday living in the heart of the world of human places."[115] For Sheldrake as for me, the place that concerns us is the city, which "both represents and creates a climate of values that defines how humans understand themselves ... and also shapes their sensibilities and ways of seeing the world."[116] The disciplined practice of corporeal generosity (that is, responsiveness to this "curve" thrown up from below ego) is here being invoked as an alternative to that which seems to be fragmenting the city between those with and those without access to the commons of life, leaving many on both sides shivering in their self-protective cynicism.

Assuming the prosthesis of Spirit, the locus of opening and the yoke of corporeal generosity might imply practicing through the "vacuum of meaning" – here, specifically, as ways of "being with" one another in the city. Within the global city, idealization sheers off difference. As a result, we remain resolutely cool – indifferent, detached, and neutralized in relation to one another. For a life of "meaning and mattering" in the postcolonial city, we need ligatures of friendship amidst the rampant dislocation – not that we imagine a great communitarianism, but rather that through friendship we might live an alternative to the existentialist individualism, which even the "spiritual, but not religious" ethos can engender.

Friendship – breaching the enclosure aggravated by modern humanist individualism (the guarantees of a money economy and the self-protective paranoia of dislocation), without collapsing the ethical autonomy of persons developed during modernity – might provide enough affiliative sheltering to allow us slowly to entrust our vulnerable animal flesh one to another. To love, after all, does involve softening and yielding our flesh to each other. There is no civic being, no friendship, no neighbor, no public, no commons without a mutual yielding of our tissues and the shared exercise of developing the muscle of intercorporeal generosity.

Mendicants of the Free Spirit

Noting that Deleuze considers the urban flow to be one of the apparently irresolvable difficulties of the capitalist axiomatic, Todd May invites us to think toward "an urbanism that is Deleuzian" by "jostl[ing] the reins of the majority identity in order to investigate ... new ways of becoming ... to live in accordance with a difference that is always there, always subsisting within the world that is presented to us."[117] Deleuzean philosophy attends to microsociological practices; and we might consequently imagine something of a mendicant order of "Free Spirits" wielding friendship.[118] If religion's power has too frequently been used to generate a transcendent elsewhere masking sovereign power and subjected persons rather than free radicals, Spirit here invites dis-enclosure of identity, invites us to break with the wealth insulation and isolation of those identity formations so amenable to free market capitalism.

The practice of this mendicant order of Free Spirits might begin with the yoga of "becoming whale." In the words of the ancient poet, whales are the pet of the sacred (Psalm 104:26); but they have become vulnerable, in the last several centuries, to the human species. Whales – a creature in relation to the sea as humans are to the land, i.e., "a kind of parallel 'us'" – are a complex, socially structured species, each pod having its own unique culture and dialect. Like humans, they sing, they leap in joy, they are curious, they grieve, they wail in distress. Their vulnerability as a species arises, most obviously, from the increased technology enabling human hunting and ocean-going traffic. But seismic testing and the military use of high-tech sonar have become the silent bane of whale existence. Yet, among whale researchers, one of the more intriguing whale–human interactions remains whales' curious solicitation of human affection.[119]

Dubbed by researchers "the friendlies," the forty-foot long, multi-tonned mastadons make their approach toward humans, slide their hidden hulls up close to the research crafts, then lift just their slow-blinking eyes up out of the water as if in a provocative wink. "The baby gray glided up to the boat's edge," writes reporter Charles Siebert, "and then the whole of his long, hornbill-shaped head was rising up out of the water directly beside me, a huge ovoid eye slowly opening to take me in ... I'd never felt so beheld in my life," he concludes in a note of awe. Mother grays, often the first to initiate human contact, will, having established relations, retrieve their calves, showing them off – as if their own version of a stroll to the park. After taking the baby home, the whales return for a final hug: the whale glides up close, inviting humans to scratch their tongues or rub their backs; then returning touch, the whale bumps or lifts – on its back – the underside of the boat. Despite the impact of humans upon the species, they seem to remain intrigued with communicating with their land-based peers. Despite human betrayal, the ovoid eye beholds us. "A fellow mammal breaking the boundary of its domain for a long look at you is beguiling in and of itself," Siebert notes. But, he concludes, "such behavior becomes downright otherworldly ... when you consider the ... history of human–whale interactions."[120]

With the concept of "becoming-animal," Deleuze invites persons into a process of metamorphoses, into a process of undoing codes and of deterritorializing learned, habituated coordinates.[121] In "becoming whale," I invite us, within the coordinates of global city, to offer ourselves as "friendlies" – to offer one another the beholding gaze. "Basic trust in mutuality is that original 'optimism,'" writes Erik Erikson. It is the "assumption that 'somebody is there,' without which we cannot live." After detailing children's failure to thrive, their vulnerability to intellectual and emotional shut-down in an environment void of basic trust – a scene which we might relate to life in postmetropolis – Erikson concludes: The "meeting with the perceiving subject" becomes "the anchor-point" for "all the developments which culminate ... in the establishment of psychosocial identity."[122] More than a shared "civil religion," we need yoga of the loving eye.

Intriguingly, Erikson wrote this description of mutuality in his analysis of Luther's cathection to a providential God – i.e., the one "whose face shines upon us" (Numbers 6:25; Psalm 4, 31, 80, 119), which served as Luther's psychological, stabilizing chant. This "ideological formula," Erikson suggests, provides the anchor, "provides nutriment for the soul as well as the stomach." Erikson then concludes, without any arrogant disdain: "Of all the ideological systems, only religion restores the earliest sense of appeal to ... a Providence" – whether in benediction ("The Lord's face shine on you"), or as icon (e.g., the Madonna, Jesus the friend, or Buddha), or through prayer and meditation. "One basic task of all religions is to reaffirm that first relationship," he instructs us, "for we have in us deep down a lifelong mistrustful remembrance of that truly metaphysical anxiety." Erikson seems to refer to a deep anxiety of our being extraneous to the universe as also, more immediately, the simple anxiety as to whether or not we will be acknowledged.[123]

That anxiety, I maintain, can become reactivated amidst cultural dislocation, especially when, as within global cities, the scene may not provide easy means for psychosocial integration. In that vein, Erikson's prescriptive diagnostic is helpful: "One basic form of heroic asceticism, therefore, ... is to retrace the steps of the development of the I, to ... step ... back to the borderline where the I emerged from its matrix" – to shine our faces one upon another, to double bind ourselves in this way.[124] This is a *pli* of Spirit.

Nancy writes that "there is no wink of god, but ... god is the wink."[125] If Spirit transpires in the wink of an eye, might we mendicants, we urban Free Spirits, simply begin to home life in the city, to let loose the flow of corporeal generosity and trust by assuming the yoga practice of "becoming whale"? Urban mendicancy – the roving of a band of Free Spirits – might attend to persons' inchoate suffering, but also to providing "ports of trust" for the socially dislocated, those of us needing a solid, psychological base, from which we might then engender a generous public. In the wink of an ovoid eye, we might let loose love of a world in which God has been positively ruined.

Notes

1   E. W. Soja, *Postmetropolis: Critical Studies of Cities and Regions*, Oxford: Blackwell, 2000, pp. xv, 3.
2   Soja develops the notion of *synekism* from Aristotle's term *synoikismos*, meaning "the condition arising from dwelling together in one house" via insights accrued from also reading Henri Lefebvre, *Postmetropolis*, pp. 12, 19.
3   T. May, *Gilles Deleuze: An Introduction*, Cambridge: Cambridge University Press, 2005, p. 148.
4   G. Vattimo, *After Christianity*, trans. L. D'Isanto, New York: Columbia University Press, 2002, p. 104.
5   E. W. Soja, "Seeing Nature Spatially," in D. Albertson and C. King (eds), *Without Nature: A New Condition for Theology*, New York: Fordham University Press, 2009, p. 184.
6   Soja, p. 148.
7   E. Isin, cited in Soja, p. 231.
8   Z. Bauman, *Liquid Modernity*, Malden, MA: Polity, 2000, pp. 31–9.
9   Cited in M. Davis, *Planet of Slums*, London: Verso, 2007, p. 20.
10 Ibid., pp. 14, 17.
11 Ibid., p. 7.
12 T. Asad, *Genealogies of Religion: Discipline and Reasons of Power in Christianity and Islam*, Baltimore, MD: The John Hopkins University Press, 1993, p. 11.
13 M. C. Taylor, *After God*, Chicago, IL: University of Chicago Press, 2007, pp. xvi, 3, 44, 55, 64.
14 A. Giddens, *Runaway World: How Globalization is Reshaping our Lives*, London: Profile, 1999, Chapter 3. Giddens notes – as does Bruce Alexander (*The Globalization of Addiction: A Study in Poverty of Spirit*, Oxford University Press, 2008) – the proliferation of addictions worldwide in the face of detraditionalization. See also Bauman, pp. 3–4.

15 Alexander, p. 61.
16 Ibid.
17 K. Polanyi, cited by Alexander, p. 91.
18 Alexander, p. 105.
19 Ibid., p. 93.
20 M. A. Wrathall, "Between the Earth and the Sky: Heidegger on Life after the Death of God," in M. A. Wrathall (ed.), *Religion after Metaphysics*, Cambridge: Cambridge University Press, 2003, p. 77.
21 Ibid., p. 72.
22 Alexander, p. 3.
23 Ibid.
24 Bauman, p. 4.
25 L. Sandercock, *Towards Cosmopolis*, Chichester: John Wiley, 1998, p. 125.
26 S. Zabala, "Christianity and the Death of God," *Common Knowledge*, 11.1, Durham, NC: Duke University Press, 2005, pp. 35–7.
27 J. Caputo, "The Power of the Powerless," in J. W. Robbins (ed.), *After the Death of God*, New York: Columbia University Press, 2007, p. 145.
28 J. Caputo, *The Weakness of God: A Theology of the Event*, Bloomington, IN: Indiana University Press, 2006.
29 G. Deleuze, *The Fold: Leibniz and the Baroque*, trans. T. Conley, Minneapolis, MN: University of Minnesota Press, 1993.
30 T. Morton, *Ecology without Nature: Rethinking Environmental Aesthetics*, Cambridge, MA: Harvard University Press, 2007, p. 14.
31 William Connolly argues against that form of secularism which assumes "a single, authoritative basis of public reason and/or public ethics" and in this vein argues against being identified as a "secularist." See *Why I am Not a Secularist*, Minneapolis, MN: University of Minnesota Press, 1999, p. 5.
32 May, *Deleuze*, p. 35.
33 J.-L. Nancy, *Dis-Enclosure: The Deconstruction of Christianity*, trans. B. Berge *et al.*, New York: Fordham University Press, 2008, pp. 10–11.
34 S. V. Betcher, "Christianity as Path and Practice," *Canada Lutheran*, Vol. 21.2, March 2006, pp. 32–4.
35 H. Cox, "The Myth of the Twentieth Century: The Rise and Fall of 'Secularization,'" in G. Baum (ed.), *The Twentieth Century: A Theological Overview*, Maryknoll, NY: Orbis Books, 1999, p. 139.
36 H. Cox, *The Future of Faith*, San Francisco, CA: HarperOne, 2009, pp. 3, 8, 10, 13, 21.
37 See *Eve and the Firehorse*, a Vancouver-based movie about growing up religious and ethnically Chinese.
38 J. McDaniel, *Living From the Center: Spirituality in an Age of Consumerism*, St. Louis, MO: Chalice, 2000, pp. 5, 28.
39 K. Jaspers as cited in S. B. Thistlethwaite, "Why are our Cities Dying?," *Theology Today*, 51/1, April 1994, pp. 19–21. See also L. C. Schneider, *Beyond Monotheism: A Theology of Multiplicity*, New York: Routledge, 2008, p. 188.
40 B. Hooks, *Yearning*, Boston, MA: South End Press, 1990, p. 31. Cited in Soja, p. 281.
41 M. K. Gandhi, *Vows and Observances*, Berkeley, CA: Berkeley Hills Books, 1999, p. 15.
42 Neighbor-love is the essence of the observance Gandhi called "swadeshi." Ibid., pp. 90, 155.
43 Z. Bauman, p. 6.
44 A. Nandy, *Intimate Enemy: Loss and Recovery of Self Under Colonialism*, Delhi: Oxford University Press, 1983 (1988 ed.), p. 49.
45 Gandhi, *Vows and Observances*, pp. 90, 149–50.

46 Nandy, p. 51.
47 H. Smith, "Western Philosophy as a Great Religion," in M. D. Bryant (ed.), *Huston Smith: Essays on World Religions*, New York: Paragon House, 1992, p. 217.
48 R. Ravindra, *Christ the Yogi: A Hindu Reflection on The Gospel of John*, Rochester, VT: Inner Traditions, 1990 (1998 ed.).
49 W. Carter, *Matthew and Empire: Initial Explorations*, Harrisburg, PA: Trinity Press International, 2001, pp. 36, 48, 50, 113, 116. Carter insists that the NRSV translation suggesting "God's yoke is 'easy'" to be a poor translation; here I follow his suggestion that the opposition between Roman power and "infinite mercy" sets up the contrast of opposing yokes, p. 126.
50 Ravindra, p. 91, original emphasis.
51 B. Thurston, *Religious Vows: The Sermon on the Mount, and Christian Living*, Collegeville, MN: Liturgical Press, 2006, pp. 2–3.
52 Ibid., p. 90.
53 Ravindra, p. 107.
54 P. Knitter, citing J. Fredericks and F. X. Clooney, *Introducing Theologies of Religions*, Maryknoll, NY: Orbis Books, 2008, p. 209.
55 T. D. Swanson, "To Prepare a Place: Johannine Christianity and the Collapse of Ethnic Territory," *Journal of the American Academy of Religion*, LXII/2, p. 242.
56 M. E. Isaacs, *The Concept of Spirit*, London: Heythrop Monographs, 1976.
57 Swanson, pp. 244–5, 251.
58 M. Eliade, cited in Swanson, p. 242.
59 Ibid.
60 J. Moltmann, *The Spirit of Life: A Universal Affirmation*, Minneapolis, MN: Fortress Press, 1992, p. 43.
61 Swanson, pp. 257–8.
62 Ibid., p. 262.
63 Moltmann, *Spirit of Life*, p. 43.
64 Ibid., p. 43.
65 D. Ikeda, "The Age of the Internet: Interplay of Danger and Promise," in H. Cox and D. Ikeda (eds), *The Persistence of Religion: Comparative Perspectives on Modern Spirituality*, New York: I.B. Tauris/Palgrave, 2009, p. 37.
66 Alexander, citing E. Erikson and K. Polanyi, p. 58.
67 Ibid., p. 3
68 Thurston, *Religious Vows*, pp. 1–3.
69 K. MacKendrick, *Counter Pleasures*, Albany, NY: SUNY Press, 1999, p. 18.
70 S. Schneiders, *New Wineskins: Re-imagining Religious Life Today*, Mahwah, NJ: Paulist Press, 1986, pp. 99, 109.
71 R. Panikkar, *Initiation to the Vedas*, M. C. Pavan (ed.), Delhi: Motilal Banarsidass Publishers, 2006, p. 12.
72 D. Copeland, *Life After God*, New York: Washington Square Press, 1994.
73 J. D. Caputo, *Against Ethics: Contributions to a Poetics of Obligation with Constant Reference to Deconstruction*, Bloomington, IN: Indiana University Press, 1993, pp. 7–8.
74 M. Sanford, *Waking: A Memoir of Trauma and Transcendence*, New York: Holtzbrinck Publishers, 2006, pp. 145–50.
75 Sanford, p. 184.
76 M. Matousek, *When You're Falling, Dive: Lessons in the Art of Living*, New York: Bloomsbury, 2008, p. 184.
77 Matousek, pp. 6, 8, 12. See also M. Matousek "Savage Grace: The Spirituality of Illness," *Utne Reader*, Vol. 62, March–April 1994, pp. 104–11.
78 Ibid., pp. 10–13.
79 V. Woolf, *On Being Ill*, Ashfield, MA: Paris Press, 2002.

80 J. Sittler, "A Theology for Earth," *The Christian Scholar*, Vol. 37, September 1954, p. 373.

81 Connolly, pp. 16, 47.

82 Ibid., p. 65.

83 Caputo, *Against Ethics*. See also R. Diprose, *Corporeal Generosity: On Giving with Nietzsche, Merleau-Ponty, and Levinas*. Albany, NY: SUNY Press, 2002, pp. 4–5.

84 Diprose, pp. 4–5.

85 Ibid., p. 9.

86 Caputo, *Against Ethics*, pp. 26–7.

87 M. Luther, "The Freedom of a Christian," trans. and with introduction by Mark D. Tranvik, Minneapolis, MN: Fortress Press, 2008, pp. vii, 24.

88 Ibid., p. 28.

89 Ibid., pp. 29, 83.

90 A. Shrift, "Logics of the Gift in Cixous and Nietzsche: Can We Still Be Generous?," *Angelaki: Journal of the Theoretical Humanities*, Vol 6.2, August 2001, p. 114.

91 Luther, pp. 83, 89.

92 M. Abe, "Kenotic God and Dynamic Sunyata," in J. B. Cobb Jr. and C. Ives (eds), *The Emptying God: A Buddhist, Christian, Jewish Conversation*, Maryknoll, NY: Orbis Books, 1990, 2nd ed., 1991, p. 31.

93 In his essay entitled "The Cut that Binds: Time, Memory and the Ascetic Impulse," Elliot R. Wolfson addresses circumcision, the fleshy seal of Jewish males' covenant with God (*God's Voice from the Void: Old and New Studies in Bratslav Hasidism*, ed. Shaul Magid (Albany: SUNY, 2001: 103–54). He sets out to read kabbalists, specifically Nahman ben Simhah of Bratslav (1772–1810), by employing David Levin's phenomenological lens. Levin concludes that "the very essence of circumcision – the heart of the matter, as it were – lies in the fact that the incision *opens*" (emphasis added). Wolfson suggests that "the path opened by circumcision" is that of spiritual memory – the memory of a path beyond the spiritual amnesia induced by realism – specifically, the recollection of the greater mind or God-like consciousness of the everything–nothing of the universe (103). In Nahman's cosmology, Wolfson explains, "temporal consciousness is really a lack of consciousness and supratemporal consciousness is perfected consciousness." Since "the very nature of circumcision is … that it negates the natural instincts that are timebound …," circumcision "connects the individual with the spiritual root in a dimension above time" (120). Circumcision thus makes possible the path of true knowledge, which for Nahman was "the perspective of being beyond time, a seemingly impossible state of mind for consciousness to comprehend in its temporal deportment" (111). Most intriguingly for me, Nahman uses disability experience, specifically, suggestively linking "the cut that binds" with the disarticulation of disablement (the beggars all being disabled, the seventh – the one without feet – being the consummate dancer, the messiah), to encourage persons to perceive the world in a less limited way than realism imposes (121).

94 Nancy, p. 1.

95 Ibid., pp. 143–5.

96 Ibid., pp. 8–10.

97 Ibid., p. 36; Schneider, p. 162.

98 Nancy, pp. 5–6, 11, 146.

99 Schneider, pp. xi, 162.

100 L. Irigaray, *I Love to You: Sketch of a Possible Felicity in History*, trans. A. Martin, New York: Routledge, 1996, p. 15.

101 Nancy, p. 73.

102 Ibid., p. 10.

103 In his sermon on "Blessed are the poor in spirit," Meister Eckhardt describes this poverty of spirit as wanting, knowing, and possessing nothing, even as it applies to his God concept: "The authorities say that God is a being, and a rational one, and that [God] knows all things. I say that God is neither being nor rational, and that [God] does not know this or that." Meister Eckhart, "Sermon 52: Beati Pauperes spiritu, quoniam ipsorum est regnum caelorum (Mt.5.3)," *Meister Eckhart: The Essential Sermons, Commentaries, Treatises, and Defense*, trans. E. Colledge and B. McGinn, Mahwah, NJ: Paulist Press, 1981, pp. 199–203.

104 J. E. Bruns, *The Christian Buddhism of St. John*, Mahwah, NJ: Paulist Press, 1971, p. 28.

105 Ibid., pp. 30–1.

106 Luke 17:5, translated as "Increase our faith," reads in Greek as *"prostheses emin pistin."*

107 D. Haraway, *Simians, Cyborgs, and Women: The Reinvention of Nature*, London: Routledge, 1991, p. 249.

108 D. M. Halperin, *Saint Foucault: Towards a Gay Hagiography*, Oxford: Oxford University Press, 1995, p. 66.

109 Connolly, p. 54.

110 V. Westhelle, *Scandalous God: The Use and Abuse of the Cross,* Minneapolis, MN: Fortress Press, 2006, pp. 40–1.

111 Paul Tillich's existentialist insight regarding courage is here yoked with Jean-Luc Nancy's "being with." P. Tillich, *The Courage to Be*, New Haven, CT: Yale University Press, 1952.

112 D. Wells, *Prosthesis*, Palo Alto, CA: Stanford University Press, 1995, p. 1.

113 T. Roberts, *Contesting Spirit: Nietzsche, Affirmation, Religion*, Princeton, NJ: Princeton University Press, 1998, p. 70.

114 Ibid., pp. 66–8.

115 P. Sheldrake, *Spaces for the Sacred: Place, Memory and Identity*, Baltimore, MD: The Johns Hopkins University Press, 2001, p. 147.

116 Ibid.

117 T. May, Gilles Deleuze, p. 150.

118 "Free Spirits" names a movement across the rapidly urbanizing scene of northern Europe in the late Middle Ages. These religious mendicants assumed a panentheist perspective and emphasized, among other things, voluntary poverty.

119 C. Siebert, "Watching Whales Watching Us," *The New York Times Magazine*, July 12, 2009, pp. 26–35, 44–5.

120 Ibid., pp. 30–2.

121 R. Bogue, "The Minor," in C. J. Stivale (ed.), *Gilles Deleuze: Key Concepts*, Montreal: McGill-Queens, 2005, p. 115. The notion of "becoming-animal" echoes the sensibilities of some indigenous peoples who contend that humans must learn from the animals, our elders, which were born or learned to be content, to be at peace, with nature. Song and mask rituals enact this teaching.

122 E. Erikson, *Young Man Luther: A Study in Psychoanalysis and History*, New York: W.W. Norton & Company, 1958 (1962 ed.), p. 118.

123 Ibid., pp. 118–19.

124 Ibid.

125 Nancy, p. 119.

5 Be a multiplicity

Ancestral anticipations

Catherine Keller

A dog sitting in a patch of sun licking itself, says he, is at one moment a dog and at the next a vessel of revelation. And perhaps he speaks the truth, perhaps in the mind of our Creator (*our Creator*, I say) where we whirl about as in a millrace we interpenetrate and are interpenetrated by fellow creatures by the thousand.

(J.M. Coetzee, *Elizabeth Costello*)

But a Creature, because it needs the assistance of its Fellow-Creatures, ought to be a multiplicity, that it may receive this assistance: for that which receives something is nourished by the same, and so becomes a part of it, and therefore it is no more one but many.

Anne Conway, *The Principles of the Most Ancient and Modern Philosophy**

Be neither a One nor a Many, but multiplicities!

(Gilles Deleuze)

To be in relation is already to be a multiplicity: who had recognized this, before Anne Conway? But there she lies, increasingly immobilized by the headaches, composing her slim volume. Her darkened bedroom doubles as salon, where she converses passionately with some of the most adventurous thinkers of the seventeenth century. Her former mentor Henry More, the great Cambridge Platonist, visits. Because only men were allowed at university, he had tutored her – immediately recognizing her brilliance – by mail. They became lifelong dialogue partners. This, despite a difference urgent enough to provoke her writing of this book. It was More who sent to her the renowned "gypsy scholar" and physician Francis Mercury van Helmont, hoping he might heal her worsening headaches. While his treatment failed, their

---

*   Anne Conway, *The Principles of the Most Ancient and Modern Philosophy*, P. Loptson (ed.) The Hague/Boston/London: Martinus Nijhoff Publishers, 1982. The text has a complex transmission history. A translation of the original notebook into Latin was undertaken by More and van Helmont after Conway's death in 1679, published in Amsterdam in 1690 anonymously, and retranslated into English that year by one "J.C." I take the liberty, where noted, to adjust the English to the Latin, as in translating "*multiplex*" above as "multiplicity," translated by Loptson as "manifold." Deep thanks to Dr. Ernie Rubenstein for help with texts and contexts.

friendship grew. He introduced her to the deeper Kabbalah of the *Zohar* (with More she had already studied the Christian Kabbalah),[1] and came to reside at Ragley, the Conways' home. And the Quakers – the great religio-political radicals of the first generation, including George Fox, especially George Keith, the most intellectual of Friends, and numerous women activists – began to frequent her home. Despite his distaste for the Quaker dissidents, Conway's husband acquiesced. Out of dogged respect for the Lady Conway, the Viscount bought several out of prison. As her illness progressed, finding it "incredible how very seldom I can endure anyone in my chamber," she wanted few beside her but these Friends.[2] For they understood suffering and brooked no pat pieties. Had she gathered around herself the nourishing multiplicity she is writing into the elemental structure of the creation? More was also disturbed by her growing involvement with these "schismatic enthusiasts" who would not doff their hats before nobility, who flagrantly challenged the authority of ye Church and Kingdome. Ragley Hall became, as Carol Wayne White writes, "the epicenter of intellectual and theological innovations, as well as a haven of social progressiveness."[3] What a polydoxy she hosted.

Through the wide-angle lens of a present intellectual context, the Conway story appears as an anachronistic map of manifold social issues: here is a female writer in a misogynist context, suffering physical disablement, inspired by a Jewish counter-tradition, supporting dissenters against her own class and religious establishment. This quadruple jeopardy marks her voice as rife, for all her privilege, with subjugated knowledge. But of themselves, these issues would not quite warrant her revival as more than a subject for specialized histories and feminist archaeologies.[4] Indeed even when Conway was discovered in the 1930s, it was not her ideas but her relationship to other (male) thinkers that drew scholarly attention.[5] Exceptional as these men were, such geneology ironically reproduces the conditions that had blocked her public voice. Seventeenth-century Europe was aggressively averse to women intellectuals. A "learned woman is thought to be a comet, that bodes mischief whenever it appears," wrote one discouraged reformer.[6] Conway's slim book was published posthumously and anonymously on the continent. Leibniz, however, because of his friendship with van Helmont, referred to its author by name, and with admiration.

What first stunned and captured me in the story of Anne Conway lies beneath and between her "issues." It is what enigmatically postdates her text as a treatise in early modern polydoxy: her cosmotheology of the multiple. I find in no other text before, and in a certain sense after, this explicit teaching of the inherent *multiplicity of each creature* – as the condition and the effect of *a nourishing interdependence of creatures*. Her insight is crystal clear: "a Creature, because it needs the assistance of its Fellow-Creatures, ought to be manifold, that it may receive this assistance."[7] A proto-Deleuzian imperative, supplemented with compassion? Drawing from her intensive study of the Kabbalah with van Helmont,[8] she understood every creature to be a multitude. Indeed "in the least Creature there may exist, or may be comprehended Infinite Creatures …"[9] Her vision of this irreducible multiplicity, even as she prophesies the unfathomable macro and microscales of current physics, runs to the theological. "Indeed the Nature of a

Creature is such, that the same cannot be merely one single Thing, in case it ought to act or do something, and so enjoy that Goodness which is prepared for it by its Creator."[10] The participation of the creature in the divine requires of us, in other words, our participation *in each other*.

This idea, that the creature cannot be "merely singular" if it is to actualize its gifts, remains almost as obscure as Conway herself. When, for example, Jean-Luc Nancy declares, splendidly, that "a single being is a contradiction in terms,"[11] the thought is fresh. Like Whitehead's "mutual immanence," her nourishing connectivity resists the root substance metaphysics of Western common sense, of its identities religious and political. The root morphs into a rhizome. "Each multiplicity is symbiotic," write Deleuze and Guattari. "Its becoming ties together animals, plants, microorganisms, mad particles, a whole galaxy."[12] Such a symbiosis suggests the *togetherness of life*, the *bios* of co-existence, disclosed in the recent theory of symbiogenesis.[13] Indeed the buzzing life of this multiplicity belies even the boundary between the organic and the inorganic. "The plant sings of the glory of God, and while being filled all the more with itself it contemplates and intensely contracts the elements whence it proceeds. It feels in this prehension the *self-enjoyment* of its own becoming."[14]

A polydoxical theology will register, in its own methodological symbioses, the creaturely multiplicity of us all, now, becoming. But in Conway the symbiosis, the together-life, of all creatures becomes what we may call the *con-viviality of the creation*, in which living together takes on an atmosphere of gracious commensality, of unsentimental care and celebration. Across all species and particles of life, the convivial manifold evinces, in what Conway calls, not accidentally echoing Quaker language, a "Society of Fellowship." Its "nourishment" or "assistance" renders each creature manifold by virtue of its multiple relations. We have, then, not to do with a mere many, a plurality of ones, but with the enfolding, the *pli*, of the multi*pli*city between and within its members.

And what on earth is the point of theology, now, today, if not the cultivation of this convivial manifold? Amidst the mounting perils of our social, ecological, and spiritual multiplicities, can theology in its Christian morphology now come – despite our more demoralizing histories – to nourish our planetary symbiosis? If I bring a surprising old bit of polydoxy into conversation with the likes of Leibniz, Whitehead, Deleuze, and rather more contiguously, of Schneider and Betcher, it is as an offering to that hope. At any rate, it will turn out that Conway's posthumous, anonymous little volume is not so much the subject of this chapter as its "vessel of revelation" – evanescent as Coetzee's offbeat dog in the sun and radiant with interpenetrations.

Her bodies

Our present context has shifted from the beginning of modernity to its end. But Conway's text is barely readable in isolation from its Baroque context. She has written one concentrated answer to the defining modern segregation of body and spirit, just as it arrived. It still might have gone otherwise. Conway's title makes ironic appeal at once to past and future, as though to thrust her text into an immense temporal orbit: *The Principles of the Most Ancient and Modern Philosophy.*[15] With her impossibly wide loop of signification, she proceeds to contest the emergent modernity of dispirited matter and dematerialized spirit. She is trying to pry open an alternative to the notion of separate, singular entities (mental or physical) and of dead, exploitable materiality. Even More, also in correspondence with Descartes, embraces the new science of inert matter – indeed he effects the synthesis of Cartesian and Platonic dualisms. That did it.[16] While expressing respect for Descartes' physics, she describes her treatise forthrightly as "anti-Cartesianism."

> First, Cartesian philosophy claims that body is merely dead mass … This great error must be imputed to all those who say that body and spirit are contrary things and unable to change into one another, thereby denying bodies all life and perception. This is completely contrary to the fundamentals of our philosophy.[17]

Those fundamentals become coherent antecedents of our present polydoxy when read as a response to the prestigious new dualism. For an elite of Christian intellectuals, Cartesianism seemed to secure pathways for free enquiry and empirical science without atheism. But Conway wanted that without the disembodied spirit and the dead mass. She railed against a modernity purchasing its knowledge at the expense of living bodies.

In that conceptual context one is after all haunted by her story. Her community dramatizes the multiplicitous and reciprocal "assistance" Conway theorizes. Given the poor collective health of the multiplicity of micro-creatures making up her own body, her solidarity with bodies is remarkable. One might expect her to have resigned from this world, to have abstracted herself (of this she would have been eminently capable) from the animal body. Instead she remained disclosively attuned to ailing bodies – her own and the bodies of others.

Through such mindful embodiment, cosmology gets entangled in politics. White shows that Conway's "sense of shared bodily suffering" is inseparable from the "potentially emancipatory nature of the mystical religiosity in blurring, even dissolving, traditional lines and divisions between respectable and disrespectable philosophies and religious systems, between high and low culture, and between politics and faith." Conway's "reflective relationship" to her own suffering female body "allowed her to understand and share in the extended effects of unjust suffering by collective bodies that were bound and classified together as Friends – those deemed enemies of the state."[18] In letters she writes repeatedly of their importance to her:

> The particular acquaintance with such living examples of great patience under sundry heavy exercises, both of bodily sicknesse and other calamatys (as some of them have related to me) I find begetts a more lively fayth and uninterrupted desire of approaching to such a behavior in like exigencyes, than the most learned and Rhetorical discourse of resignation can doe.[19]

Listening to the Quaker women recount their experiences with the authorities, writes White, "moved the feeble, bedridden Conway to action. During her last years, she unceasingly advocated for the Quakers, who were persecuted and imprisoned for their stance against social conventions."[20] Far from "resignation," Conway's "fayth" practices a contemplative courage whose "patience under sundry heavy exercises" – like the long history of Quaker activism – nourishes movements for social justice. The theological, indeed incarnational, link between a relational cosmology and progressive movements lies close to the heart of polydoxy.

The rigorous practice of convivial embodiment is further illumined by Sharon Betcher's theology, developed in the present conversation, of "the *pli* of intercorporeal generosity." The warmth of this concept is – like that of Conway's affirmation of the mutual aid of bodies – existentially hard won. And similarly, it ties multiplicity together – *religare* – with an inter-religious "yoga" or "yoke."[21] When Betcher entrains her postcolonial approach to disability studies with a Deleuzian sense of the multiple, she moves close to the lineage of mystical naturalism. Her ecologically embodied pneumatology lets feminism outgrow its rhetorical tendency to reduce all suffering to a subjugation to be resisted. Certain profound forms of co-existence, needful for us all, may perhaps only be learned from sufferers of serious disablement. There is, however, no question here of an idealization of suffering, let alone of a naïve harmony of creatures.

Conviviality under the friendliest conditions remains close to the struggles, competitions, and predations that make it possible. That we must be multiple in order to receive the help of our fellow creatures does not guarantee that either our own multiplicity or theirs will prove benign. For a theology of multiplicity, the early modern wrinkles of gender and class politics, disability, religious difference, and dissent fold into contemporary flows of sex, race, economics, and ecology: into our *issues*. They issue across centuries, right into our bodies. Reflecting on "incarnate divine being," Laurel Schneider notes that "bodies, whether human or not, like cultures and languages, are porously open to each other." Boundaries "exist temporally and spatially, meaning that they are always in a state of emerging and passing away."[22] The boundaries of the bodies to which we belong (even of the Body of Christ) no longer serve to cut off and unify the multiplicities. Instead, they serve as living skins, sensitive, permeable, scarred, differentiating one collective from others without pretending to segregate.

The theopolitical hope here lies in an honesty that *minds* this bodied and spirited multiplicity, that not only notices it but *cares* for it. This honesty exposes the hybridity, not only the plurality, of teachings – as for instance in Conway's mix of Anglicanism, gospel-driven Quaker dissidence, Renaissance Neoplatonism, Kabbalistic heterodoxy, and natural philosophy.[23] As John Thatamanil puts it, "Religious goods do not sort themselves out one per tradition."[24] The multiplicity of teachings (of and about the multiple) may run up and down into infinity. But what of the singular finitude of the Infinite's creatures?

Shudders of the self

> But how I ask you can I live with rats and dogs and beetles crawling through me day and night, drowning and gasping, scratching at me, tugging me, urging me deeper and deeper into revelation – how? … sometimes I too creep through. *Presences of the Infinite*, he calls us, and says we make him shudder.
>
> (J.M. Coetzee, *Elizabeth Costello*)

Shuddering on an edge between orgasm and horror, this letter of Lady Chandos (dated September 11, 1603) concludes Coetzee's 2003 novel. The fictional Lady is describing, to none other than Francis Bacon, the primitive mysticism her husband has drawn her into, "where we whirl about as in a millrace we interpenetrate and are interpenetrated by fellow creatures by the thousand." This porosity of the creation, with its entangled creatures, has its creepy crawly aspect. It also stirs vibrations of pleasure: "And indeed I have those shudders, in the throes of my raptures I have felt them."[25] Such ecstatic experiences of the intercreaturely manifold have Lady Chandos reaching out for help, in fear of madness, to the father of the new empiricism. In him knowledge has become power, animals mere meat and matter. In this novel of altogether contemporary characters, a meditation on human betrayal of nonhuman creatures, the letter is an enigmatic conclusion.[26] Both of our seventeenth-century British Ladies address us from the threshold of modernity and the precipice of illness, where revelations of creaturely interpenetration flash in and out of impossibility. But how radically these confessions differ. While the fictional Lady turns to Bacon, the single-minded mechanist, for salvation from insanity, the historical Conway offers a more manifold rationality than Bacon or Descartes could have tolerated.

Neither the constituent relationality nor the infinity of its pluralities make for comfortable help, then or now. Might we "creep on through" – even if the opening is dis/closure, apo/calypse? But what if this "we" includes the rats and dogs and beetles? The animal revelation has been less traumatic among indigenous and shamanic peoples, with their theriomorphic iconography. Would Derrida's "divinanimality" help?[27] Sharing the goods of revelation with the nonhuman creatures does not come easily to the children of Abraham – particularly in a Protestant dispensation overlaid with the modern grid of power/knowledge.

Nonetheless, the vitalism of which Conway is a foremother has accrued a legacy in the philosophies of process. Its developing chaosmos consists of possibilities, virtualities, in process of self-actualization through inter-activity. We will see that Whitehead recaptures an intuition resonant with Conway: the mutual immanence of creatures expresses a primal *sym-pathos*, a pulsating emotional energy whereby the many become a particular one. In passing. Temporality churns on, and there is no hiding the savagery that rips through the delicate orders of conviviality. The creatures help each other, feed each other, feed *on* each other. So before leaping into this vortex of creatures, we had better pause and ask: Will any mystical cosmology, indeed any polydoxical manifold, ultimately betray the particular – and especially, the human – individual? The

human creature may knowingly offer care to emergent multiplicities, societies, ecologies. But how would this care touch Kierkegaard's "really existing
individual?" Will its endless multiplicity ultimately penetrate, crowd, engulf,
confuse, escape, madden? Will it entangle, and possibly strangle, theology in
all the *issues* of the day? Will these multiplying ethical demands that infinitely
elude satisfaction, these politics that expose us to the contradictions of our
priorities (ethnicity vs economics vs sexuality vs ecology), really nourish the
concerned persons? If this care – this love – issues into a networking infinity of
relations, all requiring my assistance, then truly I (any *I*) am lost. Hail Many,
mother of us all. Polydoxy may multiply munificently, but will not assist. If it
abandons us to an infinite multiplication of infinities.

Theologically speaking it might, at best, attain to Kierkegaard's caricature of
Hegel; the ethical self-emptying of the subject sacrificially yields an impersonal
acceptance. Then let the shudder turn to *Fear and Trembling*. The "knight of
infinite resignation" renounces the particular for the sake of the eternal. But, then,
"the knight of faith" – not before having gone the ethical route of the infinite –
twists "impossibly" back to the particular: "Temporality, finitude, that is what it
is all about."[28] Twisting further, however, might we hear a consonance with this
knightly double movement in Conway's respectful refusal of the counsel of mere
"resignation?" Was it not in the face of her impossible suffering that her "fayth"
opened possibility?

According to Conway, however, that possibility depends upon our multiplicity: for we do not exist, let alone grow and thrive, without the help of the others
and therefore of God. Such cosmological conviviality is distant from the anthro-
pocentric clashing of the Hegelian dialectic. Yet Kierkegaard would also reject a
theology of mutual assistance. For the knight of faith "this trifling participation in
the woes and welfare of other people that is extolled under the name of sympathy"
is "nothing more than vanity."[29] Faith, beyond ethics, allows only silent "witness"
(de Silentio). Without reducing the difference to gender, we note that Conway's
multiplex creature abides suffering in a conviviality modeled on the living solace
of Friends. These "fellow creatures" witness, both silently and in words, to an
infinity of care. They may not eliminate suffering. But they do relieve despair.
Kierkegaard's faith concentrates itself into "one single desire," in order that the soul
not be "dissipated in multiplicity." This is the ancient Augustinian concern – amidst
our "manifold distraction amid many things" to "be recollected ... to follow the
One."[30] Indeed it is the worry of all classical thought. It should worry us too, as persons, as activists, as thinkers. The multiplicity of issues can exhaust, in this century,
the very theologies they had so energized in the last. But the point is that it is not
multiplicity that dissipates the self, but mistaking it for a many of *ones*.

Conway hints at how the actual multiplicity of a creature makes *possible* its
concentration. Indeed a creature in its bodily finitude *is* a concentration of the
multiple. Contrary to convention, a self is not comprised by its being "one only
Atom ... having Dominion over the rest." Rather "this Centre it self, or chief,
and governing Spirit *is manifold*." This is a wild flight of thought: "All the other
spirits concur to it, and Lines from all parts of the Circumference do again depart

or proceed therefrom." Like Deleuzian lines of force or flight, the lines replace points along the creases of the fold. So the manifold yields a force of cohesion, not of dissolution: "And indeed the unity of the Spirits that compose or make up this Centre, or governing Spirit, is *more* firm and tenacious." In other words, to be multiplicities is not to have multiple personality disorder! But she may over-state the case: "yea, in Man this Unity is so great that nothing can dissolve it!"[31] Even if, in fact, human identity is frequently dissolved in personality disorders, traumas, transformations, Conway's polydoxical point is well taken. That I func-tion identifiably as "myself" during most of my waking moments and many of my dreaming ones is all the more impressive, given the multiplicity of "spirits" (influences, genes, memories, complexes, not to mention issues and theologies) comprising this figure of "me." Might we now imagine – in the place of a merely singular individual – a *plurisingularity*?

Kierkegaard did not reflect upon the relational multiplicities comprising the divine promise: God would make your issue as "numerous as the stars of heaven and as the sand that is on the seashore." (Genesis 22:17; and Abram himself mul-tiplies – from Avram to Abraham to Ibrahim.) The very pressure of the multiple – in the relations of its history and the lure of its promise – demands my tenacious singularity: "Here I am." It is not that I was already there, a centered substance. I *become* in response to this call. Not *ex nihilo* – though in my dissipation it may feel so – but out of the indefinite welter of my interdependencies. Plurisingularly.

If it is to "enjoy that Goodness which is prepared for it by its Creator," a crea-ture cannot be "merely one single Thing." Far from steering us toward relativism or insanity, a polydoxical pluralism may be required now, in the toxic dregs of matter-deadening modernity (I finish this chapter as the oil spreads in the Gulf of Mexico) for planetary sanity. But this good is not delivered, as Kierkegaard so clearly states, by any ethical universal. His paradox of ethics and faith does not disappear. It multiplies. For it is no longer reducible to a tension between duty to neighbor and love of God. As per the great commandment, the love of God (that ambiguous genitive) comes folded together with love between creatures finite and temporal. Here our ferociously competing multi-responsibilities to one another may find the grace with which to meet them. In time. That is what it is all about.

Conway's emanations

If to be at all is to be, in Nancy's friendly phrase, "singularly plural," Conway also linked this plurisingularity to a *constituent relationality*. It is that fold, or flow, between internal and social multiplicity that calls now for our deeper attention. The nourishing interdependence of creatures brooks no impermeable boundary between mind and matter, spirit and body. For our most conscious moments are alive with heart, energy, perception – not to mention all the supportive apparatus of the brain still so mysterious to science. And the simplest, unconscious units are still – creatures. I am hoping that a closer reading of her visionary anti-reductionism will help us to press into contemporary language the elusive excess of our deeper convivialities.

The notion that there could exist "Dead Matter" at all, in a universe that participates in the divine, strikes Anne Conway as "mere Fiction."[32] Repeatedly she argues "that Spirit and Body *differ not essentially, but gradually.*"[33] That graduation, which she calls "modal," signifies a difference of degree rather than a separation between substances. "*Every Spirit hath its Body, and every Body its Spirit*" – that, itself, is an extraordinary answer to both ends of dualism. Body is inherently spirited (remembering the linguistic overlap of "spirit" with mind, *esprit, Geist*), not merely and occasionally infused with a prior spirit. Her sentence continues:

> And as the Body of a Man or Beast, is nothing but an innumerable multitude of Bodies, compacted together into one, and disposed into a certain order; so likewise the Spirit of a Man, or Beast, is a certain innumerable multitude of Spirits united together in the said Body.[34]

Again we read that the alternative to dualism hinges not on a simple oneness, but on a constituent multiplicity.[35] It is for that very move, which renders nondualism as multiplicity, that she refers repeatedly to the "*Hebrews,*" the *kabbalah denudata*, and the "*Nizuzoth*, or Sparks" which are the multiplicity of spirits in a person. The sparks become more opaque, denser, "thicker," as they become "compacted" into body. Thus, "every Body is a Spirit."[36] It is in the lavish multiplicity comprising any body that the boundary between spirit and body dissipates. So the nondualism is accomplished precisely not by a reduction of spirit to body, or an abstraction of body into spirit, but a refusal of reduction of either spirit or body to "the logic of the one" (Schneider). It is the *interdependence* of each creature on "its fellow creatures" that makes for each creature's *internal multiplicity*. And this relationality does not appear as a bare ontology, a formal structure of relations. For the motive force, the dynamism of this multiplicity, is called "assistance." A creature "must be multiple to receive this help." Let us return to that key passage: "*For that which receives something is nourished by the same, and so becomes part of it.* Therefore it is no more one but many, and so many indeed as Things received, and yet of a greater multiplicity."[37]

We get a glimpse, here, of a universe of mutual participation, in which all creatures become members of others, "part" of each other. If it hints at Whitehead's mutual immanence of becoming creatures, he was undoing the Western presumption that reality is divided into units of substance, mental or physical. For the constituent relationality of things belies the metaphysics of static identities. His "principle of universal relativity" displaces Aristotle's dictum that "a substance is not present in a subject." He claims that philosophy "is mainly devoted to the task of making clear the notion of 'being present in another entity.'"[38] Thus Conway's "becoming part of" another foreshadows Whitehead's relationalism, despite a still essentialist framework. Each creature has internalized the multiplicity of its relations. Therefore it has prehended, enfolded, the many that have "nourished" it. But when the single creature adds something "even greater," it becomes more than the sum of the given relations. It therefore anticipates a principle of "creative advance."[39]

"Let us suppose but one Atom to be separated from its Fellow Creatures, What can it do to perfect it self and become greater or better?"[40] What an absurd question, from the point of view of that modernity producing a world of separate, lifeless, and impenetrable atoms. But she is arguing that only in its "Fellowship" with other creatures can a creature have motion and take part in perception – as, for instance, in my own. I have knowledge of which the atom is incapable because it is "so small that it can receive nothing within it." As part of me, however, it participates in the "variety or multitude, which is the Subject or Receptacle" of knowledge.[41] Something different from the morphology of parts within a whole is appearing in her receptive multiple – as the allusion to Plato's receptacle (the *khora*, so intriguing to Kristeva and Derrida).

Conway returns repeatedly to the intuition of the transhuman relational multiplicities. "Every creature which has any Life, Sense, or Motion, must be multiple or numerous; indeed, from the perspective of every created intellect, it must be numerous without number or infinite."[42] Always, the argument is theologically driven. If it is objected that "God made all Things in Number, Weight and Measure; wherefore there cannot be an infinite multitude of Spirits in one Man nor an innumerable multitude of Bodies in one Body" – Conway answers with mathematical panache: "certainly every Creature will have its Number, Weight, and Measure; and by consequence we cannot say of any creature, that it is but one single Thing, because it is a Number, and Number is a multitude, or more than one."[43] Or as Nancy puts it, "the One is more than one." For 'one' cannot be counted without counting more than one."[44]

Are we yet learning to count differently? Are we learning to count in multiples always less and more than one? If so, is it because we begin to realize that bodies count? That I, who do the counting, am a permeable commune of spirited bodies and embodied spirits?

The delivery of that multiplicity through the nourishing interdependence of all creatures conjures the atmosphere of conviviality: the thematic of sociality, of sentient, intercreaturely cooperation in the symbioses of becoming. "Therefore there is a certain *Society of Fellowship* among Creatures in giving and receiving, whereby they *mutually subsist* one by another; for what Creature in the whole World can be found that hath no need of its Fellow-Creature? Certainly none."[45] In other words, the assistance that creatures offer each other expresses the dynamism of the "society of fellowship" that is the universe. This "mutual subsistence," so close to mutual immanence, knits creatures together in a continuum, not just of being, but of active and receptive inter-becoming. It is from this sociality of creatures that there follows for Conway their infinity: not just of all of them together, but of each of them – in their relation to each other. In other words, each creature is a complexity, an enfolded multiplicity, indeed an "Infiniteness of Spirits in every Spirit, and Infiniteness of Bodies in every Body." As though anticipating current speculations on the scale of the multiverse, she unwraps these embedded infinities into an "Infinity of Worlds or Creatures made of God."[46] The infinity of each creature did not signify its divinity. In this she marks her philosophy off from Spinoza's pantheism as sharply as from Descartes' dualism. The finite creature's internal infinity suggests, rather, its enfolding of the boundless multiplicity of its relations.

In the mutual subsisting of creatures, Conway discerns a virtually infinite interactivity: "none can be separated from his Fellow Creatures."[47] This statement of radical inseparability follows from her argument for the "Infinite Divisibility of every thing, into parts always less."[48] This, again, is not an argument for reduction to single or simple units but for its opposite. Here she positions her stunning *theological* argument against reductionism: "So far as [God] co-operates with the Creatures ... he *never reduces Creatures into their least parts; because then all Motion and Operation in Creatures would cease,*" which would make the Creature "a mere *non ens,* or nothing."[49] In other words, a theology of cooperation, of divine creaturely synergy, precludes a God who would reduce anything to the paralyzing isolation of a mere unit or unity.

Folds and tangles

In this refusal of the minimum unit of atomism, Conway has a grand ally in Leibniz, who read her with great respect. His calculus of infinities had been developing across the channel from her, in a related anti-Cartesianism. Consider the following passage from Leibniz:

> The division of the continuous must not be taken as of sand dividing into grains, but as that of a sheet of paper or of a tunic in folds, in such a way that an infinite number of folds can be produced, some smaller than others, but without the body ever dissolving into points or minima.[50]

Here was another alternative to the pointillist atoms that had already gained control of modernity's "nature": the countervision of a tissue of inseparable differences, along an infinitely divisible continuum.[51] This Leibnizian insight is key now to *The Fold*, where Deleuze explicates – in the light of chaos mathematics and Whiteheadian chaosmology – a Baroque origami of drapes, whorls, spirals, envelopes. The Leibnizian monad – not a point, not a minimum building block – enfolds the universe from its own point of view. Each is animate.[52] The derivation of Leibniz's monadology from the Kabbalah, by way of his long-term dialogue with van Helmont, is now well documented.[53] But Leibniz at a later point had the benefit of Conway's book, whose "rationalist" method was closer to Leibniz's own.[54] Thus he writes that "my philosophical views approach somewhat closely those of the late Countess Conway ... [in that I also hold that] all things are full of life and consciousness, contrary to the views of the atomists." The monadic microcosm in Leibniz has influenced Whitehead's resistance to classical atomism as well: "Thus the continuum is present in each actual entity, and each actual entity pervades the continuum."[55] The difference between Conway and Leibniz however is critical. Hutton, in her intellectual biography of Conway, seems to think it is just a matter of her retention of a cosmic Christ as mediator of the creation, which for Leibniz would appear extraneous.[56] But Hutton fails to mention the more fundamental divergence.

It is the free interactivities of Conway's creatures that distinguish them from Leibnizian monads. As though to protect the delicate intuition of his folds from the regnant atomism, with its machinery of external relations, Leibniz has deprived his monads of windows. Even the most miniscule live. But none see or feel each other. There is a magnificent mathematical relationality, but no interaction, no influence, no mutual immanence. These monads can give each other no assistance. Conway, by contrast, embraces the active and becoming interactivity of mutual need and influence. The relations do not determine outcome, only inflow. A relation may be horrendous or helpful – but the possibility of help will flow or fold itself into her creature through and as its own complexity. These virtual webs of relation are, in Conway, internalized through *nourishment* for the finite creature: the *need* of each for the others. This care is infinitely more than human, and as such permeates the universe.

In this interactive motion bodies interpenetrate and change into one another, spirit into body and vice versa, disaggregating and recombining.

> For however Bodies or Spirits may be divided or separated from one another in the whole Universe, yet they still remain united in this separation; seeing the whole Creation is still but one Substance or Entity, neither is there a Vacuum in it: How then can any thing be separated from it self?[57]

Yet this nonseparability of each from the "self" that is its universe must not be misread, we have noted, as only a relation of each part to the whole. It is at this boundary of her thinking that she plunges into an insight that should not have been possible:

> A thing of very great moment ... how all Creatures from the highest to the lowest are inseparably united one with another, by means of Subtiler Parts interceding or coming *in between* which are *the Emanations of one Creature into another, by which also they act one upon another at the greatest distance.*[58]

If I am not mistaken, Lady Conway has just chanced upon the cosmic enigma that in our century physicists call "nonlocality." The French quantum physicist Omnes calls it "nonseparability."[59] In the 1920s, Schroedinger named it "entanglement"; Einstein, trying to make it go away, called it "spooky action at a distance." It did not go away, but instead tested out: and that, says Brian Greene, "boggles the mind."[60] In a nutshell: at the level of minimum matter, particles, once they have been together, continue to act as though they are yoked. That is, if you provoke a response in one of them, its twin will instantaneously react as though *it* is the one you have interfered with – *even if they are light years apart*. Most physicists admit that they lack any intuitive grasp of the phenomenon. In this they may be helped by considering Conway's "Emanations of one Creature into another," by which one creature participates interstitially into the becoming of another.

The "coming in between" is the "Foundation of all Sympathy and Antipathy which happens in Creatures."[61] Spooky? Indeed it is, she avers, that "which ignorant Men call occult Qualities." She is arguing already against the assumption that "mere Local or Mechanical Motion"[62] is sufficient explanation of the interactivity of the universe. That mechanical localism got so set in stone as to seem unquestionable to Einstein. Of course, quantum entanglement need not imply a mystical natural-ism, or even a convivial relationalism. However, Conway's account of sympathy and antipathy between even the microcosmic bodies (the kabbalistic monads) does anticipate what Whitehead calls the "aversions and adversions" relating each actual entity to others; and which the quantum physicist Shimon Malin, combining neo-platonic mysticism and Whiteheadian cosmology, considers a crucial lens upon a universe in which no matter is dead. "Even when the events take place very far apart they seem to be 'entangled,' they seem to 'feel' each other."[63]

I am, however, only suggesting that any pluralism responsive to the multiplicity of the universe and the ecology of the earth will encode some version of this social cosmology – and of its convivial manifold. For theology, a primal sympathy remains the condition, the gift and as such also the lure for intercreaturely evolution.[64]

Our acts of conviviality do not compete with divine care. They actualize it. There is no zero sum game of infinite transcendence versus finite immanence. The mutual finite immanence of the creatures provokes their transcendence of themselves, their becom-ing "greater or better." Their *becoming*: the temporal, finite content of the infinite.

Divine conviviality

> Multiplicity is a dialect of porous openness, implicating a divinity that is streaming, reforming, responding, flowing, and receding, beginning … again.
> (Laurel Schneider)

Our first thinker of the convivial multiplicity did not, however, contemplate the multiplicity of God. Conway's notion of plurality, porosity, and penetrability was limited to the main subject of her theology, the Creature. When it comes to God, she presumes a neoplatonically stabilized One, orthodox in its omnis. Indeed its classicism provided her, as it has provided theology all along, an intellectual bar-rier against the more vulgar idolatries of divine power, "in which he is like to those Cruel Tyrants which are in the World, who act many things out of their mere Will or Pleasure, relying on their Power."[65] One might say that the immu-table and noncomposite divine eternity lends her kabbalistically kaleidoscoping cosmic infinities an anchor. If the theology of multiplicity today, and differently, is beginning to articulate a "divine manifold,"[66] it may prove more consonant with Conway's multiplex cosmology than was her own doctrine of God.

Yet the divine manifold would not here be signified either by monotheism or by polytheism – terms turning out to be modern European neologisms.[67] The bet-ter to discern the possible multiplicity of the holy One, the polydoxical project loops at certain junctures back to biblical antiquity, before any omni-rhetoric had supervened. The divine plurisingularity hinted at in the name *Elohim* and its first person plural ("let us create"), bears the trace of a prior history of divinity.[68] It also encodes a Hebrew potentiality that lends itself – not necessarily, and in resistance to Christian supersessionism – to trinitarian explication. In the origi-nal Christian dogma set forth by Tertullian in third-century Africa, the logic for any polydoxical relationalism breaks into a linguistic formula: "Different not separate, distinct not divided." Schneider's own reading of Tertullian roots her pathbreaking narrative of divine multiplicity in a surprisingly orthodox origin (among many origins).[69] Our experiment in polydoxy pits itself not against monotheism, not against orthodoxy, but against a temptation besetting both: that of a *monodoxy* that actually sabotages the full operation of its own trinitarian logic. Tragically, much of the tradition has repressed the relational radicality of "distinct not divided" – by enclosing it within God, rather than following deity into the interrelations of creation. The iconic cliché of three single "Persons" became superimposed upon the steely surface of the One. By contrast, to break open the dynamism sealed into the *ménage à trois* is to release its eros into its boundless cosmological body – the universe. *Ménage à multiplicité*?

With an interreligious respect startling in her time, Conway proposed that "we should neglect that Phrase of *Three distinct Persons,* which is a Stone of Offense to Jews as well as Turks, and other People, and indeed in itself hath no sound reason, nor can be anywhere found in Scripture."[70] As an alternative, she develops a triad of "species": God, Christ, and the Creatures. "Christ" designates the "middle nature," rendered in a polydox, judaizing hybrid, the "Messias," as the kabbalistic male–female, Adam Kadmon.[71] "God is infinite," and is such *in* the Messias and also "*with* the Messias *in* the Creatures."[72] That latter third species, "Creature," can be read as the primary subject matter of Conway's little book. In this way, each "species" is characterized by the same divinity. Process theologians have similarly questioned the biblical, intellectual, let alone ecumenical integrity of the three Persons in One.[73] Yet Whitehead found a clue to his quantum cosmology of inter-creaturely immanence in the original "unassimilability" of the theological logic of the trinity to Greek metaphysics. "The accepted solution of a multiplicity in the nature of God, each component being unqualifiedly Divine, involves a doctrine of mutual immanence in the divine nature."[74] It is the idea of the mutual immanence of creatures that Whitehead and Conway share. Differently, Whitehead deploys its relational logic against the Greek immutability of the divine. He proposed "the consequent nature of God," according to which God enfolds the becoming world at any moment – and is therefore relationally composed *of* its multiplicity.

Might we now read the interlinkage of complex creatures as the manifestation of a Supreme Conviviality? As another way of translating "God is love?" The Augustinian formula of Lover – Beloved – Love itself already jams the three Person dogma. We might also borrow Nicholas of Cusa's name for the infinite (and therefore unknown) depth of divinity: the *complicatio* that "folds together" all things in itself. It designates a relationality within the Godhead, hospitable but not reducible to the trinitarian symbol.[75] It is, at the same time, the internalization of the multiplicity of the world, which complicates God. If we then envision a trinity of *complicatio*, *explicatio*, and *implicatio*, the divine complexity at once enfolds and unfolds. The *explicatio* – as the logos or *principio* embodied in every creature – unfolds in and as the unpredictable finitudes of the multiverse. The finite creatures "explicate" the infinite, which always at the same time "complicates" – co-implicates – them in its divinity and itself in them.

Such panentheistic difference of God and world has proved a hospitable category. Maintained *avant la lettre* in varying forms by the church fathers, Aquinas, Cusa, Conway, and *to* the letter by Whiteheadians, panentheism also expresses the relational logic of "different not separate." If all is in God then of course multiplicity is also in God. But in its classical form, even the proto-panentheism (as distinct from either dualistic theism or monistic pantheism) insists on the divine simplicity and aseity, the immutable independence of the One from the many. For the classical theism that Conway presumes, God cannot in any sense depend upon the creature. If love offers assistance responsive to need, God does not need love. God does not *need*. And perhaps we do not need to question Conway's classical distinction of creator and creature, at that level. "God" cannot be meaningfully said, even now, to depend upon any set of creatures to exist, and to do so with the integrity of an abstract perfection.

Nonetheless, in certain convivial ways, the divine may indeed "need" the creature. Surely, first of all, the creatures do "help" God – not to improve *herself*, but *our*selves. Are we creatures not called – from the start, earth, waters and all – to bring forth, to cooperate, to *help* in the endless creativity of genesis? In "all our geneses" (Hélène Cixous)? Furthermore, does there not groan around us the desperate need to which prophetic teachings direct us, the deprivations and degradations near and far, in which the multiplicity of issues, relations, and demands registers urgently? Finally, inasmuch as this God cares, she *gets* something from our efforts. For love means nothing if it does not signify both giving and *receiving*. The Lover receives some impression, some feeling, joy or pathos, some offering from the Beloved – or else "He" is immutable substance, hardly different from dead matter. A love-God, unlike the platonic Good, must be *affected*; something must register, as in an infinitely sensitive medium. Something therefore subtly shifts with every exchange; and, so, the divine properly speaking is *becoming*. What does not become does not live. The constitutive relationality of genesis that goes all the way down also goes all the way up. (In this way we may even retrieve some meaning from the nearly ubiquitous, blood-soaked ancient symbols of sacrifice: we do actually "nourish" God.)[76] If, then, we may speak of Love along the biblical trajectory of its ultimacy, divinity does, after all, "need the assistance" of the creatures to assist each other, and thus to nourish its own interactive Life.

"If the origin is irreducibly plural, if it is the indefinitely unfolding and variously multiplied intimacy of the world, then not gaining access to the origin takes on another meaning."[77] Nancy may only seem to hint at an apophatic theology of creation. But what would be this other, non-prohibitive meaning of the inaccessible? Intimacy and infinity seem to converge in an original multiplicity. "Divine promiscuity," writes Laurel Schneider – as though theologically amplifying that primal intimacy – "is an economy of 'more-than-enough,' but it is also a negative gesture."[78] There appears, again, the fold between the unknown and the excessive, the apophatic and the multiple, where our polydoxical possibility is nourished *now*. "There is no 'control' that doctrine can place on divinity, especially in the theory-resistant multiplicity of divine immanence."[79] Negative theology *doctrinally* protects that uncontrollability. The "knowing ignorance" knows its own incapacity to know the infinite, and so offers an intimate, rather than reifying, knowledge of its finite embodiments. For in each of them the "contracted infinity" of the world is microcosmically unfolded.[80] So if, in the *complicatio*, all creatures are encompassed in a bottomless, a tehomic, unknowing – in the *explicatio* the logos matters, materializes. The word becomes flesh, always does. Nothing unfolds without it. But all things unfold out of the inaccessible origin, clouded by an uncertainty principle knowingly foreshadowed in apophatic mysticism.

Yet if the rhythm of complication and explication exhausts the creative process, what of that "third species?" If we call it the *implicatio*, the enfolding, we do not identify it as the creation, but rather as the *Life of the relations constituting the creaturely manifold*, which is to say, as the Spirit. The membranous intimacy of these relations may hold at any distance. This infinite intimacy characterizes Conway's concept of intercreaturely emanations. (We noted how such an intuition is now being quite empirically "explicated" in the physics of entanglement.) Here, then, the mutual immanence of creatures may be signified by the mutual immanence within the divinity, in Cusa's Augustinian sense of the Holy Spirit as "connection itself." This third signals the contraction, or enfolding, of "each in each and all in all."[81] Here is the connectivity, whose coherence is at work in the "sticking together" of the creatures for the sake of their manifold becoming – despite their occasional paroxysms of separation. ("Presences of the Infinite, he calls us." Shuddering.) And yet these "Virtual Extensions" that Conway discerned everywhere, these "Emanations of one Creature into another," these "interpenetrations," are not of blunt and prolific beings barging through one another's ontic boundaries. As Whitehead clarifies, every actuality is a *potential* for the becoming of other actualities. In other words, the mutual immanence as *implicatio* is the signifier of the *possible*. It makes actualization possible – sometimes as the smooth unfolding of a code, the elegant predictabilities of orbits and tides, the lawful stabilities of the social order, or the faithfully fulfilled promises. But such predictably realized possibilities hardly exhaust the spirit – the *Spirit* – of the possible. At its edge it rocks and riles us. It foments the improbabilities we creatures might actualize. Together. Or not.

Too much, too late

Possibility irrupts from, and returns to, that excess, that infinity, which recedes into the impossible. Impossible, at least, to master theologically or to mirror personally. So if the third genre "coming in between" (Conway) makes persons possible, it itself escapes personification. It is the interstitial life of the nourishing multiplicity. In a pneumatological language that is not Conway's, its conviviality is the gift that vivifies, counsels, blows, or vibrates intimately over the face of the ... multiplying beginnings.

Any theism risks saying too much, in order to say anything at all. About its Manifold One. Perhaps Conway, along with most panentheisms, gives insufficient attention – even as they negate the literalism of divine persons – to the limits of her own God-talk. Yet the apophatic practice of the Quakers permeates her theological process.[82] An apophatic panentheism may help us articulate a conviviality that affirms the radical potentialities of the One while negating any merely singular actualizations. In the words of the leading contemporary philosopher of the Kabbalah: "the One is negated in relation to everything to the extent that everything is affirmed in the One."[83] Manifold are the signs of a theology that neither blanks out multiplicity in an ascent to the One, nor blacks out, in moods of manic self-sufficiency, all singular transcendence.

In between and beyond the religions, our entangled polydoxy affirms its multiplicitous spirit. Here in particular we offer a self-critically Christian conviviality, as one messianically explicated host for the larger *convivencia*: for the nourishing, today, of the planetary multiplicity of vulnerable bodies. Each plurisingularity – "interpenetrated by fellow creatures by the thousand" – enfolds in itself, variously, uncertainly, responsively, its world of others. Spirit seems to urge us, with an urgency amplified in every ecological or existential emergency, every religio-politico-economic contradiction, to welcome assistance and to offer it abundantly. Might a systemic evolution beyond the needy, greedy collective of modern *ones* yet alter the human manifold? In time? We slice through the cloud of impossibility perilously.[84] Finitude is what these infinities are all about. We actualize something here and now – careless or grateful for the manifold that in its eerie beauty assists us.[85] Multiplicity becomes us.

Notes

1   R. H. Popkin, "The Spiritualistic Cosmologies of Henry More and Anne Conway," *Henry More (1614–1687): Tercentenary Studies*, S. Hutton (ed.), Dordrecht/Boston/London: Kluwer Academic Publishers, 1989.

2   #257, Letter from Lady Conway to Henry More, (#257, February 4, 1676 [year uncertain]). *The Conway Letters: The Correspondence of Anne, Viscountess Conway, Henry More, and their Friends (1624–1684)*. Marjorie Hope Nicolson and Sarah Hutton (eds), Oxford: Clarendon Press, 1992, pp. 421–2.

3   I am indebted to Carol Wayne White both for my discovery of Anne Conway and for her superb mapping of Conway's work and life. *The Legacy of Anne Conway (1631–1679)*, Albany, NY: State University of New York Press, 2008, p. 11.

4   As in the work of Duran, op. cit.; see also P. Findlen, "Ideas in the Mind: Gender and Knowledge in the Seventeenth Century," *Hypatia*, 17 (1), Winter 2002, pp. 183–96.

5   Duran notes that the "odd concomitant" of the first scholarship on Conway has been "that well-known philosophers of her time were actually more cognizant of the work and the abilities of women thinkers of their time than many male philosophers have been of contemporary women thinkers." J. Duran, *Eight Woman Philosophers: Theory, Politics, and Femnism*, Urbana and Chicago, IL: University of Illinois Press, 2006, p. 73.

6   Thus, Bathsua Makin, lamenting the loss of the Tudor celebration of female erudition, in "An Essay to Revive the Antient Education of Gentlewomen in Religion, Manners, Arts and Tongues." White, p. 8.

7   Conway, here in the original translation into English, pp. vii, 4, 209.

8   Van Helmont's serious engagement of the Kabbalah (and of its Jewish interpreters) cost him two years of imprisonment by the Inquisition on the charge of "judaizing."

9   Ibid., III, 4.5. p. 159. Here is one of multiple allusions to the Kabbalah: "Concerning Infinity see Philosoph. Kabbal. [ref to chapter in Kabbalah Denudata] ... Whence Creatures are rather termed Indefinite than Infinite."

10   Ibid., p. 208.

11   J.-L. Nancy, *Being Singular Plural*, trans. R. D. Richardson and A. E. O'Byrne, Palo Alto, CA: Stanford University Press, 2000, p. 12.
12   G. Deleuze and F. Guattari, *A Thousand Plateaus: Capitalism and Schizophrenia*, trans. B. Massumi, Minneapolis, MN: University of Minnesota Press, 1987, p. 250.
13   Symbiogenesis is the emergence of a new organism out of the merging of two separate ones. Lynne Margulis argues for its primary importance in evolution, and therefore for the priority of cooperation over competition in natural selection. "Origins of Species: Acquired Genomes and Individuality," *BioSystems*, 31 (2–3), 1993, pp. 121–5.
14   Gilles Deleuze, *The Fold: Leibniz and the Baroque*, trans. T. Conley, Minnesota. MN: University of Minneapolis Press, 1993.
15   It had earlier included the subtitle: *Concerning God, Christ, and the Creature; that is, concerning Spirit, and Matter in General.*
16   More sought to subsume the new mechanical Cartesian philosophy into a Neoplatonic metaphysic.

> Descartes' physical system, which he first encountered in about 1645, appeared to complement his Platonic "Cabbala" because it was based upon a similarly dualistic assumption, that bodies were metaphysically "dead" or in themselves 'non-existent,' and that the natural world was moved by "res cogitnas" – for More, spiritual being.

> R. Crocker, "Henry More: A Biographical Essay," *Henry More (1614–1687) Tercentenary Studies*, S. Hutton (ed.), Dordrecht/Boston/London: Kluwer Academic Publishers, 1990, p. 5. So Conway's discovery through van Helmont of the Jewish Kabbalah, different from More's idiosyncratic version, supported her critique of the dualism.

17   Conway, p. 48.
18   White, p. 31.
19   Letter from Conway to More, op. cit.
20   White, p. 30.
21   See S. V. Betcher's chapter in this volume.
22   L. C. Schneider, *Beyond Monotheism: A Theology of Multiplicity*, New York: Routledge, 2008, p. 159.
23   In the present context I cannot elaborate on the brilliant and varied seventeenth-century symbioses of Neoplatonism, Kabbalah, alchemy, and natural philosophy which form the background of the thought of More, van Helmont, Conway, and indeed Isaac Newton, hence the emergence of science as well as religious toleration. See F. Yates, *The Art of Memory*, London: Routledge and Kegan Paul, 1966; also Yates, *Giordano Bruno and the Hermetic Tradition*, London: Routledge and Kegan Paul, 1964; and more recently A. P. Coudert, *Leibniz and the Kabbalah*, Dorderecht/Boston/London: Kluwer Academic Publishers, 1995. On the ferment of Quaker theology vis à vis Conway and van Helmont, see D. Byrne, "Anne Conway, Early Quaker Thought, and the New Science," *Quaker History: The Bulletin of Friends Historical Association*, 96 (1), Spring 2007, pp. 24–36.
24   See J. Thatamanil's chapter in this volume.
25   J. M. Coetzee, *Elizabeth Costello*, New York: Viking, 2003, p. 230.
26   This invented letter was penned as an addendum to another letter, purportedly from her husband Philip Lord Chandos to Francis Bacon – a lamentation on the limits of language that was to become critical text in literary modernism. But what has come to be called the *Lord Chandos Letter* was, in reality, the 1902 creation of Austrian novelist and dramatist, Hugo von Hofmannsthal.
27   J. Derrida, *The Animal that Therefore I Am*, M. L. Mallett (ed.), trans. D. Wills, New York: Fordham University Press, 2008.
28   S. Kierkegaard, *Fear and Trembling*, H. V. Hong and E. H. Hong (eds), Princeton, NJ: Princeton University Press, 1983, p. 49; also Chris Boesel on the double movement, *Risking Proclamation, Respecting Difference*, Eugene, OR: Wipf and Stock, 2008;

and Helene Russell on Kierkegaard's polynimity/multiplicity, H. T. Russell, *Irigaray and Kierkegaard: On the Construction of the Self*, Macon, GA: Mercer University Press, 2009.

29   *Fear and Trembling*, p. 80. This cancellation of a participatory relationalism (and by implication the Pauline metaphor of bodily members) is perhaps compensated by the relational intensity of Kierkegaard's parables, where hope is for the hand of the princess, the return of Isaac.

30   A. Augustine, *The Confessions of Augustine*, trans. J. K. Ryan, Garden City, NY: Doubleday, 1960, Book 11, p. 302. See also my feminist analysis in *From a Broken Web: Separation, Sexism and Self*, Boston, MA: Beacon Press, 1986, p. 164.

31   Conway, p. 210.

32   Ibid., p. 197.

33   Ibid., p. 211, emphasis added.

34   Ibid., p. 190.

35   Historians routinely refer to her absorption of the kabbalistic "monism." For instance, Hutton argues that "for someone exposed to the orthodoxy that monism was symptomatic of atheism, and that a properly conceived dualism was essential to sustaining theism, the kabbalah was a vital means of endowing monism with theistic credentials," p. 166; also see historian of science C. Merchant's pathbreaking essay, "The Vitalism of Anne Conway: The Impact on Leibniz's Concept of the Monad," in which she posits "Conway's Monistic Vitalism," *Journal of the History of Philosophy*, July 17, 1979, p. 258. But such helpful readings occlude the irreducible multiplicity in which Conway's spirit/body continuum unfolds.

36   Ibid.

37   Conway, p. 209, emphasis added.

38   A. N. Whitehead, *Process and Reality: An Essay in Cosmology*, D. R. Griffin and D. W. Sherburne (eds), New York: Free Press, 1978 (1929), p. 50.

39   Whitehead's "principle of the ultimate," distinguished from his concept of God, as the keystone of his radical pluralism: "The many become one and are increased by one." *Process and Reality*, p. 21.

40   Conway, p. 208.

41   Ibid., p. 209.

42   Ibid., p. 210, translation adjusted to Latin, p. 122.

43   Ibid., p. 208.

44   Nancy, p. 40.

45   Conway, pp. 209–10, emphasis added.

46   Conway, p. 158.

47   Ibid., p. 207.

48   Ibid., p. 164.

49   Ibid., p. 162, emphasis added.

50   Leibniz, cited in G. Deleuze, *The Fold: Leibniz and the Baroque*, trans. T. Conley, Minneapolis, MN: University of Minnesota Press, 1993, p. 6.

51   Conway, p. 164.

52   In his New Essays Leibniz refers with approbation to "the late Platonist Countess of Conway" as one of "those who put life and perception into everything." See the discussion of Conway and Leibniz in S. Hutton, *Anne Conway: A Woman Philosopher*, Cambridge: Cambridge University Press, 2004, p. 233.

53   Especially *Leibniz and the Kabbalah*, in which Coudert summarizes the debates about the degree, phases, and chronology of kabbalistic influence upon Leibniz. She also considers the special appeal of Conway's concept of infinity and theodicy upon Leibniz, p. 119.

54   See C. Merchant, op. cit., for the stronger account of how "van Helmont and Anne Conway served to confirm and buttress [Leibniz's] vitalistic view of nature and to stimulate the coalescence of his ideas into a 'monadology,'" p. 269.

55   Whitehead, p. 67. Deleuze does not mention the Leibnizian influence on Whitehead (*Science and Modern World*) even as he mates them in *The Fold*, as the rare geniuses of the "event."

56   Hutton, op. cit.

57   Conway, pp. 206ff.

58   Ibid., p. 164, emphasis added.

59   R. Omnes, *Quantum Philosophy: Understanding and Interpreting Contemporary Science*, Princeton, NJ: Princeton University Press, 1999, pp. 227–30.

60   B. Greene, *The Fabric of the Universe: Superstrings, Hidden Dimensions, and the Quest for the Ultimate Theory*, New York: W.W. Norton & Company, 2003, p. 115.

61   Conway, p. 164.

62   Ibid., p. 229.

63   S. Malin, *Nature Loves to Hide: Quantum Physics and the Nature of Reality, a Western Perspective*, Oxford: Oxford University Press, 2001. "Yet the theory requires that the influence propagate faster than light, which was for Einstein impossible."

64   The trope of "perfection" developed by way of the ancient tradition of *theopoiesis*, or *theosis*: "becoming divine." Of course English, or rather Anglican, sensibility remained quite Catholic in emphasizing sanctification, as the process whereby one aims at "perfection" in grace – over and against the absolute Reformation gesture of justification. And of course the Quakers developed early a strong doctrine of perfection. The Wesleyans would amplify the call to "perfection" a century later. But her catholicity is broad indeed. From her readings with van Helmont of the Lurianic Kabbalah, she draws a strenuous sense of the developmental obligations laid upon every last creature – following the fall or *zimzum* – to grow, to evolve, to exceed itself.

65   Of this apathetic and coercive concept of omnipotence she particularly accuses the "schoolmen," presumably the medieval voluntarists, with their notion of divine "indifference of will." Conway, p. 157.

66   See R. Faber's chapter in this volume, and his [forthcoming] *Divine Manifold*.

67   Schneider, p. 19.

68   The plural grammar of Gen – "let us create man and woman in our image" – cannot be written off as a "royal we." See my *Face of the Deep*. The opportunity to derive trinitarian theology from this strand of Hebrew scripture poses an alternative to the supersessionist Christian practice of reading "types" of Christ and Trinity onto prechristian passages; or in contrasting Jewish monotheism to the subtler three-in-one. In fact the plurisingular potentiality of Elohim was never erased, despite the need in the face of imperial pantheons to protect the novel intuition of the universal deity from cultural dissipation.

69   Schneider, pp. 60–73.

70   Conway, p. 150, emphasis added.

71   Hutton, "Kabbalistical Dialogues," p. 172.

72   Conway, p. 151.

73   J. Cobb, *Christ in a Pluralistic Age*, Eugene, OR: Wipf and Stock, 1975/99.

74   Whitehead, *Adventures of Ideas*, p. 168.

75   I articulate this trinity in *Face*, Chapters 12 and 13; the terms *complicatio* and *explicatio*, not their deployment in this triune form, are from Cusa, *The Knowing Ignorance*, or *de docta ignorantia*, in *Nicholas of Cusa: Selected Spiritual Writings*, trans. L. Bond, Mahwah, NJ: Paulist Press, 1997.

76   Evidently I am not recuperating a metanarrative of the saving blood, of the crucifixion as atoning sacrifice, but rather suggesting a perspective from which the whole range of sacrificial rites and symbols become readable sympathetically enough to make possible their con-vivial transmutation.

77   Nancy, p. 12.

78   Schneider, p. 162.

79 Ibid.
80 Thus, when Cusa names the unknowable excess, or "negative infinity," the *complicatio*, he also intensifies the intimacy of creation, in its folded togetherness, as a "contractedly infinite." *The Knowing Ignorance.*
81 The orthodox fathers installed in the Logos a classical panentheism of "all things in God." But all-things-*in-God* did not yet imply all-things-in-*all-things*: not until Nicholas of Cusa in 1420 made that cosmological connection, wrapped in a boundlessly multiple universe. *De Docta Ignorantia* II, 5, credits Anaxagoras with "each thing in each thing." See C. Keller, "The Cloud of the Impossible: Embodiment and Apophasis," in *Apophatic Bodies: Negative Theology, Incarnation, and Relationality*, C. Boesel and C. Keller (eds), New York: Fordham University Press, 2010, pp. 25–44.
82 Thanks to friends L. B. Callid Keefe-Perry and Lloyd Lee Wilson for the concept of "quaker apophaticism."
83 Elliot R. Wolfson, from whom I receive back illumined the language of an apophatic panentheism, in *Open Secret: Postmessianic Messianism and the Mystical Revision of Menahem Mendl Schneerson*, New York: Fordham University Press, 2009, p. 90.
84 A phrase from Cusa, *de visio dei*. I am currently finishing a monograph called *The Cloud of the Impossible*. There I also engage the tensive implications of Jacques Derrida's "impossible possibility of the im/possible," for apophatic panentheism.
85 And thanks to Beatrice Marovich, my Research Assistant, for particularly insightful assistance in restructuring this chapter.

Part II
The unknown

6   Undone by each other

Interrupted sovereignty in Augustine's *Confessions*

Mary-Jane Rubenstein

A tenuous "we"

In a collection of essays written shortly after September 11, 2001, Judith Butler explores the ethical and political importance of vulnerability.[1] Much like Emmanuel Levinas, Butler suggests that exposure to violence and loss actually conditions responsibility by interrupting the sovereignty of the subject. The vulnerable self remains open to the needs of others and the care they offer, even as it remains exposed to the violence they may inflict. The ethical task, then, is not to consolidate one's sovereignty and singularity, but rather to refuse it – to live into the self's constitutive vulnerability to a shifting multitude of others. Unlike the Levinasian self, however, Butler's ethical agent is not the infinitely subjected "me," more responsible than anyone and called to stand in for everyone.[2] Rather, it is a fragile community, formed and deformed through our common vulnerability to loss. "Loss," she writes, "has made a tenuous 'we' of us all."[3]

This suggestion – that loss makes a "we" of us all – means at least two things. First, it posits a basis for community that cuts across the usual foundations of identity (nation, race, religion, gender, class, age, ability), opening out new possibilities for compassion and alliance. To be more precise, "loss" is not a "basis" of community at all, but something more like an abyss of a foundation, an inessentiality at the heart of who "we" are – which nevertheless lends "us" a powerful coherence, both between and within our interrupted selves. This leads to the second meaning of the sentence at hand: loss makes a tenuous "we" of *us all*, that is to say, of each of us. As Freud eventually discovered, each of us becomes herself by introjecting the people and places and things that she mourns, establishing the ego through the very process that disestablishes it.[4] This is not to say that my self does not exist, or that it is present only as absent, or that it subsists, zombie-like, as a series of gaping holes. Rather, as Jean-Luc Nancy would phrase it, my inessentiality amounts to my co-essentiality.[5]

Consider, for example, the process of mourning. The moment I enter into it, I am thrown against its impossibility. For if I mourn you, whom I have lost, it is because I cannot imagine living without you. But insofar as mourning services my ability to go on living at all, I also cannot imagine mourning you without you. I need you to help me get over you. What is happening here? As Butler explains it, "I not only mourn the loss, but I become inscrutable to myself. Who 'am' I, without you? ... On one level, I think I have lost 'you' only to discover that 'I' have gone missing as well."[6]

What grief reveals, in short, is that I am not myself. I am only me in and through you, and through a multitude of yous, so that I "myself" am a tenuous we. Grief therefore runs us up against a relational ontology, exposing the extent to which I am exposed to others. To be clear, grief does not perform this ontology; it uncovers it. Mourning hits me over the head with the extent of my heteronomy, but it does not put it there to begin with. I do not start out complete and then end up fractured as I lose the ones I love. Rather, grief reveals the ego as dependent and undone because, in Butler's words, "it was already the case with desire."[7] Desire kicks in the very moment we do, installing our selves from the outset as dependent on others. From the outset, we want to be held, fed, warm, dry – and we cannot fulfill these desires ourselves. We are, as Butler mysteriously phrases it, "given over."[8] Given over (although it is not clear by whom or what) to the care of others, the neglect of others, and the desires of others – which we in turn fulfill, reciprocate, or exploit.

What the forces of mourning and desire therefore make clear for Butler is that the self is *fundamentally* ecstatic, outside of itself and in others.[9] If otherness and externality constitute selfhood, however, they deconstitute it at the same time, preventing the self from being itself in the very gesture of establishing it. This, then, pushes beyond a simple logic of "relationality," and even Butler is at a loss for a new word as she explains that ecstasy renders us ourselves only as outside ourselves, even "*beside ourselves*, whether in sexual passion, or emotional grief, or political rage."[10] So this ecstatic structure of selfhood is at once ontological, affective, and ethical. "Let's face it," she writes, "we're undone by each other. And if we're not, we're missing something."[11]

Of course, we miss something all the time. The extent to which we are undone by each other is missed, in particular, by the sovereign subject upon which most western ethico-political systems rely – not to mention the sovereign state that mirrors it. Solid egos and strong nations depend upon a foreclosure of vulnerability – a pretension toward self-determination that ignores, appropriates, or obliterates anything that threatens to compromise its independence. So, when it is exposed to loss, or even the possibility of loss, the "violent and self-centered subject ... seeks to reconstitute its imagined wholeness ... denying its own vulnerability, its dependency, its exposure."[12] Such a violent assertion of sovereignty is precisely what we have seen in the United States' protracted military response to the attacks on the World Trade Center and Pentagon.[13] And, as most of the other contributors to this volume have argued in different ways, this western "value" of sovereignty is in large part an inheritance of Christian orthodoxy, which posits a single, static, and immutable God who makes the whole world out of nothing at all.[14] This vision of God both reflects and endorses an all-too-human pretension toward sovereignty and untrammeled will to power.

The task of "polydox" thinking is not to oppose this inheritance, but rather to point out its internal instability. There is a constitutive multiplicity at the heart of the Christian will-toward-oneness, an irreducible inessentiality that fuels orthodoxy's efforts to hyper-essentialize itself; that is, to *be orthodoxy* in the first place. One way to get at this anxious heart of orthodoxy and the multiplicity it covers over is to focus on its two ontological lynchpins: the purportedly autonomous human self and its purportedly autonomous God. Twin, and ultimately identical subjects that sustain one another's illusions of sovereignty, yet are ultimately undone by each other.

In his genealogy of western subjectivity, Charles Taylor traces the formation of this singular, self-reflexive "individual" to the work of St. Augustine. It is Augustine, Taylor suggests, who forms the crucial link from Platonic recollection to Cartesian cognition, interiorizing the Good and enclosing the subject within itself.[15] This claim, which has been roundly opposed by those who seek to salvage trinitarian theology from the post-Heideggerian dustbin (the radically orthodox in particular)[16] nonetheless draws us into a fascinating cluster of polydox possibility. Augustine, architect and defender of Latin orthodoxy, certainly *seems* to consolidate the individual human self as singular, static, and invulnerable: a narcissistic reflection of his singular, static, invulnerable God.[17]

Following Butler's lead, however, I propose that these "sovereign" figures are far more fragile than they appear. Reading Augustine's *Confessions*, I suggest that a kind of ecstasy can be detected in the text's crises of mourning and desire. Far from presenting us with a stable ontotheology, the *Confessions* opens in spite of itself onto a constitutive host of others: multiplicities that compose and undo Augustinian selfhood – and the divinity at its inscrutable core.

Lost in multiplicity

At its face value, the *Confessions* is an account of conversion – of Augustine's protracted, occasionally comic and often ridiculous effort to turn (*vertere*) from what is not-God back to what *is* God. Throughout the book, Augustine explains this process as a journey from created things to their creator, which carries Augustine himself from distraction to singularity and from dispersion to unity. Speaking to the one God who has finally made him one, Augustine exclaims, "You gathered me together from the state of disintegration [*dispersione*] in which I had been fruitlessly divided [*discissus sum*]. *I turned from unity in you to be lost in multiplicity* [*in multa evanui*]."[18] Multiplicity, then, is a mark of sin. The soul *in multa evanui* is lost, dis-integrated, fractured. The process of conversion, by contrast, entails a gradual renunciation of multiplicity. Turning to God, the soul becomes unified and unchanging *in imitatio Dei*:

> for you are supremely "the selfsame" in that you do not change. In you is repose which forgets all toil because there is none beside you, nor are we to look for the multiplicity of other things which are not what you are. For "you, Lord, have established me in hope by means of unity [*singulariter in spe constituisti me*]."
>
> (9.4.11)

Of course, Augustine has not always understood God to be so singular and unchanging. In his errant youth, he thought God to be mutable (4.15.26), dispersed (7.1.1), physical (3.7.12), and even tehomic:

> I visualized you, Lord, surrounding [creation] on all sides and permeating it, but infinite in all directions, as if there were a sea everywhere ... which had within it a large but finite sponge, and the sponge was in every part filled from the immense sea.[19]
>
> (7.5.7)

It is not until he is converted, which is to say "collected together and brought to the unity from which [he] disintegrated into multiplicity" (10.29.40), that Augustine discovers God similarly to be "wonderfully simple and immutable" (4.16.29). In other words, the journey from plurality to singularity takes place on an existential and a theological level at once. Augustine's personal dispersion mirrors his "misapprehension" of God's dispersion, and his conversion delivers both of them – Augustine *and* his conception of God – from the treacherous waters of multiplicity.

The *Confessions'* journey from plurality to singularity has become something of a paradigm within the western theological tradition – so much so that William James writes it into the very core of his *Varieties of Religious Experience.* For James, religious experience is marked primarily by conversion, and conversion is "the process, gradual or sudden, by which a self hitherto divided, and consciously wrong inferior and unhappy, becomes unified and consciously right superior and happy, in consequence of its firmer hold upon religious realities."[20] As he puts it elsewhere, conversion unifies the "divided self," homogenizes the "heterogeneous personality," and forms a "stable system" out of the "chaos within us."[21] Citing as evidence the text that clearly gave rise to this definition in the first place, James tells us that

> St. Augustine's case is a classic example ... distracted by the struggle between the two souls in his breast ... he heard a voice in the garden say, "*sume* [sic], *lege* (take and read)", and opening the Bible at random, saw the text ... which seemed directly sent to his address, and laid the inner storm to rest forever.[22]

There are two major problems with this (again, not uncommon) interpretation: first, as Virginia Burrus has suggested, the "shameful" process of conversion produces the very division it purports to expose and heal.[23] Second, and this issue I will take up here, the healing never arrives; Augustine's "inner storm" simply *isn't* "laid to rest forever." Such rest, promised in the opening lines of the first chapter ("our hearts are restless until they find rest in you" [1.1.1]) seems rather to be infinitely deferred: even after his conversion, Augustine admits to being disturbed by nocturnal emissions, plagued by "occasional gluttony," enthralled by the admiration of others, carried away by beautiful sounds, and distracted by the sight of dogs chasing rabbits (10.30.41, 10.31.45, 10.37.61, 10.33.49, 10.35.57). "My life is full of such lapses," he writes, realizing that the only sense over which he has fairly good control is that of smell.[24]

Generations of readers have puzzled over these remnants of multiplicity in the converted self that Augustine and his God have labored so long to unify. As Marinus Burcht Pranger puts it, it is quite a surprise that "Augustine judges his *après*-conversion to have been quite a mess and full of broken promises."[25] Was conversion supposed to fix this mess, this brokenness? For his part, William James borrows the solution offered by one Louis Gourdon, telling us in a footnote that Augustine's conversion scene in the garden "is premature," marking his adoption of a kind of neo-platonism rather than full-strength Christianity.[26] Augustine's final conversion, along with his internal unity, comes along later. It must come along later, otherwise Augustine is never fully converted. Or – in a more polydox register – perhaps conversion does not bring about the static unity it promises. Perhaps, far from annihilating multiplicity, the confessional journey uncovers and reconfigures it.

For the moment, however, the "plain meaning" of Augustine's text construes multiplicity as sinful, and unity as godly. After all, Augustine explicitly tells us that he became "evil" by virtue of his various entanglements with others. There were the women, the Manicheans, and of course, the pears he stole as a teenager. Plagued with guilt, Augustine realizes he neither wanted nor needed these pears, but took them merely to impress his friends. Over the course of two chapters, he repeats with near-obsessive insistence,

> *Had I been alone I would not have done it* – I remember my state of mind to be thus at the time – *alone I would never have done it* ... I would not have needed to inflame the itch of my cupidity through the excitement generated by sharing the guilt with others ... *alone I would not have done it, could not conceivably have done it by myself.* See, before you, my God, the living memory of my soul. *Alone I would not have committed that crime*, in which my pleasure lay not in what I was stealing but in the act of theft. But *had I been alone*, it would have given me absolutely no pleasure, nor would I have committed it. Friendship can be a dangerous enemy.
>
> (2.9:16–17; emphasis added)

Clearly, solitude is configured as blameless in this passage, while relationships assume the burden of sin. Friendship becomes "a dangerous enemy" for Augustine when it threatens the self's autonomy, leading a person to do what he would not or could not do "alone." Friends are dangerous when they are motivated by one another, egged on by one another, smitten with one another, carried away by one another. Better, then, to remain within oneself: "*Alone I would never have done it.*"

It is striking here that what Butler construes as the *sine qua non* of responsibility is precisely what Augustine construes as the source of irresponsibility. Being-outside-oneself is not to be abided – far less to be cultivated, for it is what gets Augustine in trouble in the first place. Conversely, the responsible subject to which Augustine gestures would be a solitary individual in full control of himself and invulnerable to the influence of others: precisely the sovereign subject that Butler construes as the source of violence and irresponsibility. In short, the heteronomy that Butler extols as a virtue is for Augustine the quintessence of vice. To be sure, Augustine's suspicion of heteronomy is not surprising; his panic over sexual ecstasy is well known, as is his suspicion of excessive grief, which I will address shortly. As we will see, whether in desire or mourning, Augustine *will not let himself be beside himself.*

To be clear, what Augustine and Butler share is the notion that affective ecstasy is a sign of existential ecstasy: if grief and desire leave me beside myself, it is because I *am* beside myself – inextricably bound up with (and unbounded by) the others I want, love, and lose. While Butler claims this condition as an ineradicable good, however, Augustine sees in ecstasy a sign that the soul is mired in sin. "My soul was in rotten health," Augustine tells his God. "In an ulcerous condition it thrust itself to outward things [*se foras* – literally, it went outside itself]" (3.1.1). He deepens his critique of ecstasy by adding to it a sexual valence: "I had stumbled upon that bold-faced woman … She seduced me, for she found me living outside myself [*invenit foris habitantem*], seeing only with the eye of the flesh" (3.7.12). Again, then, to be living outside oneself is to be living in sin, which is furthermore characterized here as an excessive attunement to the physical world. The deeper one goes into materiality, the farther one is from oneself; and the farther one is from oneself, the farther one is from God: "Where was I when I was seeking for you? You were there before me, but I had departed from myself [*a me discesseram*]" (5.2.2).

If being outside oneself is a mark of sin, then one would imagine that turning back toward oneself would be the means of salvation. This certainly seems to be the case with the passage Charles Taylor cites from *De Vere Religione* ("Do not go outward; return within yourself. In the inward man dwells truth")[27] or indeed with Book X of the *Confessions*, where Augustine scans the whole cosmos before ultimately finding God in his own memory. In fact, it is God's dwelling in *memoria* that leads Taylor to charge Augustine with internalizing the Good, making this proto-Cartesian self its own source of truth.[28] What this accusation forgets, however, is that turning toward the self is *also* the original sin for Augustine, both historically and typologically. In the *City of God*, he explains that the sin of Adam and Eve was "falling away from the work of God to [their] own works."[29] From their quest for immortality to Augustine's own love of public acclaim, turning toward oneself is the work of pride, and pride is "the fountain-head of all … evils."[30]

So while the *Confessions* describe the sinful soul as being lost outside itself, it also describes the sinful soul as being stuck within itself. At some points Augustine tells God, "I had departed from myself"; and at others, "I could not escape myself" (4.7.12). Sometimes, his error is "seeking for you outside myself," and other times it is *not* seeking God outside himself ("I did not know that the soul needs to be enlightened by light outside itself, so that it can participate in truth" [4.15.25]). Perplexingly, sin is a matter both of being outside oneself and of being stuck within oneself. How, then, does one get out (or in)? If sin were simply a state of either ec-stasis or in-stasis, then the remedy would be the other. But somehow, the sinful soul that wanders outside itself also remains pridefully within itself. This can only mean that the redemptive return-to-oneself will also deliver the self outside itself; the gathering into inner unity will also be an opening onto the externality of multiplicity. In other words, *pace* James, conversion is not nearly so simple a process as moving from heteronomy to autonomy. Rather, it is a movement from one sort of heteronomy to another, making Augustine's "own" *Confessions* a catalog of the manifold others that compose, undo, and reconfigure him.

Boy, interrupted

"'You are great, Lord, and highly to be praised [*Magnus es, Domine, et laudabilis valde*]'" (1.1.1). Thus opens the *Confessions*, and any effort to locate in Augustine an early formulation of the *cogito* is compromised from the start. First, this is not, as Jean-Luc Marion would say, a statement about God; it is an address *to* God.[31] The text opens not in the mode of predication, which knows before it speaks, but of praise, which loves what it cannot know. Our speaker is overwhelmed, unknowing from the beginning. Second, the praise he offers is a quotation from Psalm 47:2. This renders the utterance doubly dispossessing; not only does Augustine not know the God he praises, but his praise is borrowed, not his own. And finally, we should note that the first words of this purportedly personal confession of a purportedly single, pre-modern individual are not "I am," but rather "You are." The moment Augustine begins to account for himself, he finds himself interrupted; far from the Cartesian thinker who serves as his own Archimedean point,[32] Augustine cannot get to himself except through another.

Without referring explicitly to this text, Judith Butler has theorized this sort of interruption as the mark of *any* account of oneself: "If, at the beginning … *I am only in the address to you*, then the 'I' that I am is nothing without this 'you,' and cannot even begin to refer to itself outside the relation to the other."[33] Just like affective ecstasy, narrative interruption is a sign of ontological interruption. My inability to speak without another indicates my inability to be without that other. But is this dependency the same thing as the ecstasy we have been thematizing? Augustine is not entirely clear: "I would have no being, I would not have any existence, unless you were in me. Or rather," he stammers, "I would have no being if I were not in you" (1.2.2). Hence the simultaneity of ecstasy and instancy we saw a moment ago; just as the sinful and godless Augustine is at once lost outside himself and stuck within himself, the converted and prayerful Augustine cannot tell whether he is outside himself in God or whether God is outside Godself in him. Internality and externality fold in on one another because, in its truest "essence," the human self is *both* inside itself with, and outside itself within, an unassimilable other. Augustine has his being within the ecstatic God within him. Either way, Augustine is not simply himself, which means (to return to the problem of narrative interruption) that his story is not simply his own: "if it is an account of myself, and it is an accounting *to* someone, then I am compelled to give the account away, to send it off, to be dispossessed of it at the very moment that I establish it as *my* account."[34]

As Book I moves from praise to narration, we see that this account is not, in fact, Augustine's "own" – not only because he does not tell it *to* himself, but also because he cannot tell it *by* himself. Hoping to account for his whole life, Augustine starts at the very beginning – and hits an immediate impasse: "I do not know where I came from" (1.6.7). Once again, this text operates in the unsovereign mode of unknowing. Augustine does not know where he comes from, both because he cannot comprehend the God from whom he came and, less loftily, because he was an infant when he did. Far from installing a stable link to Cartesian reason from Platonic anamnesis, Augustine does not know and cannot remember.

Butler writes, "When the 'I' seeks to give an account of itself, it can start with itself, but it will find that this self is already implicated in a social temporality that exceeds its own capacities for narration."[35] So it is with Augustine, who "starts with himself" by appealing to his parents and nurses. Rather than finding infantile memories within himself, he will rely upon the stories they have told him, "for I do not remember" (1.6.7). His infant self wept. He smiled. "This at least is what I was told" (1.6.8) and he believes it because he has observed as much in other children. He sees now that infants "revenge [themselves] upon" their parents by crying, and concludes that he must have done so, too (1.6.8). Once again, then, Augustine is recollecting himself by means of others: "Who reminds me of the sin of my infancy? ... Any tiny child now, for I see in that child what I do not remember in myself" (1.7.11). All of this is to say that Augustine's memory – the driving force of the *Confessions* and the place Augustine will ultimately find God – is not his own. His "own" memory is rather the work of countless others, who supply him, either in act or story, with the recollections he does not have alone. Moreover, each of these "others" opens onto God, who filled the breasts of his mother and nurses (1.6.7), who allows other people's stories to supplement his own (1.6.10), who dwells within all of them, and in whom they all dwell. Augustine is gathered together – and in the same gesture dispossessed – by each of these others. In this sense, Augustine can say of any of the events related here, and of the act of confession itself, "alone I never would have done it."

The unwork of mourning

Clearly, however, this dependence upon others is not a condition with which Augustine is comfortable. As every first-time reader of the *Confessions* remarks with a degree of horror, Augustine denies innocence even to the state of infancy. From the very beginning, he describes himself as sinful: flailing his arms, weeping excessively, and demanding the attention of others. The infant Augustine is, one might say, beside himself, and it is a condition he will spend his mature years trying to escape – but not before his heteronomy deepens, multiplies, and throws him into crisis. Leaving his mother and nurses, Augustine is handed over to all sorts of others, from the slave who takes him to school (1.19.30) to abusive teachers (1.9.14, 1.14.23), to the lusty streets of Babylon (2.3.8), the pear-stealing thugs (2.4.9), and the "slick-talking" Manicheans (3.6.10). Then, from the depths of distraction and sin, Augustine tells us, "I had come to have a friend" (4.4.7).

Like Augustine's romantic partner of 15 years, this young man remains unnamed throughout the book. All we are told about him is that Augustine had seduced him from "the true faith" and that the two of them shared "identical interests" (presumably, sports, theatre, rhetoric, and whatever other activities were leading Augustine so far from his God [4.4.7]). Yet the chief failing of this friendship was not so much its quality as its intensity, for which Augustine spends the rest of Book IV reproaching himself. Like the incident with the pears, what troubles him most is not what he and his friend did, but how they did it: "I never left his side," he confesses, "and we were deeply dependent on one another [*pendebamus ex invicem*]" (4.4.8). What troubles him, in other words, is the deepened heteronomy into which this relationship threw him. Worse than the pear tree friends whose provocations led him to *act* in a way he would not *act* alone, this friend causes him to *be* in such a way that he cannot *be* alone. Far more radically than "alone I would not have done it," Augustine now laments, "my soul could not endure to be without him [*non poterat anima meo sine illo*]" (4.4.7).

Since this friend effectively constitutes the 16-year-old Augustine, his untimely death unravels him. In what is arguably the least controlled and most poetic passage in the *Confessions*, Augustine mourns:

> "Grief darkened my heart." Everything on which I set my gaze was death. My town became a torture to me; my father's house a strange world of unhappiness; all that I had shared with him was without him transformed into a cruel torment. My eyes looked for him everywhere, and he was not there. I hated everything because they did not have him, nor could they now tell me "look, he is on the way," as used to be the case when he was alive and absent from me.

It is at this point that Augustine famously declares, "I had become to myself a vast problem [*factus eram ipse mini magna quaestio*]" (4.4.9). Something about the death of his friend splits him from himself, makes himself inscrutable to himself. Augustine fumbles around and tries to explain:

> I was surprised that any other mortals were alive, since he whom I had loved as if he would never die was dead. I was even more surprised that when he was dead I was still alive, for he was my "other self." Someone has well said of his friend, "He was half my soul." I had felt that my soul and his soul were "one soul in two bodies." So my life was to me a horror. I did not wish to live with only half of myself.
>
> (4.6.11)

We will recall that for Butler, grief reveals the extent to which one does not exist independently of another, a realization that renders the whole process of mourning impossible. In losing his friend, Augustine discovers that he has "gone missing," as well. He is tormented, fractured, horrified, and undone. Both emotionally and ontologically, this death leaves him beside himself.

In time, Augustine will attribute his youthful restlessness to his flimsy conception of God. The young Augustine could not let God solidify his "lacerated and bloody soul" because "when I thought of you, my mental image was not anything solid and firm; it was not you but a vain phantom … If I attempted to find rest there for my soul, it slipped through a void and again came falling back upon me" (4.7.12). This image of God was effectively an image of Augustine himself, and neither of them was anything substantial. Again, then, we see that the figures of God and self mirror one another, so that Augustine's efforts to secure his own integrity parallel his efforts to secure God's. And the only God who will ultimately manage to gather him together is one who promises not to change, move, or abandon him, who is a place of "undisturbed quietness" that will keep him invulnerable to further loss (4.11.16).

In the aftermath of his friend's death, we therefore find Augustine doing his best to change his cathexis – to transfer his emotional and libidinal investment from earthly things to an increasingly immutable God. This is not to say that Augustine advocates hatred of created things, or even detachment from them. The process is not so much one of turning *from* the temporal to the eternal as it is one of turning *through* the temporal to the eternal. "Let these transient things be the ground on which my soul praises you," Augustine tells his God. "But let it not become stuck in them and glued to them with love through the physical senses. For these things pass along the path of things that move towards non-existence" (4.10.15). And when they do cease to exist, the soul that loves them for their own sake will be torn apart. Augustine therefore entreats us to love created things as created: "if physical objects give you pleasure, praise God for them and return love to their Maker … If souls please you, they are being loved in God; for they also are mutable and acquire stability by being established in him" (4.12.18). By loving temporal things *in God*, the soul finds an eternal guarantor for its affective investment: the things that are loved may come and go, but the God in whom they are loved remains the same forever.

In the background of this emerging picture of the single, unchanging God of orthodoxy, we can therefore detect something like a refusal of mourning. By insisting, first, that others must be loved in God and, second, that this God "cannot in any way be subjected to violence" (10.5.7), Augustine tries to secure a world in which nothing is truly lost. Turning from the heteronomy of sinful attachments to the unity of conversion, the human self becomes invulnerable in relation to its invulnerable God.

Back to the garden

We will recall that William James defines conversion as a journey from division to unity, of which Augustine's conversion in the garden is paradigmatic.[36] The story is a familiar one: having finally found in Bishop Ambrose an intelligence that rivals his own, Augustine abandons the Manicheans and resolves to convert to Christianity – only to find himself unable to do what he resolves. Just like Saint Paul, whose writings he has begun to carry around with him like a security blanket, Augustine finds within himself two opposing forces: the law of God pulls him away from sex and festivities and public acclaim, while the "law of his members" draws him right back (8.5.12). Augustine compares himself to a person who tries to get out of bed in the early morning, half of him knowing what it needs to do while the other half presses the snooze button, mumbling, "'At once' – 'But presently' – 'Just a little longer, please'" (8.5.12). Augustine is, as he recounts and James reaffirms, divided against himself: heteronomous. "I was neither wholly willing nor wholly unwilling," he recalls. "So I was in conflict with myself and was dissociated from myself [*ego contendebam et dissipabar a me ipso*]" (8.10.22).

This dissociation, which has been the mark of sin from Augustine's needy infancy through his grief-stricken early adulthood, reaches its final crisis point in the conversion scene of Book VIII. Appalled that scores of others are winning salvation while he wallows in the muck of sin, Augustine resolves to take his split self into a garden, and not to emerge until only one of him remains. He struggles, contorts himself, weeps, rips his hair out, and finally throws himself in exhaustion under a fig tree, whereupon he hears a child's voice telling him to "take and read" (8.12.29). Reaching for the Epistles he has pored over for months, Augustine opens at random to Romans 13:13–14: "Not in riots and drunken parties, not in eroticism and indecencies, not in strife and rivalry, but put on the Lord Jesus Christ and make no provision for the flesh in its lusts." He is instantly converted, "all the shadows of doubt dispelled" (8.12.29), and is able, in James's words, "to quell the lower tendencies forever."[37] From the chaotic turmoil of heteronomy, Augustine has suddenly and rather anti-climactically "emerged into the smooth waters of inner unity and peace."[38]

As we have already seen, however, James's conclusion seems hastily drawn. Augustine displays neither unity nor peace after his conversion, tortured as he remains by his residual sensual attachments.[39] But even if we were to say that Augustine manages "to quell the lower tendencies forever," we would see that the converted Augustine has not overcome his heteronomy; he has transferred it. This is evident from the (singularly uninspiring) passage that converts him, in which Paul entreats the Romans to give up drunkenness, eroticism, and anger and "put on the Lord Jesus Christ." Augustine admits as much, confessing that "what I once feared to lose was now a delight to dismiss. You turned them out and entered to take their place" (9.1.1). In other words, Augustine ceases to fear loss once he is permanently insured against it – once he has shifted his desires from the mortal many to the eternal One "in [whom] nothing dies" (1.6.9). But again, this substitution in a sense reconfirms the very heteronomy Augustine (and James) denigrates. As Karmen MacKendrick argues, God is a "hotter" love than his earthly ones, a master seducer to whom Augustine enslaves himself with a fervor that only deepens after his conversion.[40] In short, Augustine becomes "unified" only by giving himself over; insofar as he is established in God, he is thoroughly dispossessed.

What is more, Augustine's libidinal transfer is not complete; God is not the only "other" interrupting his converted self. Even continuing to bracket his residual sensual distractions, we can find in and around the garden scene a host of others who enable and sustain Augustine's conversion. There is, of course, his mother Monica, who has followed him from shore to shore, weeping over his soul. There is the saintly Ambrose, to whom Augustine attaches himself in order to detach from the Manichees (5.8.34). And there is Alypius, a student of Augustine's who accompanies him on his quest for conversion.

Augustine describes his relationship to Alypius without a shadow of self-reproach. This is surprising, considering how clearly their inseparability recapitulates his boyhood friendship: "So I found Alypius at Rome. He attached himself to me with the strongest bond [*adhaesit mihi fortissimo vinculo*] and was to accompany me to Milan, so that he would not be parted from me [*nec me desereret*]" (6.10.16).[41] As the Latin makes clear, Alypius's refusal to be parted from Augustine reflects Augustine's longing not to be abandoned. In fact, the desire of both men for one another's company is so strong that Alypius convinces Augustine not to marry the young woman his mother has selected for him: "his theme was that, if I did that, there would be no way whereby we could live together in carefree leisure for the love of wisdom" (6.12.21). While these passages clearly echo the ones surrounding the death of his codependent friend, there is no criticism here of excessive attachment, of loving another as though he would never die, or of being unable to live without the beloved. In fact, even though Alypius is clearly motivated by his refusal to live without Augustine, he is so lauded in this book as to be credited with having secured Augustine's chastity. The question is, why does the Bishop interpret this friendship so favorably? In what way does Augustine's attachment to Alypius differ from his attachment to the friend without whom his "soul could not bear to be?"

Ostensibly, the friendship with Alypius escapes Augustine's condemnation because, however inseparable, these two friends share a "love of wisdom," which is to say, a love of the God they both seek.[42] What is important for our purposes, however, is to see in Alypius (as in Ambrose, as in Jesus Christ) a network of substitutions. Refusing to live apart from Augustine *for the sake of God*, Alypius becomes for Augustine an acceptable libidinal investment: he is the boyhood friend, the abandoned lover, and the forbidden spouse, all purified and eternalized through the superegoical filter of God the Father. It is not surprising, therefore, that Alypius effectively mediates Augustine's self-abandonment to this God. Were the *Confessions* adapted for the theater, the staging of the garden scene would look downright farcical: Augustine resolves to go into the garden and unify himself "where no one could interfere," adding, "Alypius followed me step after step." Still, Augustine is convinced that this story should concern him-alone, so he qualifies, "although he was present, I felt no intrusion on my solitude" (8.8.19). Even in his solitude, Alypius is there – even as Augustine sets himself apart to wrestle with himself, he is together with another person. Hence the baffling declaration: "This debate in my heart was a struggle of myself against myself. Alypius stood quite still at my side" (8.11.27).

Moments before he gives himself over, Augustine decides that even Alypius is too distracting, and moves "farther away" so he can be completely uninhibited (8.12.18). Unlike the road that has led him there, Augustine imagines that the precise moment of conversion will be his alone. So like Descartes before his solitary fire, Augustine strips himself down to himself.[43] The moment he tries to do so, however, he receives a vision of "the dignified and chaste Lady Continence, serene and cheerful and without coquetry, enticing me in an honorable manner to come and not to hesitate" (8.11.27). This utterly queer appearance becomes even more "Broadway" as it grows to a proverbial chorus of thousands:

> To receive and embrace me she stretched out pious hands, filled with numerous good examples for me to follow. There were large numbers of boys and girls, a multitude of all ages, young adults and grave widows and elderly virgins ...

And she smiled on me with a smile of encouragement as if to say: "Are you incapable of doing what these men and women have done?"

(8.11.27)

Here too, then, we see Augustine preparing to make a series of substitutions. This "pious" lady will allow him to give up the impious ones, and the "chaste" multitude will entice him away from the sinful others he has spent his life pursuing. But Continence is still a woman and *the multitude is still a multitude*. The good lady concludes, "why are you relying on yourself, only to find yourself unreliable? Cast yourself upon him [*proici te in eum*], do not be afraid. He will not withdraw himself so that you fall" (8.11.27). Casting (literally, pro-jecting) himself upon the immovable "him" of God, Augustine also casts himself with and upon all these others. In other words, Augustine's conversion does not in any simple way "unify" him within himself. Rather, it throws him outward – toward his mother, toward Ambrose and Alypius, toward the holy throng within the fabulous bosom of Lady Continence, and toward the God who contains them all – or whom each of them contains.

It is at this point that Augustine takes, reads, and "put[s] on the Lord Jesus Christ." This moment tends be read either as a final capitulation to God the Cosmic Moralist or as a massive act of sublimation (who needs riots and drunken parties when you've got Jesus?). Insofar as this passage contains one of the few references to the person of Christ in the *Confessions*, however, I suggest reading Augustine's self-abandonment instead as an ecstatic act of mimesis. Exhausted from his struggle in the garden with an omnipotent God, Augustine gives himself over to the *incarnate* God, renouncing his own sovereignty for the God who renounces *his* … and then he bursts into tears (8.7.28). "Alone" with a swarm of others, given over to the God given over to the multitude, Augustine is once again beside himself.

Mourning revisited

As we have seen in Judith Butler's work, one mark of the purportedly sovereign subject is its refusal to mourn. Owning up to the vulnerability of mourning, the subject is forced to face its constitutive relation to the lost object: mourning runs us up against our irreducible heteronomy. Because he aligns heteronomy with sin, Augustine the Bishop chastises his younger self and sublimates his earthly affections into eternal ones. In the process, his conceptions of God and himself increase in stability, immutability, and immateriality. In a Butlerian register, these efforts shore up Augustine's own autonomy: by routing all of his desires through a God whom he insists does not move or change, Augustine effectively insulates himself against loss, which is to say against relation *tout court*. In this vein, David Bakan has accused Augustine of staging a "vaulting assertion of self … a vaulting struggle to identify the limited ego with all of the grandness and timelessness which he attributes to God."[44] As I have been trying to argue, however, Augustine's pretentions do not exactly succeed. Rather, his journey toward unity and autonomy opens him instead into something like a reconfigured heteronomy, preventing the solidification of a "grand," "timeless," sovereign self.

To test this hypothesis with respect to his conception of the self, I propose that we examine the first major event after Augustine's conversion: the death of his mother. If it were the case that Augustine's conversion had, in Bakan's words, "alienated [him] from all existence," or in James's terms, "laid to rest the inner storm forever," we would expect to find Augustine's approach to grief transformed after Book VIII. Rather than the tortured cries of his young adulthood, the unified Augustine would respond to the death of a mortal with detachment, offering placid thanks to the immortal God. Indeed, this is how Augustine reacts to the death of his son – or at least, it is the way he *recounts* his reaction to the death of his son, whose very name points to his creator. Adeodatus: given by God. Or, in the lexical indeterminacy Latin affords, given *to* God. Either way, Augustine loves his son the way one "ought" to love created souls: "in God," and in God alone, "for there they acquire stability" (4.12.18). Augustine gives voice to this stability when he writes of his son, "His intelligence left me awestruck. Who but you could be the Maker of such wonders?" As we see here, Augustine's amazement at his son's intelligence opens him *directly* onto God: Adeodatus is wonderful; God is the source of that wonder. Augustine, his sole focus on Him, reports being untroubled by his son's death, redirecting his attachment to God-alone. One sentence later, however, he tells us of the great floods of tears he wept, not after his son's death, but *after his own baptism*, which had taken place two years earlier. One cannot help but think of this bizarre and unchronological diversion as a way for Augustine to channel his grief into piety.

But Augustine's sublimation proves incomplete and his invulnerability a fantasy – not just in the rerouted tears over his dead son, but even more forcefully after the death of his mother. The narration here is strange: again we are presented with an event that happened before Adeodatus's death but is recounted after it, and again, Augustine tries to relate the news with total dispassion: "While we were at Ostia by the mouths of the Tiber, my mother died. I pass over many events because I write in great haste" (9.8.17). Then, in a two-chapter detour that reads like a clinical evaluation, Augustine details Monica's adolescence and young adulthood, her dalliance with alcohol, her growing piety, and her conversion of his pagan father. All of this culminates in the equally unlyrical "window" scene, with Monica and her favorite son ascending to eternity together: talking, panting, and sighing at the height of spiritual attainment before descending again to the created order (9.10.24).

Having recounted their joint mystical union, Augustine can now return to the story of his mother's death: "On the ninth day of her illness, when she was aged 56, and I was 33, this religious and devout soul was released from the body" (9.11.29). Unlike the ataraxic speaker who first gave us the news, however, the Augustine who finishes the story is pathetically divided:

> I closed her eyes and an overwhelming grief welled into my heart and was about to flow forth in floods of tears. But at the same time under a powerful act of mental control my eyes held back the flood and dried it up. The inward struggle put me into great agony.

> (9.11.29–30)

As Catherine Keller has shown, this "inward struggle" wells up into an outward silencing of Adeodatus, who lets out the cry his father suppresses.[45] But the inward struggle itself is also remarkable, considering it was precisely such division that Augustine's conversion ostensibly healed. Although it takes place after his unification in the garden, then, Monica's death reveals Augustine as *still divided*.

Facing the loss of his mother, Augustine is, as he always has been, torn between his passions and what he imagines to be the passionless will of God. The changeless and eternal God forbids mourning – at least over those souls who will dwell with him forever. Indeed we have repeatedly witnessed Augustine's efforts to shore up God's stability and filter his desire through Him, precisely in order to inoculate himself against mourning. "Why then did I suffer sharp pains of inward grief?," Augustine asks.

> It must have been the fresh wound caused by the break in the habit formed by our living together, a very affectionate and precious bond suddenly torn apart … my soul was wounded, and my life as it were torn to pieces, since my life and hers had become a single thing [*sauciabatur anima et quasi dilaniabatur vita, quae una facta erat ex mea et illius*].
>
> (9.12.30)

So once again, grief reveals an ontic togetherness: just as the loss of his friend revealed the extent to which his sinful self was bound to him, the loss of his mother reveals the extent to which his converted self is bound to *her*: the two of them are *una facta*. Once again, we can hear Augustine wondering, "who 'am' I, without you?"[46] The difference, of course, is that like his relationship with Alypius, Augustine's "affectionate and precious bond" to his mother is marked at every turn by his (supposedly) primary bond to God.

Augustine's nameless young friend, like his lover and his son, are all objects and products of his sinful attachments. His mother, on the other hand, is in a sense the source of the substitutionary attachments he adopts (by means of Alypius) under the fig tree. It was Monica who introduced Augustine to his divine Father, who pleaded for his life with a local bishop, who ended his non-marital relationship, who followed him weeping all the way to Milan, who waited in the house while he struggled in the garden, who climbed the ladder of creation with him at the window, and who was ultimately *united to God with him*. If Augustine cannot manage in this instance to suppress his grief by turning from her to immortal things, it is because his vision of the immortal is mediated by her in the first place. His relation to the eternal is, in other words, scandalously contingent upon the temporal. In Augustine's inability *not* to mourn Monica, she and God fold heretically in on one another, causing orthodoxy's ontological distinction to tremble. God and Monica become so identified, in fact, that the God before whom Augustine eventually breaks down is one who rocks him maternally, morphing briefly from a *fundamentum inconcussum* into what Keller dubs a "tehomic waterbed."[47] Moreover, at the same time that he identifies God with his mother, Augustine identifies himself with his mother as well. Pleading with God to "forgive her her debts," Augustine is remade in her image, weeping and praying for the soul that has always wept and prayed for his (9.13.35). Then, rather abruptly, Augustine concludes "And now, Lord, I make my confession to you in writing" (9.12.33). In losing and introjecting Monica, Augustine has finally found himself. Far from being unentailed, however, this self is haunted by her and the others who undo him. And it is in this wholly interrupted self that Augustine will finally find God.

"But I was outside myself"

From the beginning of the *Confessions*, we have seen that Augustine's effort to get himself right is paralleled by his effort to get his God right. His attempted journey from division to unity, change to stability, and sensuality to spirituality is contingent upon a similar transformation in his conception of God. When he was young, he confesses, he thought that God was material, mutable, liquid even, and just as dispersed as he (4.15.26, 7.11.1–2). But this God proved too slippery to hold him – most dramatically in the wake of his friend's death, when he found "no rest" in his "phantom" God (4.7.12). A divinity that is itself subject to loss could not possibly protect human beings from loss. In search of certainty and security (8.1.1), Augustine therefore begins to solidify his understanding of God. As his mature and unified self asserts throughout the *Confessions*, the true God is "immutable" rather than changing (1.4.4), "being" rather than becoming (1.6.10), eternal rather than time-bound (1.6.10), simple rather than composite (2.6.13), spiritual rather than material (3.7.12), "immune from injury" rather than vulnerable (7.1.1), and single rather than multiple (9.4.11). It is in this uniquely substantial God, rather than his old oceanic phantom God, that Augustine hopes to secure his own "permanent solidity" (4.16.29). As I have suggested, however, this solidity never arrives. The very conversion that promises to return him to himself opens him out constitutively to others (both human and divine), a holy heteronomy that preserves, and one might say sanctifies, Augustine's vulnerability to loss. What, then, does this mean for the God whom the human self mirrors? In this final section, I turn away from Augustine's assertions about God and toward his experience of God – from the static oneness he posits throughout most of the text and toward the dark mystery he encounters in Book X: in memory.

It is only after the death of his mother, once he has become "what I am now" (10.4.6), that Augustine undertakes a sustained quest for God.[48] He gradually scans the whole cosmos, asking the earth, the sea, their creatures, the wind, the sun, moon, and stars, "What do I love when I love my God?" (10.6.8). Each of them answers, "It is not I" (10.6.9). Having searched the whole world, Augustine therefore turns to the only place left to look: himself. Rejecting out of hand the possibility that God might be found in his body or even his senses (10.7.11), Augustine dives all the way in – "to the fields and vast palaces of memory" (10.8.12).

Ultimately, it will be in these fields and palaces that Augustine's God dwells. It is therefore striking that the first thing we learn about memory is how *crowded* it is. The moment Augustine enters into it, a flood of images "pour out to crowd the mind ... leap[ing] forward into the centre as if saying 'Surely we are what you want?'" (10.8.2). Unsurprisingly, Augustine does not linger with the multitude that greets him at the gates of memory. Rather, "with the hand of my heart I chase them away from the face of my memory until what I want is freed of mist and emerges from its hiding places" (10.8.12). As it turns out, however, Augustine does not so much "dismiss" these memories; he asks them to get in line. With everything in its proper place, Augustine walks us through the chambers of memory in ascending order – from his base sense perceptions, through the events of his life, to the skills and ideas he has learned, to his feelings (10.8.13–10.14.21).[49] Examining all of these in turn, Augustine begins to marvel at what one might call memory's ability to make the absent present, for example, memory enables one to remember "red" or a tune in a pitch-black, silent room.

As Augustine works his way toward feelings, memory gets even more impressive. "What is going on," Augustine asks, "when in gladly remembering past sadness, my mind is glad and my memory sad?" (10.14.21). Stranger still, Augustine discovers that memory can remember itself. For I can remember times that I have remembered, say, a name or a book or a set of keys that I had forgotten. What this also means, of course, is that memory can remember forgetting. I can remember that I forgot my lunch, or my mother's birthday. I can even remember that I am a forgetful person, without neglecting to remember as much or canceling my forgetfulness as such. Augustine therefore entreats us to wonder along with him, *what on earth is the memory doing when it remembers forgetfulness*? He approaches the problem as systematically as possible: forgetfulness is the failure of memory. So in remembering forgetfulness, does the memory fail to remember? No; it actually *remembers* forgetting. Forgetfulness is present without causing forgetting – like red in a pitch-black room. And from the depths of astonishment, Augustine cries, "Who can find a solution to this problem? Who can grasp what is going on?" (10.16.24).

What we have reached here is a thick cloud of inscrutability at the heart of the Augustinian self – a failure of reason at the heart of reason. Unable to think, Augustine shifts to praise. "This power of memory is great, very great, my God. It is a vast and infinite profundity. Who has plumbed its bottom? This power is that of my mind and it is a natural endowment, but *I myself cannot grasp the totality of what I am*" (10.8.15; emphasis added). With this marvelously uncartesian exclamation, we are thrown back upon the opening chapters of the *Confessions*. There, we will recall, Augustine confessed to an unknown God that he did not remember – either where he came from or what happened to him as a child. Now, in this meditation on memory, Augustine confesses that memory *itself* is unknowable. This is to say (if we push "*memoria*" out to its full range of neo-Platonic meanings) that the power by which we come to know anything cannot itself be known. Augustine is "astonished" and "amazed" (10.8.15).

As I have argued elsewhere, amazement or wonder in the Platonic tradition is the philosopher's response to the sudden inscrutability of something she had thought to be self-evident.[50] What amazes Augustine is that there is a place within him that is totally inaccessible to the efforts of his mind, *yet it is his mind*. And it very nearly drives the man mad. It makes sense, he says, not to understand things outside oneself – the rotation of planets, for example (10.16.25). It makes very little sense not to understand what is closest to oneself. At the deepest core of myself, I am outside myself. And it is here that God must be. God must be in memory because memory is the innermost part of me that nonetheless exceeds me. And what is God but that unknowable force that inheres in creation yet exceeds it, who is in me yet outside of me, and who establishes me within myself by casting me outside myself?

Considering that memory is at once the unassimilable essence of himself and the unknowable dwelling-place of his God, it is remarkable that memory is not a point of stillness, oneness, or sameness for Augustine. Rather, this "awe-inspiring mystery [*quid horrendum*]" is a "profound and infinite multiplicity [*profunda et infinita multiplicitas*]. And this is mind," he marvels, "this is myself [*hoc ego ipse sum*]" (10.17.26). Perhaps as shocked as his readers, Augustine goes on to praise the multiplicity he "is":

> What then am I, my God? What is my nature? It is characterized by diversity, by life of many forms, utterly immeasurable. See the broad plains and caves and caverns of my memory. The varieties there cannot be counted and are, beyond any reckoning, full of innumerable things … I never reach the end.
>
> (10.17.26)

Having found these "innumerable things" to constitute the very essence of himself, Augustine asks, "What then ought I to do, my God? You are my true life" (10.17.26). But here, the transitive principle gets Augustine into a bit of a bind. If memory's "infinite multiplicity" is Augustine and God is Augustine, then God must be an infinite multiplicity. This is most likely the reason that Augustine suddenly resolves to "transcend even my power which is called memory. I will rise beyond it to move toward you, sweet light" (10.17.26). But the moment he tries to move from the dark plurality of *memoria* to the "sweet light" of God, he gets stuck. "What are you saying to me," he asks, and the answer seems to be that there *is* no beyond to memory. "As I rise above memory, where am I to find you? … If I find you outside my memory, I am not mindful of you. And how shall I find you if I am not mindful of you?" (10.17.26). In other words, God cannot be above or beyond the thick multiplicity of memory.

So God is in memory. But of course, the *Confessions* have been a work of memory all along: God has been the power fueling Augustine's efforts to recall God. It is oddly akin to the final scene in the *Wizard of Oz*, in which Glinda tells Dorothy she could have gone home all along, but "had to learn it for herself."[51] Like some ontological pair of ruby slippers, Augustine's memory has propelled this journey through the strange terrain of his soul, all the while containing the very thing he was looking for. Totally overwhelmed, Augustine cries out, "Late have I loved you, beauty so old and so new, late have I loved you. And see, you were within and I was in the external world and sought you there, and in my unlovely state I plunged into those lovely created things which you made. You were with me, and I was not with you" (10.17.38). Now at its face value, this passage seems to uphold the received reading of this text: finding God delivers Augustine from external things to internal things, from others to himself-alone.

As we have seen, however, when Augustine finally gets to himself, he is beyond himself, for there he stumbles upon the God who transcends him, who dispossesses him in the very gesture of establishing him.

Furthermore, we should remember what Augustine confessed at the outset: the memory that "is" him is not simply his own. Rather, it is supplemented, rewritten, and constituted in the first place by others. In other words, it is not just Augustine and God who exist in and as his memory; there are also *all those other others* – from the boyhood friend to the "continent" chorus of saints – populating this work of recollection. More radically, God is *in* all of it – and all of it in God.[52]

Frustratingly, Augustine does not go so far as to sustain what he has discovered. Rather, he reverts to the pursuit of the oneness that will become orthodoxy's inheritance. Recovering from his amazement and dusting himself off, Augustine declares with philosophic dispassion that "by continence we are collected together and brought to the unity from which we disintegrated into multiplicity" (10.29.40). And so we have returned to that world in which "continent" unity opposes the excess of multiplicity. But the very heart of this monodox world seethes with polydox potential. For the "continence" that "collects" us gives us over to the "multitude" she contains: the multitude for whom the One God renounced his sovereignty, his eternal immobility. And so our "unity" is not oneness, but something like a "tenuous we." A crowded, haunted collection, folded into the God folded into us, interrupted and undone by each other we desire, mourn, and remember.

Notes

1   J. Butler, *Precarious Life: The Powers of Mourning and Violence*, New York: Verso, 2004.
2   See, for example, Levinas's insistence that "I substitute myself for him, whereas no one can replace me," E. Levinas, *Otherwise Than Being: Or Beyond Essence*, trans. A. Lingis, Pittsburgh, PA: Duquesne University Press, 2002, p. 158.
3   Butler, p. 20.
4   Sigmund Freud initially distinguished the processes of mourning and melancholia, arguing that the former finds a replacement for the lost object whereas the latter incorporates it. S. Freud, "Mourning and Melancholia (1917)," in P. Gay (ed.), *The Freud Reader*, New York: W.W. Norton & Company, 1989, p. 584. A few years later, however, he discovered that the ego is only ever formed in relation to incorporated others. S. Freud, "The Ego and the Id (1923)," in *The Freud Reader*. Mourning, melancholia, and ego-formation itself are therefore all processes of psychic introjection. The others I love and lose constitute the core of what "I" become.
5   J.-L. Nancy, *Being Singular Plural*, trans. R. D. Richardson and A. E. O'Byrne, Palo Alto, CA: Stanford University Press, 2000, pp. 28–41.
6   Butler, p. 22.
7   Ibid., p. 23.
8   Ibid., p. 32.
9   While I am referring here to Butler's more recent articulations of the ecstatic self (in addition to *Precarious Life*, see J. Butler, *Undoing Gender*, New York: Routledge, 2004, pp. 17–39), she initially framed this formulation in more straightforwardly

Hegelian terms. See J. Butler, *Subjects of Desire: Hegelian Reflections on 20th Century France*, New York: Columbia University Press, 1987, p. 48.

10   Butler, *Precarious Life*, p. 24, original emphasis.

11   Ibid., p. 23.

12   Ibid., p. 41.

13   In addition to Butler's *Precarious Life*, a variety of reflections on the political alternatives to violent self-assertion can be found in S. Hauerwas and F. Lentricchia (eds), *Dissent from the Homeland: Essays after September 11*, Durham, NC: Duke University Press, 2003.

14   C. Keller, *God and Power: Counter-Apocalyptic Journeys*, Minneapolis, MN: Fortress Press, 2005; and L. C. Schneider, *Beyond Monotheism: A Theology of Multiplicity*, New York: Routledge, 2008.

15   "*Noli foras ire, in teipsum redi; in interiore homine habitat veritas*" (do not go outward, return within yourself; in the inward man dwells truth) cited in C. Taylor, *Sources of the Self: The Making of Modern Identity*, Cambridge, MA: Harvard University Press, 1989, p. 129.

16   See, for example, J. Milbank, *The Word Made Strange: Theology, Language, Culture*, Oxford: Blackwell, 1991, p. 207.

17   This sort of charge is usually issued in relation to the *Confessions*. It would have to change course entirely in relation to the very different picture of subjectivity that emerges, say, from the *De Trinitate* and *De Vere Religione*. In this work, the human soul is configured as irreducibly tripartite. The question then would be whether this trinitarian structure secures real relation to otherness, or whether it confirms the subject's inviolable interiority. Augustine of Hippo, *The Trinity.*, J. E. Rotelle (ed.), trans. O. P. E. Hill, Vol. 5, *The Works of Saint Augustine*, Brooklyn, NY: New City Press, 1991. See also J. Milbank, "Sacred Triads: Augustine and the Indo-European Soul," in *Augustine and His Critics*, R. Dodaro and G. Lawless (eds), New York: Routledge, 2002; R. Williams, "*Sapientia* and the Trinity: Reflections on the *De Trinitate*," in M. Lamberigts, B. Bruning, and J. Van Howtem (eds), *Collectanea Augustineana: Mélanges T. J. Van Bavel*, Leuven: Augustinian Historical Institute, 1990.

18   Augustine of Hippo, *Confessions*, trans. O. Chadwick, Oxford: Oxford University Press, 1991, 2.1.1, emphasis added. Subsequent references will be cited internally. Latin phrases refer to the Loeb Library edition: Augustine of Hippo, *Confessions*, J. Henderson (ed.), trans. W. Watts, Vol. 2, Loeb Classical Library, Cambridge, MA: Harvard University Press, 2006.

19   Keller glosses this fleeting image of divinity as follows:

> The divine ocean, the Infinite, permeates all finitude, utterly soaks and saturates the creation: God-in-All, All-in-God. To be sure, this imaginary of divine imma-nence subsides in Augustine's thought … Yet within this God-soaked topos of creation *the deity flows freely.*

C. Keller, *Face of the Deep: A Theology of Becoming*, New York: Routledge, 2003, p. 81, original emphasis.

20   W. James, *The Varieties of Religious Experience*, New York: Penguin Books, 1982, p. 189.

21   Ibid., pp. 169–70.

22   Ibid., p. 171. The passage actually reads, "*tolle, lege*" (8.12.29).

23   V. Burrus, *Saving Shame: Martyrs, Saints, and Other Abject Subjects*, Divinations: Rereading Late Ancient Religions, Philadelphia, PA: University of Pennsylvania Press, 2008, p. 112.

24   "The allurement of perfumes is not a matter of great concern to me" (10.32.48).

25   M. B. Pranger, "The Unfathomability of Sincerity: On the Seriousness of Augustine's *Confessions*," in M. B. Pranger (ed.), *Actas Do Congresso International as*

Confissões De Santo Agostinho 1600 Anos Depois: Presenca E Actualidade, Lisbon: Universidade Católica Editora, 2002, p. 209.

26   James, pp. 171–2.

27   See note 16.

28   Taylor, p. 129.

29   Augustine of Hippo, *Concerning the City of God against the Pagans*, trans. H. Bettenson, New York: Penguin Books, 2003, 14.11.

30   Ibid., 14.3.

31   J.-L. Marion, "Idipsum: The Name of God According to Augustine," in G. Demacopolos and A. Papanikolaou (eds), *Orthodox Readings of Augustine*, Crestwood, NY: St. Vladimir's Theological Seminary Press, 2008, pp. 169–70. J.-L. Marion, *God without Being: Hors-Texte*, M. C. Taylor (ed.), trans. T. A. Carlson, Chicago, IL: University of Chicago Press, 1991, pp. 106–7.

32   R. Descartes, *Meditations on First Philosophy*, trans. D. A. Cress, 3rd ed., Indianapolis, IN: Hackett, 1993, 2.24.

33   J. Butler, *Giving an Account of Oneself*, New York: Fordham University Press, 2005, p. 82, emphasis added.

34   Ibid., p. 36.

35   Ibid., p. 8.

36   See note 19.

37   James, p. 173.

38   Ibid.

39   See note 22.

40   K. MacKendrick, "Carthage Didn't Burn Hot Enough: Saint Augustine's Divine Seduction," in V. Burrus and C. Keller (eds), *Toward a Theology of Eros: Transfiguring Passion at the Limits of Discipline*, New York: Fordham University Press, 2006, pp. 206, 208, 214.

41   See Augustine's earlier confession with respect to his friend: "I never left his side, and we were deeply dependent on one another" (4.4.8).

42   While recounting his grief over his nameless friend, Augustine contrasts this sinful obsession with "true" friendship, which would "bond together those who cleave to one another by the love which 'is poured into our hearts by the Holy Spirit who is given to us'" (4.4.7).

43   Descartes, 1.18.

44   D. Bakan, "Augustine's Confessions: The Unentailed Self," in D. Capps and J. E. Dittes (eds), *The Hunger of the Heart: Reflections on the Confessions of Augustine*, West Lafayette, IN: Society for the Scientific Study of Religion, 1990, p. 113.

45   Keller, *Face of the Deep*, p. 72.

46   Butler, *Precarious Life*, p. 22. See notes 6 and 32.

47   Keller, *Face of the Deep*, p. 43.

48   On the strange turn the *Confessions* take after Augustine mourns Monica, see V. Burrus and C. Keller, "Confessing Monica," in J. C. Stark (ed.), *Feminist Interpretations of Augustine*, University Park, PA: Pennsylvania State University Press, 2007, pp. 120–1.

49   It is certainly remarkable that, of all things, "affectations" are last and presumably highest.

50   M.-J. Rubenstein, *Strange Wonder: The Closure of Metaphysics and the Opening of Awe*, New York: Columbia University Press, 2009, pp. 1–4.

51   Upon hearing this, Dorothy resolves, "if I ever go looking for my heart's desire again, I won't look any further than my own backyard. Because if it isn't there, I never really lost it to begin with!" Victor Fleming (dir.), L. Frank Baum, Noel Langley, Florence Ryerson, and Edgar Allen Woolf, "The Wizard of Oz," Metro-Goldwyn-Meyer, 1939.

52   "If they are not in you, they are not at all," 10.27.38; translation modified.

7 "Empty and tranquil, and without any sign, and yet all things are already luxuriantly present"

A comparative theological
reflection on the manifold Spirit

Hyo-Dong Lee

Pneumatology and the problem of one and many

One of the fundamental biblical affirmations about God is that God is Spirit (John 4:24; 2 Corinthians 3:19). The original biblical terms for Spirit, *ruach* and *pneuma*, have rich metaphorical connections to natural and material phenomena such as breath, wind, fire, water, energy, life-force, and winged creatures. At the same time, in close connection with other biblical terms often representing Spirit, *hochmah/sophia* and *dabar/logos*, they capture what are normally considered "spiritual" phenomena such as consciousness, language, intellect, reason, and wisdom.[1] Given that the latter phenomena presuppose a sense of focus, centered activity, and coherence, unity (or unicity) here becomes a prominent interpretive category for the notion of Spirit, reinforcing the monotheistic impulse of the entire biblical tradition, epitomized by the traditional rendition of the Shema – "Hear, O Israel: The LORD our God is one LORD" (Deuteronomy 6:4).[2] Yet the natural and material connections of Spirit contextualize and spatio-temporally "incarnate" its connotation of unified activity as the reflective, interpretive, passionate, and vital responses of a self to its relational environment. The biblical idea of Spirit – and, by implication, the biblical idea of God – can therefore be adequately explored only when the categories of unicity and unity, on the one hand, and multiplicity and difference, on the other, are employed.

It has been the function of the doctrine of the Trinity in Christian theological traditions to serve as a reminder that God is not merely One – that reality on both the metacosmic and the cosmic planes is both one and many, as the dynamic triadic structure of the "immanent" Trinity and the "economic" Trinity indicates. Especially in the Augustinian reading of the Spirit, the Third Person as the loving union of the First and Second presents a picture of the agency of Spirit that bridges one and many (i.e., embraces unity and difference, in order to produce the divine Whole as a harmonious, not discordant, patterning of divine relations).[3] However, this delicate pneumatological balance between one and many, rooted in the biblical pneumatological tradition, is obscured, by and large, in the Christian monotheistic development of the doctrine of Trinity. Under the essentialist–substantialist rubrics of classical Western thought, with asymmetrically binary and excessively dualistic constructions of one and many, transcendence and immanence, ideal and material, mind and body, spirit and nature, eternity and time, permanence and change, and substance and phenomena, the unity of God is seen as originary and self-subsistent while divine multiplicity is regarded as derivative and dependent. The First Person of the Trinity, God the Father, is understood as a unified and singular agency that eternally "begets" the Second Person, God the Son, who acquires a body in the unique historical event of incarnation. The being of Spirit is conceptualized as "spirated" or breathed into the world by the Father and the Son as their mutual relational love, one pole of which is originary and the other derivative.[4] Given that the Father is the unoriginate origin and the Son the eternally derived Word or Logos, the Spirit as their love comes to represent the ultimately – if not explicitly – subordinate mode of being of the essentially immaterial, self-sufficient, unitary, unrelated, impassable, unchanging, omnipotent sovereign Father who freely begets His divine counterpart and creates the material world *ex nihilo*.[5] A notable consequence of this subordination of the Spirit to the essentially disembodied and unrelated unitary God of classical Western theism is that the Spirit in the world is sacramentally confined to the Christ the incarnate Son and the church as his body, all in the name of their unity.

One of the important theological tasks today, then, is to recover the balance between one and many found in the biblical intuitions of Spirit and retained, however dimly, in the doctrine of Trinity. The question is how to articulate and affirm the dynamic, liberating, immanent, historical, earthly, fluid, processional, relational, and pluralistic character of Spirit's being in the world and its all-inclusive universal reach as the intrinsic being of God who is at the same time a unitary agency. Appeals have been made to a wide range of resources in answering this question, from the pioneering nondualistic constructions of spirit by Hegel and Tillich to contemporary liberationist, feminist, ecological, process, scientific, postmodern, and postcolonial thoughts.[6] In this chapter, I turn to the nondualistic traditions of thought within the so-called "Eastern" religions, in this case Neo-Confucianism.[7] More specifically, I propose that the Neo-Confucian notion of ultimate reality, the Great Ultimate (太極 *taeguek/taiji*),[8] offers a thought-provoking relational and dynamic vision of Spirit that is both one and many, and that in so doing can serve as a transformative critic of the bias toward oneness prominent in classical Western theism and show us a way to reconstruct the trinitarian doctrine. To argue this, I focus on the way two Neo-Confucian thinkers, Zhu Xi and Yi Hwang, interpret the famous Neo-Confucian dictum widely seen as a commentary on the symbol of the Great Ultimate – "Empty and tranquil, and without any sign, and yet all things are already luxuriantly present."[9] I argue that the Neo-Confucian debate on this dictum, especially the way it unfolds among these two thinkers, presents helpful conceptual resources for Christian theology in exploring the possibilities of the kind of Spirit-centered trinitarian panentheism that does justice to both the unifying and the pluralizing motif found in the biblical pneumatological tradition.

Zhu Xi: the omnipresent Great Ultimate

Neo-Confucianism uses the symbol of the Great Ultimate to explain the ultimate structure or "logic" of everything that is.[10] The symbol depicts the two primordial forces of the universe which, as complementary opposites, are intertwined and constantly in the process of turning into one another – i.e., the receptive or negative force (陰氣 *eum gi/yin qi*) and the active or positive force (陽氣 *yang gi/ yang qi*).[11] As the ceaseless dynamic union of complementary opposites that cannot stand independent of each other, the Great Ultimate expresses the thoroughly relational and dynamic yet at the same time fundamentally harmonious and unified character of the universe. In other words, the Great Ultimate points to the fact that, while reality is at root differentiated and plural, that plurality consists of harmoniously interrelated and unified multiplicity, not sheer, unrelated multiplicity devoid of unity.

As can be seen from the fact that the Great Ultimate depicts the "logic" of the relationship between the two primordial, constitutive forces of the universe, the symbol is first and foremost a cosmological symbol. It is based on the East Asian notion of *gi/qi* (氣) which is an idea for world-explanation ubiquitously found in East Asian cultures and religions.[12] The notion of *gi* is etymologically rooted in the words for "steam," "breath," or "wind" and is usually translated as "material force," "vital energy," or "psychophysical energy."[13] It is similar to the biblical *ruach* and *pneuma* in the sense that it retains much of its metaphorical roots in pre-Axial Age cultures, in this case the pre-classical, indigenous cultures of East Asia despite its sophisticated philosophical developments in Daoism and Confucianism.[14] *Gi* is what the universe is made of, the psychophysical "stuff" that constitutes whatever exists, both ideal and material, living and non-living, organic and inorganic. But this psychophysical "stuff" is to be understood not in terms of static elements but in terms of constantly changing creative processes. What appears to be solid and unchanging forms possessed by worldly entities are only temporary coalescences of psychophysical energy's own bifurcated and mutually complementary modalities of the receptive and active forces. One coalescence of psychophysical energy is constantly changing into another, as its balance of receptive and active energies shifts in an unceasing interaction and communication with the larger environment. One can witness this in the universal phenomena of birth, growth, decay, and death. Admittedly, the creative and transformative operations of psychophysical energy can be extraordinary, subtle, and mysterious as, for example, in the operation of human consciousness and imagination. In such cases, psychophysical energy is said to have become *sin/shen* (神) usually translated as "spirit."[15] Nevertheless, spirit here merely points to a mode of psychophysical energy's operation, not to an independent metacosmic substance or entity. In other words, nature is constantly becoming a spirit that is no other than nature's own wondrous creativity.[16] Furthermore, with notable indifference to the question of the radical contingency of the world, psychophysical energy is viewed as comprising a self-sustaining and self-organizing universe.[17] In sum, psychophysical energy, whose logic of operation the symbol of Great

Ultimate captures, is both one and many, transcendent and immanent, spirit and nature, mind and body, ideal and material, object and event, and *natura naturans* and *natura naturata*.

Despite a fundamentally nondualistic worldview shaping its cultural milieu, Neo-Confucianism does exhibit the tendency to place the creative–transformative power of psychophysical energy in the derivative and dependent position within a hierarchically structured binary relationship, resulting in a form of metaphysical or metacosmic transcendence. In explaining the workings of the Great Ultimate most, if not all, Neo-Confucian thinkers appeal to the analytic dyad of principle (理 *li*), which is also called "way" (道 *do/dao*), and psychophysical energy. The dominant philosophical tradition of Neo-Confucianism represented by Zhu Xi posits principle as the metaphysical ultimate, which is logically and ontologically prior to psychophysical energy and upon which the cosmic creativity of the latter is dependent. Principle, according to Zhu Xi, is a kind of dynamic ontological creativity giving birth to the ceaseless dynamic union of the complementary opposites of the receptive cosmic force and the active cosmic force.[18]

In contrast to the apophatic construal of the metaphysical ultimate as vacuity, emptiness, and nothing that exists in Daoism and Buddhism, Zhu Xi emphasizes the reality and rational determinability of this dynamic ontological creativity as dynamic "patterning," "structuring," or "harmonizing."[19] Rather than utterly undifferentiated and ineffable oneness, principle itself consists of a repetitive series of constantly harmonizing movements between the interdependently differentiated binary principles of the receptive and the active. In other words, the Great Ultimate is the symbol not only of psychophysical energy but also of principle.[20] The symbol of Great Ultimate here functions for Zhu Xi as the single interpretive lens through which the two levels of the same reality are read. On the cosmic level, it symbolizes the fundamental workings of psychophysical energy constituting the universe, while on the metacosmic or ontological level, it points to the very ground and "logic" of the movements of psychophysical energy, that which makes psychophysical energy move the way it moves, which is no other than principle.[21] In this sense, the Great Ultimate represents not only the unity of the differentiated binaries of the receptive and the active but also the unity of the metacosmic and the cosmic, of principle and psychophysical energy. Zhu Xi expresses this insight by affirming that the Great Ultimate is everywhere, in every single being or process in the world.[22] In this way, Zhu Xi's reading of the Great Ultimate reinforces the fundamentally nondualistic thrust of East Asian thought in general.

But precisely in what manner is the Great Ultimate present everywhere, in every single thing or process in the world? As has been indicated, on the one hand individual thing-processes are what they are because they are each endowed with their principles, their individually unique patterning of the receptive and active forces that enable them to be harmonies (和 *hwa/he*) and constitute their respective natures (性 *seong/xing*). The Great Ultimate, on the other hand, represents the one Principle or Harmony, i.e., the shared "logic" of such diversely harmonious patternings of multiplicity that give rise to the thing-processes of the world.[23] It is, in this sense, somewhat similar to Plato's Idea of the Good, the Idea of perfection in which all the individually perfect ideas participate.²⁴ Zhu Xi employs the Buddhist metaphor of the moon and its many reflections to make the point: while there is only one moon in the sky, when its light is scattered upon rivers and lakes, it can be seen in many places. But that does not mean the moon has been split, as what is seen upon the surface of rivers and lakes is the moon in its entirety.²⁵

A question, however, remains regarding the precise relationship between the one Principle and many individual principles. While the images of the moon upon the surface of rivers and lakes are identical to one another, reflecting the same moon in the sky, the individual principles in the ten thousand thing-processes of the world are not identical to one another, even though there may be degrees of similarity among them. In order to explicate this relationship, Zhu Xi utilizes one of the key concepts in East Asian thought, namely, the substance–function (體用 *che-yong*/*ti-yong*) distinction. The substance–function distinction refers to the difference between the original state of a thing, its nature or potential to act, and the state after it has been activated or put into use in response to another within a relational context.²⁶ An important point to note here is that, for Zhu Xi, substance and function are interrelated and interdependent concepts, inseparable from each other and, strictly speaking, without either having logical or temporal priority.²⁷ For the sake of analysis, they can be isolated from one another and examined as abstractions, but in concrete reality they are indivisible.

Zhu Xi's deft use of the substance–function distinction to explain the workings of the Great Ultimate is well demonstrated in his highly consequential reading of the famous dictum of one of his Neo-Confucian precursors, Cheng Yi: "Empty and tranquil, and without any sign, and yet all things are already luxuriantly present."²⁸ The saying is meant, by Cheng Yi, to capture the gist of another of his famous sayings that expresses the thorny ontological problem of one and many: "Principle is one, but its manifestations are many."²⁹ Zhu Xi reads Cheng Yi's sayings as referring to the Great Ultimate, and renders an original interpretation of the Great Ultimate in terms of substance and function:³⁰

> The receptive force and the active force, [the relationship between] the ruler and the minister, the father and the son – these are all concrete things and affairs, what people do. They are with physical form, i.e., they constitute the differentiated assembly of the ten thousand figures of the world. All of these [things and affairs] each have a principle according to which they ought to be, the so-called "way" or the path upon which they ought to travel. It [principle] is what is without physical form; it is what is "empty and silent, and without any sign." *If we are to speak in terms of what exists without physical form, then that which is "empty and silent" is in essence substance; and its activation among concrete things and affairs is function.* If we are to speak in terms of what exists with physical form, then concrete things and events constitute substance, and the manifestation of their principles is function.³¹

According to Zhu Xi's interpretation of the saying, through the prism of the substance–function distinction, the phrase "empty and tranquil, and without any sign" points to the Great Ultimate as substance. When taken by itself totally in abstraction "before" its operation in the world, the Great Ultimate may be seen as an indeterminate and inactive One, the so-called Ultimate of Non-Being (無極 *mugeuk/wuji*) interpreted by Zhu Xi not as pure emptiness or nothingness but as representing the undelimited, chaotic, and non-concrete nature of the Great Ultimate.[32] As function or in concrete reality, however, the Great Ultimate is always already in the world, enfolding and unfolding into an infinite number of mutually differentiating and dynamically coalescing harmonies of receptive and active psychophysical energies. They unfold in relation to one another, as captured by the phrase, "all things are already luxuriantly present."[33]

What is notable here is that, although Zhu Xi posits principle as the metaphysical ultimate in the sense of dynamic ontological creativity or ground, he denies principle its own creative dynamism independent of that of psychophysical energy.[34] Principle is, here, allowed only an abstract status of ontological formal and final cause, to borrow Aristotelian terminology, which needs to be activated by the dynamism of psychophysical energy to be effective.[35] That is how Zhu Xi unites principle and psychophysical energy in a thoroughly interdependent fashion. He assigns to principle the status of substance, the potential to act, minus the "potency" of that potential and gives that potency over to the other, i.e., psychophysical energy, by whose power principle becomes functional. In this interdependent relation, principle as metaphysical ultimate functions merely as the ideal horizon of becoming for the cosmological creativity of psychophysical energy without itself actually being an agency in its own right. Principle can be called dynamic ontological creativity only insofar as it is inseparably united with psychophysical energy in concrete reality. In other words, principle as dynamic "patterning," "structuring," or "harmonizing," refers to principle as function, not to principle as substance.

Given that the Great Ultimate is the symbol of the dynamic union of differentiated binaries, strictly speaking it is only the latter half of the saying (i.e., the part pointing to principle as function in which "all things are already luxuriantly present") that can be properly and effectively represented by the symbol. Nevertheless, principle in the state of being "empty and tranquil, and without any sign," principle as substance, can also be represented by the symbol of the Great Ultimate on the strength of Zhu Xi's strictly interdependent reading of substance and function that firmly upholds the unity and inseparability of principle and psychophysical energy. In this way, by means of the substance–function distinction, Zhu Xi crafts a holistic vision of reality that is both one and many around the symbol of the Great Ultimate.

A question emerges here, however, casting a shadow of uncertainty over the ontological status of principle's multiplicity. In Zhu Xi's account, principle as substance is the indeterminate and quiescent One. It is only when principle is activated, when it is united with psychophysical energy, that multiplicity is introduced into it. If multiplicity is introduced into principle only when principle is activated by psychophysical energy, for which multiplicity is intrinsic, then does that not imply that principle is originarily and primarily one, and only derivatively and dependently many? There is an added force to this question, as long as Zhu Xi posits principle as the metaphysical ultimate in the sense of dynamic ontological creativity or ground that has logical if not temporal priority over psychophysical energy. Despite his use of the symmetrically construed substance–function relation, an undercurrent of ontological asymmetry is undeniable in his bestowal of logical and ontological priority to principle. Although Zhu Xi argues firmly against speaking of principle alone in abstraction, insofar as principle is the metaphysical ultimate, it is hard to dispel the suspicion that multiplicity belongs to principle only penultimately, only by virtue of its association with psychophysical energy. Given the presence of ontological asymmetry that makes psychophysical energy – and its inherent multiplying dynamic – depend for its being on principle, the possibility that principle's multiplicity may not be ultimate threatens the ontological status of multiplicity as such. When Zhu Xi's moral assessment of the differentiating and multiplying dynamic of psychophysical energy as the source of evil is taken into account, the derivative status of multiplicity is even more strongly implied.

Zhu Xi, however, does make allusions that seem to draw a picture of the Great Ultimate as multiple in and of itself, referring to it sometimes as the *sum or totality* of all the individual principles rather than the one Principle.[36] The most prominent reference of this kind goes like this:

> In general, the Great Ultimate is the unfathomable wonder of the original state; and activity and tranquility constitute the mechanism of its riding [psychophysical energy]. The Great Ultimate is metaphysical Principle; and the receptive force (*yin*) and the active force (*yang*) are physical implements. When looked at from the perspective of its [the Great Ultimate's] manifestation, therefore, activity and tranquility are not co-present at the same time, and the receptive and the active do not occupy the same place, yet the Great Ultimate is present everywhere. *When looked at from the perspective of its concealment*, it is "empty and tranquil, and without any sign," but *the principles of activity and tranquility, of yin and yang, are all already furnished within it.*[37]

In other words, from the perspective of the Great Ultimate in its "manifestation" in the world (i.e., as function), while each concrete thing-process has its own individual principle that cannot be mixed or confused with another, the Great Ultimate as the one Principle is always co-present with each individual principle in each thing-process, because it transcends the determinate concreteness of individual principles.[38] At the same time, however, from the perspective of its "concealment" (i.e., as substance), the Great Ultimate is undifferentiated and without movement, yet it nonetheless contains within itself the sum or totality of all individual principles. What this implies is that when each individual thing-process partakes of the Great Ultimate on account of its principle participating in the one Principle, all the other individual principles of all the other thing-processes of the world are co-present within each at the same time.[39]

Given Zhu Xi's appeal to the substance–function distinction, this exposition is somewhat confusing. The reason lies in the fact that when he makes the distinction between the Great Ultimate in its "manifestation" (i.e., as function) and the same in its "concealment" (i.e., as substance), he describes the latter as plurisingular, *both* one indeterminate Principle *and* the totality of individually differentiated principles. Does he mean that there can be found yet another layer of the substance–function distinction within the Great Ultimate as substance itself? Zhu Xi never says so and thus fails to clarify, and for an understandable reason: the substance–function distinction is not meant by him to be used solely on the level of abstraction, because for him principle (or the abstract potential to be of a thing-process) cannot be actualized without the involvement of the concretizing power of psychophysical energy. To speak of another layer of the substance–function distinction within the Great Ultimate as substance would not have made sense to him.

Because of the cloud of uncertainty hanging over the ontological status of multiplicity, Zhu Xi's account of the Great Ultimate makes us pause, its attractive holistic and nondualistic vision notwithstanding. It poses a problem for the present comparative–theological attempt to appeal to the conceptual resources of Neo-Confucianism to find a way toward a Spirit-centered trinitarian panentheism that pays homage to both the unifying and the pluralizing motif found in the biblical pneumatological tradition. Here I turn to another Neo-Confucian, Yi Hwang, and his reading of the Great Ultimate that deviates from that of Zhu Xi whom he regards as his intellectual and spiritual master and whose true intention he believes he follows. Yi Hwang's interpretation of Cheng Yi's saying restores to principle its own dynamism and agency, and in so doing makes it easier to affirm multiplicity as originary and truly intrinsic to principle's own being. Admittedly, it is not out of a concern with multiplicity that he comes to disagree with Zhu Xi. It is out of the what may be called soteriological concern widely shared by other Neo-Confucians, including Zhu Xi himself, but found in Yi Hwang with a much more "religious" tone, i.e., in an attitude of reverence and even worship. It is therefore imperative that this concern be examined.[40]

Yi Hwang: the manifold heart–mind of the way

For Confucians, the ultimate goal of human life is to become fully human, which is to become a person of *yin/ren* (仁), usually translated as "humanity," "humaneness," or "benevolence." According to Confucius, the humanity of human beings consists in the integrity of the self without guile and empathetic response to (or sympathetic understanding of) others, both of which are *sine qua non* of a harmonious social order.[41] In other words, humanity is an ideal of ever-expanding, all-embracing selfhood that is empathetic, open, and related all the way to the entire cosmos.[42] Zhu Xi identifies this humanity with the human nature (性 *xing*) universally shared by all human beings, and the human nature with principle as it is embodied.[43] As a matter of fact, Zhu Xi goes a step further to identify humanity with the other principle-endowed natures of all beings and processes of the world, which are understood to be no other than their ceaseless and harmonious creativity (literally "life-giving will [生意]" but also called "the fecund heart–mind of Heaven and Earth [天地生物之心]").[44] The ultimate goal of human life, human fulfillment, lies in achieving an empathetic and harmonious unity with the cosmos by participating fully in the universally and harmoniously transformative creativity of principle that is found everywhere and represented by the symbol of the Great Ultimate.

It is precisely here that the issue of principle's creative–transformative agency emerges for Zhu Xi. It is an accepted fact, for him, that everything in the universe consists of psychophysical energy. If the entire universe is made up of psychophysical energy, then whatever unity and commonality one finds in the world or deems achievable in it can be explained in terms of the communicative possibility of one psychophysical energy shared by all.[45] Many Neo-Confucians acknowledge that psychophysical energy, at least in its original condition of clarity and purity, does feature balance, resonating power, and communicative possibility. At the same time, however, psychophysical energy's own bifurcated modalities of receptive and active forces in myriad combinations and patterns give rise to the myriad thing-processes of the world. In other words, psychophysical energy is the source of difference in the world.[46] It is the principle of differentiation and individuation in accordance with which the one Principle (or the Great Ultimate as substance) becomes delimited and concretized into many actual creative patternings of psychophysical energy.[47]

The dominant tendency among the Neo-Confucians, including Zhu Xi, is to train exclusively on this latter observation and so deny psychophysical energy any unifying and harmonizing function of its own. They assign that function to principle, regarding it as never losing its original condition as one abstract unifying potential even in the midst of its concretizations into myriad actual patternings of psychophysical energy.[48] Furthermore, they view psychophysical energy as the source of evil in the sense that its excesses and deficiencies in differentiating and coalescing movements continually lead to a loss of the balance, resonating power, and communicative possibility characteristic of its original condition of clarity and purity. The loss of psychophysical energy's original condition gives rise to the kinds of psychophysical energy that are opaque, turbid, indolent, and therefore less open and communicative. The source of evil, which is understood as selfishness, is located in these non-resonating and uncommunicative kinds of psychophysical energy – the kinds of psychophysical energy that would obstruct the full realization of humanity as empathy.[49]

Seen in this way, human fulfillment requires a cultivation of one's psychophysical energy. The path toward humanity lies in resisting and controlling the excesses and deficiencies of one's psycho-physical endowment in order to transform it gradually into its original condition of perfect equilibrium. This makes one perfectly resonant with the "pulsation" of the human nature (principle) vibrating from within to creatively harmonize the self with the rest of the world.[50] According to Zhu Xi's moral anthropo-psychology, such self-cultivating moral agency resides in the human heart–mind (心 *xin*), which, as the most clear and responsive coalescence of psychophysical energy, possesses the extraordinary, subtle, and marvelously receptive and creative quality of "spirit" (神 *shen* or 靈 *ling*). As such, it is the seat of consciousness and the somatic vessel of principle as the human nature.[51] In the Neo-Confucian picture of the self-cultivation process, the most fundamental and initial activity of the human heart–mind consists in feelings and desires that are activations of the human nature by one's bodily psychophysical energy in response to concrete relational contexts. The heart–mind follows up on its initial affectational responses to the environment in the form of intentional deliberation and discrimination in order to oppose those feelings unbefitting the particular relational context (i.e., self-oriented and unempathetic) while nurturing those feelings appropriate to the context (i.e., other-oriented and therefore conducive to harmonious relations).[52] A continued exercise of rational discrimination, opposition, or nurture over the long haul, through trial and error, accumulates relationally correct psychosomatic judgments to such an extent that one's psychophysical energy is conditioned to spontaneously respond in a proper manner. It is in this way that the moral agency of the heart–mind transforms one's psychophysical energy into its original, empty, open, perfectly balanced, and perfectly responsive condition, allowing the human nature within to be activated to its full creatively harmonizing potential.

Nevertheless, Zhu Xi's denial of an independent dynamism to the metaphysical ultimate, or principle, presents a serious challenge to the moral agency of the heart–mind. The problem lies in the fact that the heart–mind itself is psychophysical energy, albeit of the most clear and responsive (i.e., "spiritual") kind. According to Zhu Xi's account, the moral agency of the human subject – which is precisely the activated human nature or principle within the heart–mind – can neither be activated nor act without the dynamism provided by the very thing that it is supposed to control by its activity, namely the spontaneous dynamism of psychophysical energy. If principle is only the a priori, abstract, and general values of "unity" and "harmony" made determinate in diverse ways by the delimiting dynamism of psychophysical energy, and not an independent agency with its own dynamism to shape harmonious patternings of relations, then human moral agency is in fact completely dependent on the power of psychophysical energy in order to be active. But, since Zhu Xi takes psychophysical energy solely to be the principle of difference and denies it any spontaneously unifying and harmonizing function, the reduction of principle to the status of ontological formal and final cause without any dynamism of its own raises a serious question about the effectiveness and reliability of human moral agency. Strengthening this doubt is the common Neo-Confucian observation that the vast majority of people are born with opaque, turbid, and indolent – i.e., unbalanced, non-resonating, uncommunicative, and therefore involuted – kinds of psychophysical energy to begin with, which makes the guiding beacon of principle in them all the more dim. Their self-transcendent moral agency largely falls under the sway of their spontaneously self-centered psychosomatic responses and fails to achieve the empathetic, relational, harmonizing, and solidary agency characteristic of the fulfilled human beings, i.e., the sages and the "superior persons."

It is out of such a concern with the effectiveness and reliability of moral agency, on which the ultimate dependability of the project of self-cultivation is premised, that Yi Hwang allows principle an independent dynamism of its own, conferring upon what has been merely a moral map the actual power to implement its directives.[53] When human agency fails, the project of self-transcendence is not lost, because the transhuman agency of principle is efficacious apart from human agency. In arguing for this claim, Yi Hwang makes the same appeal as Zhu Xi to Cheng Yi's saying, employing the same substance–function distinction but applying it in a variant manner at one crucial point. Unlike Zhu Xi, who sees principle's function only in its union with and activation by psychophysical energy, Yi Hwang envisions principle's "own" function without psychophysical energy's involvement:

> Principle has movement and rest. Substance refers to its rest; and function designates its movement ... There are two levels of substance and function. If we speak on the level of principle, the substance–function distinction is parallel to "Empty and tranquil, and without any sign, yet all things are already luxuriantly present." If we speak on the level of concrete things and events, the analogy would be the capacity of ships and carriages to travel across water and land on the one hand and their actual travels on the other.[54]

Yi Hwang agrees with Zhu Xi's reading to the extent that he also claims that the phrase, "empty and tranquil, and without any sign," points to principle as substance in abstraction from concrete reality. He adds, however, that the latter half of the saying, "all things are already luxuriantly present," also points to principle "before" its operation in the world. In other words, Yi Hwang argues that Cheng Yi's saying is meant primarily to describe both principle's substance *and* function on the same ontological, metacosmic level, apart from its involvement in the world via its union with psychophysical energy. On the level of concrete cosmic reality, by contrast, he explains both principle's substance and function always in reference to principle's union with psychophysical energy, in terms of a concrete thing-process' potential and its actualization.

The substance–function distinction, as it is employed to account for the workings of principle and psychophysical energy, therefore has two levels for Yi Hwang.[55] On the ontological, metacosmic level, substance and function both refer to principle in abstraction from the world. Substance names principle as the indeterminate and quiescent One "before" it has aroused itself, a kind of undelimited chaotic plenitude often called by the name of the Ultimate of Non-Being, while function designates principle in an active state, principle as the Whole enfolding and unfolding into an infinite number of potential harmonies. This implies that principle has the capacity to act on its own, to introduce movement, difference, and multiplicity without having to depend on the dynamism of psychophysical energy. Furthermore, principle's capacity to act is such that principle could even be envisaged as actually "producing" psychophysical energy, as implied in the following exchange between Yi Hwang and a student:

[Question:] Master Zhu says, "Principle is without feeling, intention, and productive activity." If principle is without feeling, intention, and productive activity, then I am afraid that it would not be able to produce *yin* and *yang*. [Huang] Mianzhai says, "To speak of the Great Ultimate producing *yang* and *yin* is like saying that *yang* and *yin* arise." Does this not reflect his profound dislike of attributing productive activity to the Great Ultimate?

[Yi Hwang's answer:] "In general, Master Zhu's reference to principle being without feeling and intention points to principle's original state of substance; its capacity to activate itself and produce, by contrast, is its extremely wondrous function. Mianzhai's explanation need not be like that, because principle has function in and of itself, and therefore spontaneously produces *yang* and *yin*."[56]

In other words, to borrow Aristotelian terminology again, principle can exercise efficient causality of an ontological kind in addition to formal and final causality. On the level of concrete cosmic reality, by contrast, substance and function both point to the operation of principle united with psychophysical energy. Here substance designates the nature or capacity of thing-processes to be the way they should or aim to be, which is no other than principle as "incarnate," while function names the actualization of that capacity in the infinite unfolding of differentiating and coalescing movements of the receptive and active psychophysical energies in relation to one another.

An argument can be made that, in recognizing principle's own capacity to move independent of psychophysical energy, Yi Hwang is not so much concerned about securing the ontological status of multiplicity as about principle's capacity to be an active and effective source of unity and harmony in the world. Nevertheless, the practical impact of his dynamic interpretation of Cheng Yi's saying is that change, difference, and multiplicity can be seen to belong to principle originarily, not derivatively. By a repetitive series of self-transformative and self-creative movements, principle spontaneously multiplies itself into many principles without relying on the differentiating dynamic of psychophysical energy that is devoid of unifying power and therefore morally ambiguous. This enables the symbol of the Great Ultimate to represent the whole of reality without reserve, since the metaphysical ultimate, the creative ground of all, is itself both one and many, a unifying and pluralizing force. This implies that, when each individual thing-process partakes of the omnipresent Great Ultimate on account of its principle participating in the one Principle, all the other individual principles in their potentiality are co-present to each thing-process – the insight confused in Zhu Xi because of his denial of a substance–function distinction that is based on principle's own dynamism. From among the infinite number of harmonizing possibilities presented to it by the plurisingular Great Ultimate, each thing-process actualizes a finite and determinate number of them that make it uniquely what it is in each moment.

Furthermore, Yi Hwang's affirmation of principle's own dynamism opens up a path toward something akin to panentheism within the rubrics of the Neo-Confucian worldview. This occurs in the way Yi Hwang applies his affirmation of metaphysical dynamism and multiplicity to the problem of self-cultivation. By conferring an independent dynamism to principle, he assuages doubt about the feasibility and ultimate effectiveness of the Confucian project of being fully human in face of the seemingly insurmountable human predilection toward self-ishness and discord. The human heart–mind, whose moral agency comes under suspicion due to its constitution by psychophysical energy, becomes more than human in Yi Hwang's account, as the human nature embodied within the heart–mind acquires its own power to implement its *telos*, i.e., the value of humanity as empathy. Without any involvement of the dynamism of psychophysical energy, human nature within the heart–mind activates itself and "issues" in the four "good" feelings of sympathy, shame, deference, and approval (or disapproval), all of which are diverse relational articulations of humanity as empathy. Given that these so-called Four Sprouts (四端 *sa-dan*) of humanity issue in response to relational contexts, for instance seeing a child about to fall into a well, they are always mixed in with and hard to distinguish from other feelings activated and carried by psychophysical energy within the same relational contexts, such as the Seven Feelings (七情 *chil-jeong*) of pleasure, anger, sorrow, fear, love, hatred, and desire.[57] Nonetheless, since the human heart–mind relies solely on the incarnate principle's own power to issue the Four Sprouts, they are in effect offspring of a *transhuman* moral agency, which Yi Hwang names "the heart–mind of the Way (道心 *do-sim*)."[58]

Because it is the human heart–mind that must deliberate upon and either oppose or act on these feelings of transhuman origin, the heart–mind of the Way or transhuman moral agency is not an entity separate from the human heart–mind or human moral agency – the two are nondual. It is simply that the psychosomatic responses of the human heart–mind to relational contexts have a more-than-human origin when those responses, as in the case of the Four Sprouts, are conducive to empathetic and harmonious patternings of social and ecological relations despite the human penchant for conflict and discord. Yi Hwang goes so far as to speak religiously – in a worshipful, reverent tone – of "Lord on High" (上帝 *sangje*) in reference to the transhuman agency of principle within the human heart–mind,[59] which in his view one can encounter via the practice of cultivation of "mindful-ness" or "reverence" (敬 *gyeong*).[60]

One can, here, see that Yi Hwang has taken Zhu Xi's Great Ultimate and turned it into a moral agency. The human moral subject finds itself in relational contexts, having always already responded spontaneously and psychosomatically in and through a welter of heterogeneous feelings, which may or may not help guide its action toward social and ecological harmony. Many of those feelings have issued from the activation of the human heart–mind driven by the dyna-mism of its own psychophysical energy, and are deliberated and acted upon by the same heart–mind. Some others, however, have issued from the transhuman moral agency of the Great Ultimate, which is no other than principle incarnate within the human heart–mind as the pluralizing and unifying power of empathy, although these feelings are also carried by the same psychophysical energy of the human heart–mind as others.[61] These feelings of transhuman origin are empathetic, other-oriented, and relationally appropriate psychosomatic responses to a variety of concrete situations. They emerge when principle's activation into a multiplicity of potential patternings of harmonious relations, which happens on the abstract, metacosmic plane, becomes actualized without distortion in the concrete cosmic reality of the human heart–mind.

Because they are various articulations of empathetic understanding, when deliberated and acted upon by the human heart–mind, they are all conducive to harmonious patternings of relations in specific local contexts. Moreover, precisely because these feelings articulate empathetic understanding despite the amazing plurality of their situational appropriateness, they all contribute to a harmonious configuration of an overarching socio-ecological whole. Perhaps the name Spirit may be given to this transhumanly "spiritual" (*sin/shen*-like) working of the "heart–mind of the Way." Especially when taking into account the prevalent Neo-Confucian tendency to identify humanity as empathy with cosmic creativity (the "life-giving will"), one could go as far as to identify the "heart–mind of The Way" with the "fecund heart–mind of Heaven and Earth," thereby giving the transhuman moral agency a truly cosmic reach and generative function. If one ventures to name such cosmic creative agency of the Great Ultimate "Spirit (*sin/shen*)," the Spirit envisaged here is both one and many, human and transhuman, ideational and somatic, just as the Great Ultimate is both one and many and embraces the cosmic and metacosmic planes of reality.

Such a Neo-Confucian conception of the divine Spirit is panentheistic in the sense that, while principle is a dynamic creativity logically and ontologically prior to psychophysical energy, this creativity is never active outside of that to which it has given birth. While principle has the capacity to activate itself without relying on the dynamism of psychophysical energy, it activates itself always in response to concrete relational situations. Principle as function on the metacosmic level, captured in Yi Hwang's interpretation by the phrase "all things are already luxuriantly present," refers to principle's natural capacity to move and to become many, its originary and potential manifoldness, not to the concrete actualization of that capacity or potential. Its actualization always comes in union with psychophysical energy in the form of the unfolding of the natural capacity of concrete things and processes in a web of relation. It is on account of this that the spiritual agency of principle, the heart–mind of the Way, is always found within the human and creaturely heart–minds, and is in that sense always related and embodied. The Spirit in this Neo-Confucian sense is never a disembodied agency that might crack open the door through which a dualism of substance, which the whole tradition has consistently fought to keep at bay, may creep in and gain a foothold. Consequently, this Neo-Confucian conception of the Spirit cannot be employed to construct a view of God as a creator who creates the world out of nothing in the classical sense of the doctrine in the Christian tradition.

A trinitarian panentheism of the plurisingular spirit

What can the Neo-Confucian conception of the panentheistic Spirit suggest for the Christian theological task of constructing a Spirit-centered trinitarian panentheism that honors both one and many as ultimate? First and foremost, the Neo-Confucian conception of the Spirit helps us deconstruct the monarchical formulation of the Trinity dominant from the classical period up to now. If we use the symbol of the Great Ultimate to represent the divine life of the "immanent" or preworldly Trinity,[62] the Father as the unoriginate origin can be thought of as the Great Ultimate as substance (or the Ultimate of Non-Being), while the Spirit as the loving power and efficacy of the Father can be re-envisaged as the Great Ultimate as function. A subtle shift takes place in such a reconception, for the Great Ultimate as substance, i.e., the indeterminate One, is not logically and ontologically prior to the Great Ultimate as function, because of the interdependent and symmetrical construction of the substance–function distinction.

In other words, the Spirit can be conceptualized as itself the unoriginate origin, the fountain and wellspring of all thing-processes that is fully alive and active in the present, and whose transcendence of the determinate past or whose creative openness and receptivity to novelty is captured by the notion of the indeterminate One. The Spirit's creative activity consists in unfolding *out* of the undelimited chaotic plenitude of the One *into* an infinite multiplicity of potentially harmonious or empathetic orders (principles or ways [*do*/*dao*]), to which the traditional doctrine of the Son as the eternally derived Word or Logos corresponds, albeit now genuinely pluralized. Of course, this conception of preworldly Trinity, the chaotic One – the plurisingular Spirit – many Ways,[63] is still an abstract though real notion. In concrete reality, there is only the economic or worldly Trinity, as principle is always already found united with psychophysical energy. The Spirit's creative activity, which enfolds and unfolds into infinite potential harmonies or "ways," always actualizes them in concert with the dynamism of psychophysical energy. It does so by unfolding the natural creative capacity of concrete thing-processes to be harmonies that are always drawn toward one another in empathy. The omnipresent Spirit co-presents an infinite number of harmonizing possibilities to each thing-process, which in turn responds (or fails to respond) by actualizing a determinate number of possibilities relevant to its own creative potential to become in a harmonious web of relation.

This reconceived notion of the Trinity can be fruitfully compared and contrasted with Hegel's idealistic and panentheistic revamping of the Western doctrine of the Trinity. Hegel's concept of God features the divine logical Idea which, when taken by itself in abstraction from the world, is the always-active universal One. This One consists in an infinitely repetitive series of unceasing dialectical movement to posit the other of itself (the particular), and reunite itself with the other – i.e., the universal with the particular – to produce the singular or individual as internally differentiated unities of multiplicity, "concrete unities" or harmonies. The Idea, in other words, is in fact plurisingular, as an incessant activity of becoming Harmony of harmonies. However, this repetitive (self-) creative activity of the Idea is not randomly or chaotically repetitive as there is an orientation toward ever greater complexity. In concrete reality, the infinitely repetitive series of the Idea's differentiating and reuniting movements in nature give rise to infinite multiplicity of thing-processes that are all "subjects" (spirits or *Geist*), i.e., concrete unities in varying degrees of complexity. These harmonies, in turn, weave themselves further through the differentiating and reuniting dynamics of the Idea into ever larger and more complex harmonies, until the logical Idea is turned into the Subject or Spirit (*Geist*). The Spirit is the name for the Whole that consists in the overgrasping (*übergreifende*) or mutual self-emptying and self-recovering relation between being and nothing, one and many, identity and difference, essence and existence, substance and phenomena, subject and object, spirit and nature, Spirit and spirits, and the divine and the human.[64] In that sense, the Spirit is an emergent divine subject–agency that, on the one hand, *precedes* the world as its dynamic and internally multiple ontological ground and, on the other, *proceeds* from the world as an emergent divine subject–agency that comes into being only as creaturely subject–agencies come into being intersubjectively, in evermore harmonious and increasingly complex relations to one another.[65]

The Neo-Confucian-inspired notion of the Trinity, proposed above, and Hegel's conception of the Trinity agree that the ultimate is neither One nor Nothingness but the plurisingular Whole or Harmony that precedes and grounds the universe as a dynamic activity of creating harmonies out of multiplicities. They also agree, at the same time, that in concrete reality, Harmony of harmonies as dynamic subject–agency or Spirit comes into being only in concert with creaturely subject–agencies or spirits that "incarnate" in a web of relation, which is the Spirit's unfolding into many potential harmonies. However, a significant difference lies between them on account of Hegel's notion of the logical Idea or the preworldly Trinity (which is the dialectical triad of universality and particularity and individuality, or identity, difference, and mediation). There is no analogy here to the Great Ultimate as substance: the Idea as indeterminate and quiescent One "before" it has aroused itself, i.e., a kind of undelimited chaotic plenitude that would point to the openness to transcendence and novelty of the Idea's creative activity. Certainly it can be argued that a chaotic plenitude is present within Hegel's conception of the divine life, as the logical Idea "posits" within itself its other, namely, the realm of indeterminate chaos of sheer particularity, which in concrete actuality is represented by the notion of "nature."[66]

Insofar as openness to self-transcendence and novelty is openness to what is other than the (present) self, one could argue that the logical Idea is creatively open and receptive to novelty. Nonetheless, since Hegel construes the other of the logical Idea as proceeding from or posited by the latter, there is a hint of ontological asymmetry that makes the immediate self-presence and self-identity of the logical Idea more ultimate than its openness to transcendence and novelty. The result of this asymmetry within Hegel's conception of the divine life is that his construction of the Trinity comes to lack the kind of symmetry between the apophatic and kataphatic – or between difference and identity – found in the substance–function construction of the Neo-Confucian-inspired idea of the Trinity proposed here.

Absent such a symmetrical construction, it is hard to explain how exactly the Spirit is an open infinity, not a closed totality, as Hegel himself declares at the end of one of his most famous works.[67] In other words, it is difficult to provide a compelling reason for the restlessness and refusal to be content with the status quo found in the constant "dialectical ferment" of the logical Idea.[68] The Hegelian conception of the Trinity, which is one of the most influential reworkings of the classical doctrine, can therefore be transformed beneficially in dialogue with the Neo-Confucian conception of the Trinity proposed here. By introducing the interdependently and symmetrically constructed substance–function distinction into the very heart of divine life *a se*, such a dialogical reworking can safeguard the key insight of the Hegelian conception, namely, that the ultimate is infinite activity of mediating one and many, i.e., the Spirit, while providing a needed conceptual clarification that enables a convincing affirmation of the Spirit's infinity. The kind of trinitarian concept that results from this dialogue will be able to strike a balance between the apophatic and the kataphatic by recognizing a depth in God while refusing to call that divine depth God's ground.[69]

The challenge of symmetry, however, also evokes one potential drawback in using the Neo-Confucian conception of the Spirit uncritically to construct a panentheistic idea of the manifold Spirit. In its present formulation, mainly drawing on Zhu Xi and Yi Hwang, it does not challenge the dominant Neo-Confucian refusal to recognize the existence of an intrinsically unifying and harmonizing dynamic in psychophysical energy. This results in a tendency to abject creaturely agency's dependence on the spontaneous dynamism of psychophysical energy as much as possible through the latter's devaluation. Those spontaneously emerging feelings that are not issued by principle – the so-called Seven Feelings representing ordinary, everyday emotions – are under a cloud of suspicion, because they are perceived as prone to lose the middle and to become either excessive or deficient, or unbefitting particular relational contexts. This wariness is abundantly evident in the Neo-Confucian opposition of "Heavenly principle" to "human desire" and the rigidly hierarchical social ordering of cultured male gentry as "superior persons" over women, the working mass of commoners, and nomadic "barbarians" as "inferior persons" unfit to participate fully in the work of harmoniously ordering the world.[70] What is thereby considerably weakened is the thought that the Spirit as human–transhuman agency may be understood as emerging "in concert with" many self-creative practices of somatic cultivation in relational contexts. The Spirit's creative activity that enfolds and unfolds into infinite potential harmonies is here in danger of turning into a dominating power rather than an "inspiration" (i.e., a "spiritualizing" lure and guide) for creaturely agents. A more interdependent and symmetrical construction of the relationship between principle and psychophysical energy, akin to the substance–function distinction, would give us a doctrine of the manifold Spirit that readily affirms the real plurality of harmonious socio-ecological configurations emerging from our embodied – racialized, gendered, sexualized, class-located, etc. – and therefore multiple agencies. Expounding such a vision, however, calls for another chapter.

With this caution in mind, I suggest that the Neo-Confucian conception of the panentheistic Spirit can make another significant contribution to the Christian theological task of constructing a Spirit-centered trinitarian panentheism. It suggests a promising nondualistic approach to explicating the precise relationship between creaturely agency and the agency of the Spirit, the problem of so-called divine action. To principle within the abstract, metacosmic plane of reality, the Neo-Confucian conception of the Spirit adds an independent dynamism that becomes efficacious only within the concrete context of principle's union with psycho-physical energy. In the realm of human agency, this means that the transhuman agency of the Spirit acts only "in and through" human agency. The Neo-Confucian conception explains this "in and through" by emphasizing what has been more or less sidelined in the classical Western, Christian tradition, namely the centrality of feelings in embodied, relational contexts for a theory of moral agency, be they human or transhuman.

Although both principle and human nature consist in the idea of harmony, that idea is active first and foremost as feelings in and among human agents. In other words, the transhuman agency of the Spirit influences human moral agency by presenting feelings of empathy to enact in relations rather than the idea of unity to which human agency must give assent. This means that the "logic" of the pluralizing and unifying operation of the Spirit, the very thing on which the differentiated unity of the Whole is premised, is first and foremost affectational before it is nomological as it unfolds in and through human agencies. And, precisely because it is first and foremost affectational, the circle of creaturely agencies in which the "logic" of the Spirit can be present in the full sense of the term expands far beyond the human realm. If the task of constructing panentheistic pneumatologies ought to involve an attempt to "incarnate" the centered activity of *hochma* and *sophia* in the material and somatic connections of *ruach* and *pneuma* as a series of reflective, passionate, and vital responses of an embodied self to its relations, then the Neo-Confucian conception proposed here has much to offer.

Notes

1   G. T. Montague, "The Fire in the Word: The Holy Spirit in Scripture," in B. E. Hinze and D. L. Dabney (eds), *Advents of the Spirit: An Introduction to the Current Study of Pneumatology*, Milwaukee, WI: Marquette University Press, 2001, pp. 35–44. See also the extensive analysis of the biblical meanings of "spirit" in P. C. Hodgson, *Winds of the Spirit: A Constructive Christian Theology*, Louisville, KY: Westminster John Knox Press, 1994, pp. 276–82.

2   I am using the Revised Standard Version.

3   For the Western, Augustinian doctrine of the Trinity, see J. N. D. Kelly, *Early Christian Doctrines*, rev. ed., San Francisco, CA: Harper & Row, 1978, pp. 271–9.

4   Ibid., p. 276.

5   Jürgen Moltmann has pioneered this trinitarian critique of classical Western monotheism. See his *Trinity and the Kingdom: A Doctrine of God*, trans. M. Kohl, Minneapolis, MN: Fortress Press, 1993.

6   Some examples are: Hodgson, *Winds of the Spirit*; E. A. Johnson, *She Who Is: The Mystery of God in Feminist Theological Discourse*, New York: Crossroad, 2002;

C. Keller, *The Face of the Deep: A Theology of Becoming*, New York: Routledge, 2003; P. Clayton, *Adventures of the Spirit: God, World, Divine Action*, Minneapolis, MN: Fortress Press, 2008; M. I. Wallace, *Finding God in the Singing River: Christianity, Spirit, Nature*, Minneapolis, MN: Fortress Press, 2005; S. V. Betcher, *Spirit and the Politics of Disablement*, Minneapolis, MN: Fortress Press, 2007; M. Rivera, *The Touch of Transcendence: A Postcolonial Theology of God*, Louisville, KY: Westminster John Knox Press, 2007; L. C. Schneider, *Beyond Monotheism: A Theology of Multiplicity*, New York: Routledge, 2008.

7   By "nondualistic" traditions I mean those that are neither monistic nor dualistic.

8   When the Korean pronunciation and the Chinese pronunciation differ for Classical Chinese characters or words of common usage, I put the latter after a slash. When a specific Classical Chinese word or text quoted is by a Korean author, I give the Korean pronunciation. When by a Chinese author, I give the Chinese pronunciation.

9   I use Wing-tsit Chan's translation of this saying. W. Chan, *A Sourcebook in Chinese Philosophy*, Princeton, NJ: Princeton University Press, 1963, p. 555. Unless otherwise noted, all the other translations from Classical Chinese are my own.

10 C. Cheng, "Reality and Divinity in Chinese Philosophy," in E. Deutsch and R. Bontekoe (eds), *A Companion to World Philosophies*, Malden, MA: Blackwell, 1999, pp. 185–93. For the historical origin of the notion, see J. Ching, *Religious Thought of Chu Hsi*, Oxford: Oxford University Press, 2000, pp. 32–7. The Neo-Confucian use of the Great Ultimate to name ultimate reality derives from a statement in Zhou Dunyi's *Explanation of the Diagram of the Great Ultimate* (*Taiji tushou*) in which the Ultimate of Nonbeing (*wuji*) appears to come before the Great Ultimate as the origin of all things: "The Ultimate of Nonbeing, therefore, the Great Ultimate (無極而太極)." The dominant Neo-Confucian interpretation of the text, represented by Zhu Xi, rejects a hierarchical reading of the relationship between the two that regards the structuring cosmic power of Dao as itself rooted in vacuity – the kind of reading probably intended by Zhou Dunyi himself. Reading the character as meaning juxtaposition ("and") instead of sequence ("therefore"), Zhu Xi argues that the Ultimate of Nonbeing merely names the indeterminacy of the Great Ultimate "before" its manifestation. Livia Kohn disagrees with Zhu Xi to assign the status of ultimate reality to Zhou's notion of the Ultimate of Nonbeing. L. Kohn, "Chinese Religions," in R. C. Neville (ed.), *Ultimate Realities*, Albany, NY: SUNY Press, 2000, pp. 20–1, 34, No. 20.

11 The binary of receptive and active includes soft and hard, cold and hot, dark and bright, etc. As David L. Hall's process interpretation suggests, *eum/yin* may also be construed as the data of the past actualized world (the objective immortality of actual occasions), while *yang* could be interpreted as an activity of integrating the data of the past into a novel event. See D. L. Hall, *The Uncertain Phoenix: Adventures Toward a Post-Cultural Sensibility*, New York: Fordham University Press, 1982, pp. 221–2.

12 K. Maebayashi, K. Sato, and H. Kobayashi, *Gi ui bigyo munhwa* (*A comparative-cultural analysis of gi*), trans. M. Park and H. Sekine, Seoul: Doseo chulpan hanul, 2006.

13 I will use "psychophysical energy" as the translation of *gi/qi*, although a more precise translation would be "psycho-bio-physical energy."

14 *Gi* is similar to the way *pneuma* was both material and non-material in early Greek thought. See Y. Yuasa, *Mom gwa uju* (*The universe and the body*), trans. J. Yi and H. Yi, Seoul: Jisik saneopsa, 2004, pp. 72–109; L. Zhang, *Gi ui cheolhak* (*A philosophy of gi*), trans. G. Kim, Seoul: Yemun seowon, 2004, pp. 37–44.

15 See J. A. Adler, "Varieties of Spiritual Experience: *Shen* in Neo-Confucian Discourse," in Tu Wei-ming and M. E. Tucker (eds), *Confucian Spirituality*, Vol. 2, New York: Crossroad, 2004.

16 Cheng, pp. 196–8.

17   M. E. Tucker, "The Philosophy of Ch'i as an Ecological Cosmology," in M. E. Tucker and J. Berthrong (eds), *Confucianism and Ecology*, Cambridge, MA: Harvard University Center for the Study of World Religions, 1998, pp. 187–207.

18   For the origin of the Neo-Confucian notion of principle in Huayan Buddhism, see Chan, pp. 407, 544. Although Zhu Xi insists on the logical and ontological priority of principle over psychophysical energy and the need to distinguish the two from each other firmly, he also emphasizes their inseparability in concrete reality, as is clear from the following statement:

> The so-called principle and psychophysical energy are definitely two different entities. But when looked at from the standpoint of things, the two are merged with each other and cannot be separated into their respective locations. This however does not hinder the two from each being one entity. When looked at from the standpoint of principle, before things existed, their principle had already existed.

The statement is taken from "Da Liu Shuwen (Reply to Liu Shuwen)," in J. Chen (ed.), *Zhuzi Wenji (Collected Literary Works of Master Zhu)*, Taibei: De fu wen jiao ji jin hui, 2000, Vol. 5, p. 2095 (hereafter *Wenji* – for citations from *Wenji*, I give the volume number followed by the page number). See also his reply to Huang Daofu's letter ("Da Huang Daofu") where he states, "Principle is the Way above physical form and the root from which all things are born. Psychophysical energy, by contrast, is the implement with physical form and the instrument by which all things are produced," *Wenji*, Vol. 6, p. 2798.

19   An interpretation of principle given by Don Baker in his *Korean Spirituality*, Honolulu: University of Hawaii Press, 2008, pp. 48–9.

20   Zhu Xi, *Zhuzi Yulei (Conversations of Master Zhu, arranged topically)*, J. Li Jingde and X. Wang (eds), Beijing: Zhonghua shu ju, 1986, Vol. 1, pp. 1–2 (hereafter *Yulei* – for citations from *Yulei*, I give the volume number followed by the page number). For Zhu Xi's kataphatic construal of the metaphysical ultimate vis-à-vis Buddhism, see *Yulei*, Vol. 6, pp. 2365, 2376. As mentioned, Zhu Xi rejects a hierarchical reading of the relationship between the Ultimate of Nonbeing and the Great Ultimate, arguing that the Ultimate of Nonbeing merely names the indeterminacy of the Great Ultimate "before" its manifestation. The Neo-Confucian rejection of Daoist and Buddhist "nihilism" comes from their concern that too transcendent an interpretation of the ultimate might lead to escapism, i.e., a metaphysical flight from the world. See Chan, pp. 464–5 and Ching, pp. 48–51.

21   Zhu Xi, *Yulei*, Vol. 6, p. 2374.

22   Zhu Xi, *Yulei*, Vol. 1, p. 1; Vol. 6, pp. 2371, 2374.

23   "The Great Ultimate is not a separate entity. It is present in *yin* and *yang* as *yin* and *yang*, in the Five Phases as the Five Phases, in the ten thousand things as the ten thousand things. It is [nonetheless] only one principle. Because of its ultimate reach, it is named the Great Ultimate," Zhu Xi, *Yulei*, Vol. 6, p. 2371. See also Vol. 6, p. 2372: "Question: 'How was it before anything existed?' Answer: 'There existed a shared Principle of all under heaven, not the principles of individual things.'"

24   According to Zhu Xi, "The Great Ultimate is simply the supremely excellent and perfect normative principle ... What Master Zhou called the Great Ultimate is the exemplary virtue of all that is good and most excellent in Heaven and Earth, in people and things," *Yulei*, Vol. 6, p. 2371. Fung Yu-lan compares this with Plato's Idea of the Good and Aristotle's God in his *A History of Chinese Philosophy*, trans. D. Bodde, Princeton, NJ: Princeton University Press, 1952–3, Vol. 2, p. 537.

25   Zhu Xi, *Yulei*, Vol. 6, pp. 2409–10.

26   Zhu Xi, *Yulei*, Vol. 1, pp. 3, 101. See also Zhu Xi, *Taiji Tushou jie (Commentary on the explanation of the diagram of the Great Ultimate)*, in K. Chen (ed.), Zhou Dunyi, *Zhou Dunyi ji*, Beijing: Zhonghua shu ju, 1990, p. 7 (hereafter *Tushou jie*).

27   The Neo-Confucian notion of the mutual interdependence of substance and function is encapsulated in the following dictum of Cheng Yi, an important predecessor of Zhu Xi: "Substance and function constitute one source; there is no gap between what is manifest and what is hidden." See Cheng Yi, *Yizhuan xu* (*Preface to the commentaries on the classic of change*), in X. Wang (ed.), Cheng Hao and Cheng Yi, *Er Cheng ji* (*Collected works of Cheng Brothers*), Beijing: Zhonghua shu ju, 1981, Vol. 3, p. 689. Zhu Xi interprets this dictum as follows:

> The meaning of "substance and function constitute one source" is that, although substance has no trace, function is already in its midst; the saying, "There is no gap between what is manifest and what is hidden," refers to the fact that what is hidden is present in the midst of what is manifest. Before heaven and earth come into being, the ten thousand things are already furnished – that is the meaning of substance having function within itself. Once heaven and earth are established, the principles [of the ten thousand things] also continue to be – that is the meaning of what is manifest having in its midst what is hidden.

   Yulei, Vol. 5, p. 1654. He says, "When speaking of *yang*, *yang* is substance, and *yin* is function; when speaking of *yin*, *yin* is substance, and *yang* is function," Zhu Xi, *Yulei*, Vol. 1, p. 101.

28   Cheng Hao and Cheng Yi, *Er Cheng ji*, Vol. 1, p. 153. As previously mentioned (note 9), I am using Wing-tsit Chan's translation of this saying.

29   Cheng Yi, "Da Yang Shi lun xi ming shu (Reply to Yang Shih's letter on the Western Inscription)," in *Er Cheng ji*, Vol. 2, p. 609.

30   See Zhu Xi, *Yulei*, Vol. 6, p. 2437, where he says the phrase "empty and tranquil, and without any sign" is none other than an explanation of "the Ultimate of Non-being and the Great Ultimate."

31   Zhu Xi, "Da Lü Ziyao (Reply to Lü Ziyao)," in *Wenji*, Vol. 5, p. 2186, emphasis added.

32   For his kataphatic construal of the Ultimate of Nonbeing, see notes 10 and 20. See also *Tushou jie*, p. 3, where he says,

> What is at the highest heaven [i.e., the Great Ultimate] is without any sound or smell, yet it is in fact the pivot of creative transformation and the root of the differentiation of all things. That is why Master Zhou says, "the Ultimate of Non-being and the Great Ultimate." It is not the case that there is the Ultimate of Non-being outside of the Great Ultimate.

   The Ultimate of Non-being, he adds, is "the very condition in which [the principles of] *yin* and *yang* and the Five Phases are dissolved into one another with no gap left between them" (*Tushou jie*, p. 5).

33   See also Zhu Xi, *Tushou jie*, p. 9. I borrow the metaphors of enfolding and unfolding from C. Keller's *Face of the Deep: A Theology of Becoming*, New York: Routledge, 2003, p. 206, where she speaks of the enfolding of God and the universe of each other as a state of chaotic plenitude, and of their mutual unfolding out of that chaotic plenitude as a process of delimitation (decision-making or "cutting"). Here I use the language of enfolding and unfolding to designate one indeterminate and omnipresent Principle that simultaneously unfolds into many principles on account of the delimiting power of psychophysical energy in concrete reality.

34   See Zhu Xi, *Yulei*, Vol. 1, p. 3, where he says principle is "without feeling, intention, deliberation, and productive activity" in contrast to psychophysical energy, which can "coalesce, congeal, and produce" concrete thing-processes. Principle is certainly in the midst of psychophysical energy's creative movement, he says, but without activity of its own. Zhu Xi is careful to interpret Zhou Dunyi's statement, "the Great Ultimate moves and produces *yang*; it comes to rest, and produces *yin*," in such as way to ensure that the Great Ultimate's "movement" and "rest" are understood as

referring to the *principles* of movement and rest, not movement and rest themselves which he assigns to psychophysical energy, *Yulei*, Vol. 1, p. 1; Vol. 6, p. 2373. See also Ching, pp. 29–30.

35   An analogy could be drawn with Whitehead's concept of the eternal objects in the primordial nature of God minus God's agency, i.e., without God's act of enabling their "ingression" into the process of concrescence so that they could become the initial subjective aim of actual occasions. See A. N. Whitehead, *Process and Reality: Corrected Edition*, D. R. Griffin and D. W. Sherburne (eds), New York: The Free Press, 1978, pp. 342–51.

36   In his *Conversations*, Zhu Xi makes the following statement: "The Great Ultimate is that which gathers [總 *zong*] the principles of heaven and earth, and of all things," *Yulei*, Vol. 6, p. 2375. Lao Siguang distinguishes between two meanings of *zong* (總), i.e., as "subsume" (總攝 *zong she*) and "comprise" (總和 *zong he*), and argues that Zhu Xi uses the term more in the latter sense, i.e., as pointing to the sum of all the individual principles, while criticizing him for being unclear and confusing on this matter. S. Lao, *Jung-guk cheolhaksa* (*A history of Chinese philosophy*), trans. I. Jeong, Seoul: Tamgudang, 1987, pp. 329–30. See also *Yulei*, Vol. 6, p. 2365, where Zhu Xi says, "The so-called Great Ultimate refers merely to the principles of the Two Forces [*yin* and *yang*] and the Five Phases. It's not the case that there is a separate entity which constitutes the Great Ultimate."

37   Zhu Xi, *Tushou jie*, pp. 3–4, emphasis added.

38   See also Zhu Xi, *Tushou jie*, p. 4, where he says,

> The subtlety of the Ultimate of Non-being is never absent from each individual entity … When it comes to the very condition of the Great Ultimate being what it is, which can first be spoken of as being without sound or smell, that is the way the substance of the nature of things is … But in the production of the Five Phases, what things are endowed with differs according to their respective psychophysical constitution; and that is the so-called "each has its one nature." "Each has its own nature" means that the entirety of the indeterminate Great Ultimate never fails to be present within each thing.

39   See Zhu Xi's comment in *Yulei*, Vol. 6, p. 2410: "Fundamentally there is only one Great Ultimate, yet the ten thousand things are each endowed with it. Furthermore, they each have one Great Ultimate in its entirety." The meaning of "one Great Ultimate in its entirety" is clearer in *Taiji tushou jie*, p. 5: "In general, to speak comprehensively, the myriad things unite to form one Great Ultimate; to speak analytically, each thing has one Great Ultimate. See also *Yulei*, Vol. 6, p. 2409:

> The saying, "Many and one are each right; small and large are [each] determined," refers to the fact that many are one, and one is many. In general, the unified whole is one Great Ultimate; but each single thing has one Great Ultimate.

Fung Yu-lan compares this notion of the Great Ultimate with the Huayan Buddhist concept of the Jewel Net of Indra or the *tathagata-garbha* (storehouse of the absolute), while recognizing the difference in that, while the Buddhist concept envisions within each concrete thing-process all other concrete thing-processes physically present, Zhu Xi's Neo-Confucian notion sees within each concrete thing-process only the *principles* of all other concrete thing-processes. Fung, *History*, Vol. 2, pp. 541–2.

40   The Neo-Confucian analogue to the Christian notion of salvation would be the ideal of self-cultivation aimed at being truly human. R. C. Neville, *Beyond the Masks of God: An Essay Toward Comparative Theology*, Albany, NY: State University of New York Press, 1991, pp. 115–26.

41   See Confucius, *Analects*, 4.15 (Chan, p. 27), where *yin/ren* is construed in terms of integrity (忠 *zhong*) and sympathetic understanding (恕 *shu*).

42   Tu Wei-ming defines the Neo-Confucian notion of transcendence as such. See W. Tu, *Confucian Thought: Selfhood as Creative Transformation*, Albany, NY: State University of New York Press, 1985, pp. 51–65.

43   For Zhu Xi's identification of the human nature with principle, see *Yulei*, Vol. 1, p. 67. See also his commentary on *The Doctrine of the Mean*, 1.1 – the alleged origin of that identification – in *Daehak Jungyong jang-gu* (*Collected commentaries on the Great Learning and the Doctrine of the Mean*), rev. ed., trans. with commentary by B. Seong, Seoul: Jeontong munhwa yeon-gu hoe, 2006, p. 82. For Zhu Xi's identification of humanity (*ren*) with the human nature, which can be traced back to Mencius, 2A6, see his commentary on the passage in *Maengja jipju* (*Collected Commentaries on Mencius*), trans. with commentary by B. Seong, Seoul: Jeontong munhwa yeon-gu hoe, 1991, p. 104.

44   "Humanity (*ren*) implies the spirit of life," Zhu Xi, *Yulei*, Vol. 1, p. 113. For Zhu Xi's identification of humanity with the "fecund heart mind of heaven and earth, see Zhu Xi, *Yulei*, Vol. 1, p. 111; Vol. 7, p. 2633. See also his "Renshuo (A treatise on humanity)," in *Wenji*, Vol. 7, pp. 3391–2.

45   An authority no other than Mencius has spoken about the growth of the "sprout" of humanity within humans in terms of the cultivation of one's psychophysical energy that expands it progressively until it comes to encompass the entire universe, i.e., until it becomes one with the "vast, flood-like *gi*" filling heaven and earth (2A2). See *Mencius*, rev. ed., trans. with an introduction and notes by D. C. Lau, New York: Penguin Books, 2003, p. 33.

46   See Zhu Xi, *Yulei*, Vol. 4, p. 1286. For a detailed account of the birth of the myriad thing-processes of the world from the creative transformation of psychophysical energy, see *Tushou jie*, p. 5.

47   For the various analogies used by Zhu Xi to explain this process, see *Yulei*, Vol. 1, pp. 58, 73.

48   Zhu Xi, *Yulei*, Vol. 1, p. 59.

49   Ching, pp. 98–101.

50   Zhu Xi, *Yulei*, Vol. 1, p. 69.

51   Zhu Xi, *Yulei*, Vol. 1, pp. 40, 85, 95. Zhu Xi acknowledges that non-human creatures also have heart–minds and consciousness, albeit without a capacity to deliberate upon feelings (*Yulei*, Vol. 4, p. 1431). Due to the partial and obstructed type of psychophysical energy with which they are endowed, they simply respond to their environment spontaneously without exhibiting the "spiritual" qualities of the human heart–mind. Their spontaneous psychosomatic responses, however, are in most cases conducive to harmony on account of the harmonizing principle present in them as their respective natures, although the kinds of harmony they manifest are incomplete compared to harmonies possible in human relations. *Yulei*, Vol. 1, p. 59.

52   See the succinct description of the Neo-Confucian moral psychology by M. Kalton in the introduction to *The Four-Seven Debate: An Annotated Translation of the Most Famous Controversy in Korean Neo-Confucian Thought*, trans. M. C. Kalton, O. C. Kim, S. Park, Y. Ro, W. Tu and S. Yamashita, Albany, NY: State University of New York Press, 1994, pp. xxii–xxv. For the relationship among the heart–mind, the human nature and feelings, see Zhu Xi, *Yulei*, Vol. 1, pp. 89, 92, 94–5. For the role of intentional deliberation (意), see *Yulei*, Vol. 1, p. 96. For Zhu Xi, desires are intensifications of feelings; and people have evil desires when their feelings become excessive and unbalanced to the point of being uncontrollable. *Yulei*, Vol. 1, pp. 93–4.

53   According to Michael Kalton, there was an evolution of Yi Hwang's thought over the course of his life away from his earlier, more strictly "orthodox" view. See his commentary in Yi T'oegye, *To Become a Sage: The Ten Diagrams on Sage Learning*, trans. M. C. Kalton, New York: Columbia University Press, 1988, p. 48.

54   Yi Hwang, "Sim mucheyong byeon (Regarding the theory that the heart–mind is without substance and function)," in Toegyehak chongseo pyeongan wiwonhoe (the

Committee for Publication of the Study of Toegye Series) (ed.), *Toegye Jeonseo* (*Complete Works of Toegye*), Seoul: Toegyehak yeon guwon, 1989, X, 41.17a–b, pp. 8–9, (hereafter *Jeonseo* – for citations from *Jeonseo*, I give the volume number in roman numerals, the book number and the page number in the traditional format, and then the page number in the modern pagination).

55   See J. Bae, *Han-guk yuhaksa* (*A history of Confucian Learning in Korea*), Seoul: Yonsei daehakgyo chulpanbu, 1973, pp. 94–5.

56   Yi Hwang, "Dap Yi Gong-ho munmok (Reply to Yi Gong-ho's topical questions)," in *Jeonseo*, IX, 39.28a–b, pp. 94–5.

57   Behind the rise of the Four Sprouts and the Seven Feelings, Yi Hwang sees principle and psychophysical energy each having a separate yet interdependent issuing function, as made clear in the following passage:

> And the Four Sprouts move in response to things, and in that sense definitely no different from the Seven Feelings. It's only that, as for the Four, principle issues them and psychophysical energy follows it; as for the Seven, psychophysical energy issues them and principle mounts it.

See "Dap Gi Myeongeon (Reply to Gi Myeongeon)," in *Jeonseo*, V, 16.32a, p. 63.

58   See "Seonghak sipdo (The ten diagrams on sage learning)," in *Jeonseo*, III, 7.28b, p. 48. Originating in the obscure phrase in the *Shujing* (the Book of History), "The heart–mind of the Way (*Dosim/Daoxin*)" became a widely used term among the Neo-Confucians to designate the human heart–mind fully enacting the human nature within, including Zhu Xi who wrote a commentary on the above phrase in the introduction to his *Collected Commentaries on the Doctrine of the Mean*. See *Daehak·Jungyong jang-gu*, pp. 73–4. My argument is that the common usage does not carry the specific connotation of Yi Hwang's use of it, i.e., transhuman agency.

59   "Seonghak sipdo," in *Jeonseo*, III, 7.31b, p. 50. Also "Dap Yi Gweng-jung (Reply to Yi Gweng-jung)," in *Jeonseo*, XIII, sokjip 6.6a, p. 56. He makes it clear, however, that he applies the name "Lord on High" to principle in a metaphorical sense, as a poetic way of describing principle's wondrous creativity that gives an appearance of someone in command ("Dap Yi Dal Yi Cheon-gi [Reply to Yi Dal and Yi Cheon-gi]," in *Jeonseo*, IV, 13.17a, p. 100). In this sense, he follows Zhu Xi (*Yulei*, Vol 1, pp. 5, 63), yet his conferral of active agency to principle puts the metaphor in a significantly more panentheistic light. On the religious dimension of Yi Hwang's philosophy of mindfulness, see S. Park, *Toegye Sasang ui Jong-gyojeok Songgyeok*, in *Toegyehak Yeon-gu Nonchong*, Vol. 9, H. Song and G. Shin (eds), Daegu: Gyeongbuk Daehakgyo Toegye Yeonguso, 1997, pp. 247–58; see also Y. Choe, *Toe Yul ui Yigiron gwa Segye Yinsik*, in *Togyehak Yeon-gu Nonchong*, Vol. 2, W. Yi and C. Yun (eds), Daegu: Gyeongbuk Daehakgyo Toegye Yeonguso, 1997, pp. 515–27.

60   Yi Hwang, "Dap Yi Suk-heon byeolji (Reply to Yi Suk-heon, addendum), in *Jeonseo*, V, 14.18b–19a, pp. 15–16. One important point to note here is that, for Yi Hwang, because principle is a transhuman agency it does not sit passively for the human–mind to reach it through the practice of mindfulness. Principle reaches out to where the heart–mind goes and meets up with it, so to speak. Here Yi Hwang makes a crucial point: when we speak of principle as having no feeling, intention, and productive activity, we are referring only to principle as substance. Principle's most "spiritual" function is to arrive at "ten thousand manifestations." If we deny this, he avers, we are in fact treating principle as a dead thing. See Yi Hwang, "Dap Gi Myeongeon byeolji," in *Jeonseo*, V, 18.31a–b, p. 111.

61   Yi Hwang, "Dap Yi Suk-heon," in *Jeonseo*, V, 14.35b, p. 24: "What is born of the materiality of psychophysical energy is called the human heart–mind; what originates from the mandate of human nature is called the heart–mind of the Way." See also "Dap Yi Gweng-jung," in *Jeonseo*, IX, 36.2b, p. 21: "The human heart–mind refers to the Seven Feelings; the heart–mind of the Way refers to the Four Sprouts."

62   I borrow the term "preworldly Trinity" from Hodgson, *Winds of the Spirit*, p. 151.

63   I have been inspired in this formulation by Yi Yi, who gives a triadic interpretation of the Great Ultimate as follows: "The 'Great Ultimate' is merely a forced name. Its substance is change (易 *yeok*); its principle is the way (道 *do*); and its function is spirit (神 *sin*)." This triadic formulation is originally by Cheng Hao (one of the Cheng Brothers), but unlike him Yi Yi applies the formulation to the Great Ultimate. See "Yeok su chaek (A treatise on calculating change [or divination])," in *Yulgok Jeonseo*, IV, 14.48a–b, p. 15.

64   Much of my reading of Hegel's logical "deep structure" of divine-creaturely actuality is based on Hodgson. See P. C. Hodgson, *Hegel and Christian Theology: A Reading of the Lectures on the Philosophy of Religion*, New York: Oxford University Press, 2005, pp. 6–12. See also *Encyclopedia of Philosophical Sciences*, §567–71, in P. C. Hodgson (ed.), *G. W. F. Hegel: Theologian of the Spirit*, Minneapolis, MN: Fortress Press, 1997, pp. 144–6.

65   This is a reworked version of Hodgson's "pneumatic Trinitarianism" (or "pneumatic Trinitarian pluralism"): "It may be perplexing to think of the Spirit as both the power of being that *precedes* the world and as an emergent power that *proceeds* from the world. Yet we must attempt to think this paradox. The power of being comes *into being* only in relation to what it lets be; it is an activity, a dynamis, not a static substance." "The Spirit and Religious Pluralism," in P. F. Knitter (ed.), *Myth of Religious Superiority: Multifaith Explorations of Religious Pluralism*, Maryknoll, NY: Orbis Books, 2005, p. 140. Given the deeply Hegelian provenance of Hodgson's theology, I believe this particular panentheistic conception of the Spirit also works well for interpreting Hegel's own trinitarian thought.

66   G. W. F. Hegel, *The Encyclopaedia Logic: Part I of the Encyclopaedia of Philosophical Sciences with the Zusätze*, trans. T. F. Geraets, W. A. Suchting and H. S. Harris, Indianapolis, IL: Hackett, 1991, p. 307 (§244). See also *Encyclopedia*, §574–7, in *Theologian of the Spirit*, pp. 152–3.

67   G. W. F. Hegel, *Phenomenology of Spirit*, trans. A. V. Miller, Oxford: Oxford University Press, 1977, p. 493.

68   Hodgson, *Winds of the Spirit*, p. 365 (note 5).

69   Here one may find an interesting parallel in Tillich's trinitarian conception. For Tillich, the "abyss" of God as the first trinitarian principle ("Father") is called the divine ground, and given the status of the power of being vis-à-vis the Logos of God as the second trinitarian principle ("Son") representing the meaning of being. The two principles are united (and actualized) by the third principle, the Spirit. See P. Tillich, *Systematic Theology*, Chicago, IL: University of Chicago Press, 1973, Vol. 1, pp. 250–1. It appears that there is no more ontological weight put on the abyss of God than on the other two principles in this trinitarian construction, making it somewhat structurally analogous to my Neo-Confucian construction. John Thatamanil suggests, however, that there may be a lingering substantialist conception underlying Tillich's attempted dynamic construal of the divine life, in which case the Tillichian Trinity becomes less of a parallel. See J. J. Thatamanil, *The Immanent Divine: God, Creation, and the Human Predicament*, Minneapolis, MN: Fortress Press, 2006, pp. 166–7.

70   Zhu Xi, "Da He Shujing (Reply to He Shujing)," in J. Zhu, Z. Yan and Y. Liu (eds), *Zhuzi quanshu*, Shanghai: Shanghai gu ji chu ban she; Hefei Shi: Anhui jiao yu chu ban she, 2002, Vol. 22, pp. 1842–3. See also Yi Hwang, "Dap Yi Pyeongsuk," in *Jeonseo*, IX, 37.28b, p. 54.

8 Faith and polydoxy in the whirlwind

Colleen Hartung

On the plains of Nebraska, the devastating power of wind and rain are familiar and feared. The extraordinary in the form of a tornado is an expected part of the landscape. Every spring as the storm clouds roll across the prairie, residents are reminded that they live their lives on the boundary between feeble attempts at order in the shape of seemingly sturdy houses and neatly planted rows of crops and the rule of chaos in the form of twisters, hail, flood, and drought. It really is a matter of faith for a farmer to put seeds into the ground every spring. It is faith for a family to build a home and a life on flatlands that offer little in the way of protection from the unforgiving, inevitable onslaught of the elements of nature. This practical faith that dares to face a whirlwind is not exactly a faith in the possibility of divine intervention or some ultimately benevolent outcome. It is a decision to plow forward in spite of ambiguity. This is a faith that takes on the everyday risks of living and loving in order to make a way in the context of the profoundly uncertain.

Polydox theologies foreground the multiple and the uncertain. They take seriously this deep-seated, embodied experience of indeterminacy. Faith from this perspective is other than a simple access to certainty as a mode of protection from the trials and disasters that threaten order and surety. It becomes more (and less) than a religious conviction that accepts the unpredictable tribulations of human life as evidence of the unknowable nature of God's ultimately compassionate designs. And it becomes more (and less) than a posture that gestures toward a naming of divine occurrence. With ambiguity foregrounded, individuals and communities, allied through presumed certainties that they have inherited or forged under the name of God, can find that their traditional foundations no longer support them. Traditional faith claims can founder and come up against a limit in the face of whirlwinds. Such disruption surfaces another possibility however, the possibility of an ambiguous, risky and life-filled conception of faith that holds loosely any alliances (Christian or otherwise) based on doctrinal certainties. In a polydox space, faith turns away from the absolute assurance of closed alliances and toward the outer edges of security in order to live courageously *within* indeterminacy. Here, indeterminacy is good news in that it makes possible a way that is open to something new – that is absolutely unforeseeable.

Taking up Laurel C. Schneider's challenge to assume a storyteller's posture that might heal "an estrangement between belief, imagination, story and credibility in the telling of Christian theology," I order this consideration of faith around a tale of ordinary, practical resolve and resilience in the face of a blinding whirlwind.[1] This is a personal story of making one's way in the midst of the extraordinarily uncertain where structures of surety fall apart. In fidelity to this story that attends to a faith that in the midst of ruin and revival does not make divine claims, I suggest the possibility of an opening toward a faith that assumes a sort of blindness and lives without certain assurance. Turned to the ambiguous, Christian polydoxy offers a space in which to think about a faith that might take place after all of our constructive endeavors reach their limit: a faith unhinged enough and ungodly enough to be surprised by some unexpected good news.

No news is good news

I turned 19 on May 6, 1975. That date has little significance for most people but in Nebraska it is remembered as the day a devastating F4 tornado cut a swath across ten miles of Omaha, the largest population center in the state. The storm caused over 1.1 billion dollars of damage in 1975 dollars. It ranks as the second most costly tornadic storm in U.S. history.[2] At the time I was a freshman at the College of St. Mary, directly in the path of the storm. Because of youthful negligence, my roommate and I sought shelter only at the very last minute. At that point the hallways were deserted and we were unsure about how to find protection when a nun in a full black habit appeared and said, "Children, follow me." We did as we were told and ended up in a tiny cramped cellar full of nuns praying the rosary. When the single bare light bulb in the room went out I thought, "Oh my God, I am going to die on my nineteenth birthday in a cellar full of praying nuns. What a waste." As it turned out the tornado crested the hill in front of St. Mary's and made a sharp left turn less than 200 feet from the front door of the college. Was it the faith of the sisters that turned the monster winds aside? Maybe but maybe not. Mercy Hospital at the top of the hill had taken a direct hit and it had had its own contingent of praying nuns and just half a mile down the road that ran in front of the school, the tornado took its first victim. Faith seemed to have little control over the chaos and devastation that was barreling through the city.

A picture showing my dormitory back grounded by the approaching massive tornado, hit the front page of the Omaha World Herald the next morning. The Herald was a statewide newspaper and I can only imagine how my mom and dad, who were 200 miles away, must have felt when they picked up the paper that morning. For several days after the storm, entrance into the city was blocked and there was no telephone service. When my parents finally got through to the main office of the school they were given the report that "yes" someone had seen me running around alive and well. Years later my mom told me that they figured that no news was good news: an extraordinary act of faith considering that it would have been five years that June since my brother had died of leukemia. In the process of my brother's illness, my parents had become familiar with what it was like to live life sliding back and forth across the boundary between order and chaos. They had experienced the futility of a faith that could be depended on to save their child; they knew the reality of cosmic injustice. And yet, they had faith: faith in the face of a newsworthy picture implying disaster that "no news was good news."

Making room for polydox faith

Polydoxy, a space of many opinions about belief within a body of belief, or alternatively a place of many faiths within a circle of faith, implies an openness to diversity, difference, challenge, and multiplicity. This story suggests an opening for a conversation about a faithful posture that makes a way in the midst of ambiguity without necessarily calling on the name of God. The question embedded in this possibility is whether the prefix "poly" can create an opening that loosens determinate alliances of faith enough so that we can discover room for a faith that is uncertain about and perhaps even allergic to the name of God. Such a faith is nonetheless open to the unforeseeable and so faithful in a theological sense. In this opening faith – a polydoxic faith – might find itself surprised and renewed in unexpected ways.

In relation to a mother's prosaic utterance that "no news is good news," I follow the intimate contours of a practical faith without the name of God that turns toward the undecidable and lives within the uncertain. John Caputo suggests that at the heart of the work of Jacques Derrida there is the theme of faith, perhaps even a driving passion of faith that turns about the logic of the *sans* (without) as in a faith without God.[3] Derrida's pursuit of the *sans* provides language that makes a faith without God, that is open to what is wholly other, theoretically intelligible. I lean on his thinking of religion without religion as I make my way along the polydox opening that this tale of faith suggests. Along the way, I have collected some insights – blindness, embrace, and courage – from three contemporary theologians (all of whom are also included in this volume) that, taken together, can fund a meaningful concept of polydox faith in a world of actual flux and challenge.

An experiential confession of blindness

Theology does not have to assume a God or divinity to be theological, but Laurel Schneider admits to that assumption in her own thinking. More specifically, she presumes an intentional reality that comes to human experience, a reality that far transcends whatever we humans could create for ourselves. She describes this as "a reality that intentionally tends toward … us and the world."[4] "The Divine," "divinity," "God," these are words that point, albeit provisionally, to the experience of the real, to that which comes into presence beyond any scripts of totality we could suggest for the world or for God. Such intentionality on the part of something called "God" typically describes conventional ideas of faith in a deity who controls whirlwinds, intends them for some purpose beyond human understanding, but who also is expected to protect, or even save, the faithful from their destructive force. In contrast, Schneider argues for an intentionality that does not guarantee safety from the forces of worldly being and for theological constructions of God that do not attempt to deny the incomprehensible fragility and "impossible exchange" of human life.[5]

It is, however, Schneider's emphasis on a logic of multiplicity and on experience (particularly her emphasis on experiential confession) that offers insight into this story of faith in the face of a whirlwind.[6] Here is a practical experience of dissonance between a conventional logic of the One that demands of and ascribes to divinity a responsiveness to the sisters' prayerful pleas for safety and the reality of the random quality of the devastation that either destroys faith, or requires a different posture from which to assume it.

The premise of Schneider's book is the occurrence of divinity beyond a "logic of the One" that can assure unilateral control over the world's becoming.[7] In the wake of her deconstructive project, she does not reject ontology. She rethinks it in light of the messiness and multiplicity of embodied existence. Working with a logic of multiplicity, she argues that the ontological markers that characterize divinity therein are also markers of embodied existence such as fluidity, porosity, interconnection, temporality, heterogeneity, and a-centered relation.[8] In other words, divine occurrence is known within or as ambiguous bodily experience. This is an ontological perspective that emphasizes vision and sight so that the ambiguity of embodiment – as the human condition – becomes a mode of seeing, or rather of what can be seen of divinity. Divinity comes to presence and occurs in the guise of ambiguous bodies and can be seen by those who have eyes to see. The story of a whirlwind is an occurrence of the ambiguous: it is a story of the safe and sound and of death and destruction right next to each other.

In such a context, Schneider argues for the realization of a mature faith that she states "could only be possible in the face of fragility."[9] Here, to face and to see the fragile is to realize divine occurrence as incarnation again and again. This is a faith that has "the courage to be physically present, to *be* in a place of hunger, violence, or despair" and to really see.[10] For Schneider, "the presence/s of the divine [is] available for encounter if we leave the scripts aside [and] are prepared to have our hearts broken by beauty, awe and the redemption of responsibility."[11]

This may be a posture similar to the aphoristic gesture of my mother who, in the context of this story, makes a confession of sorts: "no news is good news." This is an acknowledgment that resonates with Schneider's experiential confession because it speaks in the face of what is unspeakable. "No news is good news" does not explicitly gesture toward divinity. But I suggest that even without divine reference, it is a faithful response that, like an experiential confession, turned my mother toward the fragile, the fluid, and a making of room for hope. An experiential confession, in the context of Schneider's theology, names its object of faith. It is a confession toward a divinity that might go by many names. My mother's confession of faith is more homely, practical, and ambiguous. It is an aphoristic gesture of faith that appears to have no destination, no object of faith and yet it affirms. So what is the difference between a confession, a faithful response, that names God as the object of its faith and one, like my mother's, where the object of faith is an aporia, a "*sans*"?

On the one hand, Schneider's explication of a theology of multiplicity unabashedly takes its stand as testimony about and explication of the coming to presence of divinity communicated in the experiential confessions of embodied knowers (although this experiential confession is qualified by the metaphoric exemption which testifies that any confession is metaphoric in nature and not absolute[12]). In spite of the limited nature of human existence and the language within which we relate to each other, divinity overflows our limited boundaries and comes into presence – into the realm of experience. Faith in this context is a faith that sees the occurrence of the divine and makes a faithful confession.

On the other hand, there is the actual confession that "no news is good news," which hints at a certain blindness that might still be a provocation of faith. Seeing a picture of my dormitory backgrounded by an approaching F4 tornado on the front page of the morning newspaper left my mother in the dark concerning my well-being and brought her to tears. Blinded, by a picture and tears, she was left to feel her way. "No news is good news" is a folk remedy that allowed her to make a way within the ambiguity of this blind spot. Practical experience told her that it was probably a good thing to have heard nothing because "bad news travels fast." Yet such proverbial wisdom did not give her sight. It was only a space in which to wait, in a kind of apophatic faith, toward something that was yet nameless – toward what might come.

Michael Naas, a Derridian scholar, notes that in his book *Memoirs of the Blind*, Jacques Derrida attempts to think "belief or faith outside or at the limits of vision."[13] Derrida's question of faith, or at least one of his questions, concerns what might interrupt the vision and seeing that Schneider foregrounds in her theology. Caputo describes this interruption as the "inherent spacing and withdrawal that inhabits experience so that what we experience is never quite present, is always marked up and partially withdrawn, marked and remarked … Experience is always a matter of some faith."[14] Caputo suggests this as an interruption that leaves us always structurally blind, a little lost, and thrown toward the necessity of faith.

For Derrida there is a difference, that has to do with a critique of self-presence, between seeing and believing. From his perspective, believing or faith would be that posture or mode of proceeding in the world that realizes that knowledge about how to proceed is partial and as such one is always feeling or making one's way in the dark. This is not exactly a blind faith that would oppose knowing and believing, in which believing provides a privileged access to an absolute Truth or God. Rather this is a faith that pushes forward in spite of – or even because of – blindness. In this way, such a faith finds itself open to the surprise of what might come, to the possibility – perhaps the impossible possibility – of what "eye hath not seen nor ear heard."[15] Schneider's emphasis on presence and on seeing – "if we but have eyes to see" – considered from a Derridean perspective, might collapse this space between believing and seeing that Derrida attempts to keep open as a way of holding at bay a totalizing foreclosure that a too optical metaphysics of presence effects.[16] The space between believing and seeing is the gap, the abyss, or the aporia along which Derrida feels or makes his way.

Instead of an experiential confession of divine occurrence, what Derrida confesses is a conversion from a Judaism marked by assimilation (but still conditioned by faith in God) to a certain Judaism without God.[17] Yet, as John D. Caputo notes, in this space of conversion without God, Derrida remains impassioned by a God whose name he is always seeking. He takes up Augustine's question, "What do I love when I love my God?" but he finds he has no answer. So this is not a confession of the truth but a confession without truth. Caputo suggests that for Derrida, circumcision and, in a sense, confession, comes to represent the "cut from the truth … a cut from … the healing consolations of either a metaphysical or a religious Truth, capitalized."[18] This disorientation is a hallmark of human experience. We are all a little blind and "this is a blindness that cannot be remedied, a radical structural condition in virtue of which everyone is blind from birth … We never get out from under the textuality and structural undecidability of our lives."[19] Derrida realizes this aporia or blind spot as the passion of existence which provokes tears and prayers and is the very condition of faith.

My mother's confession of blindness and the failure of telephonic speech, writing, photography, and technology to give her assurance about her child's safety is an exemplary moment that illustrates the way in which the immediate or the real always eludes our grasp. And so we are left weeping, praying, and hoping, faithfully toward, we know not exactly what. Toward the safety of our children? Toward the hope that all is well, nothing disturbed, for a reproduction of the same? Yes, yes, of course. But in lieu of that, when no news becomes the realization of an uncertainty and a loss that is ruin, then what? Perhaps then through tears, faith puts one foot in front of the other, come what may. It feels a blind way in the dark for an impossible possibility that is a decision for and is a confession of life in the midst of, perhaps even because of, profound ambiguity.

The foregrounding of the ambiguous is something Schneider and Derrida have in common. Presence in Schneider's theology is experienced in or as the ambiguous nature of bodies. In her theology, this ambiguous experience of embodied knowers gives rise to faithful confession. This is a gesture that makes room for Derrida's suggestion of blindness as part of the structure of human experience, for a seeing that might admit to a little blindness. For both, ambiguity is the very condition of faith where faith is the decision to turn toward frailty, loss, and the possibility of the new and of life becoming. In a place of many faiths – a polydoxic place – this affinity creates an opening for a faith that is impassioned by blindness and confessed as an aphoristic testimony that could say "no news is good news."

The embrace as a surrender of arms

Mayra Rivera, like Schneider, also begins her constructive endeavor with a faith claim. She states that "the cosmos is inconceivable devoid of the divine life force … [and that it is] only within creation that the divine Other is encountered."[20] Creation – in particular inter-human relationality – is for Rivera the site of the divine–human meeting. In her project, this-worldly transcendence – part of the character of inter-human relations – is realized as a space of possibility where divine transcendence might take place.

Rivera's attention to relational transcendence, realized in the intimacy of embrace, adds a further dimension of clarity to the idea of faith that I am constructing from my story of uncertainty about a daughter's fate. Rivera states that "the other's transcendence manifests itself most dramatically where the system fails; where it cannot accomplish what it claims to do."[21] The relationship between a parent and a child is implicated in system-supporting processes that she calls "worlding and foreclosure," in a way that is similar to the dynamics in the relationship between the colonizer and the colonized.[22] These processes can and do find themselves exposed in instances of catastrophic failure. In the experience of my brother's illness, my parents realized the futility of systems that claim certainty: familial, medical, religious, and otherwise. The constructions they had adopted as the foundation of their lives were shattered. Rivera suggests that in the wake of such disruption, that which is not reducible to categories and to totalizing constructions might be realized. This wake is a space of possibility in which transcendence occurs.

In her postcolonial deconstruction of vertical models of transcendence, Rivera foregrounds the slippery nature of a relational posture that can make room for such a taking place. My story of mighty winds, a foolish child and worried parents confirms a relational juncture where we are afforded the gift of possibility. Stories like this illumine a choice that actually exists in the face of all experience. One choice is a rigid resistence to or negation of the ungraspable that can harden into relationships that appropriate and consume the other. But another choice is the realization of the ambiguous and fragile and so the possibility of a touch that is "capable of embracing without grasping."[23] "No news is good news" is a response that stands within the juncture between these poles and does not reject or foreclose any possibility. It contains within it the realization of the profoundly fragile and the persistent resilience of life. When my parents were finally able to pick me up from the devastated campus neighborhood a whole week after the storm, they embraced me furiously and then matter-of-factly packed my stuff into the car. They took me home, winding their way through the debris, only to send me on my way the next week to a distant summer job.

In the context of this story, faith most definitely has something to do with flesh and the space between intertwined bodies. My parents could have kept me close that summer; I was frightened enough to comply. But they had already claimed a realistic faith, forged by and in their love for my brother, that in the context of their relationship with me turned them toward life as uncertain, undecidable, and ungraspable. Their faithful response honored the space of difference between us and risked, again, the possibility of change, brokenness, and grief in order to set me aright, away from a paralyzing fear and toward an unforeseeable as well as risky becoming.

So a faithful gesture in Rivera's theology might be realized as or in a relationality that does not turn away from the uncertainties of life and flesh by reducing the other in its grasp but instead realizes a touch that evokes, in her words, "the possibility of the coming of the new."[24] Rivera claims, and perhaps one could say appropriates, this irreducible and categorically uncertain space of fleshly relationality as potential site for a taking place of divinity. Here faith as or in relation opens a space of incarnational possibility where, she says, the glory of God gleams in the flesh "as the manifestation of the intrinsic transcendence of creatures."[25] Both of my parents, after the death of my brother, let go of the name of God and yet in that release realized a faith that could and would, again and again, turn toward an unthinkable, unspeakable, ungraspable possibility – the death of a child. Yet this faith without the name of God is still an affirmative faith that refuses to give in to fear of loss and death, and so turns toward a risky embrace that opens a space of possibility, a space where the new might take place.

Both Rivera and my parents understand the price of faith as a turn toward undecidability. That is what they have in common but it is also a point of difference. Undecidability has a dual character for Rivera. There is the irreducibility of the flesh in the mattering of the cosmos, in the way in which a person, a thing or an experience is always more and less than a system defines it to be and there is an irreducibility that is underived: an originary source of difference that, she argues, is on the other side of *differance*.[26] Divine transcendence is how she names what is indeterminable and on the other side of *differance*. This is the source of the passion and paradox of faith. The faith of my parents, encrypted in the aphorism "no news is good news," makes no such distinction. It is a faith without nomination that clears a space for living in the context of nameless undecideability. It is a faith that might stay open to what is indeterminate and unnamed, to the intrinsic transcendence of creatures.

Rivera confesses, at the beginning of her project, that it was one of Derrida's deconstructive, disconcerting grammatical gestures – "tout autre est tout autre" (every other is wholly other) – that turned her attention toward the possibility of transcendence as a foundational characteristic of interhuman and divine–human relationality. In *The Gift of Death*, Derrida troubles the distinction that Kierkegaard makes in *Fear and Trembling*, between the religious and the ethical based on the absolute otherness of God. Derrida foregrounds the inherent transcendence of every one to every other. A neighbor is as inaccessible as God. Rivera identifies this challenge to philosophical and theological regimes of presence that would deny the transcendence of the other to the self as the impetus toward her reconsideration of transcendence.[27] For Rivera, transcendence is an interconnected realization of the wholly other as the ungraspability of human essence and the absolute irreducibility of a divine originary source of *differance*. The relational space between bodies is the potential site where God as Wholly Other might take place.

Derrida reads his own gesture of *tout autre est tout autre* differently. For him, it is a phrase that resists any definite meaning or translation and is meant to disrupt ontological, metaphysical, and theological constructions that might hold a wholly other in reserve as a divine source or origin. This is a cryptic saying meant to save, absolutely, the indeterminacy which is wholly other. He is suspicious of any theological interpretation or appropriation beyond this.

Caputo reiterates Derrida's disruption – *tout autre est tout autre* – but does claim a theological content for it, saying that "the name of God is the name of the wholly other, *tout autre*." But he goes on to say that the wholly other, *tout autre* is nobody's proper name, not exclusively saved for … any determinable faith. Indeed to a great extent it must be saved from them … Indeed it is absolutely necessary, *il faut*, to save the indeterminacy of the *tout autre* in order to keep it safe.[28]

Derrida himself is willing to recognize love in this cryptic phase. He describes this love as an "infinite renunciation which in a certain way surrenders to the impossible."[29] Caputo suggests that "to love is to respect the invisibility of the other, to keep the other *safe*, to surrender one's arms to the other but without defeat."[30] And here might be the opening that gives some theoretical substance to a faith that testifies to an indeterminacy that goes by no name.

"No news is good news" is a cryptic saying in its own right, but perhaps it could be read as a disclosure, as an opening that might make a space for love. Here love is a surrender of arms – economic, philosophic, pharmaceutic, and even theologic – employed to hold in check, but also to find (blindly) a way to welcome the often terrifying undecidability of what might come. Here the surrender of arms is an embrace (to borrow a metaphor from Rivera) without the benefit of technological or religious good news. "No news is good news" testifies to a moment when all systems of surety fail and the only thing one has left is surrender as an embrace. In Rivera's theology, faith is an embrace that prepares a place for the coming of the new. Derrida describes this preparation as love: a love that would surrender its defenses against the specter of what is unforeseeable. In the context of these faithful gestures, "no news is good news" can be read as the encryption of a preparatory movement that keeps a polydoxic space a little resistant to naming and open to a faith that would surrender its arms, embrace the impossible and realize "the possibility of the coming of the new."[31]

Courage as an uncertain bequest

Catherine Keller locates faith at the creative unfolding and enfolding edge of chaos. It is not a simple assertion of belief or a claim to certain knowledge but rather a sort of call to courage in the middle of the vast depths of divine creation. In *Face of the Deep*, she gestures toward the possibility of divinity as a "plurisingularity" or a "manyone".[32] She constructs a concept of this divine multiplicity as a tri-fold of complication, explication, and implication, manifesting a manifold creation. She describes this trinitarian *pli* as a rhythmic quivering at the margin between chaos and order where both God and world are realized. Here a faith that "approximates courage" turns us toward the story of a whirlwind once again, this time to consider the faith of a 19-year-old girl cowering in a cramped dark cellar where she regretfully anticipates her imminent demise.[33]

In Mark 4:35, in a fishing boat ravaged by wind and rain, Jesus identifies the cowering posture of the disciples as evidence of their lack of faith. Keller agrees, but in her reading of this text, the disciples' lack of faith is not, or at least not only, an expression of doubt; it is rather a manifestation of cowardice. This is a lack of courage that refuses to face fear and do what one might in the midst of raging winds.[34] It is possible that both Keller and Jesus are a little harsh on this point. The disciples' fear seems completely reasonable to me. Yet Keller's suggestive linking of faith with an approximation of courage also offers another important dimension to the possibility of a faith that can be understood as such in polydox terms.

When I emerged from that cellar full of praying nuns, at first I was amazed by our collective survival and then was quickly overwhelmed by the surrounding devastation. Everything looked oddly fragile, even those structures and people that had escaped unscathed. Everything seemed temporary and fluid amid the drizzle that followed the storm's fury. One could say that I adopted a new way of seeing in those moments, a new beginning of sorts. Yet, being 19 years old, I was soon preoccupied with the throngs of cute National Guardsmen who took up residence on the campus fields to stage their rescue and clean-up operations. Terror, as a visceral realization of finitude, quickly receded or dissipated like Keller's tehomic waves, back into a sea of possibility. But despite the resilient forgetfulness of youth, the fragile beginning-again that came with my emergence from the cellar left its imprint.[35]

That catclysmic encounter with a mighty wind stirred some oceanic depth that would and does haunt my midnight dreamings. Over time – in connection with the intricate web of relations that became my life – building waves of awareness turned all daylight certainties, over and over again, to dust. In hindsight, this experience was my own call to a sort of courage. And it remains a call to resist, in the wake of terror and shredded certainty, an ever more obsessive desire for mastery, order, and surety that tries vainly to stop the flux and flow of life. Following Keller, this call can be heard as a challenge to turn, fearful or not, into tehomic folding and the open-ended indeterminacy and unfolding of life. This is no easy feat. Nevertheless, with Keller I am suggesting that one key aspect of polydox faith is that it is akin to courage. For Keller, this is a courage that would turn us toward the fearsome edge of a fluid margin where both God and creation simultaneously create and are realized out of the deep and the flux "that is in God and yet not the same as God."[36] I would say that my faith, the faith of the woman that 19-year-old girl became, is less than this courage and maybe more than it as well. The tehomic rhythm of life, imprinted by a windy chaos, has, for me, eroded the name of God, leaving me with faith toward or maybe in – as in inside – a namelessness that is not passive and cannot be denied.

There is, however, a resonance between the faithful proceedings of Keller and my own faithful stumblings. We both resist the overburdened name of God as a marker for a theo-logic that might claim a masterful closure or debilitating dependency in the face of raging winds and tehomic surgings. Confronted by the indeterminacy that takes place at the fearful becoming edge between order and chaos, we both stay within the play of indeterminacy. We both assume faithful gestures that turn into rather than away from the tehomic rhythm of life as the realization that becoming life is fleeting and already, in its unfolding (one could say natality) oriented toward enfolding (one could say death).

For me, the tehomic rhythm of life has washed away any name that would underwrite faith with a destinal assurance. Yet this has not left me faithless. It has just left me without the assurance of the name of God and nervous about what other names

– like "life" or the "good" – I might be using as a tool of foreclosure. And so it comes down to a question of the name and the question of an alliance that would be forged in the name of God. Perhaps a faith with a little allergy to the name of God might loosen otherwise foreclosed and determinate circles of faith. This would mean that, in its polydoxy, theology risks a consideration of faith without the name of God.

Keller herself asks the question "What would theology be *without* theos?"[37] She poses it as a rhetorical question and so does not provide an answer, at least not directly. One possibility is that theology depends on the name of God, since god is its name. This gloss assumes that theological discourse can only be or is at least primarily about God, about who or what God is: an endeavor structured by a something to be known, seen, revealed, or "divined" as an unfolding–enfolding possibility.[38]

Derrida makes the same, or at least a similar, assumption about theology. Theological endeavors under the guise of Christian revelation result in determinable faiths that inscribe participants in a circle of responsibility that seeks closure by calling on the name of God. However, viewed from a certain perspective (which Caputo shares), the work of Derrida is not only about a deconstruction of the constancy, surety, and security that the name of God supplies, (constancy that, for Derrida, "is called by other names"[39]). Deconstruction is itself a form of faith that unhinges the destinal assurance of a determinate faith by testifying that the wholly other is wholly other, *tout autre est tout autre.* Here, the name of God becomes subject to what Caputo calls the "un-law of exemplarity."[40] Derrida says in *On The Name*, that

> each thing, each being, you, me, the other, each X, each name and each name of God can become the example for the other substitutable X's … A name of God in a tongue, a phrase, a prayer becomes an example of the name and of names of God, then of names in general.[41]

This is deconstruction as a form of faith that resists the determined, perhaps theological, momentum that has appropriated the *tout autre* under the name of God. According to Caputo's reading, deconstruction as faith is not interested in identifying the *tout autre* as the settled object of faith in order to "calm the storm or arrest the play in which faith takes place."[42] Rather, deconstruction as faith is an affirmation of the wholly other as wholly other, *tout autre est tout autre.* This is a faith that is impassioned by undecidability and a faith that says yes to what is unforeseeable. And by saying "yes," a determinate faith is unhinged, at least a little, keeping open a space of undecidability.

Caputo suggests that Derrida is also not interested in a deconstructive gesture that would judge the name of God and silence theological discourse. Rather, like Keller, he seeks to resituate talk of God within an uncertain space where the name of God would "tremble in the winds of undecidablility" or perhaps even be eroded by tehomic surgings.[43] Under the name of God, whatever theology says about inheritance or justice or love is always subject to translation or a recontextualization where God might be but an example of justice or justice an example of God. This uncertain space traces a logic of the *sans* that turns toward an undeciablility that does not know anything: that makes a way "*sans voir, sans avoir, sans savior*" (without seeing, without having, without knowing).[44] This is a faith that, without the assurance of a determinate religious conviction, is impassioned by the unforeseeable beyond the horizon of possibility.[45] Caputo notes that "undecidablility does not mean the apathy of indecision but the passion of faith, the urgency of forging ahead where one does not see" and one's alliances are not so determined.[46] The wholly other, *tout autre*, is not an object of faith for Derrida just as the tehomic chaos is no object of faith for Keller. Instead, the object of faith that can be called faith is without absolute determination. "What do I love when I love my God?" For Derrida, Augustine's prayer becomes his own confession of an undecidability that would be the very passion of his faith without God.

Keller is attuned to the fact that talk about God – theology – "has been growing uncertain for centuries."[47] Keller's theology of becoming has its own uncertainty foregrounded and its own enfolding in mind even as it gestures toward a "trinity of folds" that imprint the name of God on her constructive explication of the Deep. She ends her book noting that "tehomic icons ... take their divinity with a grain of salt." They unfold like waves upon the ocean only to be enfolded within a rhythmic repetition. She goes on to say that "out of the disintegration foam up other juicy beginnings."[48] This ending which suggests another beginning-again resonates with a faithful Derridean deconstructive posture that courageously turns toward the unforeseeable.

What Derrida is attending to is a question about what remains to be thought, or better, to be done when alliances of determinate faith reach their limit and leave us a little (or a lot) blind and lost. Here, at the limit is where Derrida finds the passion of faith. It is the passion that leaves him weeping tears that cloud his vision. And it is the passion that founds his writing. He suggests this as the legacy of faith that undergirds all faithful gestures and alliances, including those of Keller, Rivera and Schneider. But his is not a legacy of faith inscribed in a determinable lineage that might be Christian or Jewish or democratic. Rather this inheritance is a plea, or a prayer, or a voice that cries out in the wilderness when we are lost, cannot see where we are going and no longer know to whom it is that we should pray. This is a gesture that might be akin to courage as it weeps, prays, asks unanswerable questions and utters aphoristic uncertainties without seeing, without having, without knowing, *sans voir, sans avoir, sans savoir*. These are all courageous preparatory gestures that make room for a coming of the new that is not assured and always an undoing of one's world.

Faith: the good news of no news and the decision for life, love, and laughter

My mother's confession of faith, "no news is good news," is an inheritance of sorts, confirmed by the inescapable uncertainties of life. It is a confession that is suspicious of faithful gestures made in the name of God, although it does not deny them either. Instead, "no news is good news" resists gestures of faith that make light of a darkness, a blindness, and a grief that is the undoing of oneself and of the world over and over again. This is a legacy of faith that turns toward the uncertain and lives on even after a tehomic erosion of an assured faith in the name of God,

Religion, Science, Medicine, or Law. This is a courageous act of faith that says "yes" to an indeterminacy that takes place at the limit of constructive attempts to organize and insure life, and it surely resonates with Keller's call to courage. It is a practical acknowledgement of Derrida's faith in the blind that is impassioned by non-knowing and the impossible possibility of the arrival of something new. It is an affirmation of Schneider's faith in the fragile resiliency of embodiment as it leans into its own demise and anticipates an unforeseeable beginning-again. And here, for Rivera, is a faith that is an embrace without possession and without a determinable lineage that prepares a space for what is to come.

"No news is good news" is a practical bit of proverbial wisdom uttered in the blind that affirms what looks to be the impossible possibility of good news. Of course, I think it is right to say that when my mother spoke these words, she hoped that nothing had changed, that I was alive, safe, and sound. But in a sense everything had changed – again – the minute she picked up the newspaper that morning and saw a picture that left her and my father in the dark. In this context "no news is good news" can be read not only as negation but also as a gesture that is trying to find a way to live within the midst of a growing awareness of indeterminacy as part of the essence of the human condition. Unfolded in a certain way, it turns out that the good news might be that there is always the play of indeterminacy that is the stuff of daily living. One might call this the good news of living beyond (or at the limit) of a logic of the One, the good news of living within an embrace that surrenders its arms or the good news of living at a creative unfolding–enfolding edge of becoming. This is a good news that calls forth a weeping that provokes blindness and faith. And it is a good news that makes a place for the impossible possibility of a decision for life, for love, and even for laughter in the face of a whirlwind.

The story of a girl and a whirlwind, surfaces a response – a faithful response – that is a practical decision to plow forward in the face of ambiguity and to risk living at a disorienting boundary or fold. This is a faith before – but insight of – nomination and orientation that is not speechless; it says things and does things. In the words of a mother who can claim no certainty about her daughter's fate, this faith insinuates rather than claims. It holds on for dear life. Following the intimate contours of a story about faith in the face of a whirlwind, in the company of three polydox theologians and a philosopher of the *sans*, the possibility of a boundary faith – a faith that occurs when all constructive endeavors reach their limit – takes place.

Notes

1   L. C. Schneider, *Beyond Monotheism: A Theology of Multiplicity*, New York: Routledge, 2008, p. 111.
2   S. Hayden, *Omaha, NE – May 6, 1975 – Tornado*. Online posting, 2005, www.omaha5675.org (accessed 4 March 2010).
3   J. D. Caputo, *The Prayers and Tears of Jacques Derrida: Religion without Religion*, Bloomington, IN: Indiana University Press, 1997, p. xxvi.
4   Schneider, p. 11.
5   Ibid., p. 170.

6   Ibid., pp. 153–4.
7   Ibid., p. 1.
8   Ibid., pp. 10, 180.
9   Ibid., p. 156.
10   Ibid., p. 206, original emphasis.
11   Ibid., p. 207.
12   Ibid., pp. 153–5.
13   M. Naas, *Taking on the Tradition: Jacques Derrida and the Legacies of Deconstruction*, Palo Alto, CA: Stanford University Press, 2003, p. 120.
14   Caputo, *Prayers and Tears*, p. 322.
15   Ibid., p. 18.
16   Schneider, p. 206.
17   J. Derrida, "Circumfession: Fifty-nine Periods and Periphrases," in G. Bennington and J. Derrida, *Jacques Derrida*, Chicago, IL: University of Chicago Press, 1993, pp. 122–6, 153–7.
18   Caputo, p. 284.
19   Ibid., p. 313.
20   M. Rivera, *The Touch of Transcendence: A Postcolonial Theology of God*, Louisville, KY: Westminster John Knox Press, 2007, pp. 2–3.
21   Ibid., p. 114.
22   Ibid., p. 104.
23   Ibid., p. 138.
24   Ibid., p. 128.
25   Ibid., p. 138.
26   Ibid., pp. 36, 109–10.
27   Ibid., pp. 11–12.
28   Caputo, p. 48.
29   J. Derrida, *On The Name*, T. Dutoit (ed.), Palo Alto, CA: Stanford University Press, 1995, p. 74.
30   Caputo, p. 49.
31   Rivera, p. 128.
32   C. Keller, *Face of the Deep: A Theology of Becoming*, New York: Routledge, 2003, pp. 178–9.
33   Ibid., p. 140.
34   Ibid., p. 214.
35   Ibid., p. 227.
36   Ibid., p. 219.
37   Ibid., p. 172.
38   Ibid., p. 216.
39   Derrida, *Circumfession*, p. 155.
40   Caputo, p. 58.
41   J. Derrida, *Name*, p. 76.
42   Caputo, p. 64.
43   Ibid., p. 67.
44   J. Derrida, *Parages*, Paris: Galilée, 1986, p. 25.
45   Caputo, p. 333.
46   Ibid., p. 338.
47   Keller, p. 229.
48   Ibid., p. 238.

Part III
Relationality

9 Glory

The first passion of theology?

Mayra Rivera

Life is a luminous halo, a semi-transparent envelope surrounding us from the beginning of consciousness to the end. Is it not the task of the novelist to convey this varying, this unknown and uncircumscribed spirit, whatever aberration or complexity it might display?

(Virginia Woolf[1])

To convey the qualities of an elusive, luminous halo: this may be the aim of theology, as much as it was the goal of Woolf's fiction.[2] It is, indeed, what has led me to the image of glory. Not the blinding lights of its triumphalist counterfeits, the reflection of gold, or the glamour of celebrity, but a quality inseparable from life in all its fragility and ambiguities. Displaying both light and darkness, this halo is perhaps like the almond-shaped auras of Byzantine iconography – also called "glories."[3] It is the spectral luminosity of ordinary things, neither irresistible nor self-sufficient, but incessantly alluring. It is often barely perceptible, yet sometimes disconcerting – even terrifying. The apparent aberrations of its depictions do not diminish a theologian's zeal to convey its varying, hazy radiance. Drawn by passion to the glory that flickers in the midst of everyday life, theology speaks of its "unknown and uncircumscribed spirit." This is a spirit that cannot be confined to neatly defined theological concepts or categories. And yet theologians persist in our weak attentiveness, "resolute" (Keller) in our attempts to describe it, however inaccurately and distortedly. We seek, with feeble words and images to express the inexpressible, in a multiplicity of voices, languages, and genres.

An uncircumscribed spirit perhaps lured the words of Irenaeus of Lyon: "The glory of God is the human being fully alive." A celebration of these words lies behind the work of liberation theologians such as Elizabeth Johnson and Leonardo Boff, whose works express a passion for divine glory perceived in fully alive human beings.[4] Rubem Alves rewrites Irenaeus in his unapologetic theopoetics of the body: "The glory of God is found in happy people."[5] Perhaps we recognize the efforts to convey it also in Emmanuel Levinas's allusions to the "gleam of transcendence in the face of the Other."[6] These witnesses to glory are not expressions of writers who are distant from adversity. Quite to the contrary, they are the poignant confessions of those who have been touched by dreadful realities of injustice and cruelty: sexism, abject poverty, colonialism, genocide. Their statements are defiant; they implicitly challenge the assumed dichotomy between glory and vulnerability. Yet we may still ask, how can we celebrate wonder when even a cursory look at history reveals that systems of injustices expose the lives of some people to indescribable suffering, when claims to glory have so often been part of the very justification of unjust systems? Such allusions to human glory seem to have cast a long shadow of destruction and death.

The enormity of human injustice weighs on this exploration of glory – "*doxa*" – as I attempt to address the polydox character of theological witness. Injustice challenges me to attend to the vulnerability of life and leads me to seek concrete, material, fleshy images of the divine, for which I rely on biblical images of glory as earthy and elemental. Woolf's words remind us that too often we miss glory where it is the closest to us, when it is most familiar. Therefore, theologizing glory requires theorizing the earthy and elemental; it also means theorizing what makes encounters with glory possible and difficult, prone to failure or counterfeit. For that exploration, I cross the border into the realm of philosophy to ponder the related concept of wonder. I am assuming, tentatively, that glory is the event that lures us into the experience of wonder, which Socrates famously declared to be the first passion of philosophy.[7] But the distinction between these terms is hardly stable; philosophical descriptions of wonder, as we will see, often include the "objective" reality to which we are exposed as well as our "subjective" response to it. This argument thus necessarily moves between glory and wonder, for glory can only be conceived in relation to its effects on those who recognize it, who behold a transfiguration of the ordinary, those who open themselves in wonder.

This reflection is, thus, less about a theological position than about a theological attitude. Rudolf Otto's words about the numinous aptly describe the experiences of glory: it "cannot, strictly speaking, be taught, it can only be evoked, awakened in the mind" – or in the body? – "as everything that comes 'of the spirit' must be awakened."[8] Glory can only be evoked indirectly, through images that can never fully capture what, coming of an uncircumscribed spirit, materializes in multiplicity.

Semantic multiplicities

Even in the absence of the prefix "poly," the term "*doxa*" reveals an intrinsic multiplicity produced through iterative processes of cultural and linguistic translation. In its classical usage, "doxa" denotes both "expectation, referring to one's own opinion" and "reputation, referring to the opinion of others about oneself."[9] From these meanings emerge the well known usages of the term to refer to "opinion," "view," or "judgment." It is often noted that, because doxa is a function of perception and affect, philosophers regarded it as an inferior type of knowledge in comparison with the assumed universality of the *episteme*. Viewed as mere opinion, doxa was considered inadequate for philosophy – although perhaps not altogether absent from it. However, Judeo-Christian history complexified the sense of the term when "doxa" became the Septuagint's translation of the Hebrew "*kabôd*," in turn influencing the New Testament concept of glory.[10] Emil Brunner remained understandably surprised by the story of semantic intertwining.

When for the first time a translator of the Old Testament hit upon the idea of rendering "kabôd" by "doxa," a linguistic change took place which was of unusual significance. The Greek word began to be modified to an extent which cannot be exaggerated.[11]

In contrast to the strong cognitive qualities that define doxa in philosophical parlance, with implications for thinking and wondering, the meaning of "kabôd" arises in relation to more material, concrete images. Derived from "*kabed*," meaning "to be heavy," "kabôd" is associated with a wide range of sensible metaphors, the best known of them being luminosity and thick darkness, often represented by fire and clouds.

In Hebrew scripture, the glory of God is represented as ubiquitous in creation. "The whole earth is full of [God's] glory," proclaims Isaiah. "The heavens declare the glory of God."[12] It is perceived in wind, thunder, and floods: awesome and terrifying. Glory is also in the cloud that envelops the Sinai and the Temple, and the pillar of cloud or flame that accompanies the Israelites in the desert. It appears not only as extraordinary phenomena, but more often as the transfiguration of the ordinary. Even in cases where the allusions to glory are directly linked to theophanies, and thus considered as events of great consequence, depictions of glory maintain elemental, earthy qualities.

In touch with the elemental images of Hebrew Scriptures, doxa acquires different textures and shades. Contingent historical developments bring into semantic proximity a philosophical concept about thinking, and scriptural images for glory. The processes seem logical and yet the conceptual coincidences are startling. This "mysterious, almost incomprehensible word," as Brunner describes it, is an eerily appropriate (almost literal) example of what José Saramago says of all words in *All the Names*: "The sense of every word is like a star hurling spring tides out into space, cosmic winds, magnetic perturbations, afflictions."[13] The sense of *doxa* is indeed "radiating out in different directions that divide and subdivide into branches and branchlets" – reaching out indefinitely.

This wild polysemy – multiple in senses and sensibilities – is uniquely appropriate for a theology of the manifold. Thus my exploration does not aim to retrieve a univocal scriptural meaning of doxa at the intersection of Greek and Hebrew senses. Instead, it seeks to honor the term's complexity by keeping visible in doxa all of the associations named above – and thus its indeterminacy – and by attending to the cosmic winds and magnetic perturbations that afflict and lure us today. By reading polydoxy through kabôd-doxa, I seek to unsettle theological reifications of doxa and to quicken the relationships latent in it. I am intensifying tenuous linguistic relationships, following branches and branchlets to foreground connections that I deem crucial for a polydox theology: connections between what we know, what illuminates the things around us and what illumination obscures; between the proximity of touch and the opacity of flesh; between vulnerability and reverence; between thought and the earth. I thus regard polydoxy as a theological attitude that relates to thought, opinion, and praise, but also, more deeply, to the world's provocations and demands as well as to our affective responses to it. Such orientation necessarily gives rise to a multiplicity of voices, languages, and methodological gestures, yet polydoxy is more than a plurality of opinions or a collection of teachings in and of themselves. A polydox theology entails enduring attention and responsiveness to the glory that manifests itself in the world. It implies a "disposition and an activity" of passionate engagement, indeed of true com-passion, with the beauty and the pain, with the joy and the suffering of the world.

Compassion – an active receptivity – inflects a polydox theology's interpretation of "orthodoxy" ("right doxa").[14] Almost half a century ago, a first generation of liberation theologians understood that their ethical commitments demanded a courageous challenge to the privilege of orthodoxy. The "orthodoxy" they were concerned about had a reified meaning; it had become a synonym of merely "intellectualist" statements of belief. Liberation theologians argued that theology had often been obsessed with affirmations of "truth" at the expense of "doing the truth"; a new balance was needed, which they described as "orthopraxis."[15] As I envision it, a polydox theology presupposes liberation theology's challenge to the privilege of normative statements and, more importantly, it affirms the theological orientation that such debates imply. Faith, Gustavo Gutiérrez insists, is "not a simple affirmation – almost memorization – of truths, but a commitment, an overall attitude, a particular posture toward life."[16] Such a turn toward concrete, embodied sites where theology seeks to discern what is true and right – in relation – is at the heart of what I understand by a polydox theology. Yet this theological approach departs from the language of those early liberation theologies in that, while denouncing the idolatry of the *one* dogma, polydox theology also seeks to reclaim a scintillating, complex, relational, earthy sense of doxa.

The constructive task is not a simple one, for the world has seen and suffered much under the counterfeits of glory. Indeed all too often what has been proclaimed as glory is its very negation – traits and practices that numb our sensitivity to the spectral, luminous halo of life. Polydoxy challenges both identifications of "doxa" with statements of absolute, disembodied validity and depictions of glory as a quality of overwhelming power or spectacular presence that place glory on the side of might.

God, gold, and glory

A counterfeit of glory has lodged itself in the infamous trinity of God, gold, and glory, which is commonly used as shorthand for the motives of the Spanish conquest of America. In that history, glory is identified with the gold-thirsty imperial power, and wonder is associated with the fleeting curiosity of those who confronted strange worlds. Those moved quickly to subsume them under what was already known or believed by appropriating or destroying what they encountered.

Colonial attempts to make sense of the amazing features of the "New World" were informed by fantastic literatures of the time as well as by Christian mythologies. Images of a lost (but still real) earthly paradise and a zeal for establishing a utopian world colored the colonizers' encounters with the new land and its population.[17] But the glare of riches that the colonizers thought they could possess overwhelmed the delicate glow of life there. The movement of conquest was one of voracious appropriation and the results were catastrophic. The spectacular failures of conquistadores, settlers, and colonial powers to respond to the world they encountered, and the colossal destruction that conquest left in its wake revealed the very opposite of earthly paradise. The drive to conquer glory brought forth much deception and exhaustion, and Christian visions of glory are not untouched by such degradations.[18]

The sociopolitical dynamics of conquest cannot be neatly separated from the intellectual projects of the time of conquest, whether they are theological visions of glory or the philosophies of wonder. As Stephen Greenblatt argues, the theoretical conceptualization of the marvelous was not only the "intellectual background to Columbus and other early voyagers," but also its effect. "The frequency and intensity of appeals to wonder in the wake of [Europe's] great geographical discoveries of the late fifteenth and early sixteenth century helped to provoke its conceptualization."[19] The passion for intellectual questioning that infused early modern discussions of wonder is thus enmeshed in the "rituals of appropriation"[20] of exploration and conquest, which were in turn inseparable from greed and brutality. Such continuity between colonizing practices and intellectual production renders modern allusions to wonder and glory highly problematic for philosophers seeking now to deconstruct the colonial legacy. At stake is more than the recognition of historical complicity; it is more fundamentally a question of the inherent assumptions of modern epistemological and ontological frameworks in which theorizations of wonder are grounded. To trace these assumptions, I turn here to decolonial thinkers. I offer a very brief summary of a long and complex argument, which begins with the Cartesian ego.[21]

In his reassessment of modern depictions of modernity, Enrique Dussel has stressed the connection between Descartes' *ego cogito* and the ideal conquistador, the *ego conquiro*. Dussel argues that the *ego conquiro* precedes and sustains the *ego cogito*, and thus any decolonial project must deconstruct this modern construction of the subject. Nelson Maldonado-Torres extends this argument in the direction of philosophical method and ontology as they relate to the racialization of humanity. Descartes' certainty about the cogito is based on doubt or skepticism. "Skepticism becomes the means to reach certainty and provide a solid foundation to the self," Maldonado-Torres argues.[22] This movement from doubt to certainty also describes the formation of the *ego conquiro*. If the *ego cogito* doubts the world around him, the *ego conquiro* doubts the very humanity of conquered others. What Maldonado-Torres calls "Manichean misanthropic skepticism" is exemplified in the theological debates between Bartolomé de las Casas and Juan Jinés de Sepúlveda – known as the Valladolid debate – regarding the ontological status of the native people of the New World.[23] Whether we read the relationship between the Valladolid debate and Descartes genealogically or contrapuntally, and regardless of its official outcome, it was significant in reflecting and reinforcing the doubts about the scope of humanity. The process of doubting-on-the-way-to-certainty thus begins not in Descartes' studio, but in America, from whence it travelled back to Europe for philosophical rendering. "[A] certain skepticism regarding the humanity of the enslaved and colonized sub-others stands at the background of the Cartesian certainties and his methodic doubt."[24]

The problematics of conquest are thus brought to bear on Cartesian doubt and placed at the very heart of modern intellectual inquiry. Furthermore, the

> Cartesian idea about the division between *res cogitans* and *res extensa* … which translates into a divide between the mind and the body or between the human and nature is preceded and even, one has the temptation to say, to some extent built upon an anthropological colonial difference between the *ego conquistador* (conqueror) and the *ego conquistado* (conquered).[25]

This difference is not merely epistemological, but also a potent ontological division.

The colonial difference creates a sphere of "damnation, life in hell," where horror becomes naturalized through the idea of race. In the eyes of colonial powers, human beings marked as *damné* lack "ontological weight."[26] For those so marked, death is not an individualizing factor – as it was in Martin Heidegger's reflections about *Dasein* – but part of their daily reality. For this reason, Maldonado-Torres argues that decoloniality cannot emerge "through an encounter with one's own mortality, but from a desire to evade death."[27] Here lies the crucial difference for decolonial engagements with wonder: "If the most basic ontological question is 'why are things rather than nothing,' the question that emerges in this context and that opens up reflection on the coloniality of being is 'Why go on?'"[28] The *cry* is its existential expression.

To approach the concept of wonder – and consequently of glory – from the perspective of the cry of injustice demands careful consideration of wonder's inherent ambiguities. The questioning of wonder that I have been tracing here is based primarily on a reading of its modern versions, where doubt is a step, even a strategy to achieve certainty. But the decolonial critique raises other significant questions. Indeed Maldonado-Torres argues that the decolonial turn entails an affective element – a sense or feeling of horror.[29] "The decolonial attitude is born when the cry of terror in the face of the horrors of coloniality is translated into a critical stance toward the world of colonial death and in a search for the affirmation of the lives of those most affected by such world."[30] In Maldonado-Torres's view, the philosophical dimension of the decolonial attitude is related to, but different from, the attitude of wonder that Husserl describes. While the theoretical attitude of philosophy, as commonly conceived, emerges from wonder at the natural world, the decolonial attitude is born from scandal and horror in the face of unjust death; while the former is guided by detachment, the latter is motivated by non-indifference toward the Other.[31] In these statements, horror and compassion are assumed to be incompatible with the affects of wonder. Understandably. For how can wonder be related to the cry of terror, the scandal of horror at death unequally distributed, death that becomes the ordinary reality of some lives?

The cry of injustice weighs heavily on any thought of wonder and glory. And yet, we shall probe deeper into the assumed opposition between the horror and glory, compassion and wonder. For I suspect that the affective elements that spark the decolonial attitude – its sense of indignation and compassion – are sustained by an intuition, an apprehension of what I would call the "glory" encountered in the Other, where wonder leads to that "search for the affirmation of the lives of those most affected by such world."[32]

Enduring wonder

The conceptual and practical slippages between wonder and mastery, between glory and might, that affected modern explorers and conquerors (as well as scientists and philosophers) shape current attitudes toward wonder and glory, including the apparent split between those terms and the experiences of those who suffer oppression. Modern versions of wonder follow Aristotle and Descartes, valuing it only as a transitional step that prompts learning, but which a subject shall eventually overcome.[33] This role makes wonder subservient to the aims of certainty and mastery. But such aims are not intrinsic to wonder, but rather, an effect of its disregard.

A rearticulation of wonder should begin, in Mary-Jane Rubenstein's account, not with its modern exponents, but with Socrates, for whom wonder "arises when the understanding cannot master that which lies closest to it." Wonder arises when "an everyday assumption has suddenly become untenable: the familiar has become strange, throwing even the unquestionable into question."[34] This astonishment is not a stage that one seeks to overcome. It is always unsettling.

> Unlike curiosity or puzzlement … wonder does not vanish when the cause of the surprising phenomenon is discovered, nor does it relentlessly seek out new marvels to calculate, comprehend, or process. Rather, wonder wonders at that which conditions – and for that reason ultimately eludes – the mechanisms of calculation, comprehension, and possession themselves.[35]

Descartes is thus not a champion of wonder, but a paradigmatic figure of its demise. In contrast to Maldonado-Torres's association of philosophies of wonder with ideologies of domination, Rubenstein argues that what is related to "the will toward mastery, even toward divinity" is the "progressive eclipse of wonder." Yet this demise is not a simple suppression of wonder – which would be impossible to accomplish. Instead, what we observe is the appropriation of wonder by claiming possession of its sources – gold, curious objects, knowledge, or a piece of land. By "comprehending the source of the wondrous, the thinking self in effect becomes the source of the wondrous."[36]

The impulse to possess, in order to become the source of the wondrous, is not unrelated to the movement of consolidation of the *ego cogito* discussed above. It redirects desire. Rather than being affected by wonder, the subject reasserts mastery and distance. Indeed Rubenstein contends, the "Western philosophical tradition does not so much do away with wonder as it does *internalize* it, presenting itself as the agent, rather than the patient of wonder."[37] Thus I suggest that the attitude of detachment and indifference that decolonial thinkers decry is not one of too much wonder, but too little. Failing to endure wonder, Cartesian subjects pursue curiosity, accumulating knowledge through mastery and ultimately construing themselves as its source.[38] In contrast, wondering "passion traverses the not-knowing (not ignorant) subject," as Trinh T. Minh-ha describes it.[39] To be the *patient* of wonder, to endure it, entails a persistent exposure to the weight of the world.

It is thus crucial to differentiate between allusions to wonder that welcome an ultimate incommensurability and inappropriability of what it encounters, and those in which wonder is understood as equivalent to curiosity, that is, as a passing emotion pursued as a means of instant gratification, acquisition, or self-aggrandizement. And yet, such a distinction does not yield an unambiguous wonder. For instance, even in the context of colonization, experiences of curiosity provided energy for creative projects that, if never unambiguous, were not simple appropriations but also produced new hybrid spaces of life in the midst of destruction.[40] And the ambivalence of wonder runs deeper. It is not simply that wonder and curiosity often emerge from similar desires and merge into one another, or that they produce both positive and negative effects. A recalcitrant ambiguity issues from the fact that wonder produces both awe and terror: awe at the realization that there is something rather than nothing, a world that we cannot account for; terror at the strangeness of that world, where even our best explanations are inadequate, where what we assumed to be the solid foundations are shown to be groundless.[41]

The unsettling experience of seeing what used to be commonsense become untenable, and the familiar appear strange, tempts prompt closure by building fortresses of hypercertainties. "The experience of wonder also opens out the possibility of its closure. The groundless awe upon which thinking 'rests' can either be inquisitively endured or it can be covered over with unquestionable premises."[42] Thus experiences of wonder can impel the production of absolute or mystifying explanations to stand-in for terrifying uncertainties. Statements of universal knowledge or absolute dogma may be invoked to set limits to the terrifying depth that wonder reveals, covering precariousness over with "clear and distinct ideas," or strictly marked attributions of origin. In the case of theologies of glory, the phrase "the glory of God" may be treated as an explanation of the experience of wonder rather than an opening to its irreducible depth – as an attribution that can then be assimilated into common knowledge about power or prestige. That is, glory is construed as a (predictable) trait of a certain kind of being or reality, wonder as the (predictable) reaction at the grandeur of that kind of being or reality. Once this explanation is in place, wonder seems properly contained in what is reasonable, the world remains recognizable, and fear can be assuaged – or at least circumscribed and managed.

Delimiting the terrifying from the alluring aspects of wonder – if not suppressing the terrifying aspects altogether – is a constant temptation for philosophers and theologians. (Rubenstein offers numerous examples of this philosophical habit.) Otto's influential construction of the relationship between terror and wonder illustrates this tendency. He associates terror with glory but explains it as a realization of the inherent nothingness of humanity in relation to the divine, which he contrasts to the "wonderfulness" associated with grace. Otto invokes an image of divine magnanimity to make intelligible the perceived ambiguity. "Creature consciousness," the subjective reaction to awe, is "a feeling of one's own submergence, of being but 'dust and ashes' and nothingness." A sense of "impotence ... against overpowering might," Otto claims, is the "numinous raw material for a feeling of religious humility."[43] Terrifying, indeed.

Otto's characteristic assumption of a link between glory (or the awe that arises in response to it) and "self-depreciation" seems to confirm the decolonial suspicions that glory casts a long shadow of disgrace. Does such a claim not mirror the colonial dynamics that promote a sense of impotence against overpowering might? The legitimization of relationships of domination by claiming mastery as the basis of reverence or humility is a sadly familiar stance in Christian history. Moving away from such positions, however, shall not lead to the suppression of discussions of horror, to limiting glory to the beautiful and pleasurable. A theology of glory that seeks to be meaningful in the midst of concrete realities of injustice and pain cannot ignore the terror with which it is associated.

The structure that Otto describes maps the divide between glory and nothingness onto an ontological split between divinity and humanity (or vice versa). In contrast, liberation theologies invoke glory to illuminate and disturb worldly ontological structures. They insist that the glory does not manifest itself where normally expected, on the side of might, but among the weak – it shines in the midst of those who are excluded and thus denied access to what they need for flourishing. Dussel argues that the image of Moses facing a burning bush – one of the most celebrated images of divine glory – epitomizes the human encounter with the excluded person, who "is the 'locus' of God's epiphany."[44] The Other interpellates the self, like God in the burning bush. The Other calls the self to see (and thus move) beyond the boundaries of systems of domination. As in an experience of wonder, this encounter alters perception as the subject becomes responsive to a surplus of meaning in common reality.[45] While the luminosity of the burning bush evokes the alluring qualities of glory, the encounter is not merely a pleasurable or comforting experience. In a different context, Dussel argues:

> The cry of pain such as 'I am hungry' requires the urgent answer, an answer that issues from a sense of responsibility … It is this responsibility that exemplifies the authentic religion and worship, and the trauma that one suffers for the Other who cries out is the *Glory of the Infinite* in the system.[46]

The encounter with the Other shatters the pretensions of "the system" – the social, political, or epistemological system – revealing its dreadful effects. The phrase "the Glory of the Infinite in the system" may suggest a disembodied force channeling through a person as if from outside, consonant with Dussel's appeal to divine "exteriority" – a concept drawn from Levinas's work. However, Dussel grounds the cry firmly in the flesh. Gastric juices, pain, appetite: These "carnal, corporeal, and material desires" are the bases for the desire of the divine, he argues.[47] The source of the cry is anything but immaterial. Furthermore, whereas damnation implies a denial of the ontological weight of the colonized/racialized person, in this view, breaking through that denial entails a perception of glory, of a weight that cannot be circumscribed, to a divine alterity that cannot be appropriated, even by the one from whom it radiates. The "trauma" of the cry implicates the self in an irreducible responsibility and in the process the self is undone.[48]

For the person who perceives it, the cry unsettles what she assumed was most evident: the structures that defined her place as a person in established social arrangements, the weight of her life and that of others. The encounter can thus be terrifying, for it shows the groundlessness of the foundations on which we construct our world – and our selves. While the experience does not dissolve the self, it dis-encloses it – to use Jean-Luc Nancy's term.[49] And thus it may reveal not only our own complicity and complacency in such systems, but also the uncertainties of our own lives and common vulnerabilities, perhaps even shattering our sense of security and stability. It is a realization of our implication in complex webs of life that exceed comprehension. And the "complexification of relations" runs the risk of "a certain monstrosity," as Catherine Keller observes.[50] If glory evokes humility, it is from a realization not of impotence or submergence in nothingness, but rather of the immensity of the reality in which we are implicated.

To perceive glory is to awaken to the weight of reality, to be exposed to its insistence and resistance.[51] This is not just an intellectual process. While precluding neither doubt nor opinion, sensibility to glory entails an affective turn, indeed, a conversion. "A moment of awe is a moment of self consecration. They who sense the wonder share the wonder."[52] For decolonial thinkers, such conversion leads to a sense of self that is inherently marked by the responsibility to the human-Other. Gayatri Chakravorty Spivak extends this disposition to include the non-human world. She argues that the impossibility of mastering that which presents itself to us, a reality that does not derive from us and yet one we inhabit, leads us to see ourselves as planetary creatures, marked by a primordial responsibility to that which we cannot account for: the planet that sustains our life.[53]

The cry is not the negation of glory, but the negation of its negation. The cry of a hungry person and the groaning of creation manifest the persistence of glory, the astonishing fact that all the world's callousness and violence have not overcome it. Thus, I do not assume glory and wonder to be absent from the lives of those who suffer under severe conditions of colonial and neocolonial life or violence; such an assumption would lead us to lose sight of the inexplicable nature of resilience, of the uncommon insight, persistence, and vision that give impulse to the very possibilities of decolonial thinking and practice. Staying in wonder entails resisting the temptation to seek shelter behind our own certainties, even when those certainties pertain to the detrimental effects of oppression and the suffering of others. Wonder unsettles expectations by disrupting not only illusions regarding dominant systems, but also expectations about victimization that may close our senses to the astonishing realities that reveal themselves even in the midst of dire situations.

Luminosity, darkness, weight

Outraged by the horrors of human injustice, touched by the amazing insistence and resistance of life, we persist in our attempts to describe life's elusive glory. And so we approach, again, the site of one of the most celebrated biblical images of divine glory: an ordinary, insignificant bush. The scene is strange – the bush is burning, but it is not consumed. Moses is drawn to the mysteriously incandescent shrub and approaches it. God's glory appears in the bush. But is it simply God's? The one who speaks from the bush has been touched by the cries of the Israelites suffering under slavery. The cries reach God, and God is moved – inflamed. At that particular moment, the divine flame caught Moses' attention – and his heart. Its light and heat draws Moses into divine passion. The fire is then in Moses as it was in the bush.

I have imagined myself like Moses, wondering at the sight and warmth of the burning bush, barefoot, feeling the pebbles on the ground pressing against my feet. The hissing sound of fire is soothing. The encounter then becomes more than a visual experience, allowing the whole body to be exposed to it. A broader sensual experience diminishes the distance allowed by sight, but not the reverence with which glory is approached. I take off my sandals – and perhaps other protective garments as well; I am exposed, affected. The astonishing sight of fog and light over hills and sea, or the roaring power of a hurricane passing over a small island may evoke similar awe. Beauty and sensible pleasure are intrinsic to glory's lure. Yet glory is not simply another name for the beautiful; terror also arises from its encounter, as we have seen. The Israelites are often said to be shocked to realize they had survived an encounter with divine glory – and so are we. I have been arguing that only a concept of glory that acknowledges its inherent ambivalence can truly welcome the world as it presents itself, with indescribable pain as well as beauty. Glory, like the numinous, can be characterized as a *mysterium tremendum et fascinans*. Certainly, the terror that it inspires may prompt some to build fortresses of hypercertainties, to represent glory as might; its allure may tempt others to consume its sources – or to imagine that they could do so. Glory will always be susceptible to appropriation and counterfeit, as much as to simple disregard. Still neither terror nor fascination can be excluded from it without risking detaching glory from realities of injustice, from the vulnerability of flesh.

Glory gleams in the midst of ambiguous situations and common experiences, in flesh and matter – in finitude. Glory does not lead us away from actual, material things, nor does its perception unveil absolute, hidden knowledge. What then does glory bring to light? Glory is a quality of things in their irreducible singularity, as they impinge upon our lives without being reducible to them. Glory manifests value and gravity as well as non-knowledge and inexhaustibility. Thus, encounters with glory imply revelation and incomprehension – incomprehension that is not ignorance but the inability to fully grasp, to encompass, own, or contain. Incomprehension remains in revelation, not because some knowledge is kept hidden but because knowledge is never fully adequate for the glory's significance.[54] Glory is not an unknowable secret, but it defies closed explanations. Perceiving glory can be called revelation, not as the lifting of a veil but as "dis-enclosing" of structures of knowledge, of relations, of being.

Conveying the coincidence of revelation *and* incomprehension, glory is portrayed as both the radiance of the flame and the darkness of clouds, or as a splendor so intense that it cannot be contemplated, a darkness of intense luminosity. Moses' request to see the glory of God – possibly the earliest scriptural reference to glory – marks the coincidence in glory of revelation and inexhaustibility with delightful wit. In one of his various conversations with God, a seemingly impatient Moses asks him, "Now show me your glory." Why would someone who "speaks" with God make such a strange request? We may wonder. And this is where God seems to leave us when he responds:

> There is a place near me where you may stand on a rock. When my glory passes by, I will put you in a cleft in the rock and cover you with my hand

until I have passed by. Then I will remove my hand and you will see my back; but my face must not be seen.[55]

So Moses did not see, could not have seen the fullness of God. But he saw God's backside. Did he see God's glory? In a narrative that includes multiple conversations and even arguments between Moses and God, this detail is especially revealing for what it does not reveal. Thus the theologian is left, like Moses (I presume), moved by experiencing a glory that *passes* by. An irreplaceable event, to be sure, but one that cannot be controlled, contained, or possessed.

"Glory purely and simply gives itself, and precisely as that which is not appropriable – not even by the one from whom it emanates," writes Nancy.[56] Indeed divine glory is not something God manages as a tool to impress Moses. Surely, there are other stories where God seems to do just that, especially to intimidate enemies – stories that represent glory as a weapon of power.[57] Yet the story we are considering suggests otherwise. If God is forced to devise a strategy to protect Moses, we can assume that God cannot manipulate or constrain divine glory. Glory gives itself as it passes by. Glory, Nancy continues, "is only admirable, and perhaps admirable to the point of not being able to be contemplated."[58]

Unable to contemplate directly or comprehensively divine glory, mystical writers speak of the infinite divine light as darkness – darkness that is not opposed to light. Byzantine artists represent it as the inner darkness of the halo. Others see this radiant darkness in the biblical image of the cloud. Catherine Keller follows the "trail of clouds," which takes us first, with Gregory of Nyssa's guidance, to meet Moses yet again.[59]

When, therefore, Moses grew in knowledge, he declared that he had seen God in the darkness, that is, that he had then come to know that what is divine is beyond all knowledge and comprehension, for the text says, Moses approached the dark cloud where God was.[60]

This revelation of divine darkness is apparently as alluring as the inextinguishable flames of the burning bush, and yet more approachable. But its approachability only deepens the sense of mystery and inappropriability disclosed in the burning bush or a passing God. The metaphors of light and darkness eventually overflow the singularity of Moses' encounters with God to open theological nonknowing "into the eerie nonseparability of a boundless universe." This crucial step unfolds from Keller's reading of Nicholas of Cusa's work: "rather than the unknowable God desiriously pursued beyond the knowable universe, the universe itself 'cannot be grasped.'"[61] This affirmation of a universe inherently marked by divine mystery (or by a "contracted infinity") can potentially disenclose modern habits of objectification – possibilities that Keller proceeds to explore. Here it leads us to open glory beyond the boundaries of God-centered attributions into the cloudy realm of creaturely nonseparability, which entails further nuances to the meaning of the "admirable" qualities of glory.

Is the glory that lures Moses to the burning bush, as I asked earlier, simply God's? I asked before. Can we clearly distinguish between the flames in that incandescent bush, in the Israelites' cries, in God's voice, in Moses' heart? The theological habit of treating "the glory *of* God" as a circumscribed attribution with clear demarcations and calculations – as an unquestionable origin and cause – constrains this flame. Reflecting an imagined rift between divine glory and human nothingness, the habit of separation may seek to affirm an absolutely egalitarian ontological structure, for it equates all humanity in its subjection to God, all beings sharing the same lowly status compared to God's glory. However, such a structure mirrors an all too human dichotomy that opposes honor (the "admirable") to vulnerability, separating those whose lives are recognized as such from those who are denied ontological weight.[62]

The glory of a mysteriously excessive divinity overflows such ontology; its luminous darkness permeates creation and is perceived twinkling in vulnerable life, in the lives of those who are considered the least. The cries of pain and hunger – those cries that negate the negation of a creature's ontological weight – manifest the insistence and resistance of glory *in* the flesh. Those who respond to the cry, may perceive in the encounter divine glory and experience a dis-enclosure of relationships at the heart of the self. Such relationships are revealed as a matter of divine concern and our responses as ethical and religious obligations. Vulnerability and reverence coexist. Carnal, corporeal, and material needs, which expose our dependence on others and our exposure to injury, are fleshy sites of glory.[63]

The inherence of divine glory in corporeality manifested by pain or appetite is no less significant in corporeal pleasure, beauty, and resilience – when these are not construed as the absence of pain or suffering. Like the non-consuming fire that Moses reverently contemplated, flesh's hazy luminosity attracts those who perceive it, as it deters the impulse to consume or assimilate it. Envisioning a carnal wonder at the edges of Descartes' *Meditations*, Luce Irigaray brings Eros into the first passion. Wonder is for her the lure of the desired other as well as what protects a necessary "interval" between self and other. Wonder is both active and passive; in wonder touch respects the ungraspability of flesh. Irigaray uses the term to refer to what attracts/resists the self as well as to the subjects' response to it, thus including elements of glory and wonder. Her frequent references to illumination suggest that glory shines through her depictions of wonder.[64] Irigaray describes wonder as "[a]n excess that resists," aptly characterizing a glory that appears not only in the shock of injustice, but also in the irreducible difference of that which is closest to her, which lures her beyond herself, to wonder in the flesh.[65]

Matter and flesh are indispensable for glory. Still, even when we hear that the earth is full of divine glory, theologies tend to inattentively substitute a human face or body for a small incandescent bush.[66] But glory cannot be contained in the human sphere, either in the cry for socio-economic justice or in calls for an ethics of erotic encounters. The groaning of creation calls for com-passion toward the non-human other – indeed, for a conversion, to become reverently attuned to the non-human, to protect an interval for wonder against our appropriative and consumptive impulses.

Moved beyond the self, yet not breaking off finitude; turning toward the scintillating opacity of carnality and materiality and to their indefinite complexity; astonished, perhaps terrified, by sensing our implication in an immense, evolving, ever unfinished network of creaturely relations; delighting and suffering in the physical world of the senses. In that ungraspable matrix, each encounter with glory is unique, irreplaceable, unrepeatable – as is each and every one of its organisms and relationships. A "relative-absolute," Xavier Zubiri calls this irreducible singularity that emerges only in relations – that only *is* in relations.[67] Because it is never outside of materializations, glory is neither one nor many. Glory gives itself in finitude, experienced in unrepeatable events – not as a totality, not to be grasped or comprehended, not to be controlled or accumulated. Moses sees God's backside, a sight of glory passing by; and that passing is all we ever perceive – always the irreducible singularity of an encounter experienced as the touch of a fleeting moment. Glory is perceived as it passes; yet its passing, like the meaning of our vanishing present, weighs on us.

The vanishing present weighs on us; it draws us toward the earth and it troubles, it concerns us, as Nancy observes.[68] Building on the etymological proximity between "to weigh" (*pesar*) and "to think" (*pensar*), Nancy brings materiality to bear on thinking; it is a gravity to be felt in the seriousness of thought as in the pressures that bodies exert. "The existence of the world is grave," he says, adding the planetary force to the cluster of terms with which he addresses wonder and thought, existence and meaning. Thought is "to welcome the wonder before that which presents itself"; it is "letting what weighs weigh."[69] Feeling the weight, the heaviness of things is the very possibility of thought. Yet things weigh "outside thought," "away from the completed, personified, signified meaning"; weight is their very inappropriability.[70]

The etymological connection between kabôd and weight likewise suggests its grave import and its irreducibility to our processes of signification. We are exposed to the weight of the world, to the unexplainable reality of our very existence in relationships that we cannot fully represent and to the enormity of human injustice, to a life-sustaining planet (a gift we cannot account for) and to its unbearable devastation. If glory is that halo that envelops all existence, or the luminous darkness that surrounds all knowledge, it is also the weight of materiality, its resistance to appropriation, to the accumulation of constructions and deconstructions; the significance of its density and gravity. Yet thickness, density, mass are not what we most often associate with glory. Indeed, weight is likely to evoke the opposite feelings. We are "disgusted with our weight … The humus – the earthiness – of humanity can be so mortally humiliating," observes Sharon Betcher as she invites us to "think Spirit with the weight of the earth."[71] To think with the weight of the earth, to welcome the glory that persists here and yet beyond ourselves, entails a humility that – far from reducing human or humus to nothingness – feels its connections to gravity, to the planet, to the ground.

Glory is the trace of a divine relationship woven through creaturely life and its relationships. It is the cloudy radiance of the ungraspable excess that inheres in ordinary things – something that manifests itself, that gives itself: excessive in virtue of the extent and complexity of its relationships and of the divine investment in them; ungraspable in its irreducible uniqueness; heavy and grave. It can appropriately be called *divine* glory, as long as its divinity keeps materializing in earthly grounds, becoming vulnerable flesh.

Proscript

A dark and luminous halo envelops all life, but we seldom perceive it. "The perception of glory is a rare occurrence in our lives. We fail to wonder."[72] Indeed theology has too often placed belief ahead of wonder, and contained glory in an external realm, inaccessible to humanity except in spectacular events that display the might of God. I have been suggesting that the passion at the heart of theology, what keeps us moving toward this strange mode of speech and writing, is neither the illusion of security and stability offered by well-structured metaphysical systems, nor even our crucial social projects. It is rather the lure of an elusive, misty halo of life. Metaphysical statements and prophetic pronouncements are some of our responses in this passion for glory. As Christian theologians, we see in glory the manifestation of divinity in creation, of the investment and care of God for even the smallest of things. Other metaphors may likewise seek to convey that elusive quality that presents itself to us as alluring, excessive and worthy of profound reverence. "God" may not be integral to such metaphors. Yet we do not need to surrender our claims to perceive the back of God passing by in the ordinary events, in strange places or unlikely situations. We keep trying to convey this uncircumscribed spirit – however inaccurately and distortedly.

The experience of glory is rather frustratingly neither my own nor absolutely external to me, in as much as I can only experience it when attuned to its perception. The subtle appearance of glory would be lost for us in the absence of a capacity to remain in wonder – despite its unsettling effects. Like everything else in the world, neither glory nor wonder are protected from co-optation or counterfeit. Yet we may practice a kind of attentiveness that is not discouraged by such failures, but rather exposes them, as it remains open to the glory that might still surprise us.

The polydox theology that I am envisioning here may be composed like what Eduardo Galeano calls "Magical Marxism: one half reason, one half passion, and a third half mystery."[73] It is clearly not amenable to calculation and cannot be called a method; it might include a little bit of imagination and no less poetic folly. Such a polydox theology attends to the devastating realities of pain and oppression without losing sight of the marvelous qualities of ordinary life, without ever believing that it has at last discovered the absolutely real. It does not so much abandon traditional symbols or critical analysis as move in them, to open spaces for indeterminacy and wonder, dis-enclosing theology, to experience glory in our perennially unfinished and redeemable world. It seeks to cultivate the capacity to endure wonder – creative in its receptivity, persistent in its disposition. The flourishing of creatures may well depend on this capacity to welcome the wonder before the weight of reality, of a human face, a bush, a passing cloud, or a burning fire.

Notes

1   V. Woolf, "Modern Fiction," in *The Common Reader: The First Series*, annotated edition, Orlando, FL: First Harvest Edition, 1984, p. 150.
2   I am grateful to Michael Nausner for his insightful feedback on this chapter. The editors' incisive comments and suggestions were also vital for this version of my chapter.
3   In religious art, the combination of a halo and an aureola is called "glory," although often the distinction between halo and aureola is not maintained. It is often painted as concentric circles growing darker as they approach the center – a visual depiction of an apophatic theology idea. A. Andreopolus, *Metamorphosis: The Transfiguration in Byzantine Theology and Iconography*, Crestwood, NY: St. Vladimir's Seminary Press, 2005, pp. 83–91.
4   Liberation theology recovers the image of God as creator of life, a God whose glory is the "human being alive." Among the people for who death is not a single figure of speech but a daily reality thrust upon their attention in infant mortality, violent conflict, and torture, a theology of God as creator and sustainer of life acquires piercing relevance.

   L. Boff and C. Boff, *Liberation Theology: From Dialogue to Confrontation*, San Francisco, CA: Harper & Row, 1986, p. 25.
5   R. Alves, *I Believe in the Resurrection of the Body*, Eugene, OR: Wipf and Stock, 1986, p. 20.
6   E. Levinas, *Totality and Infinity: An Essay on Exteriority*, Pittsburgh, PA: Duquesne University Press, 1969, p. 24.
7   Socrates: "I see, my dear Theaetetus, that Theodorus had a true insight into your nature when he said that you were a philosopher, for wonder is the feeling of a philosopher, and philosophy begins in wonder," in Plato, *Theaetetus*, trans. B. Jowett, Rockland, MD: Serenity Publishers, p. 104.
8   R. Otto, *The Idea of the Holy*, trans. J. W. Harvey, Oxford: Oxford University Press, 1950.
9   W. R. Cook, "The 'Glory' Motif in the Johannine Corpus," *Journal of the Evangelical Theological Society*, 27:3, 1984, p. 291.
10 "The word doxa was used to translate twenty-five different words, but kabôd is by far the most common translation." It was also used in the Greek iconographic tradition for the mandorla. Andreopolus, *Metamorphosis*, p. 86.
11 E. Brunner, *Dogmatics I: The Christian Doctrine of God*, trans. O. Wyon, Cambridge: James Clarke and Co, 1949, pp. 285–6.
12 Isaiah 6:3, Psalm 19:1; New International Version.
13 Brunner, *Dogmatics I*, p. 286. J. Saramago, *All the Names*, trans. M. J. Costa, San Diego, CA: Hartcourt, 1997, p. 112.
14 I understand this active receptivity to be consonant with what Nancy calls "passibility," which defies the opposition between passivity and activity; a "disposition" and an "activity," a capacity of "receiving or welcoming" meaning. J.-L. Nancy, *The Gravity of Thought*, trans. F. Raffoul and G. Recco, Maherst, NY: Humanity Books, 1997, p. 69.
15 The intention … is not to deny the meaning of *orthodoxy*, understood as a proclamation of and reflection on statements considered to be true. Rather the goal is to balance and even to reject the primacy and almost exclusiveness which doctrine has enjoyed in Christian life and above all to modify the emphasis, often obsessive, on the attainment of an orthodoxy which is often nothing more than fidelity to an obsolete tradition or a debatable interpretation.

   G. Gutiérrez, *A Theology of Liberation: History, Politics and Salvation*, trans. Sr. D. Inda and J. Eagleson, Maryknoll, NY: Orbis Books, 1973, p. 10.
16 Ibid., p. 7.
17 R. N. Brock and R. A. Parker, *Saving Paradise: How Christianity Traded Love of This World for Crucifixion and Empire*, Boston, MA: Beacon Press, 2008.

18 The fate of images of paradise – those rich, creative representations of earthly glory – follows this path of degradation. As Rita Nakashima Brock and Rebecca Ann Parker observe, "after the discovery of the Americas, the location of paradise in maps shifted from Iraq and India to the New World and then disappear entirely." Ibid., p. 324.

19 S. Greenblatt, *Marvelous Possessions: The Wonders of the New World*, Chicago, IL: Chicago University Press, 1991, p. 19.

20 Ibid., p. 24.

21 The term "decolonial" has been used to name the work of a particular group of scholars who coined the term to emphasize, among other things, that the decolonizing project is an unfinished task. R. Grosfoguel, N. Maldonado-Torres, and J. D. Saldívar (eds), *Latin@s in the World System: Decolonization Struggles in the 21st Century U.S. Empire*, Boulder, CO: Paradigm Press, 2005.

22 N. Maldonado-Torres, "On the Coloniality of Being: Contributions to the Development of a Concept," *Cultural Studies*, 21, 2–3, 2007, p. 245.

23 The Valladolid debates, which took place between 1550–1, presented two opposing arguments about the nature of the natives, represented by Fray Bartolomé de las Casas and Juan Ginés de Sepúlveda. The latter argued that the natives belonged to Aristotle's category of "natural slaves."

24 Maldonado-Torres, "Coloniality of Being," p. 245.

25 Ibid.

26 Ibid., p. 247. Maldonado-Torres relies on Frantz Fanon's use of the term. F. Fanon, *Black Skin, White Masks*, New York: Grove Press, 1967.

27 Ibid., p. 251.

28 Ibid., p. 256.

29 N. Maldonado-Torres, "La Descolonización Y El Giro De-Colonial," *Tabula Rasa*, 9, July–December, 2008, p. 66.

30 Ibid., pp. 66–7, my translation.

31 Ibid. This attitude also includes a "willingness to take many perspectives and points of view."

32 This is the significance of the critique as one that entails not only epistemology, but also ontology.

> The coloniality of Being indicates those aspects that produce exception from the order of Being; it is as it were, the product of the excess of Being that in order to maintain its integrity and inhibit the interruption by what lies beyond Being produces its contrary, not nothing, but a non-human or rather an inhuman world.

Maldonado-Torres, "Coloniality of Being," p. 257. I use the term "apprehend" as Judith Butler defines it.

> "Apprehension" is less precise [than recognition], since it can imply marking, registering, acknowledging without full cognition. If it is a form of knowing, it is bound up with sensing and perceiving, but in ways that are not always – or not yet – conceptual forms of knowledge.

J. Butler, *Frames of War: When Is Life Grievable?*, New York: Verso, 2009, p. 5.

33 M.-J. Rubenstein, *Strange Wonder: The Closure of Metaphysics and the Opening of Awe*, New York: Columbia University Press, 2008, p. 12.

34 Ibid., pp. 3–4.

35 Ibid., p. 8.

36 Ibid., p. 16.

37 Ibid.

38 The identification of celebrity with glory similarly bypassed the challenges of wonder, affirming instead the search for qualities that can be appropriated and commodified. Referring to this debasement of glory, Heidegger wrote, "For us today, glory has long

been nothing but celebrity, and as such it is a highly dubious matter, an acquisition thrown around and distributed by the newspaper and the radio – nearly the opposite of Being." M. Heidegger, *Introduction to Metaphysics*, trans. G. Fried and R. Polt, New Haven, CT: Yale University Press, 2000, p. 108.

39 Trinh T. Minh-ha, *When the Moon Waxes Red: Representation, Gender and Cultural Politics*, London and New York: Routledge, 1991, p. 23.

40 S. Gruzinski, *The Mestizo Mind: The Intellectual Dynamics of Colonization and Globalization*, trans. D. Dusinberre, New York: Routledge, 2002, p. 127.

41 Rubenstein, *Strange Wonder*, p. 9.

42 Ibid., p. 23.

43 Otto, *Idea of the Holy*, pp. 20–1.

44 E. Dussel, "An Ethics of Liberation: Fundamental Hypotheses," in E. Mendieta (ed.), *Beyond Philosophy: Ethics, History, Marxism, and Liberation Theology*, New York: Rowman & Littlefield, 2003, p. 139.

45 Ironically, the need to challenge human failure to recognize divine glory in weakness and suffering – which leads Dussel to invoke glory – was Martin Luther's critique of what he deemed "theologies of glory." He argued

> That person does not deserve to be called a theologian who looks upon the "invisible" things of God as though they were clearly "perceptible in those things which have actually happened" … Because men misused the knowledge of God through works, God wished again to be recognized in suffering, and to condemn "wisdom concerning invisible things" by means of "wisdom concerning visible things," so that those who did not honor God as manifested in his works should honor him as he is hidden in his suffering.

"Heidelberg Disputations," in T. F. Lull (ed.) *Martin Luther's Basic Theological Writings*, 2nd ed., Minneapolis, MN: Fortress Press, 2005, p. 57. I am grateful to Terra Rowe for drawing my attention to this interesting reversal, as well as for her comments on an earlier version of this chapter.

46 E. Dussel, *A History of the Church in Latin America*, Grand Rapids, MI: Eerdmans, 1981, p. 307. The influence of Levinas is hard to miss. "The movement toward the Other, instead of completing me or contenting me, implicates me in a conjuncture … Whence came this shock when I passed, indifferent, under the Other's gaze? The relationship with the Other puts me into question …" These are Levinas's words.

47 E. Dussel, *Beyond Philosophy: Ethics, History, Marxism, and Liberation Theology*, New York: Rowman & Littlefield, 2003, p. 307.

48 Levinas's and Dussel's metaphysics of the exteriority cast the subject–Other relationship in ways that tend to reproduce some elements of the assumptions of mastery and impotence that I am questioning here. I develop this critique in *The Touch of Transcendence: A Postcolonial Theology of God*, Louisville, KY: Westminster John Knox Press, 2007. However, I am here interested in their displacement of glory as a way to conceptualize a moment of wonder that is not antithetical to terror.

49 J.-L. Nancy, *Dis-Enclosure: The Deconstruction of Christianity*, trans. B. Bergo, G. Malefant, and M. B. Smith, New York: Fordham University Press, 2008.

50 C. Keller, *The Cloud of the Impossible*, unpublished manuscript.

51 Insistence and resistance are the key characteristics that Nancy uses to describe meaning, in distinction from signification. Nancy, *Gravity of Thought*.

52 A. J. Heschel, *God in Search of Man: A Philosophy of Judaism*, New York: Farrar, Straus and Giroux, 1983, p. 78.

53 G. Chakravorty Spivak, *Death of a Discipline*, New York: Columbia University Press, 2003.

54 By "incomprehension" I am signaling something similar to what Nancy calls "inadequation" when he argues, "glory is the exhibition of inadequation or incommensurability," *Dis-Enclosure*, p. 58. Nonetheless, the spatiality of "comprehension," in the sense of encompassing or containing, evokes for me the appropriative impulses – in geopolitics as in epistemology – that I do not want to lose.

55 Exodus 33:18; 21–3.

56 Nancy, *Dis-Enclosure*, p. 57.

57 Giorgio Agamben's exploration of glory focuses on the relationship between glory and majesty, arguing (against Hans Ur von Balthasar) that there are no aesthetic aspects of glory in Scripture. By choosing what he calls the "liturgical" interpretation, Agamben uncovers important associations between power and glory, but may be foreclosing other aspects and, as a consequence, other interpretations. G. Agamben, *El Reino Y La Gloria: Por Una Genealogía Teológica De La Economía Y El Gobierno*, trans. A. G. Cuspinera, Valencia: Pre-Textos, 2008.

58 Nancy, *Dis-Enclosure*, p. 57.

59 Keller.

60 *Life of Moses*, quoted in Keller.

61 Ibid.

62 In Judith Butler's terms, one could say that this common dichotomy renders precarity imperceptible; those lives would not even be grievable, because they cannot be recognized as such. J. Butler, *Precarious Life: The Powers of Mourning and Violence*, London and New York: Verso, 2004.

63 "To mourn and to wonder ... that is what the spirit yearns for when it stands in the midst of trauma and breathes in the truth of grace," argues Serene Jones as she concludes her reflections on theology "in a ruptured world." S. Jones, *Trauma and Grace: Theology in a Ruptured World*, Louisville, KY: Westminster John Knox Press, 2009.

64 L. Irigaray, *The Way of Love*, trans. H. Bostic and S. Pluhácek, New York: Continuum, 2002.

65 Thus Luce Irigaray describes wonder, often blurring the boundary between glory and wonder. *An Ethics of Sexual Difference*, Ithaca, NY: Cornell University Press, 1993, p. 75.

66 I elsewhere pursue a reading that attends to the bush and the fire in their elemental significance. M. Rivera, "Elemental Bonds: Scene for an Earthy Postcolonial Theology," in T. B. Liew (ed.), *Postcolonial Interventions: Essays in Honor of R. S. Sugirtharajah*, Sheffield: Sheffield Phoenix Press, 2010.

67 I. Ellacuría, "The Historicity of Christian Salvation," in I. Ellacuría and J. Sobrino (eds), *Mysterium Liberationis: Fundamental Concepts of Liberation Theology*, Maryknoll, NY: Orbis Books, 1993, p. 276.

68 Nancy, *Gravity of Thought*, p. 2.

69 Ibid., p. 67.

70 The weight of thought is ... the weight of the thing insofar as that thing weighs outside of thought, insofar as it punctures and overflows the thought that it is, but that is can be only by being open to the thing, and its heaviness.

    Ibid., pp. 77–80.

71 S. Betcher, "Grounding the Spirit: An Ecofeminist Pneumatology," in L. Kearns and C. Keller (eds), *Ecospirit: Religions and Philosophies of the Earth*, New York: Fordham University Press, 2007, p. 316. Similarly, Catherine Keller reflects on the problem of the absence of any Christian stories of earth-epiphanies. "Talking Dirty: Ground Is not Foundation", ibid.

72 Heschel, *God in Search of Man*, p. 85.

73 E. Galeano, *El Libro De Los Abrazos*, Mexico: Siglo Ventiuno Editores, 2001, p. 209.

10 Invoking Oya

Practicing a polydox soteriology
through a postmodern womanist
reading of Tananarive Due's *The
Living Blood*

Monica A. Coleman

This chapter offers a postmodern womanist reading of Tananarive Due's science
fiction novel *The Living Blood* to suggest principles for practicing a polydox
soteriology.[1] Grounded in the strengths of womanist theologies and process metaphysics, postmodern womanist theology attends to the cosmology of Christianity
and African traditional religions. Postmodern womanist theology searches for
contextually-specific modes of creative transformation, and believes that black
women's science fiction can serve as a source for theological reflection. A
postmodern womanist reading of *The Living Blood* names divinity in the manifestations of the Yoruba *òrìṣà Oya* and in the depiction of "living blood."

Polydoxy is characterized by multiplicity, relationality, value, and mystery. A
postmodern womanist reading of *The Living Blood* therefore suggests a polydox
soteriology that is a route to health and wholeness. This salvific way reveals itself
as polydox through the intersections of multiple religious traditions, multiple
divine forces, multiple incarnations, and multiple Saviors. Multiplicity abounds.
As boundaries bend and cross in the narrative world of *The Living Blood*, this
reading also suggests that practicing a polydox soteriology is transnational,
transcontinental, postcolonial, feminist, womanish, and dangerous, while also
necessary for our health.

Polydoxy

Polydoxy is not just the opposite of orthodoxy. Just as orthodoxy indicates
"right teaching," polydoxy implies that there are many teachings. This suggests that theology and life are both more complex and nuanced than to affirm
one "right teaching" and there may in fact be many helpful teachings or many
teachings that can be equally, though differently, "right." Yet polydoxy also
implies that we can be taught by the many. That is, we can learn from multiple
traditions and we can, or even that we *must*, embrace that which is multiple in
order to learn. And if we are to be true to the "teaching" aspect of "doxa," then
polydoxy must be teachable. It must be capable of being taught, learned, and
practiced within lived communities of faith.

And yet, as the discussion on which this volume is based presupposes, polydoxy
does not affirm a neutral plurality. It declares loudly that pluralism is not enough.

The acknowledgement and affirmation of the many is just one step, an introductory step if you will, toward polydoxy. Polydoxy is a full on embrace of multiplicity – of multiplicity wherever it is found – in the divine and temporal worlds.

An embrace of multiplicity necessitates a radical affirmation of relationality. For the multiple interact with one another, with us. We are multiple. Radical relationality is a challenge. Not only does it mean that who we are is constituted by our many relationships – a reminder of the ways in which we ourselves are many – but it also reminds us that we are related to those who are different from us. The stranger may not be so strange. We have "alien affinities," as Keller and Schneider suggest in the introduction to this volume.

Polydoxy must still be a teaching, however – it must say something or some things. It need not, in fact should not, be morally neutral; rather, it retains value so that it affirms one position or positions and not another. There is a significant level of normativity within a polydox construction. A polydox construction should, therefore, not only be liveable, but it should be, to some extent, *loveable*.

As polydoxy establishes a counterbalance to the certainty of orthodoxy, polydoxy is able to live with uncertainty. It is comfortable with a level of ambiguity, or mystery. Polydoxy is transparent enough to reveal the many in what appears to be one. It is flexible enough to live with apparent contradictions. Polydoxy does not collapse in the presence of conflict; rather, it expands.

Polydox theology does not negate the religious tradition or traditions it inherits, but seeks the multiple within that tradition or doctrinal heritage. Thus, polydox soteriology may take hold of a classic theological concept, and bend it both backwards – toward its own varied heritage – and forwards – in new directions, engaging with new traditions.

To summarize, I am positing that polydox theology is both the affirmation of many teachings and the ability to be taught by many. Polydox theology is characterized by multiplicity, relationality, value, and ambiguity. It is teachable, liveable, loveable, historical, postmodern, and narrative. This polydox theology engages experimental theopoetics in its broadest sense. That is, it is willing to engage with narrative and literature in order to glean theological insights. In fact, I suggest that we can learn something about polydox theology through an in-depth exploration of a science fiction novel.

Postmodern womanist theology

I have previously argued that black women's science fiction can serve as a source for postmodern womanist theological reflection. Postmodern womanist theological reflection also attends to the presence and role of ancestors, especially as they signify African traditional religions and the syncretic practices of African American religions. Postmodern womanist theology's ability to work with Christianity *and* communotheistic traditions while searching for contextually specific modes of creative transformation lends itself to polydox practices that highlight multiplicity, relationality, value, and mystery.

In *Making a Way Out of No Way: A Womanist Theology*, I posit postmodern womanist theology as a quest for health and wholeness in the midst of violence, oppression and evil.[2] It is a theory of how salvation works. This quest is a life-long cooperative process between God and the entities of the temporal world; it occurs in teaching–healing communities for the creative transformation of the world. In short, the movement of life is constituted by the past, God and the agency of the world. God offers an ideal vision of justice, survival, and quality of life that is particular and relevant for each of us. Health, wholeness, and justice occur as we embrace God's calling. The past is a critical resource for this activity. Through our memories, and the activity of the ancestors, the past is an active participant in calling the temporal world toward creative transformation.

Womanist theologies maintain an unflinching commitment to grounding religious reflection in the social, cultural, and religious experiences of black women. Womanist theologies are ultimately grounded in, and accountable to, the religious reality of black women's lives. As a form of liberation theology, womanist theologies aim for the freedom of oppressed peoples and creatures. More specifically, womanist theologies add the goals of survival, quality of life, and wholeness to black theology's goals of liberation and justice. Womanist theologians analyze the oppressive aspects of society that prevent black women from having the quality of life and wholeness that God desires for them, and for all of creation.

Because of its grounding in the religious lives of black women, postmodern womanist theology acknowledges the pluralism within African American experiences. The reality of religious pluralism is particularly important for black religions in the United States because it represents the ways in which the slaves and their descendents interacted with African traditional religions and other religious traditions. Black religion is a syncretic movement that includes the influence of European Christianity and its adaptation by slaves and nineteenth- and twentieth-century believers. Black religion also includes significant influences from indigenous religions, particularly African traditional religions.

In the crucible of slavery, African Americans blended their African religious sensibilities with the Christianity introduced to them by their captors. As a result, African American Christianity reflects both the tenets and practices of Western Christianity and African traditional religions. In addition, African Americans currently participate in a variety of African-derived religious traditions. Thus, African American religiosity includes both the unique ways in which African American Christianity syncretized Western Christianity with the religious heritage of the enslaved Africans, and the contemporary diversity of religious practice by African Americans.

Black religious historian Gayraud Wilmore implies that African Americans, regardless of contemporary religious affiliation, encounter African traditional religions in historic and contemporary settings, and that this cultural encounter influences, to one extent or another, all black religiosity. He argues that, consequently, black theologies must go beyond discussing Christianity and give more attention to African traditional religions.[3] Postmodern womanist theology accepts this challenge and strives to address the diversity of black religion – with a specific focus on forms of African traditional religions.

Postmodern womanist theology utilizes process metaphysics as a postmodern theological framework. As a philosophical metaphysics, process thought offers a religious perspective that describes how the world works with specific views of God and human agency. Process thought discusses the relationship between the world and God, and is able to account for lived experiences across the boundaries of religious traditions. As a postmodern philosophy, process metaphysics presents a view of the world that is compatible with today's knowledge about the world.

Thus postmodern womanist theology affirms the following five principles. First, every aspect of life is in a process of becoming. All entities are continually sorting through what they inherit from the world, what is possible in their contexts, and their own self-determination in light of the past and possibilities. Second, every aspect of life has an individual ability to exercise power or agency. Third, relationality is internal. We are constituted by our relationships with others in the temporal world and God. Thus, God is a part of all of us. This is a radical concept of divine incarnation. It is not specific or unique; it is universal. Fourth, God has an eternal vision constituted by the ideals of truth, harmony, beauty, adventure, quality of life, and justice, by which God calls the temporal world. While the principles of God's vision do not change, the way God's vision is manifest in the temporal world is specific to each context. Finally, in the midst of the pervasive loss that occurs as the result of constant change, there are opportunities for immortality. We are able to preserve life as we influence those around us, by the legacies we leave behind, and in our own memories of what has occurred in the past.

Postmodern womanist theology as creative transformation

Postmodern womanist theology affirms a normative process of becoming, which is a particular way of living in the world. Process theologians have often named this concept "creative transformation." Creative transformation promotes living in cooperation with God for the constructive social transformation of the world. A postmodern womanist theology strives for tangible representations of the good, drawn from womanist theology's articulation of the goal of theological reflection: justice, equality, discipleship, quality of life, acceptance, and inclusion.

The components of creative transformation are tailor-made for the exact context in which we find ourselves. In other words, the details of creative transformation will differ in every context. Creative transformation also challenges the status quo. As creative transformation draws us into the future, it necessarily changes the world as we currently experience it. Creative transformation is never forced upon the world. Although God calls us, we have genuine freedom and agency, and we must make our own decisions about whether or not to embody it. Creative transformation is always available to every entity – it is an option present in God's continual callings to the world.

Postmodern womanist theology focuses on creative transformation in the activities of teaching and healing. It draws from the womanist emphasis on the life and ministry of Jesus to highlight the ways in which teaching and healing positively bring about change in the world. It is important to note that the activity of healing, while sometimes taking place in the body, is an activity of restoring wholeness and community where there is exclusion, corruption, individualism, fragmentation, and brokenness. Teaching and healing are the activities that lead to ideals of discipleship, wholeness, justice, quality of life, beauty, truth, and adventure. In other words, God's calling is often mediated to the world and represented in the world through the activities of teaching and healing.

Finally, a postmodern womanist concept of creative transformation occurs in and through communities. Creative transformation is communal because it is extended to everyone – not just certain members of a community. Creative transformation is also communal because it acknowledges that, in the process of becoming, we deal with more than just ourselves. We deal with the community of the past, and future possibilities. When who and what we are becomes a part of the larger world around us, we become part of the many factors that will influence the future. Thus, we cannot live, change, or become in isolation. Community is also the goal of postmodern womanist theology. Because evil occurs in a relational world, and womanist theology has always understood sin as social and systemic, salvation must respond to evil in an explicitly communal context. That is, if salvation aims at the eradication of sins and oppressions that exclude and divide people, then salvation must aim for a greater and more genuine sense of community.

As a corollary, a postmodern womanist theology extends the concept of Savior beyond the Christian affirmation of Jesus alone. Postmodern womanist theology looks for Saviors in every theological community. Postmodern womanist theology focuses on the activities of teaching and healing, suggesting that it is not the person of Jesus, but rather the activities of teaching and healing that are exhibited in the life and death of Jesus that make Jesus a Savior. The activities of a community leader who demonstrates salvation make for a Savior. Saviors lead communities that teach and they heal for the creative transformation of the world.

In sum, postmodern womanist theology affirms that salvation is found in the activity of communities. Postmodern womanist theology does not refer to individuals as saved, apart from the communities in which those individuals participate. Postmodern womanist theology speaks of theological communities as those communities that adopt, and adapt, to God's calling in order to creatively transform the world in which they live. Their leaders are the Saviors.

Postmodern womanist theology as a mode of learning

Postmodern womanist theology emphasizes two ways of learning from the past that contribute to creative transformation. First, we are called to remember our past and incorporate it into our processes of becoming. As we do so, we can use past survival techniques to help ourselves live into the future. We can also remember the destructive death-dealing aspects of the past and vow not to repeat them as we move into the future. This conscious remembering is best done in community.

A second approach to learning from the past focuses on the role that the ancestors play in our lives. In African traditional religions, the ancestors are closely related to the divine and are active in the everyday and ceremonial lives of practitioners. Postmodern womanist theology understands the visions, dreams, charismatic embodiments of the Holy Spirit, and possession by African ancestors as critical to the diverse religious experiences of black women. It also asserts that the ancestors can help us to creatively transform the world and leave it a better place than we found it.

In the realm of African traditional religions, postmodern womanist theology focuses on Yoruba-based religious traditions such as Haiti's Vodun, Cuba's Santeria, Brazil's Candomblé, African American Ifa and conjure. Through both the triangular slave trade and contemporary reversionary local faith communities, the religion of the Yoruba people (of current-day Nigeria) constitutes a base for African-derived religious practices throughout the Caribbean, South America, and the United States. Although all these different manifestations of Yoruba-based religions share a similar cosmology that structures the world and key religious concepts, due to the different historical and religious contexts of the encounter between Yoruba religion and the various New World situations, they differ in ritual detail and linguistic referrals. As Yoruba traditional religion travels through space, time, and circumstance, it syncretizes, or blends, with other religious and cultural traditions – most particularly Western Christianity and other African traditional religions.

Traditional Yoruba religion can be described as the worship of a supreme deity, *Olódùmarè/Olórun*, under various ancestors, forces or deities, the *òrìsà*.[4] There is no adequate description for the *òrìsà* outside of the Yoruba universe. They have been variously described as ministers of *Olódùmarè*, forces of nature, angelic forces, lower gods and sub-deities. According to Yoruba stories, the *òrìsà* are ancestors who did not return to earth because their *ìwà* (human character or human consciousness) was so closely aligned with the character of *Olódùmarè*. While *Olódùmarè* is neither male nor female, nor embodied, the *òrìsà* have genders, stories, geographical, and natural associations. The *òrìsà* have their own characteristics, herbs, personalities, and devotees. Veneration of the *òrìsà* is such an important part of Yoruba religion that the entire religion is often referred to as "*òrìsà* worship." The telos of Yoruba religion is *ìwà pele* or cool or good character. Yoruba religion identifies 401 *òrìsà*, with five to ten *òrìsà* having more importance and appearances than the others. The wisdom and content of Yoruba is traditionally transmitted orally in myths, songs, and the *odù*, verses of wisdom and divination.[5]

The cosmology of traditional African religions does not fit into the Western philosophical and theological categories of monotheism and polytheism, mortal and immortal. A. Okechukwu Ogbonnaya provides the most creative portrayal of African traditional religions in relation to Christian theological categories in his book *On Communitarian Divinity*. Ogbonnaya coins the term "communotheism" to refer to "a community of gods" operative in African traditional religions and in the Christian Trinity.[6] Communotheism is a divine communalism: "Divine communalism is the position that the Divine is a community of gods who are fundamentally related to one another and ontologically equal while at the same time distinct from one another by their personhood and functions."[7] In communotheism, there is immanence in that there is a radical relationality among the members of the divine community and between the divine community and the world, and there is transcendence because geographic distance and "physiologi-cal de-carnation" (death) cannot destroy the radical relationality. While there is distinction (eroding any real classification of pantheism), there is no idea of a separation between the human and the divine.

The process influences in postmodern womanist theology enable it to embrace communotheistic religions like traditional Yoruba religion. As God takes in, or incorporates, the manyness of the world into who God is (the consequent nature of God), God can relate those events with God's vision for the common good, searching for the best of what has happened in order to offer those aspects back to us in our next instance of becoming. The ancestors are part of the manyness of the world that is inside of or a part of God. Yet the ancestors are also available to the world in God's calling to the world.[8] This is particularly relevant for understand-ing the concept of the ancestors and their role in creative transformation.

Ancestors appear to be like humans in that one often assumes that they do the same things in the spiritual realm that they did while living in mortal bodies, but they are not simply human beings who maintain activity after death. Ancestors are transformed in the afterlife; they have a divine quality to them. African traditional religions affirm that human beings can live on after death. The ancestors, along with *òrìṣà* and culture heroes, have special knowledge that can be accessed by the living through rituals of remembrance, rites of divination, or spirit possession.

The ancestors can creatively transform us as they teach and heal us – helping us to be the best individuals and communities that we can be. The ancestors can also assist us as we transform the world. When the ancestors guide us toward creative transformation, they not only represent the vision of God but also become part of the transformed community itself. Metaphysically, we in the temporal world can discipline our own souls, selectively incorporate particular ancestors, and use their knowledge and agency to augment our own ability to creatively trans-form the world. The processes of remembering and spirit possession can produce destructive or creative effects within the world. Remembering and embracing the past does not always help us to move creatively into the future. A postmodern womanist theology insists that we learn from the past and then use what we have learned and experienced, toward God's ideals and the creative transformation of the temporal world.

Postmodern womanist theology and science fiction

Postmodern womanist theology expands womanist uses of literature by investigat-ing black women's science fiction for an image of its theological images. Womanist religious scholarship often invokes black women's literature (nineteenth-century slave narratives and autobiographies, Harlem Renaissance literature, black arts literature and fiction from the 1980s and 1990s) as a source for black women's experiences. As a syncretic combination of the various genres of African American literature, utopian writing, science fiction, and feminist literature, black women's science fiction offers its readers numerous resources. It critiques current society and offers an alternative vision of society. It shows the value of imagination in the process of creative transformation. The society it portrays includes portraits of justice, community, feminism, and gender and sexual equality. Black women's science fiction addresses some of the problems of the day and creatively suggests solutions.

African American literary theory argues that African Diasporic literatures distinctly portray traditional African religious imagery in the plot development.[9] As part of this literary corpus, black women's science fiction references ancestors and their activity in the context of the novel. Looking, particularly, at pan-African women's literature, literary scholar Alexis Brooks DeVita asserts that pan-African women writers, consciously or unconsciously, invoke symbols that reflect African goddesses, including the female òrìṣà of traditional Yoruba religion.[10] DeVita believes that ancestors help the protagonists of African Diasporic literature to achieve their own forms of fulfillment. DeVita argues that the influence or intervention of a female òrìṣà or her symbols indicates a heroine's access to divine power and assistance.

Postmodern womanist theology draws upon this literary theory in its examination of black women's science fiction. Postmodern womanist theology looks for overt and subtle references to syncretized traditional Yoruba religion in black women's science fiction. Because black women's science fiction includes elements of traditional African religions, it helps postmodern womanist theology to draw from multiple religious traditions. Black women's literature can also serve a prophetic function in theology. Black women's science fiction can provide concrete images, models, and proposals for what could happen or what should happen. A postmodern womanist reading of black women's science fiction will reveal polydox practices that highlight multiplicity, relationality, value, and mystery.

Within the relatively small world of black women science fiction writers, Tananarive Due is one of the most well known – besides Octavia Butler. The author or co-author of eleven books, Due's only series is the *African Immortals* trilogy. Hollywood actor Blair Underwood has optioned the first book in this series – *My Soul to Keep*[11] – for movie production. The second book of the series, *The Living Blood*, offers the most historical background on how the African immortals introduced in the first book became immortal.[12] In so doing, it is the most explicitly religious volume in the *African Immortals* trilogy.

The Living Blood tells the story of an African immortal named Dawit who confers his immortality – "living blood" – onto his pregnant wife, Jessica. Born with the blood (as compared to receiving it as an adult), their daughter Fana consequently possesses powers that greatly surpass those of any of the other African immortals. Immortality first came to the people through Khaldun, who came into possession of this blood as a mortal shepherd, in the first century CE. He is now leader of the Brotherhood, a group of 59 men on whom he conferred immortality. The Brotherhood lives in a secret colony in the ancient Ethiopian city of Lalibela, where they spend their centuries learning languages, math, science, music, and meditation.

The blood has the power to heal. Jessica and her physician sister Alexis run a rural clinic in Botswana, using the blood to heal sick children. In a converging story line, Florida physician Lucas Shepard hears of the clinic, and ventures to Africa to find the sisters and bring the blood back for his leukemia-stricken son, Jared. Unfortunately, another man named Shannon O'Neal begins searching for the blood so that he can use it to his own personal and economic gain. He hires merciless mercenaries who kidnap and kill for possession of the blood.

Things begin to go awry when Jessica becomes aware that Fana, at three years old, has fast-growing powers; i.e., she can kill with a glance. Jessica journeys to Lalibela to find out how to control her daughter's powers. Jessica's arrival upsets the balance of the Brotherhood, which scatters into rival factions. Meanwhile, evil is present in the form of "shadows" that beckon Fana. The Shadows speak to Fana during mysterious trances, teaching her to make storms. The story is resolved in the midst of a hurricane that Fana unwittingly causes. Jessica and Dawit must reunite to learn how to raise their daughter and rescue her from the destructive storm she is spinning. A glimpse into the future shows a small community of mortals and immortals living on a secluded farm where they gather their blood to help heal the world of disease.

A postmodern womanist reading of *The Living Blood* names divinity in the manifestations of the Yoruba *òrìṣà Oya*, and in the depiction of the living blood. There is a Cuban understanding of *Oya* operative in Due's depiction of the powerful hurricane spun by female power. Likewise, the living blood has characteristics similar to the Yoruba concept of *àṣẹ* – divine connection, transferable, morally neutral power. The story of the blood's acquisition reproduces the religious encounter of enslaved Africans and Catholic missionaries. Finally, we see black women as Saviors who use the blood to heal and start a community of healers.

In traditional Yoruba religion, *Oya* is the Yoruba *òrìṣà* of change. In her work *Oya: In Praise of an African Goddess*, Judith Gleason refers to *Oya* as the *òrìṣà* of change represented in radical weather conditions.[13] *Oya* manifests herself in several natural forms – wind, especially tornadoes, fire, the river, and the African buffalo. *Oya* is represented in the lightning that is partnered with the elements of thunder and rain. *Oya* is also the mother of *Egungun*, the collective spirit of the ancestors. Thus *Oya* is another guardian to the realm of the ancestors: "It is *Oya* who brings the voice of those ancestors who preserved the wisdom that leads to the development of good character."[14] *Oya* is the most powerful female *òrìṣà* and is well known for her sense of justice and intolerance for the abuse and oppression of women.[15]

Devotees of *Santeria* often associate Caribbean hurricanes with *Oya* and the slave trade. These Cuban devotees of *Oya* describe tropical storms with a particular travel pattern that begins on the Western coast of Africa and moves over the Atlantic Ocean.[16] *The Living Blood* describes the hurricane in the same way:

> In its present form, it was merely an infant struggling to survive, drawing sorely needed strength. It had all the means to preserve itself: the cooing growls of playful thunderstorms that had sprung from the coast of Africa, the balmy waters of the Atlantic Ocean stroking it from below, and the even, persistent kisses of winds whipping from above.[17]

Gleason interprets this stormy pattern as an attempt to resolve the evils of slavery:

> Now storms along the seam, at their most violent ... [drift] southwest over the Atlantic with ever-increasing amplitude, suddenly strike the Caribbean. Thus, by grace of atmospheric forces beyond human control, the tornadoes of west Africa, following the slave-trade routes along which those who first named them were hauled to the hurricane-prone islands of their diaspora, achieve in the New World their apotheosis.[18]

Devotees of *Santeria* identify *Oya* in the storm. *Oya* is a witness to both the presence of Africans in America and the unique ways in which black religions blend traditional African religions with Christianity.

Oya possesses Fana as she creates wind and rain. While playing with a friend, Fana learns she can create wind. Her friend realizes that the breeze comes from Fana. Playing with her powers once again, Fana also creates rain:

> Fana shot herself into the sky, so high she nearly became dizzy. She gently wrapped herself in the invisible mist high in the sky, making it grow cooler. She drew upon the mist, pulling on it as far as she could reach, collecting it, tugging against its natural will until she felt something above her rupture, as if she'd torn a bedsheet in half, and suddenly all the ground near her feet was shaded. A cloud![19]

Fana's cloud creation is associated with a central characteristic of *Oya*, a loud tearing sound: "*O-ya* means 'she tore' in Yoruba."[20] Fana can direct *Oya's* manifestation in the world. When Fana makes it rain, her friend becomes afraid of her powers and tells her that she should not control the weather: "Who decides when it rains, you stupid girl? ... God decides ... Spirits decide ... Not you."[21] Her friend does not realize that *Oya* is possessing Fana.

Fana can use *Oya*'s power to produce either creative or destructive effects in the world. Fana's initial response to her powers is a desire to use them creatively. Fana imagines working with *Oya* to end famine and drought and to improve the lives of the people around her. Despite the creative potential of Fana's ability to create wind and rain, her storms serve as the impetus for the destructive hurricane hitting the Caribbean and Florida. Fana's small act becomes a storm that kills hundreds of people, homes, and property. Unknowingly, Fana calls the storm and *Oya*'s destructive side is loosed. Because she is a child, Fana cannot control the storms. The creative or destructive effects of *Oya*'s powers will depend upon the actions of Fana's parents, in other words, on Fana's community.

The story of the blood's acquisition reproduces the religious encounter of enslaved Africans and Catholic missionaries. The living blood cannot be destroyed. People with the blood flowing through their veins are likewise indestructible. Although they can be injured and crippled with pain, they are immune to death. When killed, the blood causes the resurrection of the whole person with his identity. The blood also gives its carriers both a heightened physical sensitivity and the ability to read the thoughts of other people. Disciplined members of the Brotherhood can read the thoughts of people around them and gently intrude sentences and ideas into other minds. That is, the blood radically intensifies relationality.

The living blood is remarkably similar to the Yoruba concept of *àṣẹ*. *Àṣẹ* is the name given to a fundamental element in the Yoruba cosmos. It is a force found in all things. Art historian Robert Farris Thompson calls *àṣẹ* "the power to make things happen, [it is] morally neutral power, power to give, and to take away, to kill and to give life, according to the nature and purpose of its bearer."[22] It imbues all creation, empowering people, objects, and natural elements with the influence of *Olódùmarè* and the *òrìṣà*, and yet the people who possess it also determine it. It is the life force of creation and of the *òrìṣà*. It is quantifiable and transferable as if it is a substance, and yet it is also living – granting ability, creativity, and efficacy. *Àṣẹ* is found in ritual tools, words, people, *òrìṣà*, and elements of nature. Henry and Margaret Thompson Drewal state that *àṣẹ* is "absolute power and potential present in all things – rocks, hills, streams, mountains, leaves, animals, sculptures, ancestors, and gods – and in utterances – prayers, songs, curses and even everyday speech."[23]

Àṣẹ is often also associated with the blood of women. This is the basis of the fear of the *aje*, often translated as "witches." "*Aje*" are older women who are perceived to have large amounts of *àṣẹ*. *Àṣẹ* is often represented by menstrual blood – symbolizing the ability to create biologically. Menstruating women are often seen as losing *àṣẹ*; therefore those who are postmenopausal are considered to have "more" *àṣẹ* (and are more powerful). People do not want to offend them for fear that these older women might use their strong forms of *àṣẹ* against them. In the Yoruba religious worldview, *àṣẹ* is associated with the unique blood of women – blood that can be shed without causing death. Jessica, Alexis and Fana must deal with the same fear of their connection to the living blood. Even while befriending Jessica and Alexis, the southern Africans refer to them as witches. Jessica tells Fana, "[w]e are not witches. You are not a witch. You are just a very powerful child. People are afraid of power. They're even more afraid of what they don't understand."[24] When people do not understand the power of the living blood, the power of women, or the power of *àṣẹ*, they demonize the women who possess it.

In the novel, the story of obtaining the blood of the crucified Jesus also directly relates to the syncretic practice of traditional Yoruba religion in the Americas. Khaldun originally obtains the living blood from a man who had stolen the blood of Jesus. This man believed that Jesus' ability to conquer death was tied to the power in his blood. When Jesus' body was taken down from the cross, the man filled a pouch with Jesus' blood. Although the blood was cold for three days, when Jesus rose, the blood became warm. The man offered several friends, including Khaldun, the gift of eternal life through a "Ritual of Life" that involved killing the men and then sharing the blood with them until they came back to life. When Khaldun was revived from death, he was given the task of performing the ritual on this man. After killing the man with a deadly poison, Khaldun hoarded the blood for himself.

When enslaved Africans were introduced to the Americas, their captors tried to convert those who were not already Christian to Christianity. The Jesuit historian Edward Reynolds describes one of Pedro Claver's (1580–1654) catechetical methods among Africans in Cuba: "He taught them, too with pictures and especially with one: a representation of Christ on the Cross, with his blood being gathered by a priest below, who, in turn, poured it over Negro neophytes."[25] With this imagery, Claver suggests that salvation literally comes from the blood of Jesus. Claver is said to have baptized over 300,000 slaves.[26] In *The Living Blood*, this story is reflected in a syncretic understanding of Jesus, salvation, and traditional Yoruba beliefs that emphasize the power of blood (*àṣẹ*) and its manipulation for good or evil.

In *The Living Blood*, creative transformation comes about as Jessica, Alexis, and others pledge themselves to a vision of "a new world" where the sickest and poorest children receive healing. A creative transformation of the blood appears in three ways. First, Jessica and Alexis commit to sharing the blood to heal. Second, Jessica dedicates herself to raising Fana to use her power to heal, and third, the community makes a commitment to using the blood to heal the world.

Jessica partners with her sister Alexis to use the blood to heal children with terminal illnesses. Jessica and Alexis refuse to possess the blood's powers and withhold its healing potential. They live in constant fear that the clinic will be shut down by the Brotherhood, inquisitive health officials, or the violent actions of people who demand the blood's powers for themselves. Nevertheless, they share the blood.

Jessica also understands that her creative transformation of the living blood involves teaching her daughter to use the blood's gifts to heal. Because she is a child, Fana is unable to control the powers that the blood gives. On one occasion, Fana becomes privy to the child-molesting thoughts of a soldier in Rome's airport. Without even realizing it, Fana's fear kills him. When Jessica realizes that Fana has no control of her blood-given powers, she insists on taking her to the Brotherhood's colony in Lalibela to learn the best use of her powers.

It turns out that Fana need not use her powers to creatively transform the world. Khaldun describes Fana's potential in this way: "Fana is both salvation and destruction. She will either be our most awaited friend or our most fearsome enemy."[27] Jessica wants to teach Fana to engage life through the way of creative transformation. She warns Fana against destructively transforming the living blood: "Promise me right now, that you will never use your mind to hurt anyone else. You're not going to abuse what God has given you."[28] Jessica's commitment to using the blood to heal extends to teaching her daughter to use her powers to heal. Meanwhile, Fana's hurricane is destroying the Caribbean and Florida. Fana's parents must comfort Fana, and walk through the turbulent winds to rescue their family and friends in order to quell the storm.

In the novel's final chapter, the reader sees a vision of creative transformation. It is 2005 and Jessica, Alexis, Dawit, Lucas, Fana, and others live on a secluded farm. This community includes mortals, and immortals, that are not unlike Jesus' band of disciples: "Soon, all twelve of them were at the table with their heads bowed. Some of them were family by genetic blood, others by immortal blood, others by their common mission. They linked hands around the table."[29] After five years of growth, the community opens its doors to the wider world. They invite a diverse group of people – healers, a lawyer, a journalist – who know they have been summoned together to hear about a medical miracle, and to learn ways to share it with the untold numbers of people who need it.

This community is a salvific community. It represents a departure from the previous form of a living blood community – the Brotherhood. This is to be expected as Jessica and Fana themselves bring novelty to the immortal community as the first females to possess the blood. This community strives to use the blood's power responsibly and heal illnesses in the world. It is a diverse community of men, women, and children, mortal and immortals, healers, lawyers, and journalists. Salvation, in this community, is not based on the unique constitution of the immortals, but by its participation in a vision of healing. This is a community with a future.

A postmodern womanist interpretation of *The Living Blood* identifies Jessica as a Savior because she uses the blood to heal and starts a community of healers. Fana is a Savior-in-training as Jessica, and others in the community, teach her to use her powers for creative transformation. Although Jessica does not refer to herself as a Savior, she interprets her activity as the fulfillment of a divine calling. Jessica attributes it to a divine source: "God had given her this blood. That was good enough for her."[30] Jessica is a Savior because she helps to start a community that uses the blood for the positive social transformation of the world. As far as Jessica is concerned, her possession of the living blood is a gift that she must use to heal other people.

Like Jessica, Fana can serve as a Savior if she uses the blood to heal. Although Khaldun first identifies Fana as a Savior, he bases his identification upon her constitution. Khaldun believes Fana can mediate between the Brotherhood and the rest of the world. He describes Fana as "a child born with the power to stand between mortal and immortal, the two races of man."[31] Khaldun defines a Savior as the mediator between two ontologically different types of beings. Jessica rejects Khaldun's desires for Fana because they do not include using the blood to heal:

> And if she performs miracles, it'll be because that's what her heart tells her to do. It'll be because she'd had a good example from me and her aunt, who believe in helping people with this blood … I'm not going to force her to feel like some kind of traffic officer trying to keep mortals and immortals apart.[32]

Jessica and Khaldun echo the traditional Christian Christological debates – is it Jesus' unique constitution/person or activities/work that render Jesus a Savior? Jessica states that it will be Fana's creative use of the blood that will make her a Savior. Fana emerges as a Savior-in-training because her storms lead to the development of the healing community.

Polydox soteriology

A postmodern womanist reading of *The Living Blood* discloses a polydox soteriology. Here we see a route to health and wholeness through the intersections of multiple religious traditions, multiple divine forces, multiple incarnations and multiple Saviors. Such a reading also suggests that polydox soteriology is transnational, transcontinental, postcolonial feminist, and womanist.

The Living Blood illustrates a polydox soteriology that does not reject the Christian doctrine of salvation. In *The Living Blood*, salvation is connected to

Christian declarations that salvation comes through Jesus in general, and through the blood of Jesus, in particular. Womanist theologians have varied perspectives on the role of Jesus' blood in salvation. Christian womanist theologian Delores S. Williams rejects objective theories of atonement, wherein the sins of humanity are satisfied through Jesus' death on the cross. Williams boldly writes, "There is nothing divine in the blood of the cross."[33] Rather, Williams's concept of salvation is rooted in Jesus' work – the ethical ministry of words, the healing ministry of touch, the ministry of expelling evil forces, prayer, compassion, and love.[34] In *Power in the Blood?*, Christian womanist theologian Joanne M. Terrell locates salvation in the suffering of Jesus on the cross.[35] Terrell pays particular attention to the African American Christian language of Jesus' blood as one of the vehicles through which humanity is restored to the right relationship with God. Terrell believes that God reveres blood. For Terrell, Jesus' death and blood are offered as a once-and-for-all sacrifice for the sins of the world. Thus, Jesus' blood-loss has eternal efficacy. There is something of God in the blood of the cross. The lives of those who have suffered and shed blood – both Jesus and contemporary sufferers – can serve as a sacramental witness to the power of God. Salvation comes from the lessons learned after instances of suffering. The very life force, the blood, of sufferers is part of the sacred means that point us toward salvation. In this argument, Terrell affirms a subjective theory of atonement wherein salvation is achieved as human beings learn from and emulate the activity of Jesus.

The soteriology portrayed in *The Living Blood* engages classic Christian questions about whether salvation comes from the person or the work of the Savior. *The Living Blood* suggests that there is something about the constitution of the Savior, something unique about the Savior's blood, that makes the Savior both human and immortal, ordinary and divine, capable of death and resurrection. Khaldun identifies Fana as the Savior following this vein of Christian soteriology. Like the theology of Delores Williams, a postmodern womanist reading emphasizes salvation as the activity or "work" of healing – connected to the root word of salvation, "salve." Like Terrell, a postmodern womanist reading of *The Living Blood* argues that the blood can teach us something important about salvation. Yet, departing from Terrell, a postmodern womanist reading asserts that even those without the living blood can function as Saviors if they lead communities that use the living blood for healing the world. That is, no one person atones for all.

The polydox soteriology in *The Living Blood* bends backwards toward some strands within Christian soteriology – salvation as connected to the blood of Jesus; salvation as health; salvation through the person and/or work of the Savior. Yet it also bends forwards and away from concepts of salvation that focus on declarations of belief or justifying the work of God in one person or persons. Indeed part of the *poly*doxy of this salvation is that it involves salvation through many people, to many people and through more than one religious tradition.

In *The Living Blood*, salvation comes about through the invocation of multiple religious traditions and multiple forms of divinity. There is Christian imagery in the connection to Jesus, as well as clear connections to traditional Yoruba religion through the connection to the *òrìsà* Oya and *àsẹ*. *The Living Blood* reveals connections to the particular historical and religious experiences of formerly enslaved Africans in Cuba. The hurricane that Fana creates follows the same route as the triangular slave trade. Cuban *santeros* recognize *Oya* as an embodiment of angry ancestors in such weather patterns. By echoing this story about *Oya*, found only in Cuban Santeria, *The Living Blood* wrestles with the syncretic nature of black religiosity. Black religiosity often is not purely traditional African nor Christian. It is a complex mix with recognizable parent strands – in this case Catholicism and traditional Yoruba religions – while being its own novel practice.

Likewise, *The Living Blood* describes the acquisition of the blood with a story of blood stolen from the crucified Jesus Christ. A similar story is conveyed in an icon used in Pedro Claver's historical missionary practices in Cuba. It is difficult to know how enslaved Africans understood this story. On the one hand, many of them probably brought complex understandings of blood and *àṣẹ* to the encounter. On the other hand, Claver was very sympathetic toward the enslaved Africans and is still heralded as a patron saint among many Afro-Caribbean Catholic communities. This polydox soteriology occupies a third space as it speaks directly to the role of religion in the colonial activity of Spain against the enslaved Africans and the indigenous population of Cuba. This polydox soteriology draws from Catholicism, traditional Yoruba understandings of *àṣẹ* and Cuban Santeria – while quietly condemning theft. *The Living Blood* condemns the theft of Jesus' blood by Khaldun, the violent ways the mercenaries try to steal the blood, and – as postmodern womanist reading assumes – the theft of African bodies in the slave trade. Polydox soteriology becomes postcolonial as it condemns colonial activity, and yet works with its consequences to heal the world. Polydox soteriology does not eschew the conflicts of religious and political history; rather it acknowledges, assesses, and utilizes this toward creative transformation.

This reading of salvation in *The Living Blood* bears other markers of polydoxy (in addition to multiplicity). The normative goal of creative transformation gives value to the multiple options available with the use of the blood. The process roots of postmodern womanism affirm relationality and universal incarnation of divinity. Relationality can be seen in the radical incarnation of blood and divinity. Not only is incarnation universal in the way that the blood can be transferred to anyone, but divinity is evident in multiple forces. There is divine power or divinity itself in the wind, rain, the hurricane, the blood, Jessica, Fana, Dawit, and many others. Finally, there is an element of mystery. While both blood and *àṣẹ* are real in their contexts, they maintain a level of mystery. We never know how or why they are efficacious. Even the medical doctors in the novel cannot discern the composition of the blood, or why it works the way that it does.

If we read *The Living Blood* through a postmodern womanist theological lens, we can learn how to practice a polydox soteriology. We learn that the route to health will be global. It may be as transnational as Jessica's journey from Botswana to Ethiopia or as transcontinental as the triangular slave trade and the current movement of African Americans between the United States, the Caribbean, and the continent of Africa. Yet a polydox soteriology is also necessarily postcolonial. It acknowledges the colonial practices of enslavement and proselytization that led to the creation of entire religious and cultural traditions, while advocating the practices that lead to liberation, justice, and freedom.

A polydox soteriology is also feminist and womanist. It challenges the status quo and sees salvation in the activities of women. Perhaps, as in *The Living Blood*, women (and women's communities) are uniquely qualified to initiate polydox soteriology. Perhaps they can invoke female deities concerned with women's justice to destroy exclusive death-dealing practices in the world and promote healing and wholeness.

A polydox soteriology may be complex, but it is liveable and loveable. It was the love between Jessica and Dawit that created Fana, in the first place. The powerful force of salvation was created quite literally from love. The community envisioned at the end of the novel is bound together by the blood, but more so by their intentional creative harnessing of the blood, and the affections they have for one another. As they plan a way forward, they also experience the bonds of love: through marriage, sexual expression, and child rearing.

If *The Living Blood* is any indication of a polydox soteriology, then we must also understand that a polydox soteriology may be dangerous. The potential for creativity also contains potential for destruction. While there are some who are interested in the common good, there are also many who are interested in personal and private goods. Individualism and greed often engages violence to get its way. Many individuals and institutions are invested in a single "right" way. This is as true of politics and economics as it is of religion. Pursuing polydox soteriology involves risk – if only because it challenges neater, more unitary approaches toward the same goal. Nevertheless the world is complex and diverse, and a polydox way appears to be necessary – if we are to heal the world.

Notes

1   Alice Walker writes a four-part description of "womanist" which includes the phrase: "Committed to survival and wholeness of entire people, male *and* female. Not a separatist, except periodically, for health." A. Walker (ed.), *In Search of Our Mothers' Gardens: Womanist Prose*, New York: Harcourt Brace & Company, 1983, pp. xi–xii.

2   The argument in this section is a summary of postmodern womanist theology as laid out in my book: M. A. Coleman, *Making A Way Out of No Way: A Womanist Theology*, Minneapolis, MN: Fortress Press, 2008.

3   G. S. Wilmore, *Black Religion and Radicalism: An Interpretation of the Religious History of African Americans*, Maryknoll, NY: Orbis Books, 1998, 3rd ed., p. 280.

4   Many *òrìṣà* in Yoruba religion have multiple names although they signify the same force. This is partly attributable to the distribution of the religion throughout Yorubaland, and the Yoruba-based religions in the New World. This chapter may refer to *Olódùmarè/Olorun, Obatala/Oriṣa-nla, Orunmila/Ifà, Èṣù/Elegba/Elegbara*. This chapter will also use the "ṣ" to indicate the sound of "sh." There is no consistency in scholarship (usually because of the inconsistent capability of word processors and attempts to translate into English) so "*àṣẹ*" is also "ashe" and "*òrìṣà*" is also "orisha." Note *òrìṣà* is the same in the plural or singular usage.

5   For more information see: G. Edwards and J. Mason, *Black Gods: Orisa Studies in the New World*, Brooklyn, NY: Yoruba Theological Archministry, 1985; E. B. Idowu,

Olodumare: God in Yoruba Belief, New York: A and B Books, 1994; and J. Olupona and T. Ray (eds), *Orisa Devotion as World Religion: The Globalization of Yoruba Religious Culture,* Madison, WI: University of Wisconsin, 2008.

6   A. O. Ogbannaya, *On Communitarian Divinity: An African Interpretation of the Trinity,* New York: Paragon House, 1994.

7   Ibid., p. 23.

8   I have made this argument in greater detail in "From Models of God to a Model of Gods: How Whiteheadian Language Facilitates Western Language Discussion of Divine Multiplicity," *Philosophia,* 35: 3–4, 2007, pp. 329–40.

9   W. Soyinka, *Myth, Literature and the African World,* Cambridge: Cambridge University Press, 1976; and H. L. Gates, Jr., *The Signifying Monkey: A Theology of African-American Literary Criticism,* New York: Oxford University Press, 1988.

10   A. B. DeVita, *Mythatypes: Signatures and Signs of African/Diaspora and Black Goddesses,* Westport, CT: Greenwood Press, 2000.

11   T. Due, *My Soul to Keep,* New York: Eos, 1998.

12   T. Due, *The Living Blood,* New York: Simon & Schuster, 2000.

13   J. Gleason, *Oya: In Praise of an African Goddess,* New York: HarperSanFrancisco, 1992.

14   A. Fá'lokun Fatunmbi, *Oya: Ifa and the Spirit of the Wind,* Bronx, NY: Original Publications, 1993, p. 12.

15   A. Isola, "Oya: Inspiration and Empowerment," *Dialogue and Alliance,* Spring–Summer 1998, Vol. 12, p. 61.

16   J. Gleason, "Oya in the Company of the Saints," *Journal of the American Academy of Religion,* 68, 2, 2000, p. 276.

17   Due, p. 373.

18   Gleason, p. 31.

19   Due, p. 74.

20   Gleason, p. 5.

21   Due, p. 75.

22   R. F. Thompson, *Flash of the Spirit: African and Afro-American Art and Philosophy,* New York: Vintage, 1983, p. 5.

23   H. Drewal and M. T. Drewal, *Gelede: Art and Female Power Among the Yoruba,* Bloomington, IN: Indiana University Press, 1983, p. 5.

24   Due, p. 93.

25   E. D. Reynolds, *Jesuits for the Negro,* New York: America Press, 1949, p. 22.

26   Joseph Murphy reflects on this practice: "We can only imagine how Yoruba slaves would interpret this catechesis or what truth of Christian dogma they would derive from it." J. M. Murphy, *Santería: An African Religion in America,* Boston, MA: Beacon Press, 1988, p. 110. As a side note, Claver is best known for his missionary activities in Cartagena, Columbia, but he did work in other Caribbean countries, including Cuba.

27   Due, p. 271.

28   Ibid., p. 98.

29   Ibid., p. 509.

30   Ibid., p. 208.

31   Ibid., p. 273.

32   Ibid., p. 274.

33   D. S. Williams, *Sisters in the Wilderness: The Challenge of Womanist God-Talk,* Maryknoll, NY: Orbis Books, 1993, p. 167.

34   Ibid.

35   J. M. Terrell, *Power in the Blood?: The Cross in the African American Experience,* Maryknoll, NY: Orbis Books, 1998.

11 "They'll know we are process thinkers by our …"

Finding the ecological ethic
of Whitehead through the lens of
Jainism and ecofeminist care

Brianne Donaldson

There is a poignant dissonance within the hymn from which the title of this paper is derived: "They will know we are Christians by our love." Written in 1968 by Chicago Parish Priest Peter R. Scholtes, one can hardly miss the irony. Scholtes, marked by a tradition that reveres religious power and priestly piety, suggests "love" as the outward sign which most aptly demonstrates this group identity. Yet it is not the regalia of the pontiff or the sacraments at the altar, but love as unity, cooperation, and in-group team building that permeates each refrain of Scholtes' melodic vision.

However, there are no instructions in these lyrics regarding what to do when one reaches the liminal edge of Scholtes' in-group perimeter. Whether the dynamics of love or power win out when identity collides with difference is unclear. The choir is naked it seems, without the cover of any ideological garments when encountering the multiplicity that lurks outside the group's edge.

English mathematician and philosopher Alfred North Whitehead locates the creative unfolding of life at these edges, where multiplicities collide and, although he left no record of hymn writing to help subsequent generations navigate this precarious borderland, there is much about power and love to be gleaned from his considerable writings. In Whitehead's process worldview, every event in space-time uniquely creates itself from the past it inherits, always constituted and affected by an array of relationships – from a historical multiplicity – and contributing its own becoming to the future of manifold possibilities. To paraphrase Whitehead, the many become one and are increased by that one.[1]

Difference is not merely tolerated in this process, but its presence is vital to the liveliness of reality as we can, and cannot, see it. Radical relationism of this magnitude begins where, according to Catherine Keller, "the mere celebration of difference breaks down – where the exuberant affirmation of pluralism seeks more than the rupture of old boundaries and the proliferation of new ones."[2] It begins where "love" moves us beyond group identity into the margins of a wild, unruly encounter with otherness.

Counterintuitive love of this sort is not easily lyricized for the masses. In fact, exchanging the values of western culture, built upon boundaries of self-, human-, national-, and consumer-centeredness, for values that might acknowledge, say, that "the life of an insect might be every bit as valuable as my own," would be a hard sell for even the most accomplished saleswoman. It's just not easy to market, much less embody, attitudes, actions, or songs that represent "not only a rejection, but a *reversal* of the values that are dominant in contemporary Western [sic] society."³ Of course, there are still those who endeavor to do just that.

Ecofeminist philosophers in the West embody the reversal by encouraging a contextual, care-centric ethics that transgress boundaries of species, gender, race, and class. As a political and social movement that incorporates elements of American environmentalism and feminism, ecofeminism's considerable critique of domination structures that perpetuate exploitation of "others" will not be altogether unfamiliar to a mainstream audience, though its implications and ethical commitments – such as vegetarianism or veganism, political and economic solidarity in voting and purchasing, as well as correctives to symbolic/linguistic hierarchies – certainly might be.⁴

A greater leap of imagination is required to consider the lesser-known religion of Jainism. Tracing its Indian roots back as far back as the ninth century BCE, Jainism prescribes a path of peace and non-violence toward all living beings and has influenced and been influenced by the co-development of both Hinduism and Buddhism.⁵ Though these three religions share a muddled history of origins and influences, each represents a unique response to the Vedic traditions of the time. And while each of the three stress the importance of compassion and nonviolence, Jains extend these principles, as a corporate commitment held by both monastic and lay members, more widely than their Hindu or Buddhist counterparts, to include all humans, animals, insects, and even microscopic life forms.

Though there is a standard caricature of Jain monks sweeping the path clear of insects and wearing gauze masks so as not to inhale any microorganisms, many outsiders do not realize that the majority of Jains do not fit this representation, though they, too, strive to uphold high ecological and ethical principles. For non-monastic Jains in India and in immigrant communities around the world, these ethical principals are expressed minimally in choosing a vocation that does not involve injury to life, a verdant and unique vegetarianism (no meat, eggs, honey, or certain root vegetables whose cultivation either destroys the entire plant or is especially disruptive to the environment it was growing in; many Jains avoid dairy as well), charity, service, and the avoidance of waste.⁶

Insofar as the ecological ethics of ecofeminist philosophy and Jainism represent a contrast to dominant paradigms, they also offer insight into how contemporary actions might honor uncommon collisions between humans and the particular environments they live within. This contrast may prove useful to a process community seeking to embody its own radically relational worldview.

Ecofeminists, however, have historically been mistrustful of metaphysical justifications for such actions, criticizing systems that are based upon notions of universalization and transcendence, which diminish and devalue difference and particularity within relationships. I intend to demonstrate that Whitehead's metaphysics addresses these concerns, offering a helpful lens through which to discuss individual relationships and embodied care toward one's ecological surroundings.

This embodied care is similar to the Jain principle of *ahimsa*, meaning the avoidance of harm, and can be further elucidated by examining two Jain doctrines of relativity, alongside Whitehead's description of misplaced concreteness and mutual immanence. By doing this multi-directional comparison between Whitehead, ecofeminist critiques, and Jain doctrines, I contend we will discover a process view of reality that leaves us dressed in the vestments of an ecological ethic marked by individualized, embodied care and a unique spirit of responsive *ahimsa*, that can be enacted in the space where love, power, and differences collide.

The ecofeminist critique of universalization

Though Whitehead never spoke of an ecological ethic per se, we can find distinct points throughout his writings that suggest "the unfading importance of our immediate actions" within a relational, multiplicitous, process metaphysics.[7] Yet it is exactly the notion of metaphysics that makes some ecofeminists lay back their ears in warning. Ecofeminist author Jim Cheney suggests that the drive toward internal coherence in our relationship to other beings and the planet can lead to a place where "rather than an ethical voice emergent from existential encounter, from genuine relationship, we get an ethical voice grounded in the authoritarian, impersonal truth of metaphysics, of internalized vision."[8]

Rather than allowing particular situations to place their claim upon us, Cheney warns that metaphysics often lead, to a misguided search for universal maxims that can guide behavior. Consequently, the unique features of every situation are swallowed up in universalization, along with the ability to recognize the specific cares and concerns of the self or other in any given moment. The temptation to settle for the easy illusion of prescriptive generalizations can override the potential surprise lurking within each unexpected situation, person, or even a particular spider who crosses our path. One cannot help but think of the "Some Pig!" that the extraordinary Charlotte weaves in her web to celebrate her remarkable porcine companion.[9]

The realm of embodied particularity has long been associated with women and nature while the universal sovereign Self – with its masculinized ideals – is that part of a western rational inheritance that denies difference by merely incorporating the other into one's self. While this fusion of self and other might temporarily quell feelings of alienation, it also, as Cheney rightly notes, allows an impersonal authoritarian metaphysics to override the genuine differences we encounter in the "others" around us.

A solution: *anekāntavāda* and misplaced concreteness

Without giving a full explication of Whitehead's philosophy, it is important to note that his own metaphysics is exceedingly paradoxical. Roland Faber explains how, in *Religion in the Making*, Whitehead sets a stage for the paradox that runs through his entire philosophical corpus. Whitehead first defines metaphysics succinctly as "the science which seeks to discover the general ideas which are indispensable to the analysis of everything that happens."[10] Yet at the same time, Faber notes, Whitehead "warns us to *mistrust* metaphysics"[11] due to what Whitehead calls the "defect of a[ny] metaphysical system that is the very fact that it is a neat little system of thought, which thereby over-simplifies its expression of the world."[12] So, while Whitehead never gives up on the idea of metaphysics, his work suggests that metaphysics is always essentially incomplete.

This incompletion is built into the very structure of events in themselves. In a process universe, the present is created out of collisions between existing data and subjective freedom where something new, or novel, emerges from its history. Subjective freedom means that each event responds to the limitations and possibilities of its particular past and yet still uniquely creates itself from that past. In this way, Whitehead's philosophy rests upon a foundation of particular relationality in which the play between differences propels the creative un/re/folding of lives. For Whitehead, "[t]he [particular] individual is formative of the society, the [particular] society is formative of the individual."[13] Beyond a mere affirmation of difference or plurality, Whitehead suggests that the deliberate proliferation of *new* contrasts allows each event to "contribute to the massive feeling of the whole, [as] the whole contributes to the intensity of feeling of the parts."[14] Per Faber:

> This is the nucleus of the paradox of Whitehead's metaphysics: that it strives for a generality that is always already undermined by the creative passage of structures and the creative advance of a world of events beyond any structural stability, which would allow us to analyze this world in terms of universals.[15]

In a similar manner, Jain philosophy also sidesteps the critique of universalizing metaphysics because it is constructed on a foundation of relativity. In his dissertation, entitled "Plurality and Relativity: Whitehead, Jainism, and the Reconstruction of Religious Pluralism," Jeffery Long points out that in both Whitehead and Jainism, relativity should not be confused with "relativism" which "affirms either that there is no truth, or that the truth, whatever it may be, is something that is altogether unknowable by human beings."[16]

On the contrary, the paradox of *absolute relativity* affirms "the vital importance of the perspective from which a claim is made."[17] In process philosophy, this move toward relativity – or we could say relationality – shows up in the subjectivity and novelty afforded to all events, but it is also a hallmark of Whitehead's metaphysics in and of themselves as essentially incomplete, captured in Whitehead's enigmatic "fallacy of misplaced concreteness."[18] To understand this fallacy of misplaced concreteness, we can look to an analogous doctrine within Jainism called by the Sanskrit word *anekāntavāda*, which can be translated as "many-sided doctrine."[19]

As a central philosophical doctrine in Jainism with potentially pre-Vedic origins, *anekāntavāda*'s fundamental claim is that all existent entities have infinite attributes.[20] As summarized by the sixth-century Jain logician Haribhadra in the *Saddarsanasmuccaya*, "Existence is accepted as that which is characterized by emergence, perishing, and duration."[21] On account of this, it is said that an entity has infinite attributes and "cannot be reduced to a single characteristic or concept."[22]

This claim stems from the ontological pragmatism of the Jain position that reality is irreducibly complex and the apparent contradictions within our perceptions, like "continuity and change, emergence and perishing, permanence and flux, identity and difference – actually reflect the interdependent, relationally constituted nature of things."[23] There is something inherently unstable about every element in our surroundings, even as we may perceive them as stable. Where there appears to be continuity, emergence, permanence, and identity, there is already also change, perishing, flux, and difference. Thus, the number of characteristics that can be validly assigned to any element of reality is correspondingly infinite.

Accordingly, to say that "x is f," is a one-sided perception, unconditioned by rival assertions that account for infinitude. According to Jain scholars, such propositions are "to be regarded as false."[24] The truth value of any element of reality depends on the perspective from which it is viewed and must be complemented by rival perspectives. Jains use a version of "The Blind Men and the Elephant" fable to express this multi-dimensionality of truth. The blind man who feels the elephant's leg says it is like a pillar; the one who feels the tail says the elephant is like a rope; the one who feels the trunk says the elephant is like a tree branch, and so on. A wise man finally affirms all of their perceptions and illustrates the principle of living in harmony with people of different belief systems.[25]

This move toward relativity is represented in Whitehead's "fallacy of misplaced concreteness," a diagnosis he gives to philosophical systems that seek to establish an eternal order of structural integrity in the world. While Whitehead does, in *Science and the Modern World*, define a *principle of concretion* that describes the most basic characteristics of an actual world as "irrational process,"[26] he emphasizes, according to Faber, that "metaphysical structures are nothing but abstractions of the process of becoming itself, they are neither concrete nor are they actualizing forms of eternity."[27] Like the infinite characteristics assigned to reality in the Jain position, Whitehead's misplaced concreteness exists because his metaphysics is based in *incomplete possibilities*. Faber continues, "any metaphysical claim must have that status of *a possibility for actualization* and, hence, 'describes' [sic] the actual world as one that is *actually* incomplete, that is, incomplete because of the irrationality of its creative activity."[28]

Consequently, the interplay between possibility and actualization represents a relationship of mutual requirement where, for Whitehead, "the 'realm' of 'eternal ideas' is not absolute but only *relative* to the world-process in its ultimate irrationality."[29] The realm of eternal ideas is not singularly fixed but rather interacts with the breadth of actualization as "pure multiplicity, per se chaotic, without unity, lacking any definite structure, only being unified in the actual process of becoming itself."[30]

This mutual requirement between possibility and actualization is comparable to the Jain sentiment that, "unlike other Indian (and Western) notions of substance as having no real relations with any other entity," every definition of an entity from a Jain perspective "includes within itself the entity's relations, both of being and of non-being, with every other entity constituting the cosmos."[31] This multiplicity of relative interrelation is *the* universal center of Jain metaphysics described in the doctrine of *anekāntavāda*. Likewise, for Whitehead, the "fallacy of misplaced concreteness" according to Faber:

is not just a statement on the status of metaphysical claims in differentiation from "reality," but also a statement about the "reality" itself *insofar* as
it cannot be conceptualized. Hence, principles and categories ought to be
incomplete not because we are limited by culture and language but precisely
because this limitation of principles and categories is the *very condition* for
the conceptualization of *actuality as actuality*.[32]

It is worth noting the language that Faber uses in the above passages. He links relativity with *irrationality*, *incompleteness*, and *relational creativity*. In contrast to
what ecofeminist Marti Kheel names as the dominant traits of masculinity in the
modern era, namely rationality, universality, and autonomy, Faber's interpretation
of Whitehead's metaphysics parallels the corresponding female characteristics
which Kheel names nonrationality (or emotionalism), particularity, and relation
and dependence.[33] Yet, it is from the dominant traits that "a series of dualisms
emerge: culture/nature, male/female, good/evil, domestic/wild, conscious/uncon-
scious, subject/object, human/animal." These dualities share a common thread of
"transcending the female-imaged biological world."[34] It seems quite possible that
Whitehead has dissolved these dualities into a worldview of incompleteness and
mutual requirement.

Both Jainism and process thought offer universal systems that are paradoxically based in the fundamental incompleteness of relational processes. We will
now move to the ecofeminist critique of transcendence to show how Whitehead's
non-masculinized structure of reality moves us closer to an ecological ethic.

The ecofeminist critique of transcendence

Transcendence, from an ecofeminist perspective, is often burdened by notions of
progress, and height. Progress too often suggests a directional perfectability while
the "privilege of heights" imagines the transcendent as something above, using
spatial metaphors that result in hierarchy. According to Mayra Rivera:

> Hierarchical caricatures of transcendence depend on hypercertainties sup-
> ported by claims to absolute knowledge, totalizing systems that foreclose the
> openness, excess, and irreducibility that transcendence implies, for it appeals
> to a realm beyond the grasp of normative subjects, systems of thought, and
> social structures that would threaten the certainties on which these hierar-
> chies depend. Transcendence is thus relegated to an invisible realm and thus
> effectively prevented from touching our daily lives.[35]

In these cases, the whole of the natural world in general, and the lives of individual other-than-human beings in particular, are seen as the theatre upon which the
development and preservation of humanity takes place. So we are left with a hierarchical model of stewardship where humans are "managers" of "lower" matter.
Further, we are left with an instrumental view of nature and the individual beings
within it, whereby they become mere faceless means to help humans achieve our

private ends. Conservation efforts that sacrifice individual animals for the sake of the whole species is one example of this, i.e., killing wolves to save "The Wolf" or killing deer to conserve a lasting deer population for ongoing sport hunting.

Finally, standard notions of transcendence often separate the self from vulnerable interconnection and reinforce cultural and societal structures of masculine identity and dualism that distance humans from their cultural and ecological habitats as though somehow preserved in a bubble-wrap of perceived uniqueness, removed from vulnerable interconnection with support systems and fellow creatures. This is represented in Keller's work on "the separative self," in which the "subject must deny the influences that others have in it ... [and that] this can only be achieved through domination" in which subduing an other allows the self to be in "possession of itself."[36] In sum, ideas of transcendence typically separate or distinguish difference among individuals while failing to emphasize the relationship *between* co-members of ecological systems.

A solution: *syādvāda* and mutual immanence

Both Jainism and process thought, because of their perspective on relational relativity, can address the ecofeminist critiques of metaphysics discussed above. Already we see that Whitehead's work regarding subjectivity and novelty navigates ecofeminist hurdles insofar as real subjective creativity within individual processes bridges dualistic separation and hierarchy. There is no "separative self" to speak of that exists independent of particular events and networks of continuous mutual response. Rather, there is an embedded "debt toward that which gives and renews life," a give-and-take in the midst of relational multiplicity.[37]

Further, the locus of transcendence changes so that neither matter nor consciousness are best defined by what is above or ahead – something one is *progressing* toward – but rather by the *process* itself, where the spark of creative agency flashes *within* every novel moment. In fact, similar interpretations of transcendence have already influenced ecofeminists such as Ignacio Ellacuria's *intracosmic model of transcendence* – influential for later liberation and ecofeminist work – in which the "future emerges from within the matrices of relations."[38] Yet, I think, there is even more we can glean from Whitehead on this point of transcendence by looking to his work on mutual immanence.

In *Adventures of Ideas*, Whitehead describes mutual immanence as centrally descriptive of his metaphysics, and indeed of the entire universe as process. Whitehead draws upon the common ground shared by Aristotle, Plato, Epicurus, Lucretius, and Leibnitz when he posits "the diverse notions of communication between real individuals" and "the diverse notions of the mediating basis in virtue of which such communication is attained."[39] For Whitehead, if anything could be generalizable or transcendent in the universe, it is the reality of mutual immanence as "a natural matrix for all things," or a "medium of intercommunication" that unifies everything in the natural world.[40]

Ecofeminists, however, might claim that this is merely another universal, ultimately capturing everything with a transcendent category or over-arching principle. But in Whitehead's formulation, "there is no universality transcending the mutual immanence of all actualities, which already harbour possibilities, categories, and principles. It is a non-category, a non-principle. It is not a unity, but pure difference. It is not form, but only connection,"[41] where "universality defined by 'communication' can suffice."[42]

This communication results in linguistic dialectics within Whitehead, most notably the God/World relational dialectic that he constructs in *Process and Reality*. Here he sets out his antithetical proofs embodying the phenomenon of mutual immanence:

> It is as true to say that God is permanent and the World fluent, as that the world is permanent and God is fluent. It is as true to say the God is one and the World many, as that the World is one and God many ... It is as true to say that God transcends the World, as that the World transcends God. It is as true to say that God creates the World, as that the World creates God.[43]

The mutual immanence expressed in these proofs finds equivalent articulation in Jainism as *syādvāda*, or dialectic of relativity. Translatable literally as the "maybe doctrine," or more accurately as the "doctrine of conditional or qualified assertion," *syādvāda* in a non-exclusivist, non-absolutist form of speech, rooted in a metaphysics of relativity.[44] As described by Bimal Krishna Matilal, "'syat' means, in the Jain use, a conditional YES. It is like saying, 'in a certain sense, yes.'"[45] As a participle meant to convey indefiniteness, Jains use it paradoxically, according to Long, to disambiguate language or "to coordinate the exclusive, one-sided claims made by various competing schools of thought with partially valid perspectives, or nayas."[46] The seven applications of *syādvāda* (a combination of *syat* or "in some respect" with *eva* or "absolutistic import") results in seven possible truth claims that state:

1   In a certain sense, x exists.
2   In a certain sense, x does not exist.
3   In a certain sense, x exists and does not exist.
4   In a certain sense, x is inexpressible.
5   In a certain sense, x both exists and is inexpressible.
6   In a certain sense, x does exist and is inexpressible.
7   In a certain sense, x does not exist and is inexpressible.[47]

Matilal suggests that Jains use this sevenfold formula as a method of refined concession within philosophical debate:

> It concedes the opponent's thesis in order to blunt the sharpness of his attack and disagreement, and at the same time it is calculated to persuade the opponent to see another point of view or carefully consider the other side of the case. Thus, the Jain use of "syat" has both; it has a disarming effect and contains (implicitly) a persuasive force.[48]

The persuasive force embodied in the Jain employment of *syādvāda* as linguistic destabilization is similar to the paradoxical transcending principle in Whitehead's metaphysics which takes the form of mutual immanence.[49] As with *syādvāda* – the function of which is to "demonstrate the incompleteness, the partiality, of the truths expressed in non-Jain perspectives," Whitehead's idea of mutual immanence acts as a similar dialectic where, "universality and relativity, singularity and relationality, creativity and extension are differently related: they are *manifolds in mutual immanence* of which time, space, ideality (eternal objects), extension, and creativity are expressions of their mutual, universal incompleteness."[50]

Far from the hierarchy of height and progress implied in standard notions of transcendence that rightly earn ecofeminist critiques, the concepts of *syādvāda* and mutual immanence are as much a recognition of inextricable relationality as they are intellectual tools to bring to ethical contexts. Faber's interpretation of mutual immanence reinforces the point clearly, saying, "[mutual immanence] is a *critical* notion that, in refuting any transcendence of categories and principles, denies anything the status of origin, source, ground, aim or goal beyond the nexus of happenings itself. It is anti-hierarchical!"[51] It is from this point, having confronted ecofeminist concerns over transcendence as well as universalization, that we can begin to synthesize an extension of Whitehead's formula with the Jain notion of *ahimsa* and an ecofeminist ethos of care.

Whitehead's ecological ethics?

While Whitehead's metaphysics appears to address ecofeminist concerns over dominant western formulations of transcendence and universalization, the question of ethics is not fully answered. We are still left with the practical inquiry, "How do we live?" Although Whitehead recognizes ethics as one of several influences within the becoming process of the universe, he more often describes measures of beauty and intensity as the ultimate goal of processes.[52] Yet, this does not mean that Whitehead has nothing concrete to offer about how we should get on in the world.

If Whitehead's metaphysics have shown us anything thus far it is that any ethic has to be consistent with the relativity of misplaced concreteness and the dialectic relationality of mutual immanence. Once again we can look to the Jains for direction. L. M. Singhvi's "Jain Declaration on Nature" reads:

> Because it is rooted in the doctrine(s) of *anekāntavāda* and *syādvāda*, Jainism does not look upon the universe from an anthropocentric, ethnocentric or egocentric viewpoint. It takes into account the viewpoints of other species, other communities and nations and other human beings.[53]

Where the two doctrines of *anekāntavāda* and *syādvāda* begin to concretely affect action is in their location within the larger metaphysical context of Jainism. The central principle in Jainism, entailed by its overall cosmology, is *ahimsa*, often translated as "nonviolence," or more accurately "the absence of even the desire to do harm."[54] Ethically, according to Long, this is the principle which can give the Jain doctrines of relativity (and by extension, Whitehead's misplaced concreteness and mutual immanence) their "critical edge."[55]

Within the Jain *darsana* – a notion modeled after the Greek "philosophia" that denotes a total worldview and way of life – Jainism, similar to the process worldview, sees itself "as co-extensive with the nature of reality itself – with the true nature of things."[56] The Jain *darsana* describes an internally coherent system that assumes a logical relationship between the ethical principle of *ahimsa* and the dialectical relativity of *anekāntavāda* and *syādvāda*. In Jainism, the cardinal sin is, after all, one-sided interpretation.

Long uses the example of Nazism as a test case in which truth claims against others (i.e., that some groups of Jews, Gypsies, etc., are fundamentally different from the Nazi) must be conditioned by its contrary (those people who are different from the Nazi are also like him or her). A simultaneous recognition of the difference and similarity "would complete [the Nazi's] one-sided perspective, thereby logically negating the violence inherent in it."[57] In this way, the dialectics of relativity function as a philosophy of nonviolence. Writes Long:

> If one can presume, a priori, that all claims which could entail injury to others must necessarily contain a one-sided affirmation – which will, in all likelihood, typically be an affirmation of some seemingly unbridgeable distance between the speaker and the object of his intended violence – and then correct this one-sidedness with an affirmation of its contrary – namely, the common humanity, or "beingness," of the speaker and the object of his intended violence – then one should be able to avoid the problem of one's pluralistic interpretive method inadvertently justifying truth-claims which advocate or approve of violent acts.[58]

In a similar way, Whitehead's mutual immanence and misplaced concreteness posit metaphysical perspectives of incompletion that, when complemented by mutual requirement and inherent relationality, negate the one-dimensional otherness necessary to justify violence. Further, in non-anthropocentric metaphysical traditions, like Hinduism, Buddhism, and Jainism (and arguably now, process thought as well), one is:

> Enjoined to follow something like the Golden Rule because all beings – and not only humans – ultimately constitute one Being, one Oversoul – or *Brahman* ... or [as in the theistic traditions of the West], all beings are affirmed to be children of God ... [or as in Buddhism] all beings are dependently co-originated and ultimately no different from one "self".[59]

Process philosophers are not of one mind regarding violence – more aptly called "violation" by Keller, to signify uniquely human systems of power and repetitive brutality[60] – and nonviolence. But, while Whitehead himself contends that "life is robbery,"[61] the central affirmation of process thought – that experience is shared by all entities – offers not only a logical basis to avoid complicity with as much violence as possible, but also a "positive injunction to work for the good of all beings."[62]

For Whitehead, this positive injunction *beyond* non-violation might look very much like the Jain *darsana* rooted in this embodied *way of ahimsa*. It might look very much like an ecofeminist philosophy that, according to Kheel, "is not so much an ethic as a consciousness or ethos":

> It is a "way of life" or a mode of consciousness that invites us to be "responsi-ble," not in the sense of conforming to obligations and rights, but in the literal sense of developing the ability for response. It is an invitation to dissolve the dualistic thinking that separates reason from emotion, the conscious from unconscious, the "domestic" from the "wild," and animal advocacy from nature ethics. It welcomes the larger scientific stories of evolutionary and ecological processes, but never loses sight of the individual beings who exist within these larger narratives.[63]

Surprisingly, we find a strikingly similar definition of "peace" in Whitehead's *Adventures of Ideas*. As one of the five qualities of civilization, Whitehead puts the ethos of peace this way, "[h]ere by the last quality of Peace, I am not referring to political relations. I mean a quality of mind steady in its reliance that fine action is treasured in the nature of things."[64]

With a metaphysical system that describes the "nature of things" as relative in their particular concreteness to one another and in mutually immanent relations of co-dependence and creative novelty, Whitehead's ethic is not an absolute, total-izing demand. Just as his metaphysics is rooted in paradox, so too is any process ethics. Like the reality in which ethical action resides, Whitehead might well con-sider "fine action" to be that ethos of genuine responsiveness that develops out of recognizing the subjective value and interdependence – and the similarities and differences therein – of all matter and all beings, human or non-human.

Like the relationship in Jainism between the doctrines of *anekāntavāda* and *syādvāda* and the core affirmation of *ahimsa* as a lived expression of metaphysi-cal claims, a "care-sensitive" ethics in process thought honors the multiplicity of priorities within human care and concern in a given moment, even as it honors the metaphysical foundations of relationality and immanence that characterize our very existence.

This contextualized understanding of care and responsiveness is lived out eco-logically in the Jain code of conduct that stresses nonviolence in thought and deed, gentleness toward plants and animals, comprehensive vegetarianism, self-restraint, avoidance of waste, and charity.[65] It is lived out in the ecofeminist perspective that includes in its ecological evaluation the systematized violation of non-human ani-mals in food production, clothing, entertainment, and captivity, and that expands ethical exploration to social constructions such as gender identity that contribute to the abuse of animals and our shared ecological support systems.[66]

Many process thinkers have already begun to explore the rich possibilities of Whitehead's metaphysics for addressing ecological violence.[67] There is, however, still ample room for elucidating and encouraging concrete actions in our particular contexts; actions that, per Whitehead's poetic description "[dwell] upon the tender elements in the world, which slowly and in quietness operate by love."[68] Our ability to dress in such vestments of boundary-crossing care will depend on a willingness to embrace the enchanting irrationality of Whitehead's system; a system whose ecological way of being compels us beyond Scholtes' unifying vision of group identity toward disorderly collisions with the frequently invisible people, animals, or ideas that are entwined with our daily existence. It is precisely when these differences are allowed to surface and bump into one another that we need a metaphysics spacious enough to illuminate the possibilities for ethical action.

Whitehead's metaphysics implies that our ecosystems, neighbors, and animal cousins are capable of receiving and contributing to our responsiveness and care, when we offer it toward those beings who, and places which, our basic daily choices such as eating, speaking, and spending affect. In those metaphysically mundane moments with fork, flyswatter, or dollar bill in hand, the possibilities we affirm and refuse allow us to take seriously the "unfading importance of our immediate actions."[69]

Unlike Scholtes' tune, where love cannot remove the distance between the "they" and "we" named in the title, Whitehead recognizes the folly and power required to maintain such illusory, stabilizing distinctions. Love is, after all, nothing if not another boundary dissolved, however disconcerting it may be to relinquish our concentric circles of identity. So let them know we are process thinkers by our quivering chins, our clammy palms, our furrowed brows, determined but not cocksure, compelled toward unnerving encounters with the others who make and unmake us in the not-so-commonplace crossings of implausible love.

Notes

1   A. N. Whitehead, *Process and Reality*, New York: The Free Press, 1927 (corrected ed. 1985), p. 32.
2   C. Keller, *Process and Difference: Between Cosmological and Poststructuralist Postmodernisms*, New York: SUNY Press, 2002, p. 65.
3   J. Long, *Jainism: An Introduction*, London: I.B. Tauris, 2009, p. xix.
4   Vegetarianism is understood here as abstaining from eating animal flesh; veganism is abstaining from meat, milk and eggs, a movement spurred on largely by the abuse of farm animals in modern factory farming. See www.veganoutreach.org for more information.
5   M. P. Fisher, *Living Religions*, New Jersey: Prentice Hall, 1991 (5th ed. 2002), pp. 137–9.
6   There are widely diverging accounts of the number of worldwide Jain adherents, from between 4–12 million globally. For more information see: "Jains: Adherents," at University of Cumbria Division of Philosophy and Religion at http://philtar.ucsm.ac.uk/encyclopedia/jainism/jains.html or Jain Heritage Centers at www.jainheritagecentres.com or Adherents.com at www.adherents.com/Na/Na_359.html. The next Indian census is scheduled for 2011.
7   Whitehead, p. 351.
8   M. Kheel, *Nature Ethics: An Ecofeminist Perspective*, New York: Rowman & Littlefield, 2008, p. 184.

9   E. B. White, *Charlotte's Web*, New York: Harper & Row, 1952, p. 79.

10   A. N. Whitehead, *Religion in the Making*, New York: Fordham University Press, 1926 (4th ed. 2005), p. 84.

11   R. Faber, "Immanence and Incompleteness: Whitehead's Late Metaphysics," paper presented at conference Beyond Metaphysics? Transcontinental Explorations in Alfred North Whitehead's Late Thought in Claremont, CA, December 2008, p. 1, original emphasis.

12   Whitehead, *Religion*, p. 50.

13   Ibid., p. 87.

14   A. N. Whitehead, *Adventures of Ideas*, New York: The Free Press, 1933 (paperback ed. 1967), p. 252.

15   Faber, p. 5.

16   J. Long, "Plurality and Relativity: Whitehead, Jainism, and the Reconstruction of Religious Pluralism," unpublished dissertation, University of Chicago, 2000, p. 214.

17   Ibid.

18   Whitehead, *Process*, p. 7.

19   Long, "Plurality," p. 253.

20   B. K. Matilal, *The Central Philosophy in Jainism: Anekanta-Vada*, Amedabad, India: Creative Printers, 1981, p. 3.

21   Long, "Plurality," p. 253.

22   Ibid., p. 117.

23   Ibid., p. 253.

24   Matilal, p. 3.

25   Jain World, "The Blind Men and the Elephant," from Jain Stories at http://www.jainworld.com/education/stories25.asp (accessed February 7, 2010).

26   Whitehead, *Adventures*, p. 178.

27   Faber, p. 6.

28   Ibid., pp. 5–6, original emphasis.

29   Ibid., p. 8, original emphasis.

30   Ibid.

31   Long, "Plurality," p. 254.

32   Faber, pp. 5–6, original emphasis.

33   Kheel, p. 3.

34   Ibid.

35   M. Rivera, *The Touch of Transcendence: A Postcolonial Theology of God*, Louisville, KY: Westminster John Knox Press, 2007, pp. 8–9.

36   Ibid., p. 7.

37   Ibid., p. 129.

38   Ibid., p. 44.

39   Whitehead, *Adventures*, p. 135.

40   Ibid., p. 134.

41   Faber, p. 24.

42   Whitehead, *Process*, p. 4.

43   Ibid., p. 348.

44   Long, "Plurality," p. 259.

45   Matilal, p. 52.

46   Long, "Plurality," p. 260.

47   Matilal, p. 55.

48   Ibid., p. 52.

49   Faber, p. 13.

50   Ibid, original emphasis.

51   Ibid., p. 24., original emphasis

52   Whitehead, *Process*, p. 189.
53   L. M. Singhvi, "Appendix: The Jain Declaration on Nature," in C. K. Chapple (ed.), *Jainism and Ecology: Nonviolence in the Web of Life*, Cambridge, MA: Harvard University Press, 2002, p. 220.
54   Long, "Plurality," p. 32.
55   Ibid.
56   Ibid., p. 220.
57   Ibid., p. 34.
58   Ibid.
59   Ibid., p. 35.
60   C. Keller, "The Mystery of the Insoluble Evil: Violence and Evil in Marjorie Suchocki," in J. Bracken (ed.), *World Without End: Christian Eschatology From A Process Perspective*, Grand Rapids, MI: Eerdmanns, 2005, p. 52.
61   Whitehead, *Process,* p. 105.
62   Long, "Plurality," p. 37.
63   Kheel, p. 251.
64   Whitehead, *Adventures*, p. 274.
65   Singhvi, pp. 222–4.
66   Kheel, pp. 250–1.
67   Whitehead, *Process*, p. 343.
68   Ibid., p. 351.
69   Whitehead, *Process and Reality*, p. 351

12 Signs taken for polydoxy in a Zulu Kraal

Creative friction manifested in missionary–native discourse

Marion Grau

The polysemic concept of polydoxy denotes, among other things, the interactions between multiple socioreligious systems. Polydox dynamics are particularly evident in zones of vibrant interaction. The friction of "systematic misunderstandings"[1] that mark intercultural relationships are a major part of the reality of missionary environments and encounters. Encounters, that is, where movable concepts and agents interact to articulate, embody, and contest varieties of *doxa*, of opinion, custom, and engaged perspective. Reading polydox encounters as contexts that involve friction, and learning from them, is crucial for a constructive theology that aims to come to terms with the ambivalent heritage of missionary Christianity and seeks a way forward through a complex, circumspect, resolute progressive missiology.

The story of the Anglican Colenso mission in South Africa, the eventual heresy trial of its founder Bishop John William Colenso (1814–83), and the lifelong activism of his daughter Harriette give clues to the polydox dimensions of Christian evangelism in general, and to Christian missionary efforts in Southern Africa in particular. This story is unique in its particulars, tracing moments in the encounter between a specific family of Anglican missionaries with the Zulu in the province of Natal. But it offers, more generally, a picture of the polydox friction that occurred regularly in Christian mission settings. In this case, we can see it at play in debates around the history and origin of the Zulu, their religious roots and salvation status in comparison to Jews and Christians, the cultural and religious meaning of polygamy, the legal and political status of the Zulu monarchy, and the negotiation of hybrid identities between the cultures of encounter. The fact that the Colenso family so clearly adapted their own theological claims to the circumstances of the Zulu (leading to charges of heresy against the bishop) lifts up the profound mutuality of influence that takes place in these encounters.

Polydox friction

The multiplicity of embodied, but tentative, entanglements in the missionary context can be described as polydox friction positioned, similar to postcolonial discourse, "between the traps of the universal and the culturally specific."[2] It includes a sense of the apophatic, and contingent human, earthly, and divine relations. If *para*dox appears to upset, contest, or contradict formed opinions, then *poly*doxy contains a measure of the paradoxical, by virtue of holding multiple contingencies in tension. It resists claims to strict *ortho*doxy, if by that we mean the lifting up of one particular opinion as true. But it is in, and about, orthodoxy as a discourse interested in reliable, resolute, and responsible claims to validity. Paradox polydoxy is tuned to the clash of perceptions, lack of cohesion, the recognition of disorienting difference, and the coincidence of (seeming) opposites.[3] Paradox has some of the qualities of the *Unheimlichen* (alien, uncanny, literally un-homelike); it disrupts assumptions about home, perceived securities, and perceptions. This paradoxicality, disorienting difference, or friction necessitates methodological means for perceiving, interpreting, and usefully negotiating fraught encounters. A theological appetite for the polydox may well manifest as "a love for the paradox," which Rebecca Solnit identifies as a needful characteristic for any activist. It also is suggestive for theologians contemplating a progressive postcolonial theology of mission.[4]

Anna Lowenhaupt Tsing describes friction as the "grip of worldly encounter," a cultural diversity that "brings a creative friction to global connections" and produces a variety of discourses about the messy zones of interaction between cultures, ecosystems, and peoples.[5] These zones of cultural friction are "transient; they arise out of encounters and interactions," and reappear "in new places with changing events."[6] With Tsing, I contend that the "messy and surprising features of such encounters across differences should inform our models of cultural production."[7] This friction is one marker of polydoxy.

Missionaries, and their interlocutors in native cultures, engage in hermetic (sealing) and hermeneutic (unsealing) activities. I intend to explore, here, a few instances of polydox friction, using a particular example of missionary–native interaction to help illuminate larger methodological questions that are important for the development of a postcolonial theology of mission. To do so, I bring into conversation with each other several areas that are rarely connected in constructive theology: missionary history, missiological accounts, ethnography, and postcolonial theory. A viable constructive theology of mission must include a robust description of polydox, paradoxical friction.[8]

Missionary complexity

Missionaries have long functioned as scholars of religion and heresiologists. They also engage in varieties of comparative theology and interreligious conversations. Missionaries, and their native interlocutors, inhabit a stage of liminality between cultures. They create theological friction in their expressions of faith when communicating across multilayered differences. They negotiate religious, cultural, sociosexual, and socio-economic aspects of *doxa* simultaneously. My employment of the concept of productive friction already signals that anything resembling perfect coherence in such encounters is neither possible, nor, arguably, desirable. The pathways and crossroads of the "mission field" are therefore good examples of polydox spaces.

Although Homi Bhabha is widely recognized as one of the pioneering postcolonial theorists, few scholars have dealt with his use of missionary sources and scenarios in his writing. Oddly enough, Bhabha has done more with missionary texts than even some postcolonial biblical writers, and more than most postcolonial theologians. In a strange displacement, much "metropolitan" Northern (mostly progressive) postcolonial theological discourses integrate theories from colonial contexts, but neglect to engage missionary and missiological discourses. While this may follow a widespread tendency in the division between missionary evangelical and liberal mainline theological pursuits, it is worth reconsidering this opposition, especially in a time when the place, numbers, and purpose of liberal/ mainline/progressive Christian communities are embattled and their explicitly Christian sense of mission often lacking.

In Bhabha's classic essay *Signs Taken For Wonders: Questions of Ambivalence and Authority Under A Tree Outside Delhi, May 1817*, he reads a missionary report of some theological depth, illustrating the concept of ambivalence and creative friction concerning authority and identity in an interreligious encounter in colonial India.[9] In the report, Anund Messeh, one of the first Indian catechists encounters a group of potential converts in a grove of trees just outside of Delhi. Bhabha's essay revolves around the fact that native inquirers confronted with the gospel ask critical questions of a native catechist, manifesting their own cultural assumptions and their sense of polydox friction in the encounter with a European-inflected Christianity. They ask questions about the provenance of the book they have read and love. They question who can and ought to be the brokers of the Bible, what terms of conversion they are willing to accept, and which they are not. The people under the tree ask incisive questions, highlighting paradoxes in the gospel and sacraments as they had received them. At the same time, their questions highlight the clash of worldviews about sacrality and purity, challenging the assumptions at work both in their interpretations of the gospel and in their own expressions of culture.

Bhabha, on the other hand, reports on the subarboreal discussion as one in which the European provenance of the Bible, which has been made accessible to residents in translation, is questioned because of a logical difficulty: how can the British, a people of carnivores, produce a book recognized as holy by vegetarian Indians? Similarly, in their context, Bishop Colenso's Zulu interlocutors question the apparent inconsistency between the British attempts to suppress Zulu polygamy and the fact that the biblical ancestors of faith are shown as righteous, explicitly polygamous men. Bhabha writes, the "institution of the Word in the wilds is also an *Entstellung*, a process of displacement, distortion, dislocation, repetition."[10] As we will see, the theological friction of missionary encounter does not occur isolated from questions of power, gender, culture, and economics. It is this kind of multilayered friction that must be involved in every step of a postcolonial theology of mission: it must take into account the polydox factors that compound a situation.[11]

Tsing describes friction as something that necessitates two or more surfaces. Tracing friction urges us beyond a static dyad of missionary as privileged narrator and native as informant, toward a more complex view that challenges assumptions of hegemony and subalternity, Christian God and Zulu traditions, and competing economic and social systems. Historically, scholars have privileged the missionary voice, and it remains a struggle to encounter a speaking and writing native convert in particular during the times of early modern Christian missions. Many anthropologists and missionaries preserved indigenous oral traditions while transposing them, and their textual productions are densely interwoven with their own *doxa*, their perspective and interests. Perhaps, like some women's theologies, a recourse to midrash-like retroactive retellings, reimaginings, and retracings will eventually make most sense. Indeed in postcolonial literature, fiction and other scholarship voices are increasingly being articulated, through novels, contextual biblical studies, community action, scholarship, and news media.[12] This expanded, yet fragmentary archive of narrativity shows us that the seemingly incommensurable differences between Zulus and English missionaries can be parabolic for postcolonial socio-economic and theological reconciliation, "based on negotiating more or less recognized differences in the goals, objects, and strategies of the cause," and a refusal "to homogenize perspectives but rather to appreciate how we can use diversity as well as possible" today.[13]

Polydox hybrid friction includes the failure of attempts at distinguishing between "sacred" and "secular" events or realities. In fact, strict separations between these "spheres" disallows theological appreciation of the full scale of realities as entangled.[14] The interpenetration of religious and sociopolitical elements in colonized societies in particular complicates the modern myth that the religious and secular should be separate. This ideologically infused fantasy of separation of church and state turns out not only to be false in postcolonial contexts where religious concerns are manifesting in ever more complex ways within these transforming societies, but also in the return of a repressed (Christian) religious consciousness in Europe in the aftermath of wars of religion and certain rationalist and idealist ideologies in that region of the globe. The openness to a polymorphous methodology and discourses welcomed by polydoxy can help reclaim these multiple, inseparable levels of meaning in life, now organized into separate categories such as religious and secular, transcendent and immanent, difference and sameness.

Polydoxy stands in stark contrast to the modern concept of monotheism, which employs a "logic of the One" that is not false, but rather *incomplete*. Hence, as Laurel Schneider proposes, a theology of multiplicity seeks company. Multiplicity resists reduction to the one and reduction to the many. It takes incarnation seriously, paying attention to the mutability of bodies.[15] The designation of monotheistic versus polytheistic religious systems increasingly emerges as a reductionist distinction that does not capture the real complexities of each.[16] Schneider argues that the concept of monotheism arose for specific contextual purposes, to secure the dominance of one God in a world of difference, especially in a colonial world of difference, where missionaries must negotiate multiple, competing cultures and gods.[17]

Bishop John William Colenso and the Zulu: friction and ambivalence in Natal

As I have already indicated, encounters among missionaries and native peoples are highly complex, not only because of the difficulty to identify a gospel "anterior" to culture, but also because multiple dimensions of culture and religion are inextricably linked to each other.[18] One person's inculturation is another person's syncretism or heresy. While missionaries might tend to assume they are communicating "only" the gospel, they are always also communicating messages about literacy, tradition, technologies, social and political mores, and material culture.

The Anglican Church in South Africa started as a settler church and initially had no bishopric. With the foundation of the Church Missionary Society in 1799, this began to change. The Cornish mathematician, schoolbook author and cleric John William Colenso was recruited to be the Bishop of Natal in Pietermaritzburg in South Africa. Over the course of his tenure there, his engagement with the Zulu around issues of biblical truth claims as well as economic and sociosexual realities increasingly alienated him and his family from the growing white settler population. He was tried for heresy and eventually severely impaired in his function as a bishop. After his death, his legacy was most prominently carried on by his daughter Harriette (1847–1932), who worked tirelessly to defend and support Zulus. She also made a nuisance of herself to colonial authorities, advocating for the recognition and repatriation of the Zulu king who had been banished to St. Helena by the Crown.

Like any traveler to a different context, and every missionary, Colenso – and in an expanded sense the women in his life – represented a very specific embodiment of their ecclesial background. Rather than succumb to doubt or resort to the absolutisms of scriptural literalism, Colenso was interested in freeing the gospel message from convention and pushed for "a new mission to replace the old." The old, for him, meant propositions of inerrancy, insistence on conscious and professed Christianity as the only way to salvation, clinging to a biblical rather than a scientific historiography, and greater openness to the diversity of ethical social systems.

Doubts of faith that might be cloaked, or denied, when living in a predominantly Christian society can arise ever more forcefully for a missionary in conversation with native people and prospective converts whose view of the world does not accommodate easily to a Christian religious system. Hence, John William Colenso found that questions of his own were reopened in Natal. He found himself questioned by his native informants, in particular his language teacher and translator William Ngidi.[19] The missionary bishop did not react to Ngidi's questions and doubts by insisting on the need to believe without proofs or logical assent, but instead saw the questions as needing to be answered in good faith, and with the best of biblical exegetical scholarship that was at hand. This included a method that had recently been pioneered in German lands, but still viewed with much skepticism in the British Isles – historical biblical criticism.[20]

Bishop Colenso's heresy case impacted the self-understanding of the Church of England and the formation of the beginnings of what is now called the "Anglican

Communion." His story provides an interesting case study of the collision between a number of broad cultural factors in nineteenth-century European Christianity: the Church of England and attempts to disestablish it; conservative, dissenting, and evangelical movements within Britain; the Oxford Movement, attempts at ecumenical cooperation, and the rise of German historical criticism and liberal theology. In addition, British colonialism, and the thought of Charles Darwin complicated the conflicts, along with challenges to previous theories of history and historiography. In the creative friction between Colenso and the Zulus,

> the crisis was not one-sided, since the missionaries themselves also came from an England in acute intellectual and social crisis, arising out of the related phenomena of the Enlightenment and industrial capitalism.[21]

Colenso held controversial opinions before he left Britain. As a talented mathematician, he was open to new developments in Western science, and interested in Darwin's theories and observations, elements that had already set his originating society in turmoil. In South Africa, the Colenso family engaged in a "long conversation" that transformed Zulu communal ideas and the missionary family's self-understanding.[22] The Colensos supported the continuation of Zulu institutions that would allow the tribe to adapt the settler colonialism with a vital sense of tribal identity and culture intact. Converts and scholars from Colenso's mission station Ekukhanyeni "were among the vanguard of a new Zulu consciousness and resistance to colonialism."[23] The term "cool conversion" is a good descriptor for the "Colenso effect," a form of friction in which both sides were open to transformative mutual encounter. Among the effects of friction that Colenso fed back to British society was that he wanted to change missionary misperceptions of Africans. He sought to speak the truth about the complexity of biblical narratives, even if inconvenient, and offered an "exegesis of practical engagement."[24]

The Colensos practiced a liberal optimism, believing that if people acted according to their best knowledge and were just and truthful at all times, if they gave others a fair chance and respected the law given by God and held up by the Queen, then God would approve the colonial situation. Though they explicitly critiqued British colonial authorities, they appealed, ironically, to the Queen against British colonial functionaries and against the Church of England who had expelled Colenso. Many white settlers in the Bishop's diocese interpreted the Colensos' critical attitude toward colonial practices of racial discrimination and their willingness to consider Africans as fully capable human subjects as a betrayal. The settlers were suspicious of a "conversion" Bishop Colenso had supposedly undergone, a term that referred more to his lack of willingness to side with the colonial settlers and congregants, rather than to any loss of faith. The Colenso story shows what can happen if the transcultural value of the gospel is given up, but the universality of liberal bourgeois cultural values remains in place, a dilemma that continues to afflict progressive Christianity today.

The last few decades have seen the publication of the voices of African scholars who represent the intellectual descendants of the *amakholwa* – believers

– the first groups of Africans to enter the discourse of European-style intellectual training and writing life. This means that despite the paucity of first-hand material, Zulu scholars like Hlonipha Mokoena are beginning to recover the voices of the first converts.[25]

There were a few Zulu converts, the *amakholwa* who became a class of intellectuals oddly positioned in the emerging colonial rule. They represented the "success of mission acculturation and the failure of imperial liberalism and humanism" at the same time.[26] Some accounts of the *amakholwa* question the possibility of any independent indigenous cultural expression, while others see them as a class of nascent native nationalists, rendering them either as a marginalized class or dominant elite.[27]

The rising elite of *kholwa* – believers or converts to Christianity – who had been educated at mission schools, was the first generation of South African native intellectuals who consciously articulated "an ethnic nationalism" that ambiguously coexisted with an "older, broader pan-South African black nationalism and with new forms of class consciousness."[28] Some of these dynamics continue to inform and manifest themselves in contemporary power struggles between post-apartheid South African political and ethnic factions, and the continuing large gaps between educated, elite black South Africans and poor citizens.

Magema Fuze's (1840–1922) writings provide a rare, but strangely conditioned insight into some of the dynamics of the converts' negotiation of self, faith, and community. Fuze was brought to Colenso's Ekukhanyeni mission as a child, was educated there and eventually became a printer for the mission. He wrote a Zulu text ambitiously titled *The Black People and Whence They Came* which was finally translated and published posthumously in 1979.

Fuze sees his conversion and relationship to Colenso as foreordained. He describes his conversion as not merely a personal "decision" but as a move that required parental consent, thereby complicating the question on what level a conversion – *s'il y en a* – is personal, and on what level it is communal.[29] This raises questions of how aware the child might have been of settlers' encroachment or whether it was indeed a prophetic event. Some assessments of Fuze's contribution to an *amakholwa* literature emphasize the limitations of his historical purview, as well as his reliance on Colenso's religious and political stances. This may, however, underestimate the rarity of extant unredacted writings of a convert writing an autobiography, as well as an account of a missionary's life and work. It may also underestimate the influence a translator and cultural broker for the missionary could have even on a powerful mentor.[30] The piece was written long after the events and Fuse is quite defensive of his mentor in the thick of ongoing church politics of the Anglican Church in South Africa. Mokoena reads Fuse's account as an "act of incitement" by a storyteller less interested in factual accuracy than in stimulating and influencing an ongoing conversation and making a strong contribution to it.[31]

Though Fuze's account of Colenso is quite hagiographic, depicting him as "saintly and Christlike," the attending subtext offers multiple voices, among them critical assessments of colonial church politics, missionary activities, and current events. Having established Colenso as a benchmark for Christian moral agency, Fuze creates a unique bricolage that assesses the state of mission and region.[32] Fuze sees Colenso as the "Queen's bishop," that is, no longer authorized by the Archbishop of Canterbury and the Church of England, but by the monarch Victoria herself, to whom he had appealed for support when relationships with rival bishop Gray and the Church of England turned sour and he was deprived of structural support from the church.[33] Colenso was awarded honorary Zulu identity by Fuze, which includes status as fully human in the Zulu context: "He became black [human] only after he had arrived here in our country, he abandoned whiteness, and became a true human [black]."[34] Colenso then, perhaps "like his Lord," a phrase Fuze likes to use to compare the Bishop to Christ, became incarnate. To become incarnate as a Zulu meant speaking their language, understanding and defending their lives in such a way that Fuze sees him as one of his people. Colenso's legitimacy is further lifted up by Fuze for not hiding what other Anglican clerics regarded as esoteric knowledge, namely the theological problems with biblical texts and the hermeneutics of suspicion: "Sobantu did not like to withhold anything in his sermons and teaching."[35] The Colenso controversy thus "was as much about theology as it is about the 'democratic' ethos of Colenso's mission, especially where Africans were concerned," as, over time "colonial whites began to despise the Colensos and [Fuze] attributed this to the fact that Colenso did not discriminate." Hence, for the Africans Colenso was "'the king of peace,' for the colonists he was the 'king of kaffirs.'"[36]

After Bishop Colenso's loss of income and institutional and economic support for his missionary venture, the Colensos continued to spend great personal energy and economic substance to defend the Zulu monarchy, institutions, and individuals. The dismantling of Zulu social institutions under British rule eroded the self-sufficiency and sociospiritual integrity of the Zulu, while exposing them to English learning and religious culture. The family believed that the continuation of certain Zulu institutions would allow the Zulu to survive as an integrated ethnic group and lessen the culture-shattering impact of the colonial economic system. Their advocacy and agency pushed for an open engagement with local reasoning and theological questions. In this, Bishop Colenso's conviction that Zulus had a natural theology and access to deity impacted their sense of what mission meant, that is, the Colensos believed that a knowledge of the divine was already present within the Zulu people, and hence their conversion had a different shape and urgency than was assumed by many other missionaries surrounding Colenso.

Polydox friction and salvation history

Many scientists and missionaries during Colenso's time operated with, at least, a partially biblical historiography based on the view of biblical scholars who "still saw the Old Testament as an account of universal human history."[37] Native tribal groups had to be inserted into a biblical historical metanarrative, and the ten lost tribes constitute a "theological loophole on earth" full of mystery arising from their "theological significance and the theological anxieties they generate."[38] Not a few missionaries and scholars conjectured that indigenous peoples were either comparable to Jews or actually descended from the "lost tribes of Israel."[39] This insertion into Christian history, and hence Christian supersessionism over Judaism, allowed them to integrate previously unknown peoples and to slot them epistemologically under a commonplace trope that functioned like a midrash, locating a loose end in the biblical historical narrative that allowed expansion.

Though the Zulu were not Christian, they were thought by colonial authorities to have "a kind of recognizable religious life that could be distinguished from other religions." Hence, the Zulu were "represented as people living a relatively stable life like ancient Israelites," which is an ethnographic argument. They also could be "contained, and perhaps even ghettoized, under a system of Christian rule," as they had been "contained by annexation and the location system," which is a political argument. Furthermore, according to one observer, the Zulu "had not been corrupted by the superstitions of West Africa." Avoiding both idolatry and superstition, the Zulu practiced a type of religion found in ancient Israel," which is a theological argument. Thus, the Zulu were consistently depicted as "the Jews of Natal."[40] What is more, historical Israel was thought to represent the "gradual development of human society," so that Jews and their surrogate indigenous peoples represented the "earliest stages in the advancement of comparative civilization."[41] However, such links were ambiguous:

> Rooting Zulu ancestors in Palestine did not elevate their descendants to a privileged race. That Elohim's lost tribe could have been in South Africa might have confirmed assumptions of early nineteenth-century comparative philologists who reputedly traced "physiological classification of racial difference" through "historical linguistics." [...] While both Jew and Aryan supposedly had "pure bloodlines" that flowed back to one "Adamic" source, Semites were supposed to have degenerated into "darkness" for they no longer saw the light of Christian truth.[42]

In addition to this layer of anti-Judaism, settler interests and assumptions portrayed the Zulu, especially the mythical Zulu king Shaka, as degenerate and ready for the arrival of a "superior race."[43] David Chidester describes the missionary search for a so-called "unknown god" of the Zulu.[44] Multiple missionaries and colonial official reports include references to an elusive concept of a creator God. Whether the elusive quality of this concept (to the missionaries and colonists) was due to transformations of the local societies or represented, as the missionaries might have wished, a convenient and providential opening for their message of a universal God is difficult to determine. In the 1830s, freelance missionary Allen Gardiner asserted that "since their recent intercourse with Europeans, the vague idea of a Supreme Being has again become general,"[45] and one might wonder how much of that growth was due to the suggestive power of a polydox friction, or how much of its ongoing presence the colonial reporters had simply missed.

Colenso was not the only immigrant to Southern Africa who challenged assumptions about Zulu history. Wilhelm Bleek and Henry Callaway were also trained in the emerging disciplines of linguistics, historical critical studies, and ethnography and they claimed to give a more just account of native culture and religion, because of a more critical and less biased study of their subjects.[46] Colenso argued for the adoption of the Zulu terms of a locally expressed version of a "universal natural religion" for a creator god. He thereby put elements of indigenous religion into the service of Christian proclamation.[47] Colenso's universalist natural theology can be seen as a nascent "general theory of comparative religion," and he made a "significant contribution" to comparative religion, anticipating "a new comparative strategy by which the universal history of religion could be reconstructed, not from records found in the Hebrew Bible, but by evidence drawn from reports about the Zulu."[48] Of course, one problem with his theory of a "universal religion," however inclusivist its initial goals, is contained in the lingering cultural inflections of the term "religion" and the difficulty, perhaps the impossibility, to move the conversation between religiocultural systems beyond colonial terms.

Then who can be saved?

In the friction between Zulu worldviews and the Anglican ecclesial framework, Colenso's theological anthropology and soteriology came to differ starkly from the "evangelical gaze [that] perceived Africa as a 'desert.'" The general colonial view held that "[i]ts inhabitants, peoples of the wild, shared its qualities. Unable to master their environment, they lacked culture and history."[49]

Influenced by the British Evangelical Frederick Denison Maurice, Colenso adopted a universalist soteriology that dovetailed with his belief in living an exemplary life, the progressive effects of literacy and education, and an understanding that a benevolent imperialist administration provides the best possible way to interact with the Zulu. Such rereadings of the apostle Paul and the church fathers, tended to juxtapose a universalist salvation to the "backward" times of particularity and ethnocentrism, and looks toward a time of progress where industrial capitalism represents the apex of world history.[50] This grand narrative of liberal optimism underlies Colenso's critique of the mode of implementation of colonial rule and goes hand-in-hand with some of the less pungent, but no less invasive forms of modern imperial universalism. The Colenso family's struggle was not so much against imperialism per se, but against its perversion by colonist landgrabbers and racist political agents such as Cecil Rhodes and Robert Baden-Powell, a form of creative friction within Colenso's own cultural context.

Consequently, the Colensos believed that exemplary Christian lives, rather than conversionist preaching, were preferable missionary practices – a conviction that cohered with other liberal understandings of missionary presence. The Colenso mission wrought only a very few converts, as traditionally understood. Jonathan Draper argues that, in fact:

> Colenso's theology [...] undermined the logic of conventional mission work. If all are already saved whether they accept the Christian gospel or not, then what they stand to benefit from by baptism is enlightenment, knowledge of

what they already possess. [...] There was no need for an absolute break with their former way of life for his converts, no severance of family and kinship ties. [...] Instead his teaching encouraged the emergence of a Zulu national identity and cultural revival.[51]

Colenso's rejection of the evangelical theology of his contemporaries and their hellfire preaching, of their self-assured proclamation of what he considered an artificially shielded Bible propelled him to crack the texts wide open in the vulnerable setting of the missionary context, hence increasing the surface of creative friction. His missionary methodology looked for the "seeds of religious truths" in local customs as he studied Zulu, wrote a dictionary and language course in Zulu, all the while looking for compatible patterns between Zulu and English customs.[52]

His soteriology recapitulates Irenaeus's concept of *recapitulatio*. In his commentary on Romans, Colenso argues that Christ's typological repetition of the "First Adam" repudiates and entirely transforms for the entire human race sin and separation from God.[53] This leads him to assume a rudimentary natural sense of the sacred in every culture and person. Colenso gives maximum weight to Paul's use of the formulation "as in Adam all die, so in Christ we shall all be made alive, to see Christ as the Head of humanity, encapsulating and restoring humanity in his own person on the cross."[54]

Colenso includes a sustained argument for purgatory, the place in which both condemnation and the hope of redemption in the end coexist. This prolepsis also regrounds the sacraments of the church with a purpose: they are signs of the divine blessing already given, but do not confer or symbolize "special privileges" for the Christian over the non-Christian. Colenso's insistence that the entire human race is included in God's mercy and salvation "was one of the conclusions that most outraged the Anglo-Catholic orthodoxy" of his day.[55]

Bishop Colenso's daughter Harriette often identifies strongly with the Zulu and on occasion used the appellation "we Zulus" in her letters. She supported some of the indigenous church structures that broke away from colonial churches.[56] But in other contexts she clearly articulates that "she was not a native, but natives were very much like the rest of human beings," and that "her opinion was that of an outsider." She argued that consulting with herself did not release the Natal Native Affairs Commission from obtaining "the opinion of the people themselves."[57] She promoted the preservation of the vestiges of Zulu law still in place, rather than assimilating all Zulu into the colonial legal system arguing that "[u]niformity was not so important as preserving to the natives whatever was good in their own laws."[58] Quoting a Zulu proverb she argued that, for respect to exist at all it must be mutual, and that trust and respect had been eroded between the colonial government and the chiefs.

In a revealing public testimony given before the Natal Native Affairs Commission in 1906, Harriette Colenso opened her testimony by calling the hearings "an opportunity for salvation." She believed that the Natal colony had a chance to set things right and bring a measure of justice to the land. That is, her notion of salvation here includes a version of interracial justice, as much as that may be possible in a colonial setting. Using the salvific metaphor of sickness and healing she addressed the members of the commission as doctors, and encouraged them to "diagnose the complaints" of the native population appropriately so they can find the causes and "suggest a remedy."[59] Immediately thereafter, however, she criticizes the invitation of European witnesses as superfluous and repeatedly points to the need to hear native witnesses themselves, rather than rely upon her to speak for them.

Questions of secular and sacred authority were highly complex for missionaries. They generally associated themselves with colonial forces, but at times tried to differentiate themselves, if mostly unsuccessfully, from certain practices associated with colonial violence. They walked a fine line between colonial and tribal chiefly authority. An ensuing curious dynamic appears in a report by the Comaroffs. Here, early Methodist missionaries among the South African Tswana laid out a missionary strategy that promised to leave intact the tribal social organization, that is, chiefly power. The illusion of the insulation of powers ended, however, when baptismal rites and tribal naming ceremonies collided and competed. While missionaries often saw "practical advantage in a strong chieftainship" as it "assured a stable polity within which they could toil to build their kingdom of God," their interventions into regional relations as well as communal "religious" rites, "could not but erode Tswana sovereignty."[60] Missionaries often negotiated both patriarchal systems and were purveyors of temporary truces and awkward relationships with both forms of authority. But while they saw the colonial system as "secular," at least in theory, they were gravely mistaken to assume that chiefly power lacked sacral qualities, or that conversion in Africa, or anywhere else for that matter, was merely a matter of "private" religion or practice.

Friction and sexual politics

Colenso addressed the status of converts to Christianity prominently in his 1862 letter on polygamy to the Archbishop of Canterbury. In it, he argued that polygamy is not considered a sin anywhere in the scriptures, while adultery and slavery were. Yet, "the practice of polygamy is at variance with the whole spirit of Christianity, just as much as that of slavery is, and must eventually be rooted out."[61] His argument overlooks the biblical support for slavery. Colenso appears to adopt something of a double standard, though perhaps a realist, gradualist one. He rejected what he considered to be the greater evil of pushing away potential converts by making certain requirements before they would be baptized. He felt that it would tear families apart and remove the children of these unions from Christian teaching. He preferred the lesser evil of allowing polygamous men – there is little mention of the agency of women and children – to become Christians in the gradualist hope that future generations might be transformed toward monogamous marriages. Colenso argues that "polygamy was practiced by eminently pious men," that it was not against the law, biblical or otherwise.[62] Of course, the same argument was made about chattel slavery in antebellum America. Colenso appears to imply that polygamy is in a different stage of abolition than slavery, which was abolished throughout the British Empire in 1833, about 30 years prior, but still within memory.[63] Colenso noted that the ancient Christian authorities saw little reason to condemn a practice that was against biblical law.[64] Where the practice is condemned or accepted it is done so on ethnocentric bases, Colenso argued, as "polygamy was abhorrent to the habits of the Romans (and to those of almost all the nations of Europe, as the Greeks, Gauls, and Germans) in their heathen state, and was ultimately forbidden by law, when Eastern practices began to creep among them," while it continued to be tolerated among Jews, even under the Roman empire, as a national custom.[65]

As a result, Colenso stated strongly that "believing as I do, […] polygamy as found among the untaught heathen, is not […] in fact, a sin at all."[66] Colenso's overall argument might lend itself more toward a sense of gradualism in mission, rather than an overall acceptance of polygamy. He states, in the beginning of his document, that polygamy is not the ideal marital relationship imagined in the gospel. As further evidence of his gradualism, there are instances where he departs from distinguishing slavery and polygamy, arguing that one should "not refuse to a man the Christian sacraments, simply because he had a number of slaves,"[67] as if the practices stood at similar levels in terms of the missionary requirement to keep the relationship with the potential convert active.

Colenso, however, also challenged the popular colonial depiction of polygamy as a condition of slavery for wives. He quoted Theophilus Shepstone, the Secretary for Native Affairs in Natal, who argues that "to say that the married native women of this country are slaves, or sold as such, is to betray utter ignorance of the social condition of the natives."[68] Rather, the cattle given to their families is a "guarantee for their good treatments by their husbands, and a perpetual security for their being cared for, and protected by their parents and blood-relatives."[69] Shepstone continues that "a native woman is in this respect, more protected than her English neighbour," and to persons who argue that a native woman is the equivalent of slaves, "because she is compelled by her position to work as one," he replies that "almost every English lady in this colony is as much as slave, and for the same reason."[70]

Indeed both systems are patriarchal or, in Luce Irigaray's term, a "hom(m) osexual economy" exchange that involves women but occurs between men, in the sense that they require the unremunerated work of a wife for her husband's household. Colenso bluntly states that "there may be virtual 'buying and selling' in a nominally Christian land, and under a law of monogamy, as well as among these natives."[71] Monogamous heteronormativity, despite its own propensity to the exploitation of women, generally is promoted as the "missionary position," as defined by Laurel Schneider, that is, a metaphor for the "well-documented efforts by missionaries to inscribe European (white) norms on the sexual practices and beliefs of their converts."[72] Colenso resists the missionary position here up to a point, as he objects to the outright outlawing of polygamy. His reasons have to do with the general misperceptions about polygamy, as well as the violence that would be inflicted on entire communities if polygamous marriages had to be dissolved, not to mention the difficulties it would cause for his mission efforts. The multiple frictions and unclean edges of this debate invite further engagement.

Zulu institutions and the Colenso mission

As an independent minded woman, child to one of the most controversial figures of the colony, Harriette Colenso occupied a liminal position. Even more than her father, she was a boundary person, a translator, negotiator, activist and legal witness, a public author and lecturer on behalf of the Zulu monarchy. Brenda Nicholls writes:

> For Shepstone it was clear that the power of the Zulu royal house should be regarded as ended. By contrast Harriette Colenso remained loyal to her father's view. This was that the royal house was the integrating principle for the Zulu people and that it was their loyalty to the Zulu royal house that gave the Zulu people a corporate identity. She abhorred the policy of breaking up the Zulu people that had been followed since the end of the Zulu war and sought to achieve not only re-integration of the Zulu people but also reconciliation between the Zulus and the white government of Zululand, then represented by Havelock.[73]

It is important to try, as far as possible, to conceive the political impetus her support of the Zulu monarchy had. In strongly articulated contrast to Theophilus Shepstone, who had maligned the Zulu royal family and gone to pains to color its rule as bloody and tyrannical, Harriette Colenso supported the rule of "military chieftainships" over the "minor hereditary chiefs," arguing that these were a more efficient way for the Zulu to organize themselves in ways that could marshal a certain degree of power, rather than Shepstone's "divide and conquer" strategy.[74] Her counsel revealed a deep trust in peaceful political action and the colonial legal system. She used her influence to de-escalate conflicts and urged the surrender of Dinuzulu and other Zulu who were put on trial for one or another reason by colonial officials.[75]

She argued that the attempt to "abolish hereditary Chieftainships" would not only not work but would further destabilize the situation and "inflame the tribal sentiments" and in fact have the opposite effect by strengthening attachment and identification with hereditary chiefs.[76]

Not surprisingly, some colonial officials saw missionaries like Harriette as "foreign agitators," undermining colonial governance. The colonial misunderstandings and the resultant violence, abuses of natives, and confused mess cannot, so she argued, be claimed as necessary for a "superior race" to guide others:

> I wonder if any of you have been expecting me to arrive at a reference to "the white man's burden?" What I have to say on that point is that it is hypocritical for us to whine over it while it is so largely of our own manufacture, and we blindly refuse to let those bear their share who are perfectly willing to do so, and far better able than we are; and that the burden is manufactured not only by this Ministry or that, but by us all, by the Executive, by the Legislature, by Parliament's masters, the electors; by any of us who can so much as influence a single vote, and do not try to do so.[77]

Whether through confusion, colonial misunderstandings, or intentional, outright systemic injustice and notions of racial superiority, Harriette Colenso turned out to be correct. The effects of clashing symbols and customs in South Africa eventually developed into a state where the relationships between the races were severely damaged, even without the constantly progressing annexation of land, livelihood, and the accompanying impact on cultural–spiritual agency.

The impression of the randomness of change in colonial law created situations in which Zulus "in many cases only became aware of the existence of a law through being fined and flogged for transgressing its provisions."[78] Portraying colonized subjects as deceitful and unreliable has a long tradition. A discrediting dynamic appears to have manifested regarding the exiled Zulu king, who represented "*the* major obstacle to capitalist expansion," and "capitalist penetration was seen to be dependent on the king's removal."[79] The Zulu royal family retained a "powerful grip on the popular imagination," perhaps especially *because* it in fact had very little real material or political power.[80] In language commonly used to define the function of a sacrament, Harriette Colenso ironically names the imprisonment and exile of members of the Zulu royal family "the outward and visible sign to the people of their own general disgrace."[81]

He and his ancestors were believed to ensure the integrity and well-being of the people. At a time of growing exploitation, when subordinate chiefs were increasingly coming to be seen as subservient to white demands, what could be more natural than the people should turn to the king for protection. While the king "had no power to abuse;" he could continue to express national sentiment, and precisely because of the state's obduracy in failing to recognize him, people could express their resentment against white rule through their allegiance to the Zulu royal family.[82]

The colonial ideology of evolutionary superiority was built upon a self-fulfilling prophecy and the disadvantage of "having a different language and a different way of putting things." The disruption of native self-governance, not surprisingly, led for the Zulu to "a state of utter confusion as to what was his [sic] position and what were his rights, and even what tribe he belonged to," while rendering them "out of the habit of handling their own affairs." Yet, Harriette Colenso believed that there is "no greater mistake than to say that the native was a child," that "in some respects the native was a very old man indeed, and in all that related to the management of men he was a full-grown man."[83]

Conclusions

Polysemic polydox friction occurs in many places in intercultural encounters within the settings of Christian mission. Its dynamics can be observed, in fragmentary ways, as creative friction between various forms of *doxa*, by which I mean the assumptions, customs, and opinions of those involved in the exchanges. Studying the mutual transformation occurring in such encounters has critical import for the development of a progressive postcolonial sense of Christian mission in increasingly multi-religious settings. The rough edges and "cool conversions" that occur within such settings are important case studies for developing a methodology for decolonizing mission and its discourses. A methodology for decolonizing mission must include an epistemology that can account for polydox belongings, multiple commitments, fragmentary and hybrid religious existences, and theo-logics developed in such settings. The coexistence of multiple truths necessitates hospitality hospitality toward the paradox, as well as a polyphilia (Faber) that befriends the manifold. The historical case study and its contemporary implications as set forth in this chapter demonstrate how such polyphilia and paradoxy can be embodied, what its ongoing struggles may turn out to be, and how they may affect theologies that aim to decolonize mission.

The issues that come to the surface in the Colenso mission story represent fragments of paradox polydoxy in the past and with lingering implications for the present in post-apartheid South Africa still challenged by religious, economic, and sociosexual crises.

The Colensos are rare examples of a more intersubjective approach to mission, embodied at a time when modern biblical studies, racial, cultural, religious, and anthropological disciplines were emerging and moving into their next stages. They are deeply involved in intercultural complexities of gender and sexuality, struggles around custom and legality, forms of authority and leadership, and the religious and social status of Zulus in relationship to the Anglican mission in South Africa. Their approach also reveals some major issues that still haunt more progressive approaches to mission and missiology.

Their emphasis on living an exemplary life and emulation appears open-minded and tolerant and certainly stands in stark contrast to dominant conversionist preaching and mission. The Colensos promoted a civilization-based mission that has much in common with modern ideas of progressivist theories of religion, though the latter are less explicitly Christian in content. This approach leaves some seemingly more "benign" – and more persistent – racial and cultural forms of paternalism in place. The promotion of education and development is culturally located and, hence, creates ambivalent friction around the function of missionary education. It is a tool for cultural assimilation and submission; it is a resource for survival; it is a means of easing transition into colonial culture; it fractures tribal structures and traditions and leads, in characteristic ambivalence, to both transcultural breakdown and forms of transcultural liberation.

As the Zulu converts learn to write, becoming no longer voiceless subalterns, they are also entering colonial structures of cultural and religious education that moves them into liminal places between cultures. As converts and intellectual elites they are precariously poised between cultures. The Colensos, through their willingness to see beyond the colonial imperative, also became positioned between cultures. They lost the support of colonial church and much of the settler population, were seen to have "gone native," or in Fuze's more complimentary words they had "become black" by being in solidarity and fighting for vestiges of cultural institutions and legal justice for the Zulu.

For the Colensos, Paul's Letter to the Romans spoke to the racial pride of settler churches and the Church of England and their predetermined notions of the salvific and cultural status of the Zulu. Though there is certainly evidence of attitudes of cultural superiority patterned on Jewish–Christian supersessionism and an ambivalent Victorian romanticism about the ten lost tribes that they believed the Zulu might represent, the Colensos saw this identification as potential for a fuller development rather than permanent inferiority. The lingering interpretive patterns of mission as superseding pagan cult and Jewish religion haunted the Colensos and haunts missionary strategies still.

The Colensos intended their education to work for liberation. It stands to reason that this liberal approach to mission, privileged, and promoted education as a means of mobility toward colonial cultural *doxa*, even as it was seen by the Colensos as a means for survival and emancipation. This decision was certainly also pragmatic, accommodating some converts' desire to enter into colonial society in order to speak for their own people. At the same time there was great resistance among Zulus to letting children enter mission school and thus become alienated from their families and tribal culture, knowing the ties would become lengthened and frayed.

With a soteriology that was focused on a gradual progression toward Christian faith and was hospitable to certain forms of polydoxy rather than promoting a disruptive radical conversion, what, beyond mission as work for social and economic justice, can be gleaned from the Colenso story for a postcolonial, polydox vision of Christian mission? How do the gospel and biblical texts (however articulated between multiple cultures) manifest within and beyond the bounds of culture? As prosperity gospel churches mushroom in Southern Africa, the actual polydox forms of Christianity in postcolonial settings are problematically enmeshed with capitalism, just as older forms of missionary Christianity were. What function does Christian mission – and soteriology – have in the contemporary global context, and how should it be related to interreligious dialogue and transformation?

One answer comes from Harriette Colenso. Polydox elements of soteriology reside in her insistence that salvation is necessary for the colonizer as much as or more than for the colonized, and comes in forms appropriate to each situation. Salvation here manifests as contextual and relational. Its manifestations require hermeneutic skills in decoding polydox paradoxes for salvific potential, which in turn require generosity and patience. Magema Fuze articulates his own sense of Bishop Colenso's mission writing his *vita* at a time when Colenso was thoroughly discredited in the Anglican Church. He produced a native hagiography to contest the colonial dismissal of Colenso as a heretic for his theological openness both to Zulu culture and the emerging German biblical criticism abhorred by the Church of England. The contestation of narrativity about Colenso itself is an expression of the polydox friction between missionary theology and native culture. What is more, the complexity of "sexual" salvation intoned in the discussion regarding polygamy and monogamy sets the stage for profoundly complex renegotiations of gender, labor, property, sexuality, and disease in a South Africa reeling from HIV/AIDS. Such instances of polydox friction provide the context in which a constructive postcolonial missiology between North and South must be articulated.

Notes

1   A. L. Tsing, *Friction: An Ethnography of Global Connection*, Princeton, NJ: Princeton University Press, 2005, p. x.
2   Ibid., p. 1.
3   For a discussion of Nicholas of Cusa's sense of the *coincidentia oppositorum*, see C. Keller, *Face of the Deep*, London: Routledge, 2003, p. 206 et passim.
4   R. Solnit, *Hope in the Dark: Untold Histories, Wild Possibilities*, New York: Nation Books, 2004, p. 25.
5   Tsing, pp. ix–x.
6   Ibid., p. xi.
7   Ibid., p. 3.
8   I cannot here discuss African Independent Churches, which, having moved beyond colonial structures and personnel, represent even more intense forms of polydoxy with very interesting forms of friction.
9   Homi Bhabha, *The Location of Culture*, London and New York: Routledge, 1994, pp. 102–22.
10 Ibid., p. 105.
11 As such it could be compared to Tillich's method of correlation where human situations are correlated with Christian theological symbols or concepts. The polydox reality of our world then can be seen as resonating with Tillich's claim that "reality itself makes demands, and the method must follow, reality offers itself in different ways, and our cognitive intellect must receive it in different ways. An exclusive method applied to everything closes many ways of approach and impoverishes our vision of reality." P. Tillich, "The Problem of Theological Method," in M. K. Taylor (ed.), *Paul Tillich: Theologian of the Boundaries*, Minneapolis, MN: Fortress Press, 1991, p. 128. Kwok Pui-Lan demonstrates a related multi-issue approach in her book on postcolonial theology, calling for the integration of the discourses of gender, race, class, and religion. P.-L. Kwok, *Postcolonial Imagination and Feminist Theology*, Louisville, KY: Westminster John Knox Press, 2005, p. 7.
12 I am aware that the resources named here are writtten only, given the difficulty of accessing more than anecdotal evidence, and can only point to the use of written anthropology as an amelioration of this absence. Some of the novels to give voice to a post-missionary Africa are T. Dangarembga, *Nervous Conditions*, Oxfordshire: Ayebia, 1988; and N. W. Thiongo, *Wizard of the Crow*, New York: Anchor Books, 2006; and more famously C. Achebe's *Things Fall Apart*, London: William Heinemann, 1958.
13 Tsing, p. x.
14 C. Taylor, "The Future of the Religious Past," in H. De Vries (ed.), *Religion: Beyond A Concept*, New York: Fordham University Press, 2008, pp. 180–1.
15 L. C. Schneider, *Beyond Monotheism: A Theology of Multiplicity*, New York: Routledge, 2008, pp. 1, 3, 4, 5.
16 Ibid., pp. 19–20.
17 Ibid., p. 26.
18 A term used by Kvame Bediako, here quoted by A. Balcomb, "Faith or Suspicion? Theological Dialogue North and South of the Limpopo with Special Reference to the Theologies of Kvame Bediako and Andrew Walls," *Journal of Theology for Southern Africa*, 100, March 1998, p. 12.
19 J. Guy, *The View Across the River: Harriette Colenso and the Zulu Struggle Against Imperialism*, Charlottesville, VA: University of Virginia Press, 2001, p. 21.
20 R. S. Sugirtharajah, *The Bible and Empire: Postcolonial Explorations*, Cambridge: Cambridge University Press, 2005, p. 118.

21 J. A. Draper, "Bishop John William Colenso's Interpretation to the Zulu People of the *Sola Fide* In Paul's Letter to the Romans," *SBL 2000 Seminar Papers*, Atlanta, GA: SBL, 2000, p. 468.

22 This term, introduced by John and Jean Comaroff into ethnographic study, has become widely used for the ongoing nature of cultural encounters. J. Comaroff and J. Comaroff, *Of Revelation and Revolution: Christianity, Colonialism, and Consciousness in South Africa*, Vol. 1, Chicago, IL: Chicago University Press, 1991, p. 200.

23 Draper, p. 491.

24 R. S. Sugirtharajah, *The Bible and the Third World: Precolonial, Colonial, and Postcolonial Encounters*, Cambridge: Cambridge University Press, 2001, pp. 128–31.

25 H. Mokoena, "The Queen's Bishop: A Convert's Memoir of John W. Colenso," *Journal of Religion in Africa*, Vol. 38, 2008, p. 313.

26 Ibid., p. 316.

27 Ibid., pp. 317–18.

28 S. Marks, *Ambiguities of Dependence in South Africa: Class, Nationalism, and the State in Twentieth-Century Natal*, Baltimore, MD: The Johns Hopkins University Press, 1986, p. 111.

29 Mokoena, p. 321.

30 A. T. Cope wonders in his editor's preface to Fuze's book "to what extent Fuze influenced Colenso, not only in theological matters such as the capacity of Noah's Ark, but in political matters, too." See M. Fuze, *The Black People and Whence They Came,* A. T. Cope (ed.), Scottsville, South Africa: University of KwaZulu Natal Press, p. xi.

31 Mokoena, p. 314.

32 Ibid., p. 314.

33 Ibid., p. 315.

34 Translation by H. Mokoena, who notes that the term *umuntu* can refer to both black person or human. Ibid., pp. 325–6.

35 Quoted in Mokoena, p. 328.

36 Ibid., p. 329.

37 D. Chidester, *Savage Systems: Colonialism and Comparative Religion in Southern Africa*, Charlottesville, VA: University of Virginia Press, 1996, p. 141.

38 Z. B. Benite, *The Ten Lost Tribes: A World History*, Oxford: Oxford University Press, 2009, p. 14.

39 These were the tribes that were brought into exile after the destruction of the Northern Kingdom of Israel, but ceased to leave a historical trail, and are widely assumed today to have merged and vanished into the populations amongst which they were placed. The Second, Babylonian Exile, however, left a far larger and ongoing historical imprint in terms of ethnogenesis, historical, and ethnic consciousness of the Jewish people and religion. Benite, p. 6.

40 Chidester, p. 125.

41 Chidester here portrays the approach of Henry Hart Milman, a nineteenth-century historian, p. 141.

42 B. Carton, "Awaken *Nkulunkulu*, Zulu God of the Old Testament: Pioneering Missionaries During the Early Age of Racial Spectacle," in B. Carton, J. Laband, and J. Sithole (eds), *Zulu Identities: Being Zulu, Past and Present*, Scottsville, South Africa: University of KwaZulu Natal Press, 2008, pp. 143–4.

43 Chidester, p. 120.

44 Ibid., see especially Chapter 4.

45 Ibid., p. 122.

46 Ibid., p. 128.

47 Ibid., p. 129.

48   Ibid., p. 140.
49   J. Comaroff and J. Comaroff, *Ethnography and the Historical Imagination*, Boulder, CO: Westview Press, 1992, p. 268.
50   J. Guy, *The Heretic: A Study of the Life of John William Colenso, 1814–1883*, Pietermaritzburg, South Africa: University of Natal Press, 1983, pp. 168, 171–2.
51   Draper, p. 490.
52   R. Edgecombe, "Bishop Colenso and the Zulu Nation," *Journal of Natal and Zulu History* III, Durban, South Africa: University of KwaZulu-Natal, Howard College Campus, 1980, p. 17.
53   J. A. Draper, "Introduction," in J. A. Draper (ed.), *Commentary on Romans by John William Colenso*, Pietermaritzburg, South Africa: Cluster Publications, 2003, p. xxx.
54   Ibid., p. xxix.
55   Ibid., pp. xxxi–xxxiii.
56   S. Marks, "Harriette Colenso and the Zulus, 1874–1913," *Journal of African History*, Vol. 4, No. 3, 1963, p. 409.
57   H. E. Colenso, "Natal Native Affairs Commission," testimony to the Natal Native Affairs Commission, Pietermaritzburg, South Africa: Natal Archives, 1906, pp. 118–19.
58   Ibid., p. 119.
59   Ibid., p. 115.
60   Comaroff and Comaroff, pp. 258–9.
61   J. W. Colenso, *A Letter to His Grace the Archibishop of Canterbury Upon the Question of the Proper Treatment of Cases of Polygamy, as Found Already Existing in Converts from Heathenism*, London: MacMillan, 1862, p. 2.
62   Ibid., pp. 4–5.
63   From the point of view of a male missionary who considers, as Colenso does, primarily if not only the agency and life world of the men involved in this practice and its legality and the economic situation of women and children mostly as an appendix, this may make sense. Victorian mores had still little or no room for women's agency apart from home and hearth. Yet, in the irony of colonial femininity, the women in his family were far from constricted to the privacy of the home and all led active writing lives and engaged the public powerfully through lectures and publication. Their education was as crucial to Colenso as that of his son.
64   Colenso, *A Letter to His Grace*, p. 25. Yet, one might argue that while the integrity of patriarchal property (including women and children) is protected by these laws as well as Zulu laws, the economic ruin of women through frivolous divorce and widowhood is not against biblical law. In biblical women like Rahab, Tamar, and Ruth, we find figures that critically engage these structures and struggle for survival within the patriarchal system.
65   Ibid., p. 25.
66   Ibid., p. 75.
67   Ibid., p. 46.
68   Ibid., p. 89.
69   Ibid., p. 90.
70   Ibid., Shepstone and Colenso here problematically conflate brideprice with polygamy.
71   Ibid., p. 39.
72   L. C. Schneider, "Changing the Missionary Position: Facing Up to Racism and Nationalism," The Castañeda Lecture, Chicago Theological Seminary, 2007, p. 6.
73   B. Nicholls, "Zululand 1887–1889: The Court of the Special Commissioners for Zululand and the Rule of Law," *Journal of Natal and Zulu History*, Vol. XV, 1994/1995.
74   Marks, "Harriette Colenso," p. 407.
75   Ibid., p. 408.

76   H. E. Colenso, "Natal Native Affairs," p. 117.
77   H. E. Colenso, "The Principles of Native Government in Natal," an address by Miss Colenso delivered before the Pietermaritzburg Parliamentary Debating Society, Colenso Collection, Natal Archives, 1908, p. 15.
78   H. E. Colenso and A. Werner, "White and Black in Natal," *Contemporary Review*, Vol. 61, January/June 1892, p. 211.
79   Marks, *Ambiguities of Dependence*, pp. 27–8, emphasis added.
80   Ibid., p. 108.
81   H. E. Colenso, "Zululand: Past And Present," *Journal of the Manchester Geographical Society*, 1890.
82   Marks, *Ambiguities*, p. 111.
83   H. E. Colenso, "Natal Native Affairs Commission," pp. 121–2.

13 God as ground, contingency, and relation

Trinitarian polydoxy and religious diversity

John Thatamanil

the one First Cause is not split and cut up into differing Godships, neither does the statement harmonize with the Jewish dogma, but *the truth passes in the mean* between these two conceptions, destroying each heresy, and yet accepting what is useful to it from each ... For it is as if the number of the triad were a remedy in the case of those who are in error as to the One, and the assertion of the unity for those whose beliefs are dispersed among a number of divinities.

Gregory of Nyssa[1]

Trinitarianism and Christianity's others

Christian naming of divinity, even in the community's oldest baptismal formula, begins by affirming the threefold character of divine disclosure without abjuring divine unity. The one God who created the world saves that very world by way of God's Word and Breath which two cannot be collapsed into an undifferentiated simplicity of the one Father. The logic of Christian reflection, which led eventually to Nicene trinitarianism, was also driven by a commitment to safeguarding divine unity and transcendence while affirming God's real and gracious self-giving. To assert that God gives something other or less than Godself in giving Word and Spirit imperils salvation which can come about only as human beings are taken into the divine life and thereby deified.

What is striking about Christian reflection on divine accessibility is that, from the first, trinitarian considerations were never far removed from reflection on religious diversity. No less a theologian than Gregory of Nyssa characterized the trinitarian conception of divinity as a means between as well as a double refutation of the excesses of Jewish commitment to the One and a pagan commitment to the many. As the epigraph to this chapter shows, Gregory did not separate the work of formulating and defending Christian trinitarianism from reflection about Christianity's others. The work of self-constitution shows itself to be through and through dialogical, at least in principle.

Intriguingly, in our time, a time also marked by robust religious variety, the association between trinitarian reflection and religious diversity has been revivified.[2] Fortunately, contemporary conversations about trinity and religious diversity are not confined to apologetics but now hold promise for an affirmative embrace of religious difference. A variety of Christian theologians now assert that trinitarianism is the distinctively Christian way of offering a *positive* resolution to the problem of religious diversity: by acknowledging distinction within the divine life, Christians can account for substantial differences among the world's religions as varying but nonetheless legitimate expressions of an encounter with God who will be experienced diversely just because God is not an undifferentiated singularity. The abiding differences between the world religions are neither illusory nor indicative of error. Religious diversity is a natural expression of human encounter with divine multiplicity.

Of course, a trinitarian approach to religious diversity cannot be a neat solution to questions of religious diversity. How, after all, are Christian theologians to honor the Jewish commitment to divine unity and Muslim affirmations that God is without associates? Moreover, a problematic apologetic temptation remains at the heart of some trinitarian approaches to religious diversity, the temptation to assert that whereas other traditions offer a monolithic account of divine life, Christian trinitarianism, by contrast, is encompassing and polyphonic. Christians see the whole whereas others see only in part. We are once more in the territory of hierarchical inclusivism in which Christian traditions have little to learn from dialogue with other religious traditions.[3] Self-sufficiency trumps the possibility of mutual transformation.

Might it be possible for Christian theologians to envision a trinitarian engagement with religious diversity that is marked by a sense of *anticipation* that other traditions may have something to teach us about how to think even about trinity? Can we imagine the trinity as a site for interreligious exchange rather than as a prefabricated solution to the problem of religious diversity? My sense is that the trinity can indeed be an open site for interreligious dialogue and exchange but not so long as Christians bring to dialogue a finished conception of the trinity that can in no way be enriched by way of dialogue and comparative theology.

Theology has been in the midst of a trinitarian efflorescence since the work of Karl Barth and Karl Rahner. This return of trinitarianism, however, is not marked by happy harmony but is instead characterized by considerable dissensus. One conviction that drives the resurgence of trinitarianism is the notion that trinity affords a promising resource for social ontology. If to be is to be in relation, then there is no clearer paradigm for that contention than the trinity itself. But about the character of relationality within the divine life, there is no consensus. On the one side stand the social trinitarians and, on the other, are those who are adamantly persuaded that social trinitarianism is a fundamental distortion of the intentions of the ancients.[4] Given the vigorous internal debate between Christian theologians, it is natural to ask how engagements with religious diversity might bear on such controversies.

The ongoing intra-Christian trinitarian debate reminds us that trinity is better understood as a question and a problem rather than as a transparent dogmatic dictum. Rather than treat some readymade account of the trinity as a final Christian answer to questions about theology and ontology or the problem of religious difference, an alternative and more open-ended strategy would treat the trinity as itself a locus for interreligious conversation and exchange. Put otherwise, before any particular trinitarian formulation derived from intra-Christian resources alone is made to serve as the normative basis for a Christian theology of religious pluralism, we would be better advised to begin by treating trinity as a question for comparative theology.

In what follows, I advance a trinitarian formulation that draws from a comparative reading of Hindu, Christian, and Buddhist traditions. From Advaita Vedānta, I draw an account of ultimate reality as ground. From Christian resources, I offer an account of ultimate reality as contingency, and from Buddhist traditions (specifically Madhyamaka), I draw an account of ultimate reality as relation. The result is a trinitarianism of God as ground, contingency, and relation derived by way of comparative theology. Although each of these concepts can be correlated with accounts of God as Father, Son, and Spirit, the task at hand is not to defend the orthodoxy of this formulation but to launch an experiment in formulating Christian doctrine in conversation with other traditions. A glance at Gregory suffices to show that something like this process of construction with an eye to religious diversity has long been a part of Christian theology. Only now such construction can take on the character of collaborative conversation rather than apologetic contestation.

What about the number three? Does this venture hinge on positing a threefold structure to reality and the divine life? And what is the relationship between the three and the *poly* of polydoxy? Is three too few for those who love the many? In what follows, trinitarianism is meant to serve as a kind of Nyssan middle between the one and the many, albeit with a difference. I appeal to trinity as a refutation of any privileging of the One that would dismiss the exuberant diversity of creation as merely epiphenomenal or otherwise unreal and likewise hold to trinity against any vision of the many as sheer, arbitrary difference without relation. The number three itself is neither arbitrary nor absolute. This speculative trinitarianism is committed to a vision of God as ground, contingency, and relation. However, theologians would do well to remember the warning of the Fathers that number cannot mean in the divine life what it means in quotidian experience. Only finite realities can be enumerated; the infinite cannot. Neither one nor three can mean for the divine life what numbers mean in conventional experience. Nonetheless, I say three.

Regnant options in theologies of religious pluralism

Before turning to this particular trinitarian treatment of religious diversity, I wish to offer an abbreviated survey of the current state of the conversation. One way of putting the core question that drives current Christian thinking about religious diversity is this: what is the meaning of my neighbor's faith for mine? In some form or other, that question has been taken up by Christian thinkers from the very beginnings of Christian tradition. But over the last five decades or so, the query has generated a distinct sub-specialty within Christian theology variously called theology of religions or more precisely theology of religious pluralism (TRP).[5]

One particular organizing metaphor has set the terms for conversation and shaped the questions taken up by theologians working within this field. The metaphor imagines religious life as akin to a venture in mountain climbing and takes the various religions to be paths up a mountain. The metaphor in turn generates a basic question that has served to set the terms for conversation and debate: are the various world religions paths up the same mountain?

When we move from metaphor to concept, that question takes the following cast: are the different religions independent means for arriving at the same soteriological or saving end? Put simply, do the different religions all lead to healing because they all lead to God or ultimate reality? Noted philosophers and theologians have offered a variety of answers to this question. Christian exclusivists say no – only Jesus is the way to salvation and so it follows that other religions cannot lead to God. There is only one path up the mountain. Christian inclusivists, on the other hand, offer a more nuanced answer. Persons from other religious traditions may in fact arrive at God, but only because Christ or the Holy Spirit is in some way at work in those traditions. The religions are not independent paths leading to the religious summit. Pluralists have answered the question affirmatively: the religions really are independently efficacious paths up the mountain.

Arguably the most influential of pluralist theologians is John Hick.[6] He contends that the various religious traditions are soteriological vehicles that lead us from self-centeredness to reality centeredness. All the major religious traditions make this transformation possible, and no tradition is so exceptional at this work that it might justifiably claim to be superior to all others. Hence, all paths lead to the summit and none more efficaciously than any other.

What then of the various understandings of ultimate reality found in the world's religious traditions? How are the sharp differences between these conceptualities to be correlated with Hick's contention that the traditions are engaged in the selfsame project? Hick claims that they are all phenomenal manifestations of a noumenal Real that always exceeds any and all concepts that we may form about that reality. The differences between these conceptions do not bear on the soteriological work that the traditions accomplish. So, for example, ultimate reality or the Real is neither personal nor impersonal.[7] This is not to say that the religions are wrong to imagine the Real as personal or impersonal because the Real does give itself to be experienced in these ways. On their own terms, the religions are incommensurate and incompatible; traditions that claim that ultimate reality is a person really are in conflict with traditions that say that ultimate reality is impersonal. But from Hick's pluralist perspective, each is right in what it affirms about the Real and wrong when it denies the formulations of others.

We might well ask how Hick can know that the various religions are in fact oriented to one and the same ultimate reality. Hick offers a pragmatic answer: the major religious traditions all lead persons from narrow self-centeredness to reality-centeredness. They perform the same work. Every tradition successfully generates saints, none better than any other. Although each tradition will likely depict the specific features of this transformation in different ways, generically speaking they are all doing the same thing. Hence, on both the anthropological side and the theological side, Hick asserts that there is a deep underlying identity between traditions. There is but one mountain to climb and one summit to reach. There is but one ultimate reality.

The trouble with Hick's proposal is that he fails to offer a religiously deep motivation for interreligious dialogue. Religious traditions have nothing to learn about God, humanity, or soteriology in and through dialogue. If every account of the Real is equally true and equally false because none are adequate to the nature of the *Real-an-sich*, then the only reason for dialogue is neighborliness. We are not given reason to believe that anything ultimately is at stake in the different theologies available in the world's religious traditions. It is not as though a cumulative reading of the world's religious traditions might teach us more than we know within our traditions alone.

Likewise, if the differences between the concrete accounts of human healing and well-being do not matter because they are all generically the same, we need not be religiously interested in the concrete disciplines and practices of other religious traditions. The Christian who partakes of the Eucharist is generically doing the same thing as the Buddhist who engages in vipassana meditation or Zen. Each is but a tradition-specific way of moving from self-centeredness to reality-centeredness. The means differ but the end is the same. Hence, Hick fails to offer reasons for serious interest in the richly textured differences between traditional practices or between Christian conceptions of God and Buddhist accounts of Buddha-nature. Might the concrete spiritual disciplines of another tradition offer access to dimensions of ultimate reality that are not well accessed in our home tradition? Hick does not pose such questions because he cannot. His commitment to one unknowable ultimate reality trumps the importance of diversity. There is but one ultimate reality and just one worthwhile religious end. Strangely, Hick's pluralism turns out to be not so pluralistic at all.

In a provocative argument that opens up dramatically new possibilities, the evangelical theologian S. Mark Heim argues that there is a profound point of agreement between the most conservative and most liberal of Christian theologians. Both agree that there is at most one worthwhile religious goal or end. The disagreement comes elsewhere: liberals assert that *all traditions* arrive at that single end whereas conservatives believe that *only Christianity* provides access to that end.

> If two religions conflict, then at most one can be correct. Wishing to affirm Christianity, Christian exclusivists seek out conflicts and in each case affirm the error of the differing tradition. If your religion differs from mine, you must be wrong. Wishing not to attribute error to one religion against another, pluralists recognize difference but sever it from religious validity. They are convinced that where religions differ, the differences are only apparent … or are real but irrelevant in attaining the one true end of religion. If you think your religion is a real alternative to mine, you must be wrong.[8]

Neither camp takes difference seriously by entertaining the possibility that there might be multiple religious ends, many salvations. Heim shows that neither camp considers the possibility of more than one worthwhile religious end. Rather, it is a shared axiom for both camps that there *could be* no more than one. The axiom challenges religious believers to recognize that those of other faiths actually are (in all truly important respects) seeking, being shaped by, and eventually realizing the same religious end. All paths lead to the same goal.[9]

After demonstrating that both exclusivists and pluralists are impoverished in their approach to difference, Heim offers a striking reformulation of the mountain climbing metaphor. He argues that there is no good reason to suppose that there is only one religious mountain worth climbing. He contends that we ought to understand the world religions as paths up very different mountains. The religious terrain is mountainous; each of these mountains is worth climbing and leads to a different but legitimate destination. The different religions are not merely different ways to the same goal, but different ways to different goals.

But does the argument that there are different and valid religious goals, hence many mountains, imply that there is more than one ultimate reality? Heim could have taken that option but he does not. Here, he parts company with the process theologian David Ray Griffin who does in fact posit multiple ultimate realities, a position he calls "deep pluralism." Griffin traces deep pluralism to the work of John Cobb and points to Cobb's compelling claim that, "alongside all the errors and distortions that can be found in all our traditions there are insights arising from profound thought and experience *that are diverse modes of apprehending diverse aspects of the totality of reality.*"[10] Appealing to a technical distinction between creativity and God found in process metaphysics, Griffin argues that for Cobb there must be at least two religious ultimates.

The virtue of having two ultimate realities, Griffin notes, is that it permits us to recognize the difference between and the validity of both those traditions that insist upon a personal and loving ultimate reality – God, Allah, Īśvara, and Christ – and other traditions that insist that ultimate reality is *nirguṇa Brahman*, *dharmakāya*, or *śūnyatā*/emptiness. Both are right because there are two ultimate realities and neither can be reduced to the other. As Griffin argues, "the two types of experience can be taken to be equally veridical if we think of them as experiences of different ultimates."[11] Griffin goes onto show that there are in fact three ultimates in Cobb's vision – creativity, God, and the world, each undergirding a different kind of religious experience or tradition; creativity can serve as the basis for nontheistic traditions, God serves as the basis for theistic traditions, and the world as the basis for cosmic religions.[12]

I cannot here present a comprehensive engagement with and critique of Cobb and Griffin but will simply have to assert that the very idea of multiple ultimates strikes me as self-contradictory and runs contrary to the very idea of ultimacy. The virtue of a position of the sort articulated by Cobb and Griffin is this: if traditions are oriented toward different ultimates and these ultimates are real, then when traditions find themselves in disagreement, this disagreement becomes a possible resource rather than contradiction. Put otherwise, the challenge would be to find out how contradictory claims might turn out, upon further exploration, to be complementary rather than contradictory. We might be able to combine the insights of multiple religious traditions to generate a richer vision of reality than we are able to derive from one religion alone. With Cobb and Griffin, I agree that there is profound promise in the claim that the different religions enable us to get at "diverse aspects of the totality of reality."

However, against Cobb and Griffin, I would argue – as does Heim and a host of other Christian theologians – that all we need to posit in order to allow for a real variety of religious goods is that the totality of reality has diverse aspects. We need not posit multiple ultimates. It would suffice to posit one ultimate reality with a diversity of aspects, and that is what is entailed by any trinitarian conception of ultimate reality. Mark Heim, Raimon Panikkar, Gavin D'Costa, and a variety of Christian theologians have argued that trinity is the natural way that Christian theology can take up the problem of religious diversity. They contend that the genuine differences between religions are grounded in trinitarian difference. Different soteriological trajectories engage different dimensions of the divine life. Because Christian doctrine does not regard God as a homogeneous simplicity, we should expect that different traditions are rightly oriented to genuine distinctions internal to the divine life. Beyond homogeneous singularity and irreducible diversity, there lies an alternate possibility that Christian theology finds in the trinity. The divine life is neither an undifferentiated absolute nor a plurality of more or less loosely related ultimates.

A variety of trinitarian approaches have been tried over the last two decades beginning with Panikkar's groundbreaking volume, *The Trinity and the Religious Experience of Man.*[13] What Panikkar and others do well is to show that different spiritualities can be authentic ways of being oriented to different dimensions of God's trinitarian life. However, all extant trinitarian approaches, Mark Heim's included, are plagued by a variety of difficulties.

For the sake of brevity, I will simply enumerate six problems with most trinitarian approaches to the question of religious diversity before outlining my own approach. First, to date, most Christian theologians take up some fully formulated Christian trinitarianism and then give to religious traditions certain preassigned slots within the trinitarian economy. Other traditions are understood entirely on Christian theological terms, terms formulated *before* dialogue. Second, in most approaches to date, there is an insufficient appreciation for diversity *within* religious traditions. The whole of Buddhism, for example, is said to approach some given dimension of God's trinitarian life. Christian theologians have not recognized the deep internal diversities within religious traditions. Third, by failing to understand internal variations within religious traditions, whole traditions are reified as oriented toward different destinations. In Heim's case, these destinations are real, different, and persist even after death. Postmortem, Buddhists go to nirvana and Christians to heaven. Fourth, many theologians err in significant ways by misreading and misinterpreting other religious traditions, most especially Buddhism. Often this error is due to a desire to make traditions fit within a given trinitarian scheme that is formulated *prior to dialogue* with other religious traditions. Such a danger is most pronounced when theologians want to put all impersonal conceptions of ultimate reality into a single basket and all personal conceptions into another. What is inevitably lost to attention in such an approach are the deep, vigorous and indeed millennia-long debates between Buddhists and Hindus, and even between Buddhists about their different impersonal conceptions of ultimate reality. Madhyamaka Buddhists have long insisted that *śūnyatā* (emptiness) is not the Upanishadic Brahman. Still subtler are the arguments between Buddhist schools about just how to understand emptiness. Tibetan Gelugpas, the Dalai Lama's school of Buddhism, are insistent that there is nothing at all ground like about emptiness, whereas Nyingma Buddhists, who are deeply influenced by the idea that all things possess Buddha-nature, disagree. The latter insist that emptiness is not merely negative but must also be in some sense a positive reality. The subtlety of such distinctions between traditions has largely been lost on most Christian theologians.

And this brings me to what strikes me as a fifth problem with trinitarian approaches to date: Christian theologians have not thought to let the insights of other traditions play a role in helping us to revise and deepen our understanding of the trinity. Christian theologians rightly affirm that we can with confidence look for traces or intimations of the trinity in the world at large but these traces when found are not permitted to inform and revise our understanding of the trinity.

The sixth and final problem with most trinitarian accounts to date – and this will come as no surprise – is the claim to Christian superiority. Only Christians have arrived at a trinitarian vision whereas other traditions, however legitimate, manage to access only one dimension of the divine life. It does not occur to most Christian theologians that most Christian traditions and thinkers also miss out on the plenitude of God's trinitarian life. To affirm that God is trinity is vital, but if one's conception of the trinity is constrained by a monolithic account of the divine life, then the promise of affirming that divinity is diversity in unity will be lost.

God as ground, contingency, and relation

To account for and overcome these limitations, I propose a provisional, speculative trinitarianism derived not just from Christian resources but also from Buddhist–Christian–Hindu trialogue. This approach does not take some fully formulated Christian account of the trinity and then try to squeeze other religious traditions into that prefabricated vision, nor does it assume that Christians securely know just what is entailed in asserting that God is trinity. With other trinitarian theologians of religious pluralism, I agree that if ultimate reality is trinity, then we would do well to expect that we would see trinitarian disclosures in human experience and the structure of reality as such. Therefore, these other religious traditions might deepen and augment what Christians have come to know about God's trinitarian life in and through the incarnation and the dispensation of the Holy Spirit.

I would like to argue for a theological threefold of *ground*, *contingency*, and *relation*. This threefold names three dimensions of the divine life that I correlate with three dimensions of experience, an ontological threefold. This ontological threefold is *being*, *contingent being*, and *being in relation*; these three are fundamental mysteries that are intrawordly signals of transcendence pointing to the divine life.

In brief, being refers to the sheer mystery that there is anything at all. The sheer "isness" of every existent – that there is something rather than nothing – is a primordial source of wonderment. The theological conclusions that religious traditions draw from this wonderment are many and often incommensurable, but wonder about *the fact that there is anything at all* is a signal of transcendence that points to divinity. A second and primordial source of wonderment is contingency. Contingency speaks both to the non-necessary character of each and every item of experience but also to the fact that everything whatsoever – from atoms, to leaves, to persons, and galaxies – is utterly singular. To exist is to exist as an inimitable this, a concrete haecceity. A third and fundamental source of worldly astonishment is that nothing whatsoever exists in isolation. Not one of the concrete haeccities to be found in experience exists in isolation. It both is what it is and no other, but it is what it is precisely by being in relation with every other. To be is to be in relation.

Each of these mysteries points to a dimension of the divine life. The fact that there is anything at all rather than nothing, the sheer fact of being points to God's character as ground, as being itself. All that is exists because of its participation in God who is the ground and source of being. Contingent being points to God's character as (source of) contingency. God is the creator of every particular in its very concreteness. There is something in the divine life that gives rise to a world of inexhaustible particularity and diversity. Finally, the fact that creation is characterized throughout as marked by relation – that nothing whatsoever exists apart from relation – points to God as relation and the power of relation. God does not give rise to a world of isolated particulars but rather gives rise to a world that is through and through relational.

This double threefold, worldly and divine, is richly resonant with traditional trinitarian discourse. God as Father is the ultimate ground of divinity itself and the world, God as Son/Logos is the principle of distinction within the divine life and the source of particularity in the world. To speak is to speak not language in general but to say something concrete and singular. The world is the Word's utterance, an utterance marked by a rich profusion of diversity, a play of virtually infinite variation, an inexhaustible fecundity of difference for the sake of difference. But the world is not the domain of sheer monadic difference wherein each contingent particular is locked away in splendid isolation from every other particular. Nothing whatsoever exists apart from relation, least of all divinity. Spirit in the divine life is that which animates and binds the world together as a world of relation and secures the flourishing of beings.

Although the connections between this double threefold and traditional trinitarian formulations are not hard to miss, my focus here is not to establish their proper Christian credentials but to show how this double threefold both captures something integral about the nature of the Real and points to core themes and motifs to be found within a variety of religious traditions. Although for the sake of simplicity, I will associate each of these notions with particular strands from Hindu, Christian, and Buddhist traditions, I believe that every religious tradition does in some fashion register all three dimensions of this trinity though not in equal and emphatic balance. Religious thinkers and traditions are most often committed to one of these three concept-intuitions and so are unlikely to appreciate what is celebrated in the remaining pair. Indeed sharp theological tensions arise across and even within traditions because traditions and strands thereof fail to register and may even deny the equal importance of all three.

By ground, I mean to refer to what Christians have typically referred to as the first person of the trinity. I derive the term from Paul Tillich's language of God as ground of being while remembering his added proviso that the ground is also an unfathomable abyss. But rather than begin by characterizing God as ground by appeal to Christian resources, I turn to the Upanishads and the Advaita Vedānta commentarial tradition as exemplified in writing of the master teacher of that tradition, Śaṅkara. In his commentary on the famous passage from the Chāndogya Upanishad, "In the beginning all this was being (sat), One only, without a second," Śaṅkara argues that all reality is but a transformation of Brahman, understood as being.[14] Just as clay pots, jars, cups, and the like are ultimately nothing but modifications of one lump of clay, so too the world is ultimately nothing but Brahman. Elsewhere, the Upanishads and Śaṅkara also employ the image of sparks and flame to designate the nonduality of the world and Brahman.

Ultimately, Śaṅkara pulls back from the language of the world as a transformation of Brahman in order to assert the unchangeable immutability of Brahman as world-ground. Śaṅkara invites readers to distinguish between two intuitions that are given in any experience, namely the particular item of experience on the one hand and the intuition of being on the other. So, if one sees a pot and affirms that "the pot is," Śaṅkara would point out that whereas the pot comes and goes, the sense of being persists. One is never without the sense of being. That sense of being which is given everywhere points to the world ground that abides whereas the particulars come and go. To return to the metaphor of clay and pots, jars, and the like, the clay is real in a way that its modifications are not. The encounter with being in and through, and ultimately, underneath particulars points to an abiding and infinite world ground, namely Brahman, that upholds but is not equivalent to those particulars.

In his commentary on the Great Utterance (*mahāvākya*) found in the Bṛhadāraṇyaka Upanishad, "In the beginning, all this was Brahman indeed. It knew itself as, 'I am Brahman, (*ahambrahmāsmi*),'" Śaṅkara argues that this world ground is not merely being but also the true and innermost Self (*atman*).[15] The Self is understood as eternal luminous consciousness and not merely as the contingent psychophysical formations that make up quotidian identity. The latter formations are too passing to be mistaken for the true abiding Self. When one sees that the light of consciousness (*cit*) that shines in the mind is the true Self, then one stops living a life driven by compulsions. The result of understanding one's true identity is liberation from the cycle of rebirth. The transethical consequence of such knowledge is compassion rooted in knowledge of the nonduality of Brahman and self as well as nonduality between self and other. The true Self is one in all.

The human predicament as understood by Śaṅkara's reading of the Upanishads is bondage to the fundamental ignorance of this nonduality. When human beings take themselves to be exhausted by their conventional finite identities as composed of caste, gender, stage of life, and the like, they inevitably feel themselves to be vulnerable. From and out of that vulnerability, human beings become captive to craving, hatred, and delusion, the three great poisons in the Advaita tradition. They crave and are addicted to what promises to complete them, and they are averse to what threatens them. The cumulative force of this competing push and pull generates the profound disorientation called delusion. Captive to these forces, human beings perpetuate incalculable personal and social harm and are captive to cycle of transmigration. Liberation from this cycle comes from knowledge provided by the scripture that the Self (atman) is the ultimate (Brahman). That is the point made in the Bṛhadāraṇyaka Upanishad: *ahambrahmāsmi*. I am Brahman.

Ultimately, the Upanishads as read by Śaṅkara contend that Brahman is ineffable and beyond language and thought. It is immanent as ground but transcendent as mystery. One can know that one is Brahman but Brahman itself cannot be known. Though designated provisionally as being, it exceeds all name and form. It is the ground for all that has name and form, but it exceeds all name and form even as it grounds them. Human beings are thus understood to be the ultimate luminous and unknowable mystery that no words can reach – not even the words "ground" or "being" or even "consciousness." Crucial here for the Advaitin is that the sheer being of the world is mystery, but what draws the Advaitin's attention is not the particular being of things qua particular. What captivates is that the world of name and form – though name and form are themselves utterly evanescent – nevertheless points to and speaks of being as such. Being which shines in everything whatsoever – actually for the Advaitin *underneath* everything – is holy mystery.

By contingency, I refer to the Jewish and Christian appreciation not just for the wonder that anything is at all but rather the *irreducibly singular and distinctive* character of all that is. "God saw everything that he had made, and indeed, it was very good" (Gen 1:31). Contrary to the Advaita impulse to look past and underneath name and form, contingency speaks to the conviction that each and every particular is what it is and has an intensity and singularity of value: just this arch of an eyebrow, just this particular curve of the face, just this chin and no other, just this Jewish carpenter who makes all the difference. Contingency also names the Jewish and Christian conviction that God plus world is more than God alone.

Without diminishing or dismissing the divine plenitude, to celebrate contingency is to assert the worth and value of every element in creation as intrinsically good just in its very evanescent particularity. By creating the world, God generates singular and concrete instantiations of value. To insist on the otherness of the world from God is to celebrate the worth of creaturely life. The worth of contingent being cannot be affirmed in philosophical or theological accounts in which intrinsic worth and value of creaturely lives is said somehow to be already (pre)contained in the divine life and only made manifest in creation. The attempt to praise the glory and fullness of divinity at the expense of the rich world of concrete particulars is to miss the meaning of the doctrine of creation. The doctrine of *creatio ex nihilo* is not so much meant to stipulate that God, by way of an exercise of sheer unilateral power, makes creatures to be out of sheer absolute nothingness (*ouk on*) as it is meant to affirm that the divine life is enriched by the life of the world in a way that most Neoplatonic accounts of creation as an overflowing of the divine life cannot do. The world is more than the exteriorization of what is already contained in the divine life. Speaking as a father of a lovely and utterly singular daughter, I want to affirm that the meaning of the doctrine of creation is that her concrete and singular being enriches God's very life – that my Katie adds a measure of richness to the divine life by virtue of her contingent and lovely being, however evanescent. It seems entirely right to say, as a host of theologians have, that the divine life is not diminished by creation, but what is needed also is a robust affirmation that divine life is enriched by creaturely life precisely because the latter is not a mere manifestation of the former.

Those who orient themselves to the mystery of being, and hence to the mystery of ultimate reality as ground, tend to dismiss particularity as fleeting. Their focus rests on the sheer fact of being and not contingent being. By contrast, those who celebrate contingency insist that every particularity is a communicative expression of a good beyond being. Creation comes about through the Logos of God and is itself an expression of that Logos. The God whose Logos gives rise to the lovely world can be experienced as a lover who loves the lovely world into being. To acknowledge and celebrate contingency is to experience the ground not just as an impersonal or transpersonal absolute but as a personal, creative, and communicative source – as the Father and Mother of the Logos. God speaks the world into being and sustains the world in being. The world itself is a logos of God, the speech of God, and the gift of God. God gives Godself to the world by speaking the world into being and giving to the world concrete, lovely, and contingent (need not have been but now is) being. The world's being is not simply and without remainder God's being.

The human predicament when seen in light of contingency is the failure of particular persons and communities to love and reverence God's lovely world and the giver of that world. Whereas ignorance of the nonduality of self and absolute ground is the shape of the human predicament in Advaita, the human predicament under the sign of contingency is a failure to love widely as well as particularly. The shape of this failure can be variegated, but we can speak of a constricted selfhood that does not love widely and with sufficient passionate intensity. Love is of insufficient breadth should it love only what is one's own – one's family alone, one's nation alone. Even the hypocrites do that. Under the sign of contingency, there can be no mandate to renounce particular loves. Apart from contingency, there is no possibility of the erotic, of a genuine, inexhaustible, and generous desire for the other in all his or her concrete loveliness. Where there is no otherness, divine or human, there can be no eros for the other.

Śaṅkara and the Advaita tradition urge human beings to renounce particular and contingent loves for the sake of realizing nonduality. The focus of our attention is called away from our particular and contingent being to the sheer fact of being. When one has realized the nonduality of self and Brahman and so is no longer captive to the narrow and constricted ego, a universal compassion takes its place. The calling of contingency is otherwise. True, it too is a calling to move beyond constricted and egoistic selfhood, but the calling of contingency is for a deeper and, yes, erotic appreciation for the loveliness of the world and loveliness of the world's giver. The vocation is not to give up on particular loves but to expand one's range of particular loves without surrendering the call toward intensity which can only be fulfilled when we limit ourselves for the sake of reverence and piety to loving just this particular person or partner.

But is contingency also rooted in the divine life? Is the divine life itself marked by contingency and, if so, in what sense? On the one hand, the very idea of contingency as presented herein is meant to affirm the real ontological status of the world and the world's particulars as irreducible to divinity. The world both is the scene of difference and is itself a difference that makes it *not God* or at least not reducible to God. God gives rise to what is not merely Godself. That said, questions remain: is the divine life enriched by the world God creates? Is there something in the divine life that impels and receives the luxuriant prolixity of worldly particularity? Is God changed by the loving labor of creativity? Does the world birthed by divine labor remain merely ad extra, outside the divine life?

A Christian scriptural resource for thinking these questions can be found in Paul's letter to the Colossians wherein the apostle describes the Christ as:

> the image of the invisible God, the firstborn of all creation; for in him all things were created in heaven and on earth, visible and invisible, whether thrones or dominions or principalities or authorities – all things were created through him and *for him*. He is before all things and in him all things hold together.
>
> (Col 1:15–17; NRSV; emphasis added)

St. Paul portrays the Christ as the principle of contingency within the divine life. The Christ is the one in and through whom the world is created. Still more, the world is created *for him*.

What is the meaning of this *for him*? Perhaps it means that the reality within the divine life which gives rise to contingency is also enriched by that very contingency. The world is made *for* the Christ and it is sustained *in* the Christ who holds the world together. The divine life is enriched by the worldly life to which it gives rise. The principle of contingency within the divine life is "before all things" and is not itself one of those things. Those things, however, can enrich the Christ precisely because they are not what He is, and He is not what they are. He is enriched by what he is not – at least not at first. Insofar as the Christ holds them together, they now become part of his very life. In this sense, the divine life is really enriched by the distinct but not separate life of the world.[16]

Relation names the truth that nothing *whatsoever* is what it is apart from its relation. To be is to be in relation. This truth finds exemplary expression in the Madhyamaka truth of emptiness. To be more specific still, it is the Gelukpa reading of emptiness that is most resolutely insistent on the truth of relationality. Gelukpa Mādhyamikas insist that to speak of emptiness is not to posit some impersonal world-ground or ground of consciousness that is empty. To say that everything is empty is to say that no thing whatsoever has self-existence or own-being. Indeed to be is to be no thing at all, if to be a thing is to have some own-being or self-existence (*svabhāva*) that an entity possesses apart from relationship. Nothing whatsoever exists outside of relation. More rigorously still, no being whatsoever has an essence or core that is non-relationally derived, not even God. On this reading, emptiness is just another way of designating that all of reality is *pratītyasamutpāda*, dependent co-arising.[17]

The human predicament is understood under the sign of relation as craving, craving generated by the false idea that one is a disconnected and non-relational self. The ignorant notion that one is a self apart from relation generates a constricted and narrow ego that imagines the world to be made up of things that the self can then grasp. There is something tragicomic about the human predicament so understood: when human beings take themselves to be disconnected and reified entities and take the world to be likewise composed of such things, they are impelled toward grasping just those realities with which they are already intimately bound in and through relation. I seek to own you as a thing when I could instead discover that you and I are already bound up in utter intimacy. I thereby come to see that neither of us is a thing that grasps or that can be grasped. Buddhists share with Advaitins the sense that the ego is driven by craving, hatred, and delusion, but they differ radically about the cure for this ailment. The cure is not to discover the true Self that is the world's ground, but to discover that there is no self whatsoever apart from relation. There is no transworldly absolute according to Mādhyamika thinkers.[18] Posting such an absolute behind the world is to risk losing the world of relation. After all, the absolute is by definition that which withdraws from relation – that which is without relation.

Speaking here in my own stead rather than as a Mādhyamika thinker, I would argue that when the truth of relationality is obscured, then the co-herence of reality is lost. Nothing holds together. Even our theologies are radically compromised. As a consequence, we risk accounts of God as an unrelated and immutable ultimate, a God who is being God when there is no world for which God can be God. We make the mistake of supposing that the world is other than God in some non-relational sense and so suppose that God and world are marked not by internal relation but external relation. God is understood to be what the world is not and the world what God is not. As a result, an irresolvable dualism emerges. The profound temptation that lies within every theology that forgets relation is that it might so personalize God that God becomes a being, a person who loves us from without. Against this dualistic vision stands a depiction of God as Spirit-relation who is the Love with which I love God, the one who prays within me with sighs and groans too deep for words.

The fundamental tension between a theological account that resolutely insists on relation and one that insists with equal vigor on contingency-singularity is hard to miss. Speak only of relation and one risks losing a world of value that is, in some sense, other than and irreducible to the divine life. Without positing such otherness, it is hard to know how worldly existents can have a particularity that is distinct enough *from* the divine life to *enrich* the divine life. But to speak only of otherness

is to fall into dualism in which God becomes a being among beings – an infinite being – which as Tillich and others have demonstrated is a contradiction in terms.

To speak of God as contingency and relation without affirming God as ground/abyss is to run still other risks. Against the Gelukpa Mādyamikas stand other Buddhists who want to preserve some account of Buddha-nature as non-reified ground; these Buddhists rightly fear that an account of ultimate reality as emptiness alone might risk a nihilism that denies the very ground of the human capacity for transformation. To affirm that there is in the real an infinite fund for wisdom and compassion is the reason for insisting that emptiness is not merely a negation of own-being or self-existence (*svabhāva*). Of course, such Buddhists are (too) anxious to affirm that to posit such a ground is in no way tantamount to advancing a vision of ultimate reality as non-relational Being-Itself, the putative sin of Advaita.[19]

This brief treatment of the tension between depictions of ultimate reality as ground, contingency, and relation demonstrates that a trinitarian problem remains: just how does one formulate a theological vision that does not privilege one of these dimensions at the expense of others? Comparative theology is a necessary discipline precisely because traditions tend to settle such questions about the nature of ultimate reality in a dominant inflection or style leaving other options inadequately considered, at best. At worst, minority voices are dismissed as heretics for refusing the dominant account. Christian traditions in their logos-centrism offer rich resources for celebrating contingency, but under the dominance of contingency God is too often reduced to personhood, the sovereign person, or in social trinitarianism, three persons who are somehow also one. Driven by a singular focus on the category of contingency, some go so far as to subscribe to a vision of each person in the trinity as itself a center of will and consciousness. Personal otherness is inscribed into the heart of the divine life but in a way that effectively erases the character of God as ground and relation.

Comparative theology can shed rich light on these questions even as they play out in intra-Christian debates about the character of the divine life. How are we rightly to speak of God as inexhaustible (re)source and abyss, God as one who speaks and so gives rise to a world that is not identical to or a mere overflow of the divine life, and speak also about ultimate reality as relation?[20] That Spirit has throughout the history of Christian theology shaken off personal attributions – that from the first Christian theology was unable to fix the character of the Spirit – speaks to the nature of ultimate reality as relation, as the energy of the between and so not itself reducible either to abyssal depth or source of personal address.

By contrast, the forms of Hinduism and Buddhism described herein were formulated by renunciants and monastics who posit visions of ultimate reality that call for detachment from particularity. The shape of these particular strands of Buddhism and Hinduism are markedly suspicious of the erotic, if by the erotic we mean not just sexual love but intense desire for the loveliness of singular realities, most especially, of course, the female body.

Because of these differences in orientation, the texture and fruits of healing transformation in these different traditions are non-identical and may generate sharp tensions in persons who take up the practices of more than one tradition. But tension need not amount to contradiction. Theological differences between ground, contingency, and relation and the way in which human beings are oriented distinctively to these dimensions of ultimate reality can generate positive resources for interreligious collaboration.

I do not want to downplay the tensions between these spiritual trajectories. As already noted, those who are dedicated to the mystery of relation worry that orientation to the mystery of ground might lead to world loss. Spiritual practitioners who are dedicated to a vision of the world of name and form as unreal and so become caught up in a sense of the hyperreality of the transpersonal ground-abyss may deny the realm of relation and encounter and so fall prey to world-negation.

This danger is one that those oriented toward contingency can appreciate, albeit in a different key. Those who celebrate the mystery of contingency worry that lovers of relation can miss the inexhaustible singularity of lovely particulars because the latter are so intent on denying that particulars can come to be apart from relation. Might not an exclusive orientation toward relationality jeopardize attention to the particular and hence the possibility of the erotic, of love for the particular not because I am incomplete without it, but because the loveliness of the singular has its own inviolable beauty to which I owe the piety of desire?

The tension between these three mysteries notwithstanding, spiritual life lived in relation to them need not result in outright contradiction or incommensurability. This assertion is made in the key of faith and not ratiocination which must come later. By way of that latter work of reflection, theologians can and must give an account of the *perichoresis* of these three mysteries. If reality and divinity bear this trinitarian structure – if ground, contingency, and relation are distinct but not separate – then one would expect that any robust and historically deep tradition can find resources to orient persons to these three dimensions of the Real even if any given strand of a religious tradition typically errs in one direction or the other. So, as noted, we find in a variety of Tibetan Buddhist traditions thinkers who are worried that the Gelukpa understanding of emptiness is too negative and cannot give an adequate account of our innate Buddha-nature as a positive reality. These traditions argue that while it is true that Buddha-nature cannot be a non-relational entity, Buddha-nature must be understood also as a positive and luminous ground of wisdom and compassion. This internal difference *within Tibetan Buddhism* accounts for the longstanding debates between proponents of "self-emptiness" and proponents of "other-emptiness." In the tension, debate, and ultimately in efforts to synthesize these different commitments, one can find in Buddhist traditions the motifs of ground and relation together with an appreciation for the suchness of each particular.

Christian traditions are, by and large, deeply committed to a vision of contingency and so tend to configure the ground not just as creativity but as a personal creator who loves. Under the pressure of contingency, the ground is personalized and is experienced as Lover. But there are many Christian theologians, mystics in particular, who desire a unitive or nondual experience of God. In such thinkers, the experience of God as ground and relation complements a vision of God as loving creator of a contingent and lovely world. Figures like Marguerite Porete and Meister Eckhart come readily to mind.

In both Jewish and Christian thinkers, we also find theologians of the Spirit who experience and encounter God primarily not as ground or even as contingency but under the sign of relation. The Jewish philosopher of relation par excellence is Martin Buber, the thinker of I–Thou relation, the thinker of the event of meeting. Many contemporary Christian theologians, most especially process and feminist thinkers, are attempting to articulate a theology of God as relation and reality as relatedness precisely in order to correct for personalist visions in which relatedness is obscured.

In sum, this account of ultimate reality as ground, contingency, and relation suggests that religious traditions – and even strands and thinkers within them – are likely to be oriented toward one or the other of these mysteries at the expense of others. Rare is the theologian who manages to see how these three are one and yet also three. Thinkers and traditions have their particular genius and will customarily resonate with one of these mysteries at the expense of the others. Christians can take no consolation in nor assert religious superiority by appealing to trinity. Despite that commitment, Christian traditions have a long history of erring on the side of personalism under the weight of contingency, so much so that they have burned mystics like Porete who have given voice to a unitive experience of divinity best captured in visions of God as ground and relation. The characteristic spiritual distortion that comes from too narrow a focus on God as contingency, uncorrected by understandings of God as ground and relation, has been to figure God as a transcendent person (or worse still, three such persons). For those who hold to such personalist visions, the radical quest for an abyssal experience of nonduality is *verboten* because the self discovers that her true depth is the divine ground alone, or that the self can plunge directly into that abyss.

By appealing to a trinitarianism of ground, contingency, and relation, I argue that differences between *and within* religious traditions are vital and not merely phenomenal cultural variations. Religious differences are rooted in genuine distinctions within the divine life. The work of interreligious dialogue is religiously important because it is a way of gathering up differences for the sake of integral vision. If we are to understand how these mysteries might be marked by mutual interpenetration, we must take up interreligious dialogue. Interreligious dialogue cannot be motivated by the proximate work of peacemaking alone but must be seen as vital to the quest for right orientation. We cannot move fully into the life of the trinitarian God apart from a deeper movement into communion with our non-Christian neighbors.

John Hick argues that the Real is ultimately neither personal nor impersonal and that all ways of experiencing the Real fail to tell us anything about what Ultimate Reality is in itself. There is a sharp and irrevocable dualism between the One Real and its various manifestations. All are equally true and equally false which can mean that they are equally a matter of indifference. For Hick, the texture of human lives as they move from self-centeredness to reality-centeredness is not a matter of deep interest. What matters is that all traditions make a generic turn to reality-centeredness possible.

By contrast, in this trinitarian vision, the particular texture of soteriological trans-formation matters. Christian *agape* is not the same as Buddhist *karuṇā*, which is not to say that one is superior to the other. We may need both. If this trinitarian account is on the mark, then there are particular forms of healing and virtue that can come about only by engaging in the concrete practices of particular traditions. But these differences need not lead to mutual indifference. This trinitarian vision pro-vides grounds for a certain holy envy for the particular excellences accomplished by Buddhist and Hindu forms of practice. Also ruled out is any eschatological vision in which different religious communities arrive at entirely different post-mortem destinations, some of which are nicer than others or at least more complete. Such a vision is problematic not least because traditions are marked by deep internal vari-egations. Religious goods do not sort themselves out one per tradition. Moreover, any theological vision risks incompleteness, if not outright error, if it fails to become properly attuned to each of these three dimensions of the divine life. The religious quest of our time cannot be imagined as one in which each religious community engages in the work of climbing its own mountain in relative isolation from other religious communities. Only by more deeply appreciating the distinctive goods of other religious traditions can we move more deeply into the divine life. There is no movement into depth of divine life without a movement toward our neighbors, and that is why religious diversity is not a problem but is instead a source of profound promise for our collective well-being.

What then of the poly of polydoxy? Does the trinitarian vision sketched herein mean that divine self-showing can take only and at most three manifestations? Much depends on what is meant by this particular threefold. To affirm that God is world-ground, that God is contingency, and that God is relation in no way diminishes the worth of multiplicity. Quite the contrary. To turn one's gaze anywhere in the world is to see God as Being-Itself, to see God as one who gives rise to and receives the world of contingent particulars, and to see God as one who binds these particulars together in relation. This trinitarian vision is neither a monistic rejection of diversity as unreal and trivial nor a celebration of sheer profusion wherein each thing is just another monadic one, and then another, and then another. Inasmuch as polydoxy is a vision of the many-in-relation (multiplicity), a many that does not negate the one, this speculative trinitarianism is most assuredly polydoxic.

This commitment to polydoxy finds expression in the theology of religious diversity articulated herein. Against Hick, this account refuses a Kantian privileg-ing of the numinous one in which the value of religious difference is imperiled. Nor does this account uncritically embrace the promising work of Griffin and Heim. While their commitment to diversity is embraced, left behind is any account of multiple religious ultimates or multiple salvations that might privilege diversity at the expense of relation. Hence, this account does not envision religions as unre-lated homogeneities, each on parallel tracks that will not meet, each heading to an independent sui generis postmortem destination. This speculative trinitarianism, by contrast, celebrates and cherishes differences within and between traditions for the sake of mutual transformation. This hope for mutuality and transformation rests at the very heart of polydoxic vision.

Notes

1 Gregory of Nyssa, "The Great Catechism," *A Select Library of Nicene and Post-Nicene Fathers of the Christian Church*, 2nd series, Vol. V, T. W. Moore and H. A. Wilson, New York: The Christian Literature Company, 1893, p. 477, emphasis added.

2 For a helpful book that summarizes and assesses a number of trinitarian approaches to religious diversity, see V-M. Kärkkäinen, *Trinity and Religious Pluralism: The Doctrine of the Trinity in Christian Theology of Religions*, Burlington, VT: Ashgate Press, 2004.

3 On hierarchical inclusivism, see W. Halbfass's important essay, "'Inclusivism and Tolerance' in the Encounter Between India and the West," *India and Europe: An Essay in Understanding*, Albany, NY: SUNY Press, 1998, p. 411.

4 The literature on recent trinitarian disputes is now considerable. For an important collection of essays in which the question of social versus anti-social trinitarianism is engaged, see S. T. Davis, D. Kendall, S. J. and G. O'Collins (eds), *The Trinity: An Interdisciplinary Symposium on the Trinity*, New York: Oxford University Press, 1999. In that volume, see especially B. Leftow, "Anti Social Trinitarianism," pp. 203–49. On the important question of how to read Gregory of Nyssa on this question – as he is claimed by partisans on both sides – see the many compelling essays in S. Coakley (ed.), *Re-Thinking Gregory of Nyssa*, Malden, MA: Wiley-Blackwell, 2003.

5 For a masterful and fair-minded critical survey of this material, see P. Knitter, *Introducing Theology of Religions*, Maryknoll, NY: Orbis Books, 2002.

6 The most comprehensive articulation of J. Hick's philosophy of religion can be found in the published version of his Gifford Lectures, *An Interpretation of Religion: Human Responses to the Transcendent*, New Haven, CT: Yale University Press, 1989.

7 J. Hick, *A Christian Theology of Religions: The Rainbow of Faiths*, Louisville, KY: Westminster John Knox Press, 1995, pp. 61–3.

8 M. Heim, *The Depth of the Riches: A Trinitarian Theology of Religious Ends*, Grand Rapids, MI: Eerdmans, 2001, pp. 2–3.

9 Ibid., p. 3, original emphasis.

10 John Cobb quoted in D. R. Griffin, "John Cobb's Whiteheadian Complementary Pluralism," in D. R. Griffin (ed.), *Deep Religious Pluralism*, Louisville, KY: Westminster John Knox Press, 2005, p. 47, emphasis added.

11 Ibid.

12 Ibid., p. 49.

13 R. Panikkar, *The Trinity and the Religious Experience of Man*, Maryknoll, NY: Orbis Books, 1973.

14 Śaṅkara, *Chāndogya Upaniṣad with the Commentary of Śri Śaṅkarācārya*, Calcutta: Advaita Ashrama, 1983, p. 413.

15 Śaṅkara, *Bṛhadāraṇyaka Upaniṣad with the Commentary of Śri Śaṅkarācārya*, Calcutta: Advaita Ashrama, 1983, p. 100. The translation is mine.

16 This account of contingency is, of course, congruent with the Whiteheadian consequent nature of God which receives the created world into the divine life.

17 The authoritative philosophical articulation of this understanding of emptiness as dependent co-arising is to found in Nāgārjuna's *Mūlamadhyamakakārikā*. See J. L. Garfield, *The Fundamental Wisdom of the Middle Way: Nāgārjuna's Mūlamadhyamakakārikā*, New York: Oxford University Press, 1995.

18 Jay Garfield quite concisely characterizes Nāgārjuna, the founding master of the Madhyamaka school, as holding that "emptiness itself is empty. It is not a self-existent void standing behind a veil of illusion comprising conventional reality, but merely a characteristic of conventional reality." Ibid., p. 91.

19 On these internal Buddhist debates, see J. Makransky, *Buddhahood Embodied: Sources of Controversy in India and Tibet*, Albany, NY: State University of New York Press, 1997.

20 This question is, strictly speaking, not taken up here as it lies beyond the scope of this chapter. One would have to construct a complete tradition-specific trinitarian vision, a vision that would aim to do equal justice to God as ground, contingency, and relation. This chapter is a prolegomena to that larger task.

Index